Communities of Memory

COMMUNITIES OF MEMORY

On Witness, Identity, and Justice

W. JAMES BOOTH

Cornell University Press
Ithaca and London

First published 2006 by Cornell University Press

Printed in the United States of America

Library of Congress Cataloging-in-Publication Data

Booth, William James.
    Communities of memory : on witness, identity, and justice / W. James Booth
        p. cm.
    Includes bibliographical references and index.
    ISBN-13: 978-0-8014-4436-4 (cloth : alk. paper)
    ISBN-10: 0-8014-4436-5 (cloth : alk. paper)
      1. Memory (Philosophy)   2. Memory—Political aspects.   3. Identity
(Psychology)—Political aspects.   4. Justice (Philosophy)   I. Title.
BD181.7.B66 2006
128'.3—dc22   2005027430

Cornell University Press strives to use environmentally responsible suppliers and materials to the fullest extent possible in the publishing of its books. Such materials include vegetable-based, low-VOC inks and acid-free papers that are recycled, totally chlorine-free, or partly composed of nonwood fibers. For further information, visit our website at www.cornellpress.cornell.edu.

Cloth printing   10 9 8 7 6 5 4 3 2 1

For my daughter, Madeleine

Contents

Preface

Memory has been called a "vast palace" and an "immense edifice." Manifold and perplexing, "so precarious, so powerful," it is at once fragile and potent. Memory can be the weak flame of the struggle to remember, or the stable, enduring habits acquired over the long duration of relationships.[1] Its loss is greatly feared, yet often we seek the therapeutic power of forgetting. It has sustained a hidebound traditionalism in politics, but it has also been a weapon of liberation and a recognition of those who have been silenced or otherwise wronged. Memory has fueled merciless, violent strife, and it has been at the core of reconciliation and reconstruction. It has been used to justify great crimes, and yet it is central to the pursuit of justice. In these and more everyday ways, we live surrounded by memory, individual and social: in our habits, our names, the places where we live, street names, libraries, archives, and our citizenship, institutions, and laws. Still, we wonder what to make of memory and its gifts, though sometimes we are hardly even certain that they are gifts. Of the many chambers in this vast palace, I mean to ask particularly after the place of memory in politics, in the identity of political communities, and in their practices of doing justice, rather than about memory as a psychological phenomenon, as the "inner availability" of the past.

To begin with what may at first glance seem obvious: memory, as Aristotle says, "is of the past."[2] It would seem, therefore, that to look at memory and community is to reflect on a community's relation to its past. And that is of course true, but it is only a very incomplete and partial account

ix

of the role of memory. For memory is also a kind of making present of the past, an (attempted) abolition of the distance created by the passage of time and the ensuring of the persistence of the past into the present. In habits, those of the body and those of the heart, in institutions and ways of life, memory presides at the table of the present and is not just there as some remote archaeological presence, dead to who we are in the here and now. So too as a part of our enduringness as accountable agents, individual and collective, capable of owning our past actions, memory is central to our practical identity across time, in other words, to the persistence of the past in our midst. Together with future-oriented anticipation and commitment, it is a core part of the human time we inhabit. So memory is of the past, as Aristotle says, but the past is not always the past perfect, the "what was." It is rather woven into the continuity that we call identity, into our lives-in-common, and into our practices of justice. We could, in sum, freely adapt Marc Bloch's observation about the writing of history: "It is sometimes said: 'history is the science of the past.' [In my opinion] this is wrong . . . [among other reasons because of] the schism it claims to describe between the past and the so-called present."³

I have said that memory is manifold. One kind we could term (following Edward Casey) thick or autonomous. Thick memory is not the fight to hold on to the often fleeting traces of the absent, but rather a rich deposit of habit, of body memory and habits of the heart, of institutions, and so on. Here there is a solidity and a stability, a memory beyond active or conscious remembrance, and therefore often only barely visible to us in the present. Far from standing in need of constant efforts to preserve the past against erosion, this form of memory, it seems, does its work almost automatically. Such memory functions as a force shaping our perception of the present and future; it is a memory that pervades our lives-in-common, our life-world, whether that of families, professions, or political communities. Memory also has a preserving or guarding function, related to its special and fragile bond to what is absent. It is "the incessant actualization of what is not present . . . [t]he gift of absence."⁴ Memory here tries to close the distance with what is absent, to prevent its slipping away entirely.

Often, however, and even in the sanctuary of remembrance, the sense of absence and loss is never completely vanquished. Melancholy, nostalgia, the bittersweet recollection of things past are forms of memory, and so too are regret and remorse: all almost, but (crucially) not quite, the past perfect. Memory, as the making present of an absence, can be the work of guarding the unity or integrity of individual lives. Or it can be memory in the service of gathering together and preserving the binding threads of a life-in-common, threads that are often fragile and vulnerable. This struggle for persistence is intimately and in many ways bound up with the doing of justice. To investigate, to seek and preserve the vestiges of wrongs done, to keep victims and perpetrators in the light of remembrance, and to have their now past fates and deeds represented in a judicial forum: these are important elements of the temporal dimension of justice. Also central is the related duty to remember: that doing justice fulfills a responsibility to a community arrayed across time and to its members, past, present, and future. The flow of time, and the erosion it brings to traces and to memory, forgetfulness, and the willful desire to escape the memory of justice, all serve to make this work of memory especially fragile.

Memory, then, is at once a defensive struggle to preserve a connection with the absent and the dense soil of habit and institutional memory, that almost effortless infusion of the past into the present. Its work is often that of ingathering, and it protects (or seeks to protect) the identity of the person or community, the continuity of person or community across (dispersive) time. Allow me to sketch some basic points, drawing on the place of memory in the community of home and family. The family and especially its physical spaces have long been favorite tropes of writers about memory. The rooms of the family home are the original and principal locales of memory: Joseph Brodsky titled a reminiscence of his family life in Russia "In a Room and a Half." In antiquity, they were also common mnemonic devices.[5] Memory can reside in places, not mere empty spaces but ones that are intermingled with the inhabited time of human relationships. And it is to be found in a myriad of other forms of group memory: anniversary and birth dates, family trees, remembered stories, and in the material repositories of memory, in archives or photo albums in which images of the family, across years and generations, are tokens of both continuity and absence.[6] Some memories lie mute and need a narrator, for example, to turn the pages and tell a story for the images. And who tells those stories, and what they contain, how certain persons and events are made to stand out in broad daylight while others are consigned to the shadows of the forgotten, is itself a story of filiation, power, and memory within the community.

But family memories are not all the work of narration and invention. Some, on the contrary, seem to come back to us, as if the event "wants to be remembered," and not always happily or voluntarily.[7] Still others are to be found in our various inheritances, especially that of family names. Some forms of memory are, in a sense, the tectonic plates of our lives-in-common, shaping the way we receive and craft the more explicit memory narratives. The family members share in a certain habit-like memory, that is, the non-explicit, nearly invisible values, behaviors, and beliefs that are the geological deposit of enduring relationships. This habit-memory is itself a form of the persistence of the past; it is memory, but quite different from the active, deliberate work of recollection. Likewise, the family can be viewed as a form of institutional memory, as abiding in its constitution-like form, for example, its division of powers, responsibilities, and so forth. These other dimensions of the memory-life of the group interact in various ways with the more explicit narrative exercises of remembrance.

Two further observations. First, family memories in all these forms (archival, narrative, habit, and institutional) are a core part of the (related) boundedness and persistence of the group. To an outsider, they would be distant in the sense that even if the facts about them were made known to him, they would not evoke any recognition as being in some sense *his*. His relationship to them would be detached, which is not to say unmoved or without impact, but rather removed from the group whose identity is (in part) these memories. This memory defines one, delimited, community; but outside that framework it is little more than an assemblage of images, stories, and names. It is one of the locales of identity for the group whose bonds it helps to ground. Others have only an objective, detached relationship to it. Second, there is an intuition which belongs to the keeping of such forms of memory that they should be preserved and transmitted as a kind of bearing witness, as a debt owed to the community. This obligation in certain respects is closely kindred to justice, as we shall see, and might be described as a kind of indebtedness: what is owed within the context of an enduring community, an obligation incumbent on us as persons sharing a life-in-common. To neglect the memory of the community, not to preserve and transmit it, in short, not to bear witness to it, would be to damage the group's identity and violate a norm of reciprocity and co-responsibility: the debt, or quasi-contract, entailed by a life-in-common across time between the present in whose hands these memories (partially) rest and the absent past.

To reflect on the family's shared memory and identity, its enduringness and boundedness, is to see some (but not all) of the many questions at work in the study of (political) communities of memory. It shows memory in its fragile, vulnerable attempt to gather in and guard the past, lest it be lost to the passage of time and to forgetting. And it casts some light on the ways in which what is remembered and what is forgotten are shaped by power, interest, and selection in the present. At the same time, and as I just observed, this shaping itself draws on a reservoir of memories, the habit-like fruit of (and always at work in) our lives-in-common. I also remarked that ensuring the persistence of familial memory has a duty-like character about it, and thus forgetting in this context is something of a wrong, or at the very least a flaw to be remedied. Together these brief glimpses into memory's work in the life of a family point to its centrality for identity, understood as persistence and particularity, and for responsibility across time.

So memory is many things. It is the glacier-like deposits of habit-memory, of habits of the heart and body, that guard the past in the present and make it active there. It is also the flickering flame born of something absent, the struggle to keep the passage of time and the power of forgetting from effacing entirely what was. And while (or better, because) it is often about things absent, memory is central to making us whole and enduring.[8] Memory, we could say, is the fabric of a community's way of life. It can be all that in a presence as fleeting and as fragile as a trace, in the habits of the heart that we acquire as citizens, or in the monumental stone and inscriptions of the Lincoln Memorial, the Vietnam Veterans Memorial, or the Menin Gate at Ypres.

In this book I have chosen to focus my attention on memory and identity and, as a vital part of that, on bearing witness—bearing memory to others—as central to doing justice. Memory, because memory is essential to the coherence and enduringness of the community (or person), to its boundaries and persistence, in short, to its identity. Memory-identity matters because, among other things, it is the ground of imputation, of the society (or person) as owner of its past and responsible for it, as well as identical to, and thus capable of, making commitments to a future, of binding its future by a present promise. And because we are members of a persisting and accountable community, we bear witness. That is, we seek to ensure through acts of memory a certain persistence of the crime, the victim, and the perpetrator. Identity, justice, and memory thus emerge as tightly interwoven, and it is this path, among all the many corridors and avenues of the palace of memory, that I have chosen to follow. In doing so, I have had to stray from the familiar territory of the canonical memory of political philosophy. In part, this was a result of the relative dearth of philosophical writings in English on memory and politics. More important, however, questions about social memory have an expansive presence in other disciplines and places. An encounter with those literatures can be enormously enriching, and I have wanted to communicate to the reader as much of that wealth as I could manage. Finally, I have not wanted to lose sight of the deep, pervasive, everyday presence of memory in our lives as citizens, family members, and participants in professional vocations. This book is meant to illuminate that everyday reality.

Writing this volume has taken far more time than I initially thought it would, and not surprisingly I have incurred debts to many people along the way. Some I have thanked in the notes and others personally. Discussions with graduate students in an interdisciplinary seminar on memory, with colleagues in a faculty seminar on memory and society at Vanderbilt's Robert Penn Warren Center, as well as presentations to the Vanderbilt Law School and the Department of Philosophy, and at the University of California Humanities Research Institute have helped me greatly. So too have conferences at McGill University and in Paris. I owe special thanks to the College of Arts and Science at Vanderbilt, which supported this research with a sabbatical leave.

Two of my greatest debts lie outside the academy. I thank Father René Dutoc, pastor of St. Martin d'Igé in Normandy, who welcomed my daughter and me into his home and shared with us his knowledge of the village and its families. On his church walls the *mémoire longue* of the community is reflected in a plaque inscribed "Je me souviens" (I remember), followed by the names of families, including my mother's, Madeleine Belcourt's, which left from that region for the New World in the 1600s. My other debt is to Lieutenant Colonel Bruce Bolton, commanding officer of the Black Watch (Royal Highland Regiment) of Canada; the late Reggie Daigle, president of the Black Watch Veterans Association; and Terry Copp, who invited me to participate in a commemoration of the battle site at Verrières Ridge in Normandy, just south of Caen. There, in late July 1944, the Black Watch led an Anglo-Canadian attack against German positions and suffered staggering losses in the ensuing struggle. It was the second costliest day of the war for Canada, yet the place where it occurred remained unmarked for over fifty years. My father, Bill Booth, who was with the Black Watch at Verrières Ridge, read the dedication on behalf of the regiment, and a piper played the traditional lament, "Flowers of the Forest." Local officials from the villages of Ifs and St. André-sur-Orne were generous in their hospitality. I learned much from this, including the importance of place and memory, of debt and continuity, and of names.

One of those names was Gordon Hutton. Hutton was a teenager from the working-class Montreal community of Verdun. The triplex in which his family lived still stands. There are paper memories of him in the National Archives of Canada: the telegram to his mother informing her that he was missing in battle, as well as the second cable telling her that he had been killed in action. A letter to her from the Army Council reads, "We pay tribute to the sacrifice he so bravely made." There is a worn photograph of him, taken at a wedding: a tall boy with glasses. Gordon Hutton is buried in row IV.G.7 of the Canadian War Cemetery, Bretteville-sur-

Laize, Normandy. On his grave marker are the words "D83009 Private / G. Hutton / The Black Watch / Royal Highland Regiment / of Canada / 28th July 1944 Age 19 / Not only today / But every day / In silence we remember" / *In grateful remembrance.*

CHAPTER ONE

Identity and Memory

A passage in John Steinbeck's *Grapes of Wrath* describes a group of Dust Bowl–era tenants sorting through their things before the move westward: a pipe, a plow they used for planting mustard during the war, a picture: in short, all the bric-a-brac of their everyday life.[1] For some, these possessions are irretrievably tainted, the reminders of a life that failed them; for others, there is a powerful need to keep them. There is anguish even for those who want to get rid of their belongings, for their possessions, though burdensome to carry into the open and uncertain future in California, are the repositories of memories of family and community. To throw them away is to abandon that past, perhaps even to do it an injustice. But why not be done with the past? At best, one might say, these objects are a useless weight on a journey into the future, at worst, a reminder of loss and failure, a pollution of the new lives they will fashion for themselves in the West. Yet this *is* a wrenching issue and not a trifle for them. "How will we know it's us without our past?" they ask.[2]

A few observations on Steinbeck's story: (1) To have a sense of who you are, to have an identity, is to recognize yourself across time, to have a past, and not just to dwell in the (seemingly) point-like present moment or in an indeterminate future. A world without memory would be, in the words of Wallace Stevens, a "shallow spectacle": "Today the air is clear of everything. / It has no knowledge except of nothingness / And it flows over us without meanings, / As if none of us had ever been here before / And are not now: in this shallow spectacle, / This invisible activity, this sense."[3] (2) Having a past is more than being able to enumerate one's days by the cal-

1

endar. It is being in time, according to Hans-Georg Gadamer, as "remembering, forgetting and recalling" creatures.[4] Memory, then, the gathering in of the past, would seem to be central to continuity and identity, to an answer to the question "Who am I?" or "Who are we?" The narrator of Ralph Ellison's *Invisible Man* speaks of "my identity. . . . Who was I, how had I come to be?" and further on he says, "These [now recalled] images of past humiliations. . . . They were me; they defined me."[5] (3) Although they speak of what is "burned . . . into their memories," the past they cling to is also invested in things and places: we need to "live among things which tell us stories. We need a house, whose former occupant we know of, a piece of furniture in the small irregularities of which we recognize the artisan who worked on it. We need a city whose countenance awakens at least weak memories . . ." "Without locales [*lieux*]," writes Georges Poulet, "humans would be nothing but abstractions."[6] These *lieux,* as well as the mind and habits, are places of memory which retain the past. (4) The objects and places with which their past is intertwined are already social in the sense that they are framed by and infused with the elements of a life led in common: a plow and the wartime planting of crops, a horse and a little girl, the willow tree and the land outside their home. So, likewise, Ellison describes the bric-a-brac of an evicted African American couple's possessions, a greeting card from a grandchild, a lock of hair, a newspaper picture, as awakening a "pang of vague recognition: this junk, these shabby chairs . . . all throbbed within me with more meaning than there should have been . . ."[7] This is not the stuff of grand historical or memorial narratives; indeed, in the quoted passage from the *Grapes of Wrath,* the war is referred to only in passing and as a backdrop to the tenants' daily work in the fields. It is rather the intimate, shared remembrance of the small currency of everyday life. (5) Their possessions are mute and so need witnesses to say what place they had in their lives. They are the bearers of the past, its traces or icons, the things that evoke and secure memory and identity.[8] (6) Memory seeks to preserve; it is a guarding activity. The tenants want to hold on to the things imbued with their past. Throwing away those things would be a kind of forgetting, a violation of memory's call to hold on to the past. (7) Just as the tenants want to preserve a past that is central to what they are, so too do Steinbeck's words bear witness to the events of that era in American life, seek to preserve them in the national memory, and save these people and their time from oblivion. Bearing witness as a duty to past, present, and future stands at the heart of memory's guarding work. The pages that follow are built around these observations. In this section I look at (1) the relationship between memory, identity, and time; (2) the ways in which identity matters both practically and morally; and (3) collective and political memory-identity. The section concludes with a discussion of some illustrative cases.

1.1. IDENTITY, TIME, AND MEMORY

Discussions of political identity often focus on the identity of groups, on their recognition and difference. But the language of identity employed in these controversies is frequently of a tense-less kind (though not in the practical politics of identity, where history, heritage, and so on are central). The notion that in order to answer the question "Who are we?" or "Who am I?" we must draw deeply from memory's well is little in evidence. Where it is gestured toward (often as culture), it is embedded elsewhere, for example, in Will Kymlicka's account of "our language and history" as "contexts of choice," the "media through which we come to an awareness of the options available to us."[9] What it is that constitutes the sameness, the selfhood, of the group or political community across time and change is not at issue. Relatedly, the accountability of groups for their past (allowing, provisionally, that we can make sense of the possessive pronoun) and the group's responsibility for its future members are rarely at stake in debates over identity. Yet the politics of identity and recognition seem dependent on other, more basic claims about the nature of identity, time, and the memory that binds them together. For assertions of identity normally seek to do (at least) three related things: to draw a boundary between group members and others; to provide a basis for collective action; and to call attention to a life-in-common, a shared history and future. Clearly all three of these elements of identity politics involve claims about identity across time and change, and about identity and responsibility as well. Boundary-drawing criteria allow us to differentiate ourselves as a group, and they also mark out the group as a coherent entity through time. To identify is to distinguish in time.[10] What appears to be a purely present-tense, or tense-less, statement of identity turns out to involve a strong temporal dimension. Even current time-slice identity propositions, then, point to fundamental diachronic properties.

There are still other reasons to look for the grounding of identity in something more basic. As Susan Wolf suggests, our interest in persons or groups is rarely a present-tense matter only.[11] Rather, we see them in terms of shared pasts and future projects, as associations enduring across time and immune to (or attempting to resist) at least a certain range of alterations that the dispersive character of time seems to bring in its wake.[12] This is true of the idea of a shared history, and it is also true of the future.

For deliberation over my/our future typically assumes the identity of the (deciding) agent with the agent in the future. When projects are formed in the present, this behavior is explicable only against the background of the planner's continued existence into the future.[13] We can add to this that to see the group as the subject of imputation, of responsibility for or ownership of its past actions, is to locate the trace of a continuity extending back into the past. So (future) deliberation and commitment, and (past) accountability and the boundaries of a life-in-common that mark us apart from other groups or individuals all require a certain kind of persistence across time. The groups of identity politics, then, are actors with histories and projects, groups that sometimes speak of past injustices inflicted by earlier generations of other groups, and as such they must in some sense be continuous actors. Indeed, this would seem fundamental in speaking, as Iris Young and others do, about a group as something other than a mere passing aggregate, a transient aggregate of shared interests or views.[14] Enduringness, and with it accountability, matter and are at the core of our claims about political or group membership. The absence of reflection on these issues from current identity debates is a loss of a vital element in our understanding of the moral/political life of a community. The question of identity across time and of the imputability that depends on that sameness is basic not only to thinking about difference, identity, and recognition but also and relatedly to thinking more generally about what it means for a political community to have obligations stretching through time.

1.2. IDENTITY, PERSISTENCE, AND ETHICS

I turn here to a basic challenge to questions of identity across time, a challenge that originates with David Hume and finds a powerful contemporary voice in Derek Parfit's *Reasons and Persons*, a work that carries forward and, in certain respects, radicalizes Hume's treatment. I do this in order to sharpen the contours of the concept of identity and highlight its importance to political theory, using the Parfitian critique of (personal) identity theory to draw out some of the consequences of the view that strong identity is a (quasi-)fiction. Now, for Parfit, it makes no sense to speak of an enduring self underpinning and combining the various experiences of a life into a unity prefaced by the possessive pronoun "I." There is, he says, no "further fact" called the self, no self given directly to us in intuition. Or as Hume says: "If any impression gives rise to the idea of self, that impression must continue invariably the same, thro' the whole course of our lives; since self is suppos'd to exist after that manner. But there is no impression constant and invariable."[15] The self is never given as a single impression. Rather, we are a "bundle of impressions" in constant flux, a kind of theater, Hume writes, where several impressions appear serially. The "further fact" self said to give unity to the diverse experiences of a life is a fiction. What is real is the resemblance and relatedness of these various impressions, and it is on "relations of resemblance, contiguity and causation, that identity depends."[16] Put another way, the relationship between my self now, at time T, and what I was at $T - 1$ or will be at $T + 1$ has no connectedness other than what the "relations of resemblance, contiguity and causation" provide. Indeed, the very language of an "I" at $T - 1$, T, $T + 1$ is ambiguous and misleading, since it seems to invite just the bad metaphysics of the underlying self view, of a further fact above and apart from the various connections that link a series of impressions. Where those connections are thin, or lapse entirely, then it would be odd to speak of the same self at $T - 1$, unless, that is, one could show that there is something, a Cartesian ego, for example, that survives the dissolution of connections of resemblance, contiguity, and causation.

Parfit, like Hume, rejects the "further fact," or "non-reductionist," view of the self. There is no self or person standing behind and owning its actions, he argues; no separately existing entity, no Cartesian ego, no sense or substance that constitutes a "self." And because there is no such separate self but only a spectrum of more or less related connections of a physical or psychological kind, the question of identity (of the self) is empty. What gives unity to a life is not the subject of a possessive pronoun, an "I" who "owns" the events of his or her life, but rather the related events of body and mind, related in a way that admits of a considerable indeterminacy that is anathema to those who subscribe to the robust non-reductionist account of identity. It is those relations that matter, Parfit says, not identity. One upshot of the spectrum or degrees of connectedness view is that with the weakening or radical alteration of these relations, the person is less tied to that earlier individual, or perhaps not related at all.[17] In which case we can, in a "manner of speaking," as Parfit writes, talk of multiple selves over an individual's lifetime.

We can make the notion of multiple selves somewhat more intuitive if we consider the meaning of such commonplaces as "time heals." It heals (in this Parfitian reading) because in a way we become a different person and grow past the injury. In a similar vein, we consider the passage of years and a new way of life a mitigating factor in judging what punishment is due a person who committed a crime earlier in his life. In one sense,

the stain of guilt is indelible. But in another sense, a life well lived in suc-
ceeding years makes the crime committed in one's youth *almost* the act of
another person. Note that in the mitigation that time and change bring to
our evaluation of a person's youthful misdeeds, the fact of guilt remains:
the stain is unaltered and irrevocably on his account. The person in that
sense is identical across time: a crime committed in my youth is not someone else's act but mine, no matter how many years have passed and however different I have become. Mitigation in that sense is parasitic upon
this bedrock of identity. The boundary line that marks me out as an individual and that unites "my" past, present, and future, my experience and
expectation (to use Reinhart Koselleck's terms), into the wholeness of the
lived life of one person is thereby made thinner and indeterminate, and
so too is the basis for concern for "my" future or past. With this indeterminate spectrum-like character of my being across time, there follows also
a thinning of the relevant differences between myself and others. Since I
am no more remote from them than I am from earlier iterations of "my
self," the foundations of self-preference and concern are also weakened.
Interpersonal relations become similar to intrapersonal ones: Why (since
my relation to my own future states is as if to another self) should I weigh
my future more than the future of others, given that it may well be the future of a substantially different self?[18]

In commenting on the use of identity concepts in political theory, I
noted that it rests on assumptions about identity as (relatedly) boundary
markers, the engaging of the future, and a responsibility and inheritance
from the past. In that light, we could describe those consequences thus: if
there is no enduring self but only mutable and dissolvable relations, then
it would seem also that the self as a subject of attribution, as a responsible
agent accountable for her past deeds and able to assume commitments to
a future, would also be weakened or would wither away altogether. My responsibility for my past actions or to my future states would therefore be
similarly attenuated and would, in extreme cases, simply cease to hold. In
brief, the Parfitian (and Humean) claim that identity is the connection of
physical and psychological experiences points to an understanding of attribution (though this is not Parfit's principal normative concern) in
which the extent of that person's moral ledger and desert are far more
provisional and admitting of degrees than is the non-reductionist (strong
identity) account.[19] Identity matters in one way as a practical category, as
a way of answering the question, "Who is the agent responsible for this action?" It should be underscored here that its horizon is not simply retrospective, the assigning of responsibility for past actions. Memory-identity,
the foundation of the sameness of the person across (past) time as an ac-

countable agent, is intimately bound up with the continuity of the person into the future as a promise-making agent. Both, as Paul Ricoeur notes, are dimensions of the temporally situated, imputable agent. Both have their fragility, forgetting, and betrayal through the "vicissitudes of the heart" or of circumstances, and both therefore also have a dimension of struggle about them: the one to preserve in memory, the other to bind the self to the future through commitment (to bind oneself "despite" . . .).[20] To promise presupposes the expectation of sameness and memory. It is, Nietzsche writes, the "real *memory of the will*," and so forgetting is the true antonym of promising.[21] In brief, the two are related in that they belong to the core of identity as continuity of the practical agent across time.

They are also clearly related in their role in ongoing relations between persons, in the looking forward of enduring beings with a shared past, where memory and trust in the reliability of commitments go hand in hand. How we think about our personal futures, the tradeoffs we make in the present for their sake, our commitments to one another, or (collectively) the husbanding or trusteeship over nature, fiscal responsibility, and so on, are all matters in which we think of the future as, in an important sense, a continuation of our present selves. So the continuity or identity of the self matters not only in the sense of grounding the idea of a moral ledger of responsibility for the past ("*I* did that"), but for the future as well ("*I* will do that").[22] The reductionist (Parfitian) theory of the radical variability (even multiplicity) of the self (or selves) over time would have the most profound consequences for our practical lives. Guilt, shame, pride: those moral comportments that are ours as continuous with our past would have to be rethought. Likewise, hope, expectation, fear, and commitment to the future would be much less of a concern, unless we assumed such a similitude of passion that we could reasonably anticipate the same preferences, pleasures, and pains in the future.[23] Locke writes, "In this personal identity is founded all the right and justice of reward and punishment," and, we could add, all possibility of future-oriented commitment.[24] Indeed, it is this identity of the person, a "forensic term," as Locke says, that allows her to "appropriate" actions, to be the owner, so to speak, of her past, and to be concerned for the future which is also hers.[25] The doctrine of accountability, on the one hand, and that of concern for the future, on the other, both rest on robust assumptions about time and identity. If Parfit's challenge clarifies just how much our practices and judgments are interwoven with a certain view of time and identity, it also and at the same time mounts a powerful attack on the metaphysics of identity, with the upshot of making us both more convinced of the practical importance of the personal identity of a subject

across time and less certain as to how to analyze the grounds of that identity. Let me now turn to that issue.

1.3. SOURCES OF IDENTITY

Adequate identity concepts tell us the "what it is" of someone or something. But this "what it is" has a clear temporal dimension, a persistence
through time, the "prolongation of the [self of the] past into the present,"
and of course always the possibility of the decay or transformation of that
persistent something with the resulting dissolution of identity. To have an
identity is to have a history: the story of the enduringness of something
over time, as well as an account of what it would mean to fail to satisfy that
criterion.[26] Natural objects lend themselves most readily to standing
under identity criteria of a straightforward kind, artifacts and persons
more ambiguously so.[27] That latter fact may suggest that in these cases
identity concepts are arbitrary in relation to the thing or person sub-
sumed under them. If identity is something wholly confected by a playful
invention of new concepts, this would undermine the work of answering
the "What is it?" question as a matter of persistence, of sameness through
time, and with that undermining would come political/ethical issues similar to those I raised in reaction to Parfit.

I just said that identity concepts are applicable, most uncontroversially,
to natural things and to humans insofar as they are considered as such
natural things. Yet the physical criteria typically employed to specify the
identity of natural things seem incomplete when used to account for the
identity of persons.[28] Locke captured the need for this something further
in his distinction between the identity of a man and of a person. The
identity of a man, of a human as a natural kind, consists, he wrote, in the
sameness of body or material. The identity of a person, by contrast, is that
of a being "appropriating actions and their merit; and so [it] belongs only
to intelligent agents, capable of a law, and happiness, and misery." This
forensic notion of a person, denoting a being capable of appropriating
actions and hence of accountability, clearly has a temporal dimension:
that I am accountable for past actions because they are mine, and so belong to the same person that I was then and am now. For Locke, though,
there was a sharp distinction between the material identity of a human
being and the psychological identity criteria of forensic personhood. The
latter, he held, was both a necessary and a sufficient condition of personal
identity.[29] This view, in its extreme form, has been the object of much criticism. My concern with the Lockean account, however, lies in the way its

forensic interest directs it to a certain kind of continuity: that identity underlies the possibility of moral personality.

Here, in brief, are two ways of understanding the relation between identity and moral personhood. First, identity grounds the possibility of moral accountability, of the person as the possessor of a ledger of actions for which she remains responsible across time and change and so capable of guilt, promise-making, shame, and pride. This can be expressed as identity on the ownership model, for it captures the essential "mineness" of actions, a property that lies at the heart of the person as a potential subject of moral imputation. The "mineness," a sort of boundary line marking me and my ledger apart from those of others, is made possible by a self which is continuous through time, and it is at the center of moral personhood, of moral character and its requisite stability, that is, of accountability, imputation, and commitment.[30] A second and related way of thinking about the moral underpinnings of the continuous identity of a human self focuses not so much on the notion of moral accounts and ledgers but rather on agency and deliberation. The "mineness" of authorship and accountability is closely tied to agency, for it is in our authorial relationship to these deeds that we appropriate them as ours, both those on our past ledger and those to come. We are authors of our actions, and so we deliberate about possible courses of action, all of which are or will be ours, if we adopt them. As deliberators, we choose, arrange, and order our desires and preferences and map a path into the future. It is, Christine Korsgaard argues, the unity of this agency across time that is the basis of my concern for the future. So accountability, the weight of the past on *my* ledger, my future concerns including a deliberative stance toward my future self, and my defining, individuating boundaries are intertwined in the identity or unity of my person as an ethical agent across time. Identity here emerges not as a metaphysical postulate, a Cartesian ego, or any kind of supervening "further fact," but as a practical necessity arising from the idea of oneself as an agent, together with the preconditions of this agency.[31] Central among these preconditions is that I deliberate about and make choices concerning a self arrayed across time, whose future will be mine. And that fact, the continuity of the agent past and future, is at the core of what I do now, in the present. Indeed, as Korsgaard suggests, the idea of a purely present-tense self is unintelligible from the standpoint of the person as agent because (among other things) it lacks the notion of the "mineness" of the future that allows us to make sense of deliberation.

This practical, agency-grounded concept of self and identity is absent from Parfit's account. Instead, as we have seen, he treats the person in an objective or "sideward"-looking manner, in other words, in an impersonal fashion. Action and agency, Simon Blackburn suggests, are lost in such a perspective, and so personhood and identity are reduced to an agent-less collection of experiences or ownerless events and whatever connectedness they may happen to have.[32] Once the authorial and proprietary relationship between time and self, a relationship central to the (moral) agent-centered perspective, is dropped, then a person just is a locus of experience or bundle of behaviors and states of mind within a spectrum of relatedness.[33] The "less deep" character of the Parfitian self is another way of expressing the bundle of experiences view. This self is less deep, admitting of degrees of relatedness to its past and future versions, precisely because it is a self composed of more or less related experiences. The self as moral agent has disappeared, and thus a core part of human identity across time is absent from this account.

Recall from my earlier discussion that physical criteria of personal identity, while essential, do not capture the ethical, agent-centered aspects of identity. Treating psychological identity criteria as if they were sufficient for identity, however, seems inaccurate too. The embodied nature of human life, and the tie of that sort of continuity to our existence as agents, makes a purely psychological approach unconvincing.[34] To see this, consider again what is perhaps the best known of the psychological theories of identity, Locke's argument that the identity of a (forensic) person resides entirely in memory. This view, as I suggested earlier, is bound up with his certainty that while a materialist account may, in Locke's distinction, explain the identity of a man (i.e., as a natural kind), it cannot express the duration of the person as an accountable moral agent. For that purpose, what is needed is the unity through time of our consciousness. And what does the work of binding together past and present states into moments of the consciousness of one being is, Locke contends, memory.[35] Some rejoinders to this contention point to delusional memory and draw out the odd implications raised by amnesia for a view which holds that the (forensic) person ends where her memory ends.[36] Another line of critique develops the claim that memory must be parasitic on some other form of continuity. As early as Joseph Butler's 1736 retort to Locke, it was observed that consciousness "ascertains" identity but does not constitute it. Memory according to these critiques cannot be the foundation of identity since it seems to presuppose the identity of its owner.[37] More generally, we might say that the root problem in Locke's account lies in the idea of a separable forensic personhood reducible entirely to states of consciousness. This does violence to the real-life identity of persons and hence produces some of its deeply counterintuitive results. The idea that identity could be grounded in a self-contained criterion of consciousness, as if memory (in Locke's account) were an exhaustive and self-sufficient source of identity, not standing in need of, for example, embodied agency, is its core failing.[38]

But if memory is not a freestanding or self-sufficient source of identity, it nevertheless is one key element, in concert with others, that gives a continuity or wholeness to our lives. Without it, Paul Valéry writes, "consciousness . . . would be an eternal beginning."[39] We could put this rather more generally, with Kant, by observing that self-consciousness is at its core historical in character, meaning that it involves the capacity to tie representations to one another, to weave through and judge representations from the past.[40] And it involves this capacity for an ingathering of the past not simply as a condition of continuity with that past but as a condition of self-consciousness in the present. Pascal Quignard writes, "The interior structure of human beings is cumulative. The past is the father of interiority. . . . All self is full of the past."[41] The essential historicality of ethical agency or identity closely tracks this. Recall that in discussing agency and identity, I observed that the possibility of agency (as the subject of imputable actions, a deliberator and the maker of promises) requires the idea of a persistence of this self through the past and into the future. Memory is one key way in which we gather in that morally relevant past, survey not our material persistence, not every empirical detail of that past, but rather its ethical topography.[42]

Yet memory, operative in this ethical dimension of identity, is not simply bound up with the person's persistence but is itself the object of ethical imperatives. Memory weaves narratives and judges, calls to mind both the good and the shameful, and allows us to weigh them. The person who willfully chooses amnesia about wrongs for which he is responsible, or whose recollection of them is unable to discern their evil, is a person whose memory has failed, not necessarily in the sense of being factually in error but rather as having failed morally. We judge a person in part by what and how he remembers, and we call those shameless who consider irrelevant their past bad conduct. Memory makes us whole by (among its manifold forms of presence) binding us in judging remembrance with our past and is thus itself the subject of ethical strictures, of a duty to remember. It is a way in which we secure our persistence through time, not as materially identical beings but as self-conscious, active moral agents with an accountability arrayed across time. Memory is, in brief, deeply bound up with our ethical life: it is part of the persistence of the person as agent; it casts judgment (or fails to), awakens shame (or is shameless), and responds (or not) to the imperative to remember.

Time is dispersive, as Edward Casey writes, but memory collects: it gathers in a past that is mine/ours, and that, together with future-oriented concerns and projects, maps out my/our persistence and distinctness across time.[43] It also sets defining boundaries, distinguishing one person or community from another and giving individuals a part of the foundation of their embeddedness in communities. Autobiographical memories individuate me; group memories define who we are in the world in a way that distinguishes us as a community. Memory's appropriation of a past makes it mine and distinguishes me from others: identity involves possession of a past that thereby differentiates me from others.[44] To be a person, to lead a life, then, is in an important sense to have a memory, to have the ability to tell a story, to bind past and present, and not to lead a mere point-like existence.[45] Consider Christa Wolf's observation: "How does *life* come to exist?" she asks. "Is life identical with the unavoidable yet mysterious passage of time? While I write this sentence, time passes. At the same time, a tiny piece of my life comes into being and passes away. So is my life composed of innumerable such microscopic bits of time? . . . [L]ife is more than the sum of moments, more too than the sum of all [our] days. At some point or other, and unnoticed by us, this everyday is transformed into lived time. . . . into the course of a life [*Lebenslauf*]."[46] Wolf goes on to record a mixture of autobiographical and social/political observations arrayed across the twenty-seventh of September over each of the next forty years. Her narrative, she says, is born of a fear of forgetting, a loss of the everyday, the everyday that, held together in memory, makes a whole life.

In that light, we can better understand Oliver Sacks's comment on a patient who could remember nothing for more than a few seconds, who would confect an array of always changing stories about himself: "To be ourselves we must *have* ourselves—possess, if need be re-possess, our life-stories. We must 'recollect' ourselves, recollect the inner drama, the narrative, of ourselves. A man *needs* such a narrative, a continuous inner narrative, to maintain his identity, his self."[47] It is memory that is this synthetic force, binding together the events of our lives into something like a unity.[48] It seems implausible, therefore, to think of memory simply as evidence of another, underlying identity. For to the extent that human life is historical, that, in Heidegger's words, "I *am*-as-having-been," memory is the "sanctuary of our having been."[49] Memory gathers in the episodes of a life and weaves them into a life. Indeed, it is because of memory that we are conscious of our being in time, and of its duration; there can be no duration without memory.[50] A human who suffered radical and recurring bouts of amnesia would have no history, indeed, would scarcely have a self, save whatever was given to him in the (always vanishing) present. This would, of course, be true, however much the natural facts about him allowed outside observers to describe him as a continuously existing being. Vladimir Jankélévitch adds to this that a life without traces, without memory, would be one of total innocence. Burden, debt, guilt, shame, pride, and so forth belong to creatures with a horizon greater than the present moment, to beings able to see themselves across the duration of time. So, likewise, as I have suggested, would their future-oriented counterparts; promise-making and anticipation require such a unity in time. A consciousness of "pure succession" alone would be to live, in Plato's words, like an oyster, without memory even of life's pleasures.[51]

1.4. POLITICAL IDENTITY

Similar uncertainties recur, *mutatis mutandis*, in thinking about political identity. Consider the use that Hume and Parfit make of the analogy between personal identity and the republic or nation. Hume writes: ". . . I cannot compare the soul more properly to any thing than to a republic or commonwealth, in which the several members are united by the reciprocal ties of government and subordination, and give rise to other persons, who propagate the same republic in the incessant changes of its parts. And as the same individual republic may not only change its members, but also its laws and constitutions; in like manner the same person may vary his disposition, as well as his impressions and ideas, without losing his identity."[52] The relation of causation, Hume says, is the connection between these several parts. Parfit uses this to suggest that the reductionist view is not as counterintuitive as it might at first seem. Though nations, Parfit says, are not reducible to their component parts, to their citizens and territory, say, and though we quite naturally speak of nations existing, we do not, apart from extreme forms of nationalism, normally ascribe to them some separate and enduring self. A nation is a coming together of citizens in a territory, with institutions, laws, habits, and so forth. The holding over time of these connections is what allows us to speak of a nation. There is no further fact, Parfit argues, beyond the holding of those relations. And, as in the case of an individual's life, that relatedness is a matter of degree. Since this connectedness is a matter of degree, we readily divide a nation's history into distinct parts or epochs, and presumably the more distant those parts, the more alien they are, the less we see them as parts of us.[53] So, in Parfit's view, we are (mostly mistakenly) holists when it comes to individuals but atomists with respect to nations. That is, we find the thin unity of related experiences, with its corollary of multiple selves, menacing to (among other things) our ethical experience of the world, to the unity of our lives as accountable agents, whereas we are, he continues, much less concerned to find a unity or identity of this kind for a nation or political community. Political identity, like personal identity, consists "in nothing more than the holding over time of various connections, some of which are matters of degree."[54]

I want to employ this comparison to show how similar problems emerge at the level of the political community. As we have seen, identity in a general sense is a way of speaking of the persistence and sameness of something across time and change. Identity, whether personal or collective, is (following Locke's account) in central part a "forensic" category. Identity propositions state similarities relevant to establishing agency, accountability (for the past), and commitment-making and trusteeship in relation to the future. Now if, as Locke says, the identity of the self is the basis of desert, justice, and rights, we would anticipate that holding a political community responsible for the past and as capable of trusteeship for its future requires that we understand it to be in (forensically) important respects identical. As with personal identity, a weakening of that enduring self changes the contours of accountability since there may now be such distance between the community (or person) at T_1 and $T - 1$ that they ought to be treated as two different societies (persons). By the same token, if the community at T_2 may well be substantially different from what it is at present, with different preferences, relations, and so on, it makes little sense to consider its future a direct extension of our own. It is rather the future of some other community. And since that continuity is the basis of concern for the future, it would make a concernful comportment equally problematic. We would have no more reason to be interested in it than in the future of another community, just as in the Parfitian account of individual identity, where, as I wrote earlier, interpersonal states can be on a par with intrapersonal ones in terms of their connectedness.

The "remembering, forgetting, and recalling" that is the heart of our identity and accountability across time is also, and relatedly, at the center of the relationships that make up our life-in-common. The "face that one loves . . . [is] the mirror of the past," writes Proust. "Love and moral character," Susan Wolf observes, "require more than a few minutes."[55] In Wim Wenders's *Wings of Desire,* an angel falls in love, becomes human, and at the end of the story writes, "Now I know what no angel knows."[56] In the timeless world of angels, relationships were not possible. For love to be possible, temporality was needed, and so, as he says, no angel can know it. Human relationships take time, not in some abstract sense of the measures of clock or calendar time, or merely as a means, as in "it takes time to cultivate such-and-such," but because relationships just are temporal: they are composed of past, present, and future, of experience and expectation, of the presence of the past in memory and of the future in anticipation, of commitment, fidelity, and infidelity. I mean to suggest here that lives led in common, whether political, vocational, or familial, have an enduringness about them that is anchored in the persistence of the memories which frame them and give them sense. That property they have not as a mere contingent attribute but as a distinguishing feature that separates them from the ephemeral ties of neighborhood, or the abstract, remote bonds of universal humankind and its rights. Remembered time is the depth and intimacy of relationships. From it comes the stock of what Habermas terms the life-world: the background or tacit set of convictions, the often silent "habits of the heart" as well as its more explicit traditions.[57] At times the memory of our lives-in-common resides in us, effortlessly, as something latent, not consciously recalled, almost reflex-like: in our gestures, attitudes, unreflective values, and so on. At other times, memory is work: we glance backwards in time in an effort to assure ourselves of the enduringness of our life-in-common, even through change: hence the centrality of historical memory, of scholarly canons, musical repertoires, or sacred texts and rituals to these forms of commonality. Even an everyday thing such as the family photo album expresses "the truth of social memory . . . monuments of its past unity, or, what amounts to the same thing, confirmations [retained from the past] of its present unity. . . . [It is the family's] common past."[58]

It is the habit-memory of that past, as well as explicit remembrance, that is essential to the identity of lives led in common, the persistence of the meaning and value of those relationships. When Burke writes of Britain as an inheritance of liberty held warmly in the bosoms of its citizens, in their untutored feelings and prejudices, and expressed in its "bearings and . . . ensigns armorial . . . its gallery of portraits, its monumental inscriptions, its evidences, and titles . . . our hearths, our sepulchres, and our altars," and contrasts that to the abstract, past-less (or with a past artificially preserved in museums) calculus of the French Revolution, a part of what he is suggesting is just this centrality of a life-in-common as a relationship given depth and solidity by its enduringness in the various forms of memory (sepulchres, habits, and so on), and by the awareness of that duration.[59] Indeed, his argument is that rights and liberties flourish only when rooted in such deep ground, in communities of character that unite societies across time, giving them a retrospective indebtedness and a concern for the remote future. "Abstract" principles alone, principles not embedded in the lived time of a community's relationships, cannot sustain a community in its identity, obligations, or plans. For that, something else is needed that will give a life-in-common its requisite density. Political identity, through time and change, then, is not a matter of autochthony, of getting a lineage right, nor is it only a matter of asserting our present-tense values, forms of belonging, and so on. Identity works in three tenses, past, present, and future, and in one of its central moments it is ethical. It makes us one with the past for purposes of accountability, sheds light on who we are in the here and now, and binds us as stewards over our future societies.[60] Identity is an ownership of the past, something that makes us co-responsible for it, and an expectant look toward a future that we also see as ours. It expresses an attachment to the past that is ours and a concern for our future. Both belong to Susan Wolf's observation that relationships take time.

What is it, at the level of political life, that is sufficient to avoid such ruptures in the persistence of a community, and to do the work of giving it boundedness and persistence? Paralleling personal identity, there are a number of candidates that might seem to work to establish both the boundary (individuation) and the persistence criteria of the identity of (political) communities. One could say that territorial stability, analogous to the claim that the body grounds an individual's identity, would suffice. Or we could assert that an ethnic commonality is what makes a community identical across time. These claims, rough analogues to material identity concepts, have internal difficulties, some of which were already signaled in Aristotle's discussion of the city.[61] Their more basic insufficiency, however, is that the search for the identity of a political community is centrally concerned with locating boundary and continuity properties of a forensic kind, that is, capable of grounding the kinds of relationships that sustain imputability and commitment. Lineage does not do the requisite work here, and borders do only a part of it. What then differentiates moral subjects one from the other, and what is the identity that makes a person or community the imputable author of actions across time and change? To meet this tight standard of accountability, intention, and choice exercised through a decision-making structure would seem to be essential. In other words, in order to recognize these collective entities as person-like agents capable of desert, culpability, and so forth, we must be able to specify for them the terms of their agency, of their persistence and individuating boundaries, and of the criteria relevant to discerning when they cease to hold.[62]

1.5. AGENCY AND THE ACCOUNTABILITY OF COMMUNITIES

We might begin with a problem ventured in Aristotle's *Politics*, one that closely tracks those raised by Hume and Parfit in their analyses of personal identity. His question is whether, after a regime change, the newly founded political community is liable for the past, in this instance for the debts, fiscal and others, of its predecessor. To answer that, Aristotle suggests, we first have to ask if "a city [is] the same city as it was before, or not the same but a different city?"[63] And if the same, on what basis? By virtue of being inhabited by people of one race (*genos*)? Or because they live in the same bounded space? Aristotle argues that these are important but not sufficient. He prefers instead to seek the grounds of continuity in the constitutional form of the community, its decision-making structures, membership rules, and so forth. We shall see further on that this position is not without its own difficulties, but for the moment I want to remark on one of the results of seeing identity, both individual and that of a community, primarily in light of an understanding of agency and persistence, of the "mineness" of past actions, which would make us strictly accountable for them. We can discern the consequences of this approach in Aristotle's question about the responsibility of new regimes for debts incurred by their predecessors. What this does is to link identity to a fairly tight notion of authorship of actions: that they belong, in the sense of being (intentionally) authored by a person who is continuous across time. Against that background, Aristotle's puzzle frames the issue of political identity in the language of debt, liability, and guilt. Guilt, legal or moral, and accountability of the sort being discussed by Aristotle tend to demand clear boundaries defining the identity of the responsible agent.[64] Accountability of this kind allows of no gray areas, no seeping over of the ledgers between different persons or between successor regimes.[65] This reflects the judgment that the idea of a collective guilt of persons is "barbarous," and so too the idea of blood pollution, that is, that guilt can stain a community across time and generations.[66] The language of creditors and debtors, of debts and guilt, whether individual or political, limits the relevant agent to a person, institution, or political community that can be held to be the (intentional) author and owner of these deeds. The boundary and persistence conditions, in other words the operative notion of identity, must answer the need for a stable identity required for the type of accountability just discussed.[67]

Aristotle's (not unambiguous) answer to this is, as I said, that the constitution, including the array of institutions that it specifies, gives a political community its identity as the persisting author/owner of actions and debts. Constitutions, we might say, typically establish an institutional decision-making framework for a political community and set out the mission for those institutions. It is via these two functions that a constitution and its institutional expressions individuate a community, give it a moral personality as a responsible agent, and describe the conditions of its persistence (and, implicitly at least, of the circumstances under which it would cease to exist). Constitutions and their core institutional forms are one kind of memory vector, ensuring persistence and boundedness across time. Consider the analogous idea of corporate identity and responsibility. Here we are looking at the corporation not as an aggregate of individuals, each with will and agency, but as a legal person possessing a "conglomerate" rather than a mere aggregate identity.[68] In aggregate collectivities with no corporate identity that transcends the sum of the actual individuals who compose it, only those individuals themselves are accountable, and then only for their own acts. Collective responsibility would not be acceptable, for there is no imputable collective author here but only a collection of individual wills. It is against the application of the idea of collective responsibility in such cases that much criticism has rightfully been directed. Corporate or conglomerate persons, by contrast, have a duration through time and an accountability that is not dependent on a continuity of individual agents.[69]

What is this corporate or collective identity that makes the body as a whole responsible? Plainly, the corporate (or political) equivalents of the Cartesian ego will work no better here than they did in personal identity. There simply is no further fact about these conglomerate entities, no "soul" or "spirit" of the whole, that could serve to make them collective persons capable of imputation. A credible alternative, on the model of the identity of the person, is to look at the duration and accountability of these bodies in terms of their (persistent) agency and intentionality. Peter French identifies this conglomerate agency with a corporation's end or purpose and relatedly its decision-making structure.[70] It is the continuity of these properties, even in the presence of other changes (e.g., of personnel), that makes the corporation an identical and enduringly responsible body and not a simple aggregate of individuals. That a Volkswagen corporation, for example, or a Philip Morris is in principle answerable today for actions that likely predate most or all of their current personnel's membership in the firm is explicable in terms of corporate identity.[71] So too can we, in this way, understand the meaning of a gesture such as Prime Minister Tony Blair's apology for the conduct of the British government during the Irish Great Famine or the 2001 statement by Pope John Paul II of the Catholic Church's regret over the pillaging of Constantinople in 1204.[72] And this in turn allows us to understand better Aristotle's constitutional answer to the question of the sameness or difference of a city as it bears on the transmission of obligations across time. The constitution, as the sum of political decision-making institutions and their guiding principles, defines the continuity of the body politic as an identical agent, strictly accountable, and persistent through time. It also does that other identity work of setting out the boundary conditions of the regime, differentiating this political community from others, and it provides some guidance as to defining those conditions under which this community would cease to be identical.

Thus, when we say that a country is responsible for something, we are not, according to the preceding account, committed to a metaphysics of identity, to a "soul of the community" view, nor to a repugnant notion of blood pollution, in which individuals are held accountable for the corporate actions of their community. Rather, when we say that, for example, slavery remains on the American ledger, we mean that the constitutional and institutional persistence of the United States, the continuity of a political project, confers a collective responsibility on the community in its capacity as an identical (corporate) moral person. It belongs to Americans, not individually but as members of a community defined in terms of constitutional identity.[73] This unfolding of the meaning of political identity, understood as a cluster of boundary, persistence, and accountability criteria, captures an important part of the sense in which, even in a liberal society with its understanding of individual accountability, a political community remains responsible for the actions and undertakings of its predecessors.

1.6. BEYOND CONSTITUTIONAL CONTINUITY

We have seen that at the level of the political community, identity through time can be thought of, on the Aristotelian view, as residing in a constitutional/institutional continuity understood as the locale of political agency. In an important sense, it is through institutions and their continuity that we, as citizens, are bound to a past and a future that extend beyond our own lifetimes.[74] The identity of a regime, Aristotle concludes, is the continuity of its constitutional form. But, as Nicole Loraux observes, his apparent commitment to constitutional identity is made questionable by the very phrasing that he uses to express it: "when the city passes to another constitution."[75] This suggests that there is some entity, "the city," that, remaining one and the same, nevertheless moves from one constitutional form to another. Aristotle's hesitation here is not merely of philological interest. Rather it serves to highlight the ambiguity of his formulation of political identity: on the one hand, the absence of a political commonality in the ethnic/territorial definition seems unsatisfactory, and, on the other, the claim of the possibility of a radical rupture in identity in the constitutional thesis appears overstated, as if one community ceased to exist and another came into being with the installing of a new constitutional order.

One way to approach this aporia would be to ask what is missing from the constitutional understanding of identity and responsibility. Here I want to venture that the core of our continuity and distinctiveness (persistence and boundary) cannot be understood wholly by using agency criteria appropriate to the task of establishing strong imputableness, debt, and guilt. In other words, the (stringent) criteria we use to describe the continuity of an agent as the subject of imputation, as capable of owing a debt and being guilty, do not exhaust the ways in which we understand political identity, persistence, and responsibility. It is not exhaustive for two reasons. First, as central as (tightly defined) debt and responsibility are to the life-in-common of a political community over time, there is more to its defining mutuality than this sort of accountability. That was evident, I think, to Aristotle. For he maintained that belonging to a city involved a shared perception of justice, and he argued for the importance of habituation in virtue and the political virtues of a life-in-common.[76] So the identity of a community, its boundary and persistence criteria, consists in those of its parts that make it a body accountable (narrowly and broadly) across time and in part in the elements of a mutuality, a shared view of justice, and the habituation needed to live a life in accord with that perception. It should be underlined here that there is considerable overlap in this: the cohesive time of accountability and the time of habituation can be seen as two facets of a life-in-common. Second, because the constitutional notion of responsibility is too tightly tied to agency and authorship, it misses those areas of culpability in which we are involved even though not the authors of the actions themselves. Recall that in discussing approaches to personal identity, I focused on the centrality of responsibility over time, of the unity of a person whose moral life constitutes a whole.[77] This in turn I divided into, first, an agency-centered account, in which the unifying thread is the person who has acted and who deliberates about his or her future, and second, a more diffuse moral responsibility in which I need not intentionally be the author of these actions, or even their author at all. Agency, intentionality, and shame or pride are different but related sides of the moral identity of a person. Intentionality binds her to those moments of her life in which her agency and authorship are fully in play, and in which those actions are therefore fully imputable to her. Shame and pride, via memory, show how our past actions are woven into the wholeness of the lives we lead. And it displays the ways in which we are implicated, by virtue of being members of a family, a faith, or a political community, in a mesh of responsibility extending beyond individual agency.[78]

Institutions, including constitutions, and their memory work are crucial elements of the identity (persistence/boundary) of political communities. But the character and enduringness of a political community are not rooted only in its constitutional/institutional forms of social memory. Here I want to develop the remarks I just made by setting out an overview of the wider place of memory in identity, and extending the argument that memory is a crucial element not only of individual but of collective (including political) identity as well. Consider first Ernest Renan's argument that nations are, in central part, what they remember.[79] Similar insights underpin the many references in the political philosophical literature to "historical" communities. When the word "historical" and its cognates are used in this connection, it does not mean being amenable to a chronological, causally ordered account of a third-person (the view from the outside) type such as one might give in offering a natural history of an organism or species. Rather it signifies something closer to the collective first-person (the view from the inside) recollection by a community of its own past as a core part of its identity. Collective memory consists of the varied forms in which a community is tied to its past. It involves, among other things, the storing up of the interpretative work of previous generations as part of the self-understanding of the community (traditions), the debts and responsibilities that it carries as a continuous body (justice), its institutions and constitution, its explicit memorial activities, and the near-invisible absorption of memory into the civic habits of a people.[80] Collective memory, then, comprises the manifold forms of memory of a life-in-common. At this level of identity as the fabric of a life-world, collective memory is often neither explicitly political nor even explicit at all. It is rather a "tonality" of "sentiments," a certain way of doing things.[81] In the habits and conventions that shape our daily lives, we live out the long memory of our life-in-common.

1.6.1. The Memory of a Life-in-Common

What is at stake here is not accountability as such but something related to it, the framework of a life-in-common. That life-in-common, whether of a national, strictly political, or nation-state form, implicates us in a mutuality not only of our present moment but of our shared past as well, our collective memory. Even the elective nation of Renan's "daily plebiscite" requires a common past, a rich legacy of memories in addition to the desire to live together in the present.[82] John Stuart Mill argues that the de-

sire to be under the same government and to be governed by ourselves requires "common sympathies." The varieties of identity are many, he says.
"But the strongest of all is identity of political antecedents; the possession
of a national history, and consequent community of recollections . . ."[83]
So the past gives us an enduring society in common, something particular
to us, an identity with the past that in turn serves as a foundation for our
present and future life-in-common.

   This possession of a past is the work of memory, and it yields, in Mill's
phrase, a "community of recollection." The past is recollected, appropriated, made present in memory. Now, in theories of personal identity,
there is a natural person who is the rememberer, and, at least in the central cases, memory is first-person. Here, however, I am speaking of collective memory, of the memory of a community not reducible to an aggregate of the recollections of its individual members. Consider again the
family and its memory. To be a member of a family is to share in a community stretched across generations. Marking out the enclosing limits
may be certain biological relations among its members. It may be that we
can tell a genealogical tale about them, grafting each member into a position, a place on a branch of the family tree. These are views from the outside, accurate in their way, perhaps, but not capturing the core of what it
means to live in a community that appropriates its past in a special way.
Rather, it is memory that is the characteristic mode of incorporating the
group's past. We have first-person inner memories of childhood and our
parents, memories nourished and framed by the family's shared recollection of itself, and there are also the stories, photographs, and places, the
traces of the past that are etched in space (our rooms, homes, neighborhoods, and cities), which carry us back to earlier generations. We understand these family memories as at once given to us, existing independ-
ently of us, and revisable. They are experienced as independent in that
they are, so to speak, our inheritance, something into which we are born,
or "thrown," and over which we have no further say. That our parents or
grandparents did such and such, something that we are proud of or
ashamed of, belongs to us insofar as it is given in the identity of the family.
Yet we also know that it can be received in narrative form, revisable, not
infinitely so, but in the value we attach to its elements, to what we elect to
emphasize or to leave in the shadows, choices that are themselves in-
structed by the habits of the heart already acquired in the bosom of the
family. The familial framework of memory makes our own memory as
family members possible, and at the same time leaves a space for us to
mold and reshape the narrative of which we are inescapably a part. The

character of the community of musicians or scholars allows us to make a related, but somewhat different, point. Here the quasi-natural unity and intimacy of the intergenerational family is missing. Musicians share a past that is composed of the artistic work of their predecessors. Their language, the grammar and notation of the music they read, is the imprint of the past. Likewise, the canon of their community is a narrative of that past and the core of musicians' identity. And again, as in the case of the family, they are given this past; and in its framework it shapes their group memory. That it does even amidst the change and revision that is part of the evolution of the group. So the canon changes; Bach comes into his own, Mozart is displaced; the legacy is altered, but all within a framework of memory-identity.

These are illustrations of the way in which we quite naturally speak of groups having memory, indeed having their identity constituted by a memory that is not simply reducible to the first-person, inwardly available recollections of the individuals who make up that group. Political communities have memories most obviously (though not exclusively or even primarily) in the narratives that bind their present and past, and make sense of their being over time. To say that a community is historical is to hold, among other things, that it has a shared past, one expression of which is the narrative of that past, the fruit of the community's will to remember. Here as in the case of memory and personal identity, memory appropriates the past and makes it present. The time of collective memory, whether of families, musicians, or political communities, is not homogeneous and abstract; it is not calendar time, recording the passing of identical units, days, months, and years.[84] Rather it is the ingathering of past time, relevant morally for the group and for its cohesion. Its time is often normative and didactic. Memory time is, in part, a framework of seminal events and persons, an uneven topography of the past where "seminal" does not mean necessarily as a historian would rank them but rather ordered according to their felt importance in the ongoing life of the group. Much that would belong in a chronological or explanatory account therefore finds no place here. Françoise Zonabend writes that in Minot, the village she studied, the villagers' collective *mémoire longue* scarcely includes the two world wars. Similarly, Lucien Aschieri's analysis of memory in a Provençal village records that while the Saracen conquest is still vividly (and inaccurately) remembered in the region, other major events such as World War II are absent.[85] In the passage from *The Grapes of Wrath* discussed earlier, the war is only a background framework in which to situate the planting of mustard. Collective memory in its narrative form is, then, uneven and does not always or even often map neatly onto a chronologically ordered, causal/explanatory retelling of a community's history.

I have focused thus far on the recollective and habit-like forms of memory. Here I want to sketch another two aspects, which we will encounter again in my discussion of bearing witness. Consider once more the family photo album. In one way, turning its pages and looking at its images provides a narrative of the family, its persons and events. But something else, something quite different, can happen too. "In the struggle against Time," wrote Brassaï, "this enemy of our precarious existence, attacking us perniciously and never unhidden, it is in photography, itself born of the immemorial desire to stop the moment, to wrest it from the flux of the passage of time in order to secure it forever in a sort of eternity [that we find our ally]."[86] The photograph both stops time and allows that frozen past to be evoked again, to be made present. It is thus intimately related to those sentiments of memory, nostalgia, and regret,[87] to the presence of an absence, and in that way to the doing of justice as well. So here memory tends toward the suspension of movement and change. Remembrance is "immobile," says Yves Bonnefoy.[88] And the distinction between past and present is minimized or abolished: the past is made present rather than being kept in its remoteness. Memory, then, is the immobile presence of the past (the "presence of the non-present"), the struggle to hold it as such.[89] Nowhere is this clearer than in the great acts of public commemoration. Consider, for example, André Malraux's speech of December 19, 1964, at the interment in the Panthéon of the ashes of the Resistance leader Jean Moulin.[90] Malraux addresses Moulin in the familiar voice and present tense, "Enter here, Jean Moulin . . . ," and invites the youth of France to touch his face. The effect is to make Moulin, and perhaps the moral/political fact of the Resistance embodied in him, a presence, to bring generations of Frenchmen together in a shared devotion to the Republic. At the same time, Malraux's speech is a reminder, a pedagogy in citizenship directed to his youthful listeners, for whom Moulin is little more than a name. This activity of making the past present, of rising above the flux and change that are part of historical, chronological time, is here closely tied to memory's guarding role at the core of identity.

Another property of collective memory (again tracking memory and personal identity) is its particularity. It is the arena of sameness, the ingathering of resemblances. Memory looks to similarities, and gathers and shapes character, the selfhood of the community, across time.[91] The group, whether family, musical, or political, draws its distinctiveness, its separateness from others, by the (manifold) ingathering of its past. Collective memory as the continuity of life-in-common does not readily extend beyond the group. One could say that memory is always mine/ours, though that terminology may suggest that there is an "owning" subject to whom the memories belong, whereas memory seems rather to be constitutive, at least in part, of just the identity of that (owning) subject. Nevertheless, the language of "mineness" does capture the fact that memory inscribes boundaries between persons, families, and communities, that it establishes a deep we-relation among those who share in it. To speak of a memory-time as particularizing is to point to its place in defining a community and its members.[92] This ingathering by memory particularizes, makes the past ours, and in so doing it also burdens us with responsibility. And the particularizing (boundary) and persistence dimensions of memory-identity are intimately a part of the possibility of being accountable, of bearing the moral weight of the past.

The jagged landscape of memory-time is at the core of the identity of persons and communities, of their persistence and particularity. In one of memory's labors, we pick out those moments that are of autobiographical importance, that reveal the character of the subject, moments of moral significance or those bound up with the intimacies of a life-in-common. That time is not universal but rather marks out the identity, and thus the specificity, of the community. This collective memory is more than just the intentional, willed acts of remembrance, of a sort of national/political storytelling. Just as the meaning of our membership in a family, its place in our identity-memory, runs deeper than the occasional turning of the pages of the family photo album or celebration of an anniversary, so too does our political belonging. Memorial days, statues and monuments, calendar dates and civic holidays are the most obvious ways in which memory is active in our midst. Collective memory, however, is (as Maurice Halbwachs argued) more than a catalogue of dates and conscious recollection. The past leaves its traces on our character, our values, sentiments, and habits. Habit-memory, being habituated or accustomed to act, to respond in certain ways, a way of life in the most basic sense, is one means by which (beyond intention) the past is retained and made present: "Thus the last string of the lyre resonates with the rhythm of the song emitted by the plucking of the other strings."[93] Although the past may most visibly be kept before us in self-conscious rituals of various kinds, its presence is also, and importantly, the work of a sedimentation, of a habit-memory, a mode of being. Something like this is what Edmond Jabès is pointing to in this observation: "We know that it is we alone who construct [*fabriquons*] our recollections: but there is a memory, older than recollections, which is tied to language, to music, to sound, to noise, to silence: a memory that can be awakened by a gesture, a word, a cry, a sadness or a joy, a picture, an event."[94]

This sort of memory is what Aristotle is describing in his account of habit and disposition in the *Nicomachean Ethics*, and it underpins Tocqueville's study of the mores, the manners or way of life, of American democracy. The past made present is to be found not only in the conscious gestures of remembrance or the various kinds of habituation and modes of life that act as forms of memory, but also in the institutions of a community. Such institutions, courts, constitutions and founding documents, legislative bodies, and their various practices are both the expressions and the vehicles of continuity, and serve as the institutionalized memory of society. We could say, then, with Pierre Nora that memory is a field that stretches between the conscious and unconscious, and includes remembrance, tradition, mores and habits, and institutions. Political communities are a "dense web" of such memory forms, and it is precisely that web which gives us our identity and hence our accountability across time.

Let me elaborate on these forms of common memory. I begin by returning to my earlier observation (with Aristotle) that one type of identity-conferring continuity is that of the constitution. Constitutions, legal systems, the common law, and the other varied institutional arrangements of society define both a part of what it is as a political community (and so confer identity in the "What is it?" or boundary sense) and also are the bearers of that identity across time (duration) and thus an important form of the memory of society.[95] Institutions are often seats of agency, and hence of the continuity of direct accountability, the persistence of the responsible subject. And they can remember by guarding the past and carrying it forward, transmitting and conserving it.[96] Institutions (in that latter sense), Nietzsche observed, are one form of the weight of the past on the present.[97] Some of these institutional forms of memory may be explicitly memorial in intent, designed consciously to ensure the preservation of practices, virtues, and regime types across time. Rousseau, for example, offers the Poles abundant advice on the use of civic education, memorial days, and so on as ways of cultivating patriotism.[98] Others belong among the thick, non-intentional, but deeply rooted forms of social memory. These are institutions that preserve the practices and values of their societies not via self-conscious memorial work but by informing the dispositions, the character of citizens over the long duration. The institutionalized memory of a political community and the deeper, thick memory of the habits and ways of life of its citizens are often intimately linked, and perhaps nowhere more so than in democratic polities. Democracy is not simply a constitutional form preserving itself institutionally across time, but a cultivation (deliberate or more basically as a consequence of a life-in-common over time) of the habits appropriate to citizen life in such a regime.

Aristotle recognized these manifold notions of continuity and responsibility, and in that light we can understand the ambiguity in his answer as to whether a city that has experienced regime change is the same as its predecessor or different. A core part of the continuity of the city, especially visible in its undertaking of commitments with other states, is its constitutional/institutional enduringness, the memory of its will. But there is a level beneath that, thicker if you will, that is, less permeated by conscious decision and less available to our deliberate control: the habits and dispositions of citizens.[99] Before turning to a more detailed discussion of the idea of a community of habit, we ought briefly to consider the sense of habit-memory at the individual level. Habit, we could say with Aristotle, is a state of character, a state that once formed disposes us (in an unintentional, unreflective way) to act in a certain manner. To be habituated is to preserve the disposition to act in a certain way. Its root, Casey observes, is *habere*, to have or to hold.[100] Ethical habituation, in Aristotle's account, is the disposition to feel pleasure and pain over the right things and in the correct circumstances, and it is that stable set of habits that constitutes a continually (and not merely episodically) virtuous character. Character, then, is the synthesis of our past being acted out in the present. At an even more rudimentary level is habit-memory, the silent knowledge of the body as the "living storehouse." "To walk is to remember," says Paul Valéry.[101] The abilities of the body, its gestures and elementary activities, are the tacit efflux of the past, of sedimented experience active in the present. Bergson tells us that this memory does not so much represent the past as act it out, automatically and not via the recollecting labors of the mind. Memory is the holding, the prolonging of the past, its storing, and physical habit-memory gives my bodily person an important part of its coherence over time, much as the "habits of the heart" and tradition do in the enduringness of a way of life.[102] Character, being habituated to act and think in a certain way, and body-memory, respectively the habits of the heart and of the physical person, are important aspects of our wholeness across time as individuals. Both give us a key part of the continuity, the thread, that ties us to our earlier (and later) states.

Habit and disposition are deep or thick memories, largely free of the conscious acts associated with much remembering. They are the memory that "endures in the shadows."[103] Now, of course their cultivation is sometimes urged as an explicit part of the work of the state in forging civic virtue. As I said earlier, spectacles, civics teaching, and reminders of the community's history have all been recommended as instruments of political habituation. The intentional transmission of political virtues via civics textbooks or national holidays is one way in which the habits of citizens are formed. But there is, as I have suggested, another and more pervasive way in which we become habituated to a certain manner of life-in-common and acquire a disposition to live according to its core values. This is the habituation that comes from the amassed small currency of daily experiences, ways of being and of thinking acquired in the course of a life led in common, in a context shaped by the practices of a given regime.[104] Tocqueville was referring to this in his discussion of the "habits of the heart [*habitudes du coeur*]" and "habits of the mind [or spirit; *habitudes de l'esprit*]," of a democratic people.[105] These habits, and above all those associated with equality, give (he thought) a tonality to the behavior of Americans, one learned not so much from a self-conscious education in democratic civics as from the social conditions and practices of their society. The democratic regime, its public institutional and constitutional memory, here intersect with the (thick) memories of citizens, not in the knowledge of dates or national heroes, or the civic spectacles that Rousseau recommended, but in the habits of citizens, their "community of character," shaped, given color and form, in that mix of everyday life and of institutions that is the stuff of a political community.[106]

Judith Shklar's writing on memory as the foundation of what she terms the "liberalism of fear" illustrates some of this. In the American context, she argues, the fearful memory of slavery and discrimination has contributed to the importance attached to voting and employment status among citizens.[107] It is not that citizens have first-person memories of events that shape their politics, or that they know the history of them. Rather, there is a presence of elements of the past that endure in the moral/political reflexes of citizens: the continued legacy of slavery and racial injustice in American political life; Vichy in French politics or the Nazi years in postwar German domestic and foreign policy. Robert Putnam's account of the role of civic life in the success, political and economic, of northern Italy offers still another illustration of this. That success he attributes largely to patterns of social life dating back to the early medieval period, patterns that allowed the accumulation of civic virtue as a core part of the region's social capital. The idea of social capital, the trust (with the familiar as its basis), norms, and networks of a community, encouraging the persistence and success of certain patterns of civic life and governance, can be read as a part of a wider notion of the role of institutional and habit-memory, the habits of the heart, in the enduringness and boundedness of communities.[108]

1.6.2. Place and Memory

I turn now to another kind of thick memory: its landscapes and locales. All collective memory, Halbwachs argues, has a spatial framework.[109] In a sense, the body and body-memory are already the "primordial" spatial locale of memory. Here is how Faulkner puts it: "That is the substance of remembering—sense, sight, smell: the muscles with which we see and hear and feel—not mind, not thought . . ."[110] The body and other locales offer memory (or seem to) a fixity, a stability, and a tangibleness.[111] Places hold and synthesize, they render immobile the people and events associated with them, and in so doing they become locales of the preservation of the past, sustaining frameworks for remembrance. "The land, in its depths, does not forget."[112] To inhabit the world is to live not just in any interchangeable empty space but in a place that in a myriad ways is bound up with our past. Spatialized memory attains a certain security, and in turn, dwelling places are made possible by memory. Inhabited space, which is more than simply occupied space, carries with it, Gaston Bachelard writes, the home of one's youth. Such places at one and the same time lodge our memories and are transformed by them. Casey tells us that places are selective for memory, a place and the traces that dot it will evoke memories, just as memories are selective for place.[113] Sometimes these places are the direct result of a will to fix a memory by inscribing it in space, for example, archives, museums, and memorials. But they can also be locales that are directly tied to memory. They can be as intimate as family homes, places of worship, the neighborhoods of our youth, a park or school. And they can be as much a part of the collective memory as Dealey Plaza, the Lorraine Motel, or Gettysburg. Some are the historic spaces of a people or an epoch; others are the familiar dwellings of our individual lives. And sometimes the two intersect, as in this letter from Tocqueville to his future wife, describing his family's home in Normandy: "This place is, for me, full of memories. I live there in a world of ghosts. Do you know that from the top of the tower, I see the port where William embarked on his voyage to conquer England? Do you know that all these places carry the famous names of our history or of yours?"[114]

This intersection of personal/familial memory-identity and that inscribed in landscapes, the joining of the tectonic plates of our lives with the geography of the places we inhabit, can be seen in Marc Augé's study

of the Paris Métro system as a locale of memory. "The first German soldier I remember seeing," he writes, "was at Maubert-Mutualité [Métro sta-
tion]."[115] A personal memory and a national past are here fixed and attached to one place in a city. With many of its stations named after
illustrious persons and great military victories, the Parisian Métro system
is both a map of French national memory and a cult of ancestors. But it is
also a network of locales to which a multitude of individual memories
(such as Augé's own) are attached: memories of family, jobs, relationships, and so forth. Do those tired Métro riders, getting off at the Bir-
Hakeim station, really cast their minds back to the heroic battle of 1942?
Or does this stop hold other memories for them: of their youth, a romance, or a job? Or both, perhaps? Locales of memory, in short, can be
the custodians of multiple remembrances, from those intertwined with
the most intimate of family moments to the geography of a nation's
memory. Some spaces are engraved in us, and so (not unlike habits) belong among our thick memories.[116] Others are part of a broader civic narrative, written on the landscapes of our country, appropriations of the
landscape for memorial purposes. Habits and some locales of memory belong, as I just said, to the thick memory of the individual or community.
They help to define it, give it identity both as a way of life in the case of
habits and as a dwelling place in the case of the geography of memory.
Dwelling places and our habits and dispositions, rather than memorials or
dates on a national calendar, are the enduring heart of collective
memory-identity.[117]

Habit and space are less vulnerable to the erosion that afflicts other,
more intentional acts of remembrance. The guarding, preservative function of memory, seeking to ensure the boundedness and persistence of
the person or community, appears to be solidly grounded in this kind of
thick memory. Memory and identity, embedded in habits, dispositions,
and places, seem just to be present, almost effortlessly so. Even this thick
memory, however, is not as stable as the preceding remarks might suggest. It is by no means entirely invulnerable to loss or erosion. Clearly, for
example, one of Tocqueville's concerns was that the habits of public freedom would decay in America as a result of the absorption of a commercial
people in the pursuit of material well-being. Likewise, Machiavelli's *Discourses* are driven by the certainty that the habits of civic virtue erode and
that they therefore need periodic rejuvenation.[118] So too with locales of
memory: places can lose their memory-preserving function. Baudelaire
says that "the form of a city changes more rapidly . . . than the heart of a
mortal."[119] And Proust writes, "The houses, the streets . . . are fugitive . . .
like the years."[120] The spatial shelters of memory can be transformed (ef-

faced) in their physical properties and in the hearts of their denizens. Memory, then, seems often to be related to loss or absence, and to have its own decay and loss before it as a menacing possibility.

1.7. MEMORY AND ABSENCE

Let us return briefly to the relationship between memory and absence, with a view to underscoring memory's instability and its struggles, its centrality for the possibility of being a person and a community, and the meaning of its loss. Now, many of the states associated with memory are centered on absence and loss. As I said earlier, melancholy, nostalgia, remorse, regret, and so on all convey the bittersweet fact of something at once present and absent in memory. If it were utterly missing, however, the desire or regret associated with these comportments would not take hold; securely present, and the sense of loss or distance together with the need to restore or guard would be absent. In Plato's *Theaetetus* (191cff., 197dff.), this absence is above all a problem of knowledge: the imprint on the block of wax, different from what was imprinted, or his dovecote analogy. As we shall see, absence is also a key moment in the role of memory in doing justice. In the relationship between memory and identity, however, the issue is more complex. Take the most radical case: the virtually complete effacement of memory, the opening of the dovecote (to borrow Plato's image) and the flight of the memory that gives a unity and wholeness to our lives, that informs our habits and character and gives us a dwelling place in the world. At the individual level, such a complete absence would be not the spark of desire, of longing or nostalgia, for example, but the end of the person as a character. Luis Buñuel writes of witnessing his mother's fall into complete amnesia, and of his own failing memory, that "you have to begin to lose your memory, if only in bits and pieces, to realize that memory is what makes our lives. Life without memory is no life at all. . . . Our memory is our coherence, our feeling, even our action. Without it we are nothing." That is, "without memory there is no longer a self."[121] Patti Davis, the daughter of Ronald Reagan, says of her father's Alzheimer's disease that without memory "you are unmoored, a wind-tossed boat with no anchor."[122]

In one sense, the physical person remains and retains the identity that natural things have as persisting clusters of matter and form. But without memory, the person as a unity, as having a life, the "course of a life," drifts away. Oliver Sacks describes a patient with deep amnesia, saying of him that he "wasn't aware of . . . the loss *of* himself."[123] The person is lost. Or, even more radically, the person suffers a "living death." In a celebrated case of amnesia, a French soldier, Anthelme Mangin (a pseudonym), returned from a German prisoner of war camp at the end of the First World War without any memory whatsoever of his former life. At his (second) burial service, the mayor of the town spoke of his "sad odyssey [which was for him] a twenty-five-year living death."[124] The duration of the physical person does not alter what happens when memory fails: the loss of the "'inner availability' of personal persistence," of the identity that consists in the continuity of a lived life, of character, and also of the shared time of relationships and of inhabited places, the identity that in short is intertwined with memory.[125] But where the core of the identity of a person or society remains intact, the absence of things, persons, or places past is felt in melancholy, in the longing of nostalgia, the search for revenge, or for doing justice and bearing witness. Memory, in these instances, wages a defensive struggle, a fight against the natural erosion caused by the passage of time or the artificial erosion that is the work of human hands. Remembrance seeks to guard the past, to hold on to it or to restore it from its traces. It is, as Plato writes in the *Philebus*, the guardian or savior (*sōtāria*) of appearances.[126]

If the loss of memory destroys the wholeness of a person, so too does the loss of a person (or community) undermine common memory. Chateaubriand says of the passing of his brother that with a death, a part of us disappears, "a world of childhood memories, of family intimacies [and] affections . . ."[127] This is most apparent, perhaps, in the death of a family member or close friend, or the loss of a generation: with their passing goes a piece of a shared memory of a life-in-common, of the remembered time that is such a central part of relationships. It is the loss of a wider social memory. Georges Perec says of the killing of his parents in World War II that "I don't share in any memories they might have had, something that was theirs, which made them what they were, their history, their culture, their hope was not transmitted to me."[128] The destruction or disappearance of communities leaves a void in our collective memory. Thus the annihilation of the Jewish communities of central and eastern Europe destroyed a way of life and its living place in European life and memory.[129] What is lost in these deaths, then, is not (only) something private, the property so to speak of one person, but a part of the common stock of a community, a family, a culture, a society. In that light we can better understand the efforts to gather and store the remembrances of people. Steven Spielberg's Visual History project, the 1930s Federal Writers' Project (WPA) compilation of surviving slave narratives, the Canadian government's Canada Remembers project are illustrations of an attempt not so much to save individual memories, or to secure our knowledge of who these persons were, but to safeguard who we are, including the common memories of which they are the usufruct owners.

We might say of this connection of memory to absence that it allows us to see that the relationship between the past and memory assumes two different forms: remembering as the faintest sensation left by an absence (to adapt Alain Finkielkraut's words), and the almost glacial presence of the past in habits, ways of life (the "triumphal plenitude of instinct"), and so on.[130] On the one side, the past is present in the manner of the aorist, "without limit," as never entirely completed and gone, but rather a living deposit enduring in various ways in the present, which present is therefore no longer fully distinguishable from the past. "Maybe nothing ever happens once and is finished," writes Faulkner. "Maybe happen is never once but like ripples maybe on water after the pebble sinks, the ripples moving on, spreading . . ." Or Casey, quoting Merleau-Ponty, "The past becomes 'our true present'; it loses its identity as a separate past (a past of *another* time and place) . . ."[131] On the other side, the past is the completed past, separated from us except for its traces, and struggled for precisely because of that separation. Memory and the past in the first of these senses are especially evident in habit-memory, the manners and ways of life of individuals and their communities and in the landscapes and dwellings that are a part of their identities. The second sense of memory is, as I have suggested, bound up with absence, trace, and struggle. It is the realm of justice, history writing, memorials, and so on. The former domain of memory, the thick memory of the often almost unconscious presence of the past in habits and locales, stands in marked contrast to the flickering flame of the struggle to keep the past present in memory, not to allow crimes, victims, and so on to be lost to forgetting. In thick memory, the rememberer is almost completely passive, the recipient of memory's gifts. We are, on this view, the "shoots of an invisible anteriority," the traces of a past moving forward. The latter, however, is more uncertain, more of a question or task, the work of human hands, of witnesses, narrators, and so forth.[132] This ambiguity is not simply terminological or conceptual. Rather, it reflects the underlying tension in the memory of an always near-to-absent past, a tension between imagination and reconstruction on the one side and the involuntary presence of the past, its burdensome or weighty character, on the other. Ralph Ellison writes that "we do not bury the past, because it is within us. But we *do* modify the past as we live our lives."[133] This puzzle is nicely captured in a Japanese paradox (recounted by Quignard) concerning art and time: "Art is defined as an echo of something that has already existed which one invents."[134] "Echo" and "invention," our roles as readers and scriptwriters, bearers and creators, express the duality of our relationship to the past, and to the role of memory in that relationship. "The last string of the lyre resonates with the rhythm of the song emitted by the plucking of the other strings."

1.7.1. Tectonic Plates and Narratives

I have discussed thick memory, and now I want to consider further the (often fragile) work of memory, in its multiple and invented forms, by looking once more at locales or places of memory. There is, as we saw, an evocative dimension to the spaces we inhabit, something in these places that seems to hold or conserve the past. Yves Bonnefoy gives an account of a return home, describing its rooms as a place "where sleeps a part of what I was." Further on, Bonnefoy writes of rediscovering the "land of childhood," of a "defeated time," where we are offered for one brief and happy moment "the fruit, the voices . . . the gentle wine."[135] Bonnefoy's cycle opens with "Memory" and closes with "The Task of Hope," something that lies in the future and beyond memory. And despite the reference to the "immobility of memory," the cycle echoes with its obscurity and tentativeness: "without light," almost a desert.[136] This uncertainty is signaled to the reader in the opening lines of the poem: "what to do with your gifts, O memory." These places, houses in which one has lived, the family home of one's childhood, partially secure and stabilize the gifts of memory, but never completely determine what they become for us. A key question here is whether these gifts of memory represent the living co-presence of the past in our midst or its dead, but preserved, form.[137] The past lives nervously, Quignard writes, and memory-space is fragile, a doubt, a question as much as a guardian of past certainties.[138] Writing about Ellis Island, Perec remarks that visitors come there not to learn but to find something, a trace of their history, of the place where many renounced their past. But he goes on to say that the destiny localized and inscribed in Ellis Island does not have the same meaning for everyone. For Perec, a French Jew of Polish origin who lost his mother to Auschwitz, Ellis Island is a "non-place," the absence of a place, a reminder of exile and the loss of home that has been the fate of the Jewish people. For Robert Bober, the co-author of *Récits d'Ellis Island. Histoires d'errance et d'espoir*, Judaism is an uninterrupted tradition, and that memory-identity gives his encounter with Ellis Island a different meaning as a place of memory. For others, Perec says, Ellis Island as a locale of memory holds a very different meaning: not of wandering and loss but of hope.[139]

This multiplicity of memories surrounds something as commonplace as a Métro station or as central to the experience of a nation as a site associated with immigration. Places like these, as I said, localize and stabilize the presence of the past of individuals, groups, and political communities. They can become part of a narrative (contested and multiple), but at the same time, to understand the attachment to places as guardians of one's past and as guarantors of its continuing presence is to grasp the depth of our attachment to the locales of our life and, on the part of communities, of their commitment to specific places and territories. "A person deprived of a place [*lieu*] is without a universe, without a hearth [*foyer*], having neither a house nor a home. He is, so to speak, nowhere, or rather he is anywhere, a wreck floating in the wide expanses," writes Poulet.[140] Or as Czeslaw Milosz puts it: "In a city or a village which we have known well since our childhood we move in a tamed space, our occupations finding everywhere expected landmarks. . . . Whoever has found himself as an immigrant in a big foreign city had to cope with a kind of envy at the sight of its inhabitants . . . confidently going to definite, known to them, shops or offices, in a world weaving together a huge fabric of everyday bustle."[141] Mahmoud Darwish captures some of this when he writes about the "historic space" of a people, not the empty space in which they happen to live.[142] But by "historic space" he does not, I think, mean merely the place where something happened. Rather, the phrase suggests the storehouse of the present past at the core of identity. Exile, the desire to return, and commonplace nostalgia display this. Milosz writes of exile that "it is impossible not to look back . . . [because] stripped of memory [man] is hardly human . . ."[143] For "against the wind," Darwish says, "there is nothing except memory."[144] Thus too the conflicts over memory and place. Meron Benvenisti's *Sacred Landscape* chronicles the conflict between Israelis and Palestinians over place-names and the cartography of the Holy Land. On both sides, he argues, there was ample rewriting of the region's geography and the discovery of (often fanciful) narratives for specific towns and areas, narratives designed to assert their part in the national autobiographies of one of the communities.[145] These analyses of conflict, power, and change confirm Halbwachs's observation that many such locales of memory are artificial constructions, the imprinting on space of the memory of the group.[146] On this view, locales of memory are that just by virtue of action in the present and the interests that direct it, and of conflict between competing narratives. Although this is in an obvious way true of created sites, in other instances the emphasis on the active remembrance of narration does not do full justice to the landscapes of memory-identity.

Constructivist accounts of memory miss a number of key points. Absent is the dimension, not complete but nevertheless there, of the thickness of

place-memory: that it is the place that drives remembrance, before any explicit narrative is formulated about it. Places are selective for memory.
And as well, body, habits of the heart, mores, and place are intimately intertwined with the presence of the past, and they are not something that
we intentionally inscribe on the world but rather are acted out in that
world or elicited by its memory-spaces. The narrative view of memory and
identity needs to be qualified by the weight of institutions, the unsought
evocativeness of space, and the presence of a thick memory-identity, one
there in habit or space before it is articulated: "The past can be present or
alive in the present without being present or alive as the past."[147] It needs
to be qualified in this second sense as well. The vantage point of the present and its interests, "the presence of the now," said by Walter Benjamin
to be the standpoint of the retrospective glance, might be better understood as part of the extension of human time: not, that is, as a discrete
moment, standing apart from the past, but intimately tied to it. There is
no pure present; indeed, Marc Bloch rejects the separation between the
"past and the so-called present."[148] Consider the observation that "our
character, always present in all our decisions, is just the present synthesis of
all our past states."[149] Our character, which shapes our decisions, including those involving the narratives we create as part of our memory work, is
itself the synthesis of our past states. Put more radically still: "The past is
an immense body of which the present is the eye."[150] Bergson, writing
about perception, captures the broader point at work here: it is, he says,
"never a simple contact between the mind and the present object. It is
completely impregnated by memory-images which, in interpreting it,
complete it."[151]

The present is the eye of the past. This can be read to suggest that what
we see in the present is informed by the past, and by a past that is not just
a reservoir of facts, dates, and so on to be recalled at will but also the
memory of body, habit, language, and place. I have commented on habit-
memory, and will speak more about space further on. Here I want to note
Emile Cioran's observation that language is "one's own past." To be sure,
living languages evolve and change, but language is also the most elementary and stable framework of collective memory, and it has been argued that shared language is both a country and a memory. Albert Camus
shows us how Dr. Rieux, witness and chronicler of the plague in Oran,
finds that the very name "the plague" escapes his desire for present-tense
empirical facticity and takes on the burden of two millennia of collective
memories of the disease.[152] Rieux's dilemma can be understood as saying
that language is the unintentional bearer of the past. The fact of language
means, as Quignard writes, that there is no "pure present in the soul." We

dwell in it, the "heart of life," "the unforgettable," sleep-like, as an embryo does in relation to its mother.[153] Language encumbers us, and is itself encumbered by the geology of meanings that it retains. Through body, habit, language, and place-memory, the present is part of the extension of lived time (as is, in a different way, the future), which is to say that it is different from both past and future but inseparably joined with them not as something extraneous but as integral to what it is to be in the present. So when I reflect in an autobiographical way on my life, recount it in a narrative, formal or casual, I do so not from a standpoint apart from that past (or future) but with an eye already educated by it, and by expectation too. I am the "locale of their [past and future] encounter."[154] When we write grand political narratives about ourselves as a community, we write them from within the habits of the heart and mind which are already part of our citizen character. Democratic historians, Tocqueville tells us, write the sorts of accounts they do, read the past in their characteristic manner, from a present moment that in important respects is the eye of the past itself, the summation of the tectonic plates of a democratic way of life.[155]

It would, however, be wrong to say that memory-identity is entirely sediment-like. Much of the presence of memory is a struggle: to resist erosion, distortion, and forgetfulness. Memory "saves" the appearances, and it must struggle to do so. But it would also be inaccurate to see the present and its work of remembering as a free-floating moment, pristine, unformed, and unburdened by the layers of the past that constitute our bodily memory, habits, and the other ways in which through memory the past "is interleaved with the present."[156] Casey is right, then, to argue for a middle position between passivism (the block of wax image), the notion that we are just what we inherit, and the purely constructivist/instrumentalist accounts of memory as present-driven and instrumental reconstructions of a past that has no presence apart from these imaginative reconstructions.[157] The "*past develops,*" he says. It is "carried forward (often heavily revised) by an autonomous remembering in the present that is not the mere proxy of its own origins."[158] Quignard writes in a similar vein, though pushing the power of the present still further: "The past does not renew itself as the past. The past is renewed because the present changes. And the present makes present whatever it wants . . . arbitrarily."[159] There is one, and not a minor, ambiguity here that needs clarification. Casey's references to the "autonomy of memory" and to its therefore not being a "mere proxy" for the past are important qualifiers to the tectonic plates view, if by them we are to understand that memory is often labor, not habit, the deliberate ingathering of the past, of what is mostly absent and mere trace. In that sense, memory is not a habit-like, stable, and more or less secure presence of the past. Yet if memory of a thick kind is a core part of a person or community across time, then the present of active remembering is not fully autonomous but is rather already deeply informed by the presence of the past. The world is looked at, as Quignard himself suggests, through the eyes of memory.

CHAPTER TWO

Memory, Accountability, and Political Community

Memory is at the core of identity, and in ways that go beyond the explicit and self-conscious gestures of narratives, memorials, archives, and civic history to the memory contained in habits of the heart and in locales. When we speak about collective memory, we do not therefore mean just its most obvious forms, the public recognition (in museums, days of commemoration, archives, and so forth) of the past of our life-in-common, but the presence of that past in all of the small currency of a community's existence, its way of life, values, and so on. The presence of the past in memory, and so the unity and sameness of the subject across time, have their formal and informal, quotidian dimensions. As I remarked earlier, a central part of memory-identity as the preserver of the presence of the past is its relationship to accountability, to the view of ourselves and of our societies as imputable subjects in time. But memory and the identity it grounds can be very long indeed, extending across generations. How then should we think about responsibility and memory if memory often oversteps the threshold of direct (individual or institutional) authorship? Recall that the notion of responsibility tied to agency and authorship leaves aside those areas of responsibility in which we are involved even though not the authors of the actions themselves. Let me now return to that subject and set out some further observations on shame, using it as a lens through which to see more clearly the sense of persistence, memory, and a wider responsibility across time, a dimension that is lost in too narrow a focus on guilt.[1]

Shame is a sentiment that can be present even where there is no direct, causal responsibility for the deed.[2] I can feel shame without accepting that I am directly responsible for the misdeed, or that I deserve punishment for it. Shame can attach to actions of mine that do not meet the intentionality standard typically required for guilt. While responsibility, guilt, and liability to punishment are closely tied to the authorial/ownership standard of identity, shame is rooted in a wider, enduring kind of memory-identity. And whereas guilt is a clear threshold concept, and so is a property of discrete events in our life, shame is more pervasive and seems to be bound up with the long duration of our lives and of our communities, whether familial, religious, or political. Its sources and enduringness also appear relatively immune to punishment and forgiveness, the remedies normally applied in matters of guilt. Shame endures as part of our ethical character, as a mark of having failed. It is more a recognition of the wholeness of one's life than of the discrete actions one has committed.[3] Shame, we might say, expresses a recognition of the ethical fullness of a life across time, a fullness composed of character, habits, and dispositions as much as a ledger of actions strictly authored and therefore imputable. In that sense, shame is the sign of persistence. And it is sometimes the reluctant recognition of that unity, even when we feel removed from the earlier self who committed the act: shame, Lévinas says, is "the impossibility . . . of not identifying ourselves with this being who already is alien to us and whose motives for acting we can no longer understand." It is founded, he continues, "on the solidarity of our being, which obliges us to assume responsibility for ourselves."[4] Shame illuminates a wholeness that otherwise would be lost in a collection of discrete episodes, or in a view of ethical life as the site of authorial imputation alone. It draws attention to the enduringness of the (ethical) person, and to the importance of the temporal dimensions of past and future to what we are in the present. By contrast, a shameless or wanton person, one lacking integrity (the unity of a life), dwells in the present tense alone.[5] The truly shameless individual does not see the unity or integrity of his life, but rather sees the past and future almost as if they were someone else's, as if they suffered from a moral forgetting. And forgetting, writes Lévinas, "is a means of escaping from oneself," suggesting that shame emerges where forgetting is not at work.[6] To live without the enduring and unified identity of an ethical being is to live (literally) without integrity. Shame, in short, underscores the temporal unity that stands at the core of personhood, in part by detaching the idea of our ethical unity from its modern (often Kantian) moorings in notions of guilt and causally grounded, authorial responsibility.

Shame (and pride), then, point to the wholeness of the person across time, secured in memory. From that vantage point, guilt as a wrong and a deviation from a person's character becomes fully intelligible. Because shame is a token of an ethical unity underlying the individual's biography and the sum of his individual acts, a unity that is not centered on a strict authorship account of deeds, it draws a more complete picture of what Williams terms the "whole person." At the same time, and likewise because of the displacement of the authorial/ownership model of identity, "vicarious" shame and pride serve as an index of my relationship to and ownership of my earlier states, however remote that person may seem, but also of attachment, of embeddedness in a community, of being implicated (for good or bad) in something of which one is not the author.[7] Isaiah Berlin observed, "We are ashamed of what our brothers or our friends do; of what strangers do we might disapprove, but we do not feel ashamed."[8] This can be seen, for example, in the often bitter accounts written by children of Nazi officials or of their collaborators.[9] In a collection of interviews with such children, one son says of his father, a Nazi who betrayed his own father: "I found it difficult to look my Grandpa in the eye, as though I too was responsible for what my father had done, sitting there in his place, filled with shame and a bad conscience. All I wanted to do was go home and confront my father and ask him: 'How could you do this to me? Yes, to me.' "[10] In a sense, then, we own their actions (those of our family or political community) but not on the authorship model of, for example, classical social contract theory. We understand ourselves to be a part of their projects, even though we may have had nothing directly to do with their design or execution. Identity here is the broad "mineness" of membership in the political communities of which we are a part.[11] I feel myself implicated in their agency, in their past and future.

In a manner that parallels the case of individual identity, the ethical dimension is central, but in such a way that our attention is turned from agency as authorship in a tight sense to, in the one case, the ethical life of the person over the long duration and, in the second, the wholeness of the shared life we have with family, co-religionists, and fellow citizens. Our identity is made up of what we are as ethical beings, meaning both as agents, as the owners/authors of our actions, and as characters or whole persons through time and as members of communities. Via memory, shame and pride unite us with our individual pasts, even in the presence of change and the passing of time. They also reveal our memory ties to our past-in-common: we have a sense of a past that is ours, politically, even though we had no hand in its events. Such a recognition of co-responsibility (horizontal) among members of a present community and (vertically) between the past and present of the same community speaks to an identity across time and through change, an identity that is ethical at its core yet is not dependent on notions of authorship and causal connection. From that vantage point, we can begin to make sense of our intuition that in an ethically important way, the American people (for example) are responsible for slavery in their country, and so are capable of feeling shame even today, more than a century and a half after its demise; and that we feel pride at our national accomplishments during World War II, though a large majority of us had no hand in those achievements. Shame and pride are here indices of an identity in which my biography is interwoven with that of the community in which I am embedded, uniting me thereby with its past, present, and future. They overstep the boundary criteria of identity associated with notions of guilt and narrowly defined responsibility, show how memory is bound up with the long duration of responsibility, and in so doing also illuminate the persistence criteria of identity by suggesting that we are embedded in a life-in-common that extends beyond the sphere of our authorship. As we are citizens, so we are members of communities of memory, not only of traditions, canons, habits, and institutions but also of the wider responsibility signaled by pride and shame. We have a political identity that is neither narrowly circumscribed by principles of the ownership of actions, nor as thin and tenuous as a mere bundle of more-or-less related experiences.

Shame allows us to see one way in which collective memory and identity are bound up not only in the ways of life of a community of citizens and their habits, but also with responsibility and justice broadly understood. Here I want to use Bernhard Schlink's novel *The Reader* to illustrate, at least in a rough and incomplete way, the issue of shame, responsibility, and memory. *The Reader* captures one dimension of the dilemmas of a modern, constitutional-democratic political identity as it confronts the weight of the past. The essentials of the story are these. In postwar Germany a young boy, Michael Berg, falls in love with an older woman, Hanna. They part ways, but later, in the 1960s, and in the throes of the German student movement and its condemnation of the parents' generation, he again encounters Hanna, now on trial for war crimes of which he was unaware during their earlier romance. As much as he and his contemporaries have rejected the world of their parents, as much as political change had transformed the public face of Germany after 1945, and although its laws have reached back into those terrible years and punished some of the perpetrators, the narrator leads us to see that the weight of the past, and the stain left by it, are never entirely removed. "The tectonic layers of our lives," he writes, "rest so tightly one on top of the other that we always come up against earlier events in later ones, not as matter that has been fully formed and pushed aside, but absolutely present and alive. I understand this. Nevertheless, I sometimes find it hard to bear. Maybe I did write our story to be free of it, even if I never can be."[12] Berg's identity is bound up with his lover's, and with their community and its history. These bonds, with the idea of shared responsibility at their core, are not reducible to the customary language of agency and authorship that are the common currency of much of our moral and judicial lexicon. Nor are they readily dissolved. Neither forgetting, Schlink writes, nor recollecting the past in a conscious effort to purge its ghosts can change that bond. It is, he says, "das deutsche Schicksal," "the German fate."[13]

If co-responsibility across time and outside of the sphere of direct authorship is possible, we may be able to learn from this how better to understand controversies over responsibility in cases where dictatorial regimes are involved. In democratic societies, the responsibility rooted in enduring institutions as decision-making sites and that rooted in the broader life of their peoples overlap and are expressed through voice and representation. Aberrations apart, the actions of a democratic state are owned, in a pervasive way (institutionally and in their life-in-common), by its people and so, in principle, remain on their collective account. But what of the actions of dictatorships, totalitarian regimes, and so on, that is, governments which are not (or not in any explicit sense) authorized by the people in their actions? Although in a democracy, voice links a people to its decision-making institutions and authorizes the latter's actions (in the Hobbesian sense: "owning all the actions the representer doth"), there is, as I have suggested, a wider foundation of responsibility than that encompassed in explicit acts of consent and the direct agency of political decision-making institutions, a foundation that does not require voice in order to engage a people in responsibility for their past. And that can help us to understand the idea that some measure of responsibility exists even under non-democratic circumstances. Consider post–World War II Europe. The politics of memory and responsibility that have been so central to these communities since 1945 largely concern issues of accountability outside the context of regimes of direct and explicit representation. And something similar could be said of the debates that have followed decommunization in the former German Democratic Republic, Poland, Russia, and elsewhere. If only the presence of democratically authorized political institutions (strong agency) created a web of accountability embracing both state and people, then the nations of Europe would be excused from virtually all of the deeds of the Nazi period and of Soviet control, and Nuremberg or similar proceedings would have administered justice to the only real culprits, namely, to leading state functionaries. But that is not so, and thus the recognition of a broader co-responsibility has flourished in France, Germany, and eastern Europe even though dictatorships prevailed there during most of the relevant past. Consider in this regard the 2001 speech of Aleksander Kwasniewski, president of Poland, apologizing for the 1941 massacre of Polish Jews by other Poles at Jedwabne: "There were no Polish authorities in Jedwabne. The Polish state was unable to protect its citizens against the crime committed with the Nazis' permission, at Nazi instigation. . . . We cannot speak of collective responsibility burdening with guilt the citizens of any other locality or the entire nation. Every man is responsible only for his own acts. The sons do not inherit the sins of the fathers. But can we say: that was long ago, they were different? The nation is a community. Community of individuals, community of generations. And this is why we have to look the truth in the eyes. Any truth. And say: it was, it happened."[14] We might conclude, in brief, that the Nuremberg, Frankfurt/Auschwitz, and Eichmann trials did the work of the former sort of imputability; and that sixty years of dealing with the past in Germany, France, Poland, and elsewhere has been the pursuit of the second kind of responsibility.

I will revisit some of these issues later on. For now, I want to return to *The Reader*. Under a tightly constrained use of agency and authorship, the story's principal character, Michael Berg, has done nothing; no crimes can be placed on his account. Indeed, the idea of an account shared with the past is wrongheaded. Nothing is "sent" or written. But being a member of a community with a past, and having loved and entered into a relationship with Hanna, and with her past, he is given their legacy. The "mercy of late birth" (in Helmut Kohl's phrase) cannot cleanse him of these traces, though it renders him free of guilt-based accountability.[15] There is no absolution through constitutional change; the new political self is continuous with the past and cannot expunge it. Even the long reach of the law's empire, and its rooting out of the culpable (in this story, Hanna), does not (cannot) extend to the legacy woven into identity, into the long duration of a community's responsibility, shame, and memory. That we at once grasp the sorts of obligations being invoked here, and the moral unsustainability of a wholesale forgetting of the past, *and* that we do not have a moral language to express this, likely says a great deal about the inadequacy of that language and the exercises of abstraction that it performs in reflecting about character, shame, and responsibility.

2.1. STATE MEMORIES

With these observations about memory, responsibility, and duration in mind, I want to return to the idea of (political) collective memory in its more tangible and explicit forms. Recall my earlier discussion of Aristotle on political identity and fiscal accountability across regime change. There, as we saw, Aristotle argued for a kind of persistence, one principal locus of which was the constitutional form of the city, which would include a specification of citizenship eligibility, a method and criteria for allocating offices, and so forth. As I noted, a constitutional arrangement is itself in a sense the bearer of the past, a mode of transmission linking past to present. This it can do explicitly and in a rule-bound fashion in, for example, the law and in obstacles to a too quick tampering with the constitutional patrimony of the nation. Again, statements of political values and rights serve to unite generations in the enduring present of the constitution, and to act as a reminder, legal and moral, in the case of deviation from these principles. Such institutions, founding documents, and explicit practices are not just a transmission device but a core part of the continuity of the community, and a moment in its collective memory. They are in Peter French's phrase the "decision structures," a part of society's memory, the ingathering of the past woven into the present in the form of an institutional presence. We might also observe (adapting Montesquieu), that while in the beginning it is humans who make institutions, thereafter those institutions shape human beings.[16] But as we also saw, institutions transform the habits, the reflexes, in short the unreflective way of life of citizens, and in so doing fashion an unconscious and involuntary, almost habit-like memory of themselves and of the values and ways of living they embody. In a more contemporary idiom, this would suggest that political or citizen identity is an involuntary, and often unconsciously held, memory of a way of life given to us by our principal institutions and framing documents, laws, and social conditions, and transmitted through them across the length of a life-in-common. The second volume of Tocqueville's *Democracy in America*, with its massive compendium of the mores of democratic society, can be read as an account of the habitus of American democracy, of a way of life as the bearer of a memory of democracy. As citizens, in the here and now, our instincts and habits have been educated by formal institutions and by informal practices that, inscribed in our habits and hearts, become our way of life, our mores, and thus a living presence of the past.

"State-memory," as Pierre Nora terms it, has other, more explicitly memorial dimensions.[17] These are deliberate acts: commemorations, monuments, days of remembrance and celebration, and so forth, and as such they reflect power, selection, and the effort to fashion unity and legitimacy through the forging of collective memory. This is a will to remember, and to remember in a certain way. What is remembered, and what is forgotten, in the surface inscriptions of state-memory are the result, in part, of the power of those who do the writing and sometimes of those who contest that authorial power. Dubravka Ugrešić, herself a Croatian, writes of "the *thousand-year dream of independence* (as those in power in Croatia put it, and the citizens of Croatia obediently dream)."[18] Whether in memorials or in other devices of national identity formation, archives, libraries, or museums, the state as memory-crafter seems to inscribe its narrative only on the surface of society.[19] What this does not account for is (as I urged earlier) the eye that sees with memory and the underlying fabric, the depths from which these surface inscriptions await their echo and which give them whatever utility they may have as political acts. At one time, perhaps, this form of enacted collective remembrance would have been played out against the background of a widely shared national political narrative in which explicit historical narratives and informal group memories were largely indistinguishable.[20] Whatever seeming hold such state memories may once have possessed, they clearly no longer go uncontested. To remember, to struggle over the specific content of remembrance, reflects (among other things) the importance of identity, for the continuity of the community, and to the desire to retain a continuity with one's community. The struggle for memory is a struggle (itself informed by memory) over which the past defines the community grounded in a fear of domination, mis-specification, and the corrosive effects of the passage of time and its deleterious effects on the identity-nurturing presence of the past.[21]

We can see both the (contested) willed narrative of the state-memory's surface inscriptions and the deeper place that memory holds in our life-in-common in Vassilis Alexakis's novel *La langue maternelle* (The Mother Tongue) in which an émigré, Pavlos, returns to Greece, the country of his youth. There he reflects on the education he received, the intentional surface inscription of memory, much of it oriented toward a celebration of the continuity of Greece across the millennia. On the one side, the teaching of ancient Greek was instrumental, he thinks, inspired by the nationalist goal of lessening the distance between ancient and modern Greece, as if that now disappeared world were somehow still present among modern Greeks.[22] Yet at the same time, Pavlos's search for the meaning of the enigmatic epsilon at the entrance to Apollo's Temple at Delphi is deeply intertwined with both his family's past (the silence of his mother) and his country's memories (the relationship between ancient and modern Greece). In Greece, two thousand years before Alexakis wrote, the making of the surface inscriptions of memory was often the work of public orators. Pericles' funeral oration, Nicole Loraux argues, seeks to link the past and present of (ancient) Greek history so as to reinforce both the claims of the democratic city and the (claimed) autochthony of the community generally.[23] Funeral speeches and other narrative devices are modes of invention, of the creation of identity and solidarity. The narrative of these memorial speeches plots, so to speak, the community's life, signals its greatness, and reinforces the group's civic habits. Yet Pericles' funeral oration draws its meaning and force from a background framework of shared memories attached to sites (the Keramikos), modes of presentation, and political tropes of democratic Athens (equality, but attached to the past as well).[24] His speech requires an identity, a subject that can accept these surface inscriptions as its own, a self already there, and formed in no small measure out of the thick, background memories, the tectonic plates of the community.

In sum, we could say that the surface inscriptions of state-memory (its museums, archives, and orations) provide a unifying, sustaining, and explicit narrative of the community across time, drawing out its sameness and continuity in the manner suggested by Halbwachs's "tableau of resemblances."[25] Consider again Malraux's oration at the interment of Jean Moulin's ashes in the Panthéon. His speech is only in part about Moulin. In addition, it sets out an account of the unity of France and of the Resistance under de Gaulle, and in that way makes sense, in a fashion, of the "dark years" of the Occupation by enveloping them in the Gaullist/Republican narrative of French identity and the meaning of the Vichy period. At one level, the oration is directly a political act, the invention of a wartime France of ennobling and unified resistance personified by Jean Moulin: "On that day, his face was that of France."[26] And it is a political act too: seeking to unite French citizens in the present with the Gaullist project, one central moment of which (the Resistance) is being Panthéonized before their eyes.[27] Malraux's speech, in brief, is an effort at identity construction, closely linked to the promotion of current political interests. But, as I suggested earlier, it seems incomplete to think that this is purely an act of invention, as if it were cut out of the whole cloth of present or future utility, as if the present were some free-floating moment and autonomous vantage point. Surface inscriptions of memory, such as Malraux's or Pericles', make sense, indeed would only achieve whatever instrumental ends they may have, against the background of an underlying memory-identity already there, the context of meaning in which they are inscribed. Faulkner captures this nicely: "But you were not listening, because you knew it all already, had learned, absorbed it already without the medium of speech somehow from having been born and living beside it, with it . . . so that what your father was saying did not tell you anything so much as it struck, word by word, the resonant strings of remembering."[28] This context, the words, habits, values, and so forth, are what keeps these speeches, monuments, and so on from falling on barren ground, what causes the plucked strings to resonate. Without that meaning-giving horizon of collective memory there would be no framework within which their sense would be given; the present is not "self-intelligible" but is rather the eye looking out from the immense body of the past.[29] So the official inscriptions, the dates, speeches, monuments, and archives of state-memory are embedded in, or rest upon, the tectonic plates of the long duration of collective memory, the identity-shaping memories that belong less to conscious inscription than to the habits of the heart of a community. Memory, whether of the voluntary type, the intentional calling to mind, privately or publicly, of the past, or involuntary, draws its sense and meaning from a social framework of remembrance. This sense-giving framework is itself a form of memory: a tradition, a life-world, a way of seeing and doing that are core elements of the group's identity.[30]

Collective memory envelops and informs both *pensée sociale* and individual memory.[31] Often individual memory and collective memory are intertwined: the memory of one's own past is the recollection of one's place in a family (one reason why the family album plays the role in memory that it does), a profession, a community of faith, or a political community, and it is shaped by the memory of the surrounding group. Much memory then may be a common property, shared with or framed by others, a part of a collective memory at work in a community or generation. Seeing the debris of an evicted couple's belongings, including a yellowed letter of manumission, Ellison's narrator in *Invisible Man* says, "I turned and stared again at the jumble, no longer looking at what was before my eyes, but inwardly-outwardly, around a corner into the dark, far-away-and-long-ago, not so much of my own memory as of remembered words, of linked verbal echoes, images, heard even when not listening at home." Further on, the protagonist, finding himself being seduced by a white woman, says, "And my mind whirled with forgotten stories of male servants summoned to wash the mistress's back; chauffeurs sharing the masters' wives; Pullman porters invited into the drawing room of rich wives headed for Reno."[32] And Perec wrote of his book of first-person commonplace memories, *Je me souviens. Les choses communes* (I Remember: Common Things), that these were the shared memories of his times, memories that contemporaries of his in France would recognize as their own.[33] Collective memory is present in the daily fabric of a life-in-common, and not just in the etchings on society's surface. These are the sediments, or tectonic plates, formed over the long duration, which endure even where the conscious recollection of

their origins fades: the quotidian events of a small community; a local patois, lost then rediscovered in an unexpected place; or, as Jean Améry
writes, the *Heimat* of one's childhood, of language, customs, and mores
that become one's horizon. Here memory is not an intentional act but
something akin to a current of thought, to the air we breathe: there but so
enveloping to those on its inside as to be scarcely recognizable, except
perhaps in moments of loss such as those described by Michel Ragon and
Améry.

Most apparent when missing: in exile one's past is lost.[34] Exile can
mean the loss of one's language and with it an important part of one's
memory and sense of being at home, of having a country, not as territory
but as a locale of memory and identity.[35] With the loss of these memory
markers, those that form part of the basic fabric of a life-in-common, exiles lose a part of themselves.[36] Tocqueville's account of the "privileges of
humanity" taken from Africans deported to slavery in America focuses on
just this dimension of memory: the African American slave has "lost even
the memory of his homeland; he no longer understands the language his
fathers spoke; he has abjured their religion and forgotten their mores."[37]
Dispossession and memory are also central to Ellison's *Invisible Man*. The
exile, then, does not live surrounded by his mother language and the
other habit-like forms of memory and attachment. He must do memory
work to reawaken them or mourn their loss. Yves Bonnefoy captures this
relationship between loss and memory in a reflection on a celebrated passage from Keats's "Ode to a Nightingale": "when, sick for home, / She
[Ruth] stood in tears amid the alien corn." What was I to gather, Bonnefoy asks, from this "evasive maternal presence if not the sentiment of
exile and the tears which troubled this face trying to see in the things
present the lost place [*lieu*]."[38] "Trying to see in the things present the
lost place": memory's labors, the work of recollecting, always are related
to something absent. This can be the absence of justice done to a victim,
of a truth about the past hidden under an "official story," or the absence
and loss that death or exile brings. And recollecting memory seeks to
gather in these absences, in a way to make the absent present: to do justice, tell the true story, live in the sentiments of nostalgia or melancholy.[39]

Seen from the perspective of the tectonic plates, of habit and thick
memory, the present is not so much the moment of invention as a "place
of passage" for these memory currents, a place where they become actual.[40] Of course, as Halbwachs recognized and indeed made central to
his work on memory, collective memory is crucially a reconstruction,
something designed around present needs, imposed, and just as often

contested. But it is also a horizon, the sense of a way of life in all its dimensions, transmitted to be sure, yet closer to a habit in its next-to-
invisible presence in the life of a community: a framework of remembrance rather than an intentional inscription. Marc Bloch argued that the
present itself, locale of invention and contestation, breathes the air of
memory-habit in the same moment it seeks to shape it. State-memory, to
use Nora's shorthand, is most assuredly a construction. But the present
and its needs which guide our appropriation of the past are located in a
context of meaning and significance in which they can first come to be
understood and recognized as "ours." That context is, at its heart, a horizon of memory, of the tectonic plates that ground our life-in-common.
What memory inscriptions seek to create, suppress, or transform is given
up to the present by deeper currents of memory, and these inscriptions
would work as memory-makers only in the context of a shared framework
of memory-identity. Consider a foreigner listening to Malraux's funeral
oration for Jean Moulin. Presumably many of the allusions in that speech
would not be part of this person's social capital/memory. And even if she
were learned in the references and allusions of his speech, in an important sense they would not be hers in the same way that they would belong
to a citizen. However complete her knowledge of the memory tropes of
Malraux's oration, her relation to them would be detached, the view of an
outsider. Martin Walser argues that a Frenchman or an American, looking at a photograph of Auschwitz, might say, "Those [monstrous] Germans!" But a German looking at the same picture could not dispel his co-
ownership of that history by exclaiming against the terrible evils that
humankind are capable of, or against the Nazis.[41] That picture, like Malraux's speech, belongs to the memory-identity (and memory-justice) of
the communities in which it is embedded. Halbwachs's account is helpful
here: we must share in and identify with our group's memory in order for
testimony about the past to be fully intelligible.[42] In *La langue maternelle*,
Alexakis describes an encounter in a museum in Athens where the protagonist is challenged by someone saying, "You look at these [artifacts]
like a foreigner." To look at something like a foreigner is not to recognize
oneself in it, to have it not as one's own but as somebody else's. The present, then, as a locale of interests, inscriptions, and contest, is also and at
the same time a moment embedded in memory-narrative, memory-habit,
and the possessiveness of a community bound together in the identity of a
collective memory, in the "mineness" of an enduring life-in-common. In
both the explicit and tacit facets of memory and recognition, even such a
manifestly political gesture as Malraux's funeral oration reveals itself as

possible only against the background of a memory that shapes identity, makes its utterances meaningful, and causes it to resonate as mine.

2.2. BOUNDARIES

Collective memory is not only a central element in the identity of a political community understood as persisting through time but, like individual memory (and therefore, because individuating), a boundary condition as well. As we saw in my earlier discussion of personal identity, memory adds a vital dimension to the continuity of a person, and, as I also remarked, continuity and individuating criteria overlap in identity. The attributes that permit us to see a person (or community) as one and the same through time are also those that allow us to distinguish one person from another. Territory, like the individual's physical person, particularizes the community; so too do its institutions, though in a more ambiguous and limited way. Space and institutions are the tangible boundaries of the community, malleable but essential nevertheless.[43]

We can see the boundary dimension of memory in Malraux's remark that "humans are as separated by the forms of their memories as by those of their character" or, in Stuart Hampshire's words, that we are in "the grip of particular and distinguishing memories."[44] Those memories mark out the boundaries between communities, whether the family, a professional group, or a political community. So Halbwachs's collective memory as a "tableau of resemblances" is also and crucially a way of speaking about a boundary line between communities. In mapping a tableau of resemblances, memory seeks to find the "permanence of the same," but that sameness which grounds identity is the "guardian of difference."[45] The persistence of the same, then, is drawn in demarcation from some other. Ugrešić writes of the "exclusivity of collective memory": memory is associated with, and is part of the foundation of, the particularity of the group or individual.[46] And that is hardly surprising, for implicit in having an identity (individual or collective) is being marked by just that separateness without which the identical self would, as Parfit's argument shows, spill over and meld with others, and would therefore cease to be an enduring and bounded whole. Collective memory establishes identity boundaries between one group or person and another. As a result, it resists a universalism that calls into question the moral/political legitimacy of such boundary markers in the name of abstract, universal principles. The "mineness" of memory is not that of a property of an otherwise freestanding person or community—free, that is, to discard or accept it—but rather a central element in the identity of that self: defining its character, setting out its agency/responsibility across time, individuating it in relation to others.

Memory, embedded in habits, institutions, and places, maps out the particularity, the persisting and individuating sameness of a political community. Collective memory does not maintain a detached or objective relationship to the events that are its ingathered past. Its time, as I suggested, is not the chronology of historical time but the blending of (our) past and present into the wholeness of character whose terrain is illuminated (and occasionally left in darkness) by its moral concerns, its sense of shame and pride, and its need for legitimacy. The time of the community's memory is uneven, exemplary, and sometimes selective, in much the same way that recognition of one's character is. In what Nora calls the dialectic of memory and forgetting that is collective memory, other actions, sources of shame or division, will be submerged in forgetting, suggesting that memory as an element of political identity is balanced by an attempt to forget. The contours of memory-identity, of recollection and forgetting, are jagged and uneven in the way that an autobiography would be. Some episodes stand out as identity-defining, as bathing all others in their light and investing them with a unifying meaning; some are not relevant.[47] Still others are suppressed out of shame or from fear of division or conflict. So when we say that nations, or political communities generally, have a historical "location" or continuity, we do not mean as seen from the outside, as if by an observer. Communities of memory are rather communities of (some type of) sameness defined from within by the presence of a morally/politically relevant past.[48] The boundaries of the community, shaped by its memory, are of an intimate kind in which it recognizes itself, judges itself in both shame and pride, and sometimes seeks to rid itself of the presence of the past through a willed amnesia. Where memory is alive, this self-recognition has a lived character, and is not a museum piece offered up to spectators, as Ragon describes seeing Vendéean artifacts in a Parisian museum or as in the exchange in an Athenian museum recounted by Alexakis.[49] Such memory is of the self it constitutes, and its fidelity is part of that self-recognition.[50] Principles that call on us to privilege a moral vantage point which stands above particularity coexist uneasily with this identity and its boundaries, including those constituted by memory. When Tzvetan Todorov writes that memory (in liberal democracies, presumably) has been dethroned not in the name of forgetting but in that of universal principles, the challenge he describes is one directed toward the boundary (and persistence) conditions of the selfhood or sameness (the identity-memory) of a community across time.

2.3. THE WEIGHT OF THE PAST

Now as we saw, identity is closely related to agency and responsibility, as well as to the possibility of commitments to the future. Collective memory, as a key element in the boundary and persistence conditions of communities, is an essential component of imputable political subjects across time. In the discussion that follows, I look in more detail at the question of political identity from the standpoint of continuity across time, of memory, and of responsibility for the past, in short, at the persistence of the community and its accountability as the center of doing justice. Needless to say, with the upheavals of our era, these issues of continuity and responsibility over time have secured a considerable theoretical, political, and moral saliency. Democratic regimes emerging from the rubble of the old, whether in eastern and central Europe or in South Africa and Latin America, have had to confront the past. In western Europe, the enduring legacy of the Second World War has left traces throughout the region, but especially in eastern Europe, France, and Germany. Nor are these issues exclusively of a domestic political character; they reverberate in the international environment as well. Thus, for example, while the newly founded Federal Republic of Germany chose to assume responsibility for the past as part of its recognition by, and reentry into, the community of states, other nations have been perceived as reluctant to do so. The result has been a not inconsiderable impact on their international standing, as, for example, in the straining of Sino-Japanese and Japanese-Korean relations by issues arising from the past and the recognition of it in the present. A state's standing in the international community is sometimes tied to its own recognition of the past. This suggests that at the international level, the moral continuity of political communities over time is assumed even where, as in the case of the former Federal Republic of Germany and Japan, the new regimes are radically different from those of the past.[51] And it is not only in or between those countries that have recently experienced the trauma of war or of regime transformation that the presence of the past is keenly felt: one need only consider the legacy of slavery and the seemingly intractable problem of racial justice in America, or the bitter inheritance left by Britain's entanglement in Ireland, to see how even in stable, mature democracies, the past weighs heavily.

Let me begin with a story that illustrates some of the principal features of the controversies I shall be addressing. In 1992, François Mitterrand, then president of the French Republic, was asked to lend his voice, on behalf of France, to the commemoration of the July 1942 roundup of Jews at the Vélodrome d'Hiver (Vél' d'Hiv) in Paris and their subsequent deportation to Nazi concentration camps. Specifically, he was asked to have the Republic acknowledge the role of France in the persecution of Jews and others during the dark years of the Occupation. The Republic, then, was called upon, in an act of atoning remembrance, to inscribe in its public memory the complicity of France in these crimes. Mitterrand at first resisted this appeal for public remembrance: "The Republic, across all its history, has constantly adopted a totally open attitude [with regard to the rights of all its citizens]. Therefore, do not demand an accounting of this Republic."[52] At the core of this refusal of responsibility and rejection of public remembrance was the claim that France was identical with (as de Gaulle expressed it) "une certaine idée de la France" (a certain idea of France), namely, that of free, Republican France. The Vichy regime was thus a parenthesis in the continuous history of the Republic, "a new regime, different and temporary," as Mitterrand described it. The France that is the Republic is not, on this view, the proper locus of responsibility for these crimes.[53] In the end, a commemorative plaque was installed at the site of the Vél' d'Hiv, and the Republic's homage to the victims of these crimes referred to Vichy as the "de facto authority called 'the Government of the French State.' "[54] Here the intertwining of boundary and persistence dimensions of identity, in their moral/political form, are plain to see. On one conception of political identity, roughly the sort offered by Aristotle and Peter French, and discussed earlier in this book, the sameness of the country across time is grounded in its institutional and constitutional-normative continuity. Regime forms that break with that continuity also thereby cease to be "ours." They are not part of what "we" were and so are not the objects of public remembrance, of our collective memory of ourselves as we were. We are not the inheritors of this past which is someone else's, Nazi Germany's or the Vichy regime's. Because we are not one with the perpetrators, because we do not share with them a past that would give us a common political identity, we are not accountable for their injustices. Bearing witness to them, in atoning remembrance, is not an obligation. Yet as I also suggested, it is not just institutional continuity that grounds identity and responsibility, as if, for example, the question of French (partial) responsibility for the events that occurred in France during the war years could be exhaustively determined by a legal determination of the constitutional legality of the Vichy regime.

2.4. LIBERALISM, DEMOCRACY, AND MEMORY

We are thus led to consider the issues invoked by the presence of the past in political identity and the ethical burdens that it brings with it. I start by laying out a cluster of prominent theories of political identity, sketching for each the moral weight of the past that it allows.

The first centers on nationalism and its variants ("the most aggressive, the most passionate" form of the quest for identity) in which identity is rooted in some (usually nonpolitical) notion of autochthony and shared traits (ethnicity, culture, language) and territory.[55] Such an identity easily absorbs the long duration of a community's existence and sees sameness even in the midst of the most radical changes. Memory of a certain kind, the ingathering and making present of that sameness through time, is a central motif of nationalist politics. It also erects very high barriers to admission, and is typically exclusionary in its conception and practice of belonging. If humans are in "the grip of particular and distinguishing memories and of particular and distinguishing local passions," and their political identity includes a common history and memory, a "community of recollections," a union with the dead and the yet-to-be born, then immersion in such a community and its mores cannot "be shared, exchanged or acquired—and that is precisely why [it has been made into] the locus of national identity."[56]

(2) At the other pole is a hyper-liberal belonging in which the only morally relevant form of sharing is a roster of rights, universal in scope and thus available, at least in principle, to every human *as* human. Accordingly, our particular space in the world (our country), our interests, our past or future together, our common time, all these carry no special moral weight. For if indeed humans are all similarly situated as rights bearers, then particularity of historical time, place, religion, ethnicity, and so on, and the self-preference that flows from these strong, non-rights type markers, are extraordinarily difficult to justify in the public sphere. The only past relevant for (political) identity and belonging would be the succession of rights-governed events and transactions. History of the "blood and soil" type would clearly be meaningless and repugnant. But even a more benign cultural history would be publicly irrelevant, being at most a heuristic vantage point on the impartial and universal code of rights.[57] This view is, in principle, suspicious of thick notions of membership, that is, notions in which are embedded identity markers other than those derived from a table of rights. Or better, it is suspicious of granting such notions any regulative status over our ideas and practices of citizen-

ship. Since all human beings are rights bearers, and because that is the dominant and publicly relevant definition of membership, the world should, in this account, resemble a collection of rights holders for whom a shared past would be only of folkloric interest. Memory and the long duration of that sameness, things particular to us as members of this political locale, are irrelevant here. Such a hyper-liberal world would be a neighborhood of the rootless and memory-less rather than a high-barrier, closed (bounded by their "thick" identities) community of citizens.

(3) Occupying something like a middle position stands a constitutional patriotism that seeks a reconciliation between the universalist demands of liberal principle and the need for a robust political identity, including a shared history, which is required for a flourishing democratic life. French Republicanism is the canonical illustration of this middle path, but its contours can also be discerned in elements of the American political experience.[58] Constitutional patriotism, centered on universal-democratic principles, aims to unite the universalist aspirations of liberalism (broadly construed), and its emphasis on willed or voluntary membership, with the republican idea of a political life-in-common, an identity-conferring *patria*. To be citizens of such a regime is to subscribe to a set of locally instituted but nevertheless universal principles. When I say "locally instituted" here I mean rooted not only in space but also in time, that is, having a deep memory of historical continuity of a political/constitutional type. Consider, in this regard, a passage from Lincoln's speech of July 10, 1858: "We have besides these men—descended by blood from our ancestors— among us perhaps half our people who are not descendants at all of these men . . . finding themselves our equals in all things. If they look back through this history to trace their connection with those days by blood, they find they have none . . . but when they look through that old Declaration of Independence . . . [they feel] . . . that it is the father of all moral principle in them, and that they have a right to claim it as though they were blood of the blood, and flesh of the flesh of the men who wrote that Declaration, and so they are."[59] Of course, closure and the distribution of membership remain features of this regime, though the barriers are themselves now understood as deductions from (and constrained by) the universal-democratic principles that are the constitutional core of this society. Citizenship of the constitutional-patriotic sort stands midway between, for example, national membership of the kind in which the boundary markers are defined according to some cluster of exclusionary, nonpolitical attributes, and the nomadic world of itinerants and their neighborhoods. The horizon of membership is traced using only those properties that would be counted as legitimate among the members of

that society, while, at the same moment, that limited horizon itself and the memory of a life-in-common are seen as preconditions of any healthy form of democratic political life: "Memory is indeed central [even] to constitutional patriotism itself."[60]

As I have argued, continuous selves are the foundation of identity ("who we are") and relatedly of holding individuals and political communities to account for their past ("what do we owe?"). So we should expect that in the three classes of identity theory sketched here (nationalist, hyper-liberal, and constitutional-patriotic) are also embedded sets of propositions about identity and its relationship to liability for the past, and responsibility for the future. Plainly, these propositions about responsibility would mirror the duration and denseness of the relevant past in their foundational accounts of identity: with nationalism, at least in principle, making us one with our past and thus fully accountable for it; liberalism picking out only a narrow band of continuity, with a corresponding thinness of responsibility for that past; and, finally, constitutional patriotism, in which identity, shared memories, and responsibility are dense but strictly within the limits of the past of the constitutional order and its practices of freedom.[61] How these understandings of the temporal-moral dimension of identity, of the presence of the past, accountability, and memory, shape their respective positions on matters of identity, difference, and citizenship will be a theme of the pages that follow.

Here I will put aside two of the approaches I have sketched, a stylized nationalism of the "blood and soil" sort and an equally stylized hyper-liberalism (the world-as-neighborhoods view) which holds that the cement of the community is a mesh of voluntary agreements. I leave them to one side because they do not allow us to see fully the friction, the perplexities, that arise as the boundaries of memory, the particularizing presence of the past, and its attendant ethics encounter the universalist, open aspirations of a functioning liberal democratic society or the purely political understanding of belonging (the constitutional patriotism) of a republican regime. They do not permit us to see the source of this friction because both, in their different and opposed ways, wash the problem of memory and the past out of their theories of identity. On its face, what I have termed the hyper-liberal view, with its understanding of continuity as the expression of iterative free engagements, seems all too light. Under its corrosive jurisdiction, the notion of a continuous self all but vanishes since it lacks the conceptual language to give substance to such a self, except as the episodic product of the will. And specifically, the idea of responsibility for the past, outside the context of explicit agreements, strong agency, and contracts, finds little room in this argument. In a mirror-image fashion, the heavy weight accorded memory and the past in, for example, nationalist theories also renders them less illuminating for my purposes: what we have been just defines who we are and what we owe and, in one single mesh of belonging, points the direction to our future. What I want to focus on instead is the manner in which this middle path of constitutional patriotism understands a community's ties with its past as the core of its identity and as the source of moral burdens to be assumed. In particular, I want to discuss its fundamental ambiguities when faced with issues of continuity and responsibility, that is, with the political community as the subject of attribution over time.

With this in mind, let me now return to the Vél' d'Hiv commemoration dispute and venture that there is something unsettling in the exculpatory claim Mitterrand made on behalf of the Republic. That the Vichy years belong to France and are part of its history and identity seems a natural, almost a compelling intuition. We may grant that the sense of being ours and a source of enduring responsibility is heightened when the current regime stands in an uninterrupted relation to its predecessors (in the way that the years of slavery belong to the United States, although slavery and its principles have long since been decisively rejected). But does a rupture in regime form alone sever the bonds of memory, continuity, and co-responsibility, and absolve a political community of the wrongs that occur during this constitutional hiatus or prior to the act of constitution-making? Do the deeds of the *ancien régime* or of an interloper government cease to be its deeds? The affirmative answer appears unsatisfactory, for just the reasons suggested in Aristotle's discussion of continuity: democratic Athens and Athens under the Thirty seem, in an important sense, one and the same city, though it is also true to say of them that they are profoundly different variations of this common self. Yet if we attempt (in other than nationalist discourse) to construct a theory of identity that would make this (constitutionally discontinuous) past ours, see the present "we" as the subject of attribution for past deeds, and burden us with the remembrance of this past and the duty of atonement, we are brought up short. If not in the regime form, then where are we to find that sameness across time that renders this past ours and not someone else's? The "blood and soil" response provides one sort of account, though dubious empirically and at odds with the normative underpinnings of a liberal democratic society. By the same token, the republican thesis of identity as constitutional continuity (implied by Mitterrand's response), that this "was not ours, but another community's past," a thesis that rests on the possibility of a radically new political and moral birth, seems in its own way untenable and morally repugnant, since it holds out before us an easy path to the forgetting of injustice and to a facile self-absolution.

For evident reasons, these issues are still more salient in Germany's post–World War II history. On the one hand, the moral burden of the past weighs heavily there, and with it the ideas of identity, continuity, and memory. "Nowhere in the world (except, perhaps, in Israel or Russia) does history weigh as heavily, as palpably, upon ordinary people as in Germany. Sixty years after the end of the Second World War, the disaster of Nazism is still unmistakably and inescapably inscribed upon almost every town and cityscape, in whichever direction you look."[62] On the other hand, Germany has moved toward a greater openness to immigration, and it is part of the progress toward the creation of a supra-national European identity. The friction between the community of memory, drawn to the particularity of the past and its burdens, and the emerging openness of membership in a new kind of constitutional political community (domestic and Europe-wide) is perhaps most apparent there. In exploring the German variant, I draw on Jürgen Habermas's writings related to German identity and the "historians' debate." The direction and content of Habermas's work on these topics are familiar, and so I sketch only their outlines.[63] Their uneasy core consists of the demands of openness and diversity on the one side and the ethics of remembrance and responsibility on the other. The first set of imperatives is placed on the agenda by increasing immigration, from both eastern Europe and the developing world; by German reunification; and by the move toward a European political community. These have combined to sharpen the tension between the exclusionary nation-state (bounded by ethnicity, language, a community of fate, and so forth) and the universalist underpinnings of liberal democracy.[64] They lead us to ask how a liberal state, committed to a type of indifference to any particularist markers, can justify the criteria by which it excludes immigrants. [65] To ask how, in a liberal society, German reunification can be viewed as the bringing together of a pre-political ethnic group. Finally, we are asked to reflect on what is to become of the nation-state and its practices of citizenship in a Europe moving toward a supra-national political life.

While this first clutch of questions clearly requires its own response, there is nevertheless a common thread running through Habermas's treatment of them. And that is the guiding thought that citizenship and national consciousness, united in the first republican experiments of early European modernity, can (and need to) be separated. The liberal democratic political community and membership in it are shaped by principles that abstract from any non-rights type markers, from, as John Rawls wrote, "our place and history in society."[66] Not only does it abstract from these varied nonpolitical properties, but also it assumes the character of a "community of will" (*Willensgemeinschaft*), as Habermas terms it. The past survives, under this new dispensation, as cultural identities, as traditions to be appropriated critically, and as heuristic vantage points from which the universal principles of the public sphere are (within limits) interpreted. But the publicly relevant sense of identity and belonging is constitutional (universal-democratic) in character, and so in principle porous and open to outsiders; it understands German reunification as the extension of democracy and not as the ingathering of ethnic Germans under one political authority; and, at least in principle, it is available for political life at the European rather than the traditional nation-state level. In short, the possibility of Germany's becoming a multicultural society and of its becoming part of a European political community depends precisely on the adherence to a constitutional-patriotic pattern of identity and belonging.[67]

If that were the end of it, then Habermas's interventions in these matters would amount to the claim that identity and its expression in citizenship are constitutional (normative and institutional) in character, that they are strictly a matter of adhesion to a set of publicly recognized political values of an abstract (universal) democratic type. Such a view (in its first part) would be close to that which underpinned Mitterrand's understanding of France as the Republic. But in fact, as I remarked earlier, there is a second set of issues here, those centered on the past, including an ethics of remembrance and responsibility. The past and its relation to (German) identity haunt Habermas's work: on the political level, the reunification of Germany has, in Habermas's view, reawakened the nationalist temptations of the past, and nationalism in the German context has historically not been a friend of democracy.[68] And not only has the nationalist construction of identity not been amenable to the flourishing of political liberty, but also in the near-to-impermeable closedness of the *Volksgemeinschaft*, it is fundamentally hostile to the diversity of a modern democratic society. Along one dimension, then, the past matters because in its surviving traces it can threaten the democratic present. Its temptations are poisonous and must be expunged from our midst. Yet along a second dimension, Habermas sees a need not to jettison the past in the name of a secure post-national political identity but, quite the contrary, to embrace it, to keep the memory of the past alive in the face of the amnesiac seductions of the "normalizers" of German history; to underscore that it is ours, something for which we are responsible and no one else. To "normalize," or to treat one's past objectively, from a detached perspective, is to distance oneself from responsibility for the deed. It is, in Fernand Braudel's words, to speak of one's community "as if it were another country . . . [and the historian] an 'observer' as detached as possible."[69] One central moment of the identity problem is evident here: the tension between the vision of a "rational identity" centered on universal norms of (roughly) a liberal democratic type, the ideal of a post-1949 German political identity, and an identity laden with responsibility and remembrance, the legacy of the unmasterable past. To follow Habermas as he wrestles with this is to understand the depth of the conflict between the liberal-constitutional patriotic construction of identity(and likely that of modernity more generally) and the enduring role of (collective) memory and responsibility for the past.

One strand in Habermas's reflection on past and present offers us the relatively uncontroversial notion that the relationship between constitutional patriotism on the one side and the past on the other can be expressed in the proposition that the specific institutionalizations of universal principles have particular and varied historical roots. Virtually every regime has its own *ancien régime.* Thus in postwar Germany there has been a special path to constitutional democracy: the appeal to democratic constitutional patriotism emerges out of defeat and from the rejection of the bitter legacy of another, earlier way of belonging, the *Volksgemeinschaft.* Henceforth, there can be only one kind of patriotism and belonging, that framed by the Basic Law of 1949.[70] Is this all there is to the relationship of past and present, that this public sphere, constitutional in character, and inclining toward a universalizing democracy of human rights, has a history? That it is a result of a decisive rejection of earlier forms of belonging? That it has a defeated antecedent regime? Such a past need not weigh on us, however; it is not a burden, indeed hardly even a presence, and it certainly does not necessarily give rise to debts or moral obligations. The historical past, a terrain mapped along a grid of causally linked series of events, across a linear, homogeneous time, does individuate us, as persons and communities; but it is memory, individual or collective, whose landscape is uneven, marked by trauma, conflict, and guilt, and always eliding the past and present, that by gathering in this past, by appropriating it, gives us identity and a moral narrative of pride, shame, and indebtedness, that ties us across time to *our* past and the burdens this past imposes simply by virtue of being ours.

But Habermas himself, in his interventions in the "historians' debate," and in his praise of Daniel Goldhagen's *Hitler's Willing Executioners* in the midst of controversies over its assertion of a distinctive (annihilationist), long-enduring, and culturally embedded form of German anti-Semitism, directs us to a second idea of the presence of the past, one that lies beyond a merely genealogical relation to it. In the pages that follow I use Habermas's engagement in the *Historikerstreit* to urge that propositions such as the one that the universal has particular roots do not do full justice to the presence and weight of the past in our political lives. The identity question, in its temporal/normative dimensions, suggests that for all of their abstractness and impersonality, the constitutional project and its related citizenship practices are deeply embedded in a community of memory and in the sort of identity that such intergenerational communities have at their core. And specifically, they are embedded in the moral claims of remembrance and responsibility that a sameness, an identity across time bequeaths to members of a political community. Now the original impetus for the "historians' debate" was the issue of the "normalization" of recent German history through both a recovery of the long horizon of that country's pre-1933 past and a comparative study of the National Socialist period, seeing it not as unique but as part of the twentieth century's experience of totalitarianism in the Soviet Union and elsewhere.[71] "Normalization," as I said, meant in part the possibility of treating German history in a detached and scientific fashion.[72] Habermas answered that what was at stake was the issue of memory, identity, and politics. For Habermas's opponents, a German identity grounded in a sense of the past obsessed with the National Socialist years, with the Holocaust at their core, would make a life-in-common next to impossible.[73] Normalizing German history was essential to the making of a healthy political identity. Habermas too recognized the essentially public character (moral/political identity) of this debate and he responded, insisting on the burden of the past, and on the imprescriptible nature of the Holocaust within it. It was a debt-producing, incorrigible legacy to the community's collective memory and identity, and one to be sheltered from the erosion of time, forgetting, and normalization. Normalization was, from this latter vantage point, a way of relieving the moral burden of the past, of de-centering Auschwitz in the collective memory of this past.[74]

What then is the character of this past of debt and remembrance? We might begin with Habermas's observation that "we cannot simply pick and choose our own traditions," though it is ours to decide what future to fashion out of them.[75] We are given the totality of our past, whether as individuals or as members of a community, and even though our comportment to its varied parts may differ, sometimes applauding, other times repudiating, it is at the center of our identity in its entirety. An American memory with Emerson but without slavery would scarcely be intelligible; a

German memory with Goethe but without the National Socialist years would be unthinkable.[76] It is something given to us, into which we are "thrown." That this is our past is a fact at once non-elective and unalterable: "It is not given to man to make for himself another cradle."[77] We are, at least in that sense, members of a "community of fate." One (though not the only) way in which this fated past is present among us is in the traditions, the forms of life, in the memory-identity fabric woven of past and present, which are core parts of what it means to share in an identity.[78] The past, then, is present in our traditions, and again in what is often a non-elective manner: in habit, modes of thought, and so forth that are part of that legacy. And of course, it is also present in those chosen moments when, by deliberate decision, we put the past into words, monuments, days of remembrance.

Here we might well still be on the terrain of an archaeology of political identity, giving an account of its origins and transmission. But Habermas suggests that the presence of the past involves something more than an account of our origins. And he intimates (with the uncertainties to be discussed later on) that it is not simply present as the remnants of a cultural tradition. It is rather the wellspring of accountability: burdening us, giving us pride or shame, making us accountable. We think back to that past, commemorate it in public, atone for it, and, occasionally, try to forget it. And we do this because, in an important sense, it is *ours*: not somebody else's past, memories, or debts, but ours. Remembrance (and forgetting) depend on the fact that the past can be prefaced by the possessive pronoun "our." However much we may have changed as a political body over time, those changes are scalar in relation to our past self: they modify us but do not constitute us as a new (political) self.[79] Not only, then, are we bequeathed traditions, but also we inherit responsibility, a liability for the past and for those deeds that were produced from the core of "our life together."[80] The presence of the past is here moral and not genealogical or traditional. Because it is ours, it is with us always, even through the changes we undergo in the passing of the years. The past and the dead (like those yet to be born) make claims on the living, long after they and the events around them have entered the historical past.[81] And, we might add, long after those traditions that are our inheritance have been transformed beyond all recognition.

Consider the contrast between Habermas's argument and Karl Jaspers's 1946 essay "Die Schuldfrage." In that essay, Jaspers was addressing an audience who were contemporaries of the National Socialist years. There guilt and responsibility (*Haftung*) were perhaps more assimilable to notions of will and agency, since the parties concerned were actors in, or bystanders to, the events.[82] Habermas's audience, by contrast, born mostly after the war, is free of all agency-based responsibility. The extension of co-responsibility to them involves an ethics of intergenerational identity and accountability that is not on its face consistent with the idea of a constitutional political identity, with a "community of will" fashioned by the constitution-making of 1949.[83] For if it were simply a matter of an elective community, endowed with a "flexible" identity, and critically received traditions and memories, one would have expected the discussion to be directed to the cleansing of whatever traces remained of the life forms that had made National Socialism possible (as in the analogy of curriculum reform that Habermas uses to discuss the role of tradition in modernity).[84] Here we push the past away from us, divest ourselves of it, and seek to expunge its remnants from our midst. In so far as we continue to hold on to that past, to appropriate it, we do this not because we see it as an abiding part of our identity as a community across time, but rather because we can use it as a storehouse of lessons. Memory yields imperatives of the "Never again!" type, and its importance lies not in an act of atonement but in its ability to help us avoid repeating the injustices of the past. The prospect that the evils of the past might reappear in the present, and thereby threaten the achievements of the democratic regime, lead us both to hunt down and purge its traces and to employ it as a warning. That past would be a matter for public concern, but since it is not "ours" in the strong sense related to identity, it would be essentially indistinguishable from, let us say, the past of other societies, for example, of anti-democratic ideologies originating elsewhere, that might menace our political community. In short, our relationship to it is instrumental and pedagogical, that is, it is something from which we can learn, and not a moral burden woven into our identity.

In fact, Habermas's arguments in this area are ambivalent. On the one hand, his account is of the ethics of the debt to the past. The National Socialist period polluted Germany and left those born after the war with a responsibility for the past which cannot be expiated, and whose call is answered, in the first instance, with atoning remembrance. It is almost as if what is at work here is the idea of collective shame. Yet Habermas, while seeming to invoke just that idea, nevertheless calls it an "archaic" sentiment.[85] Perhaps, though, it is not so archaic. For shame, as we saw, is bound up with the wholeness of a life, and not the narrower connection between agent and act. At the level of the community, the sense of shame (or pride) in the deeds of one's family or fellow citizens points to a shared community of fate and memory, something that is enduringly ours. In that respect, the unity of our lives, and the shame or pride that accompanies that unity, are irreversible, and so the presence of the past, and like-wise the duty to remember, are unchangeable features of the landscape of identity.[86]

In these discussions, Habermas sometimes adopts another vocabulary, a language of responsibility rather more assimilable to the idea of constitutional patriotic identity than the notion of shame, as when he speaks of "life forms" and the "web of cultural threads" in giving an account of the mark left on the community by the past.[87] Christian Meier has remarked that this language allows for a way of addressing the presence of the past which invokes tradition not as a stained community, not as a source of shame and an object of remembrance, but as a cultural artifact. As if, were these life forms to be sufficiently transformed in the course of a long-term, successful experiment in democracy, then the burden of the past would be lifted too.[88] Why, Meier asks, does Habermas, in discussing the responsibility of the present generation for the deeds of their predecessors, not say simply that they "live in a state called Germany . . . [and] our responsibility comes to us from being German"?[89] Or in the words of Philipp Jenninger, then speaker of the Bundestag, on the fiftieth anniversary (1938–1988) of *Kristallnacht,* "The past is part of our identity" and (quoting an Auschwitz survivor), "Young Germans must accept that they are Germans, they cannot stand apart from this fate." Or, as Willy Brandt told young Germans, "No one is free from history."[90]

The response to Meier's question is surely not just that it is the archaic quality of the idea of shame that leads Habermas to seek out another way to express the presence of the past. Yet an answer as to why he finds such language difficult to accept is by no means straightforward, all the more so since it seems a principal concern of his to foreclose a therapeutic but immoral forgetting of the past. Atonement and remembrance are duties, forgetting an evil. His interventions both in the "historians' debate" and in urging a positive reception of Goldhagen's book in Germany have had as one of their central motifs an adamantine resistance to any effort to lighten, modify, or relativize the burden of the past, to be rid of the tectonic plates of German history. How then to understand this? A partial explanation is that Meier's language of Germans and Germany as a community extending across generations asserts, from Habermas's standpoint, just the wrong (*Volk*-like) sort of continuity. Something further in the way of a response can be drawn from Habermas's reflections on constitutional patriotism and national identity. Modern identity, he writes, has no fixed content given in advance; it is revisable and flexible and involves a critical appropriation through the open, discursive life of a community.[91] The openness of identity to critical revision, coupled with the separation in late modernity of national identity and political membership rooted in universal-democratic principles, rests uneasily with the idea of the past as a present, imprescriptible burden. That idea, seen from the vantage point of identity as culture and culture as imagined, willed, and revisable, appears to be almost a form of Sophoclean *miasma* or collective pollution. And in its denseness and impermeability, in its strengthening of the possessive and particularist pronoun "our," it ill serves the desiderata of universality and openness.

2.5. THE BURDEN OF THE PAST AND REVISABLE IDENTITIES

Let us take this idea of revisable identities one step further. Consider again this influential current of thought. The most widely accepted approach, as Barry Schwartz writes, "[sees] the past as a social construction shaped by the concerns and needs of the present."[92] Collective identities are interpreted as constructed, as things made, manipulatively, by mobilizing elites or in open democratic debate. Likewise the collective memory that is part of these identities is constructed and contestable.[93] The emphasis on the present weaving of the past, memory, and political identity is clearly a commodious one for modernity and liberalism, which have difficulty accepting ideas of shame, burden, and fate, and the obligations they claim to impose. The idea of the nation as, in Ernest Renan's phrase, "a daily plebiscite" has a compelling ring for those who find the idea of the burden of the past in the present to be deeply inconsistent with an underlying commitment to autonomy. For it suggests the possibility of a *Willensgemeinschaft* as, in principle, a liberal form of belonging, no longer burdened by the weight of the past, grounded in archaic (i.e., involuntary, exclusionary, often violent, and false if not irrational) notions of a community of fate arrayed across generations. The imagined, and always revisable, identities and memories of this post-traditional view have yet another advantage: being malleable, they are also porous and open to pluralism. The barriers that surround communities thus understood would be sufficiently flexible, because so little rooted in a community of memory and fate, of necessary identity, so that change within, and admission to, them would hardly be troubling. Not surprisingly, those who search for political legitimacy in the past and a community's memory of it find these arguments repugnant. Witness some of the hostile Greek nationalist responses to Anastasia Karakasidou's assertion of the recent origins (as opposed to its eternalness) and constructed character (rather than its nature-like quality) of the Greekness of Macedonia.[94] For this translation of the weight of the past into a construct, an invention, and a quasi-ideology would immediately strip that past of its mobilizing and legitimizing functions.

While objections of the sort just sketched show the implausibility of an extreme form of the view that the past just is something given to us, it is important to see how partial and incomplete are *both* the ideas of the past as simply given and of memory as a confection. Here let me venture a provisional, and by no means exhaustive, bit of clarification. On one account, we always see the past from the vantage point of the present, and from its needs and conflicts. The contours of our appropriation of the past change, then, according to what presses in the here and now. Related to this is a second claim, namely, that the past, at least in its public and political form, must be called into existence, put into words, or commemorated in stone, provided a vocabulary that will allow it to emerge. Indeed, among its original significations, the classical Greek word for remembering, *mnaomai*, meant to mention something or someone.[95] The past needs a maker of words, a poet or historian, Homer or Herodotus, to save its deeds from the oblivion of silence. The constructivist reading is surely right in this sense: that all of these actions contain at least in principle an element of will, of artifice, in the present. It is just not the case, then, that we are, strictly speaking, bequeathed or thrown into our past, that we are (in Plato's image) blocks of wax on which the past is imprinted. We appropriate it, with all that entails about the mechanisms, the power, and the passions that fuel both forgetting and remembering, and determine which pieces of the past will be hallowed and which consigned to obscurity.[96] At the same time, I have suggested that the thick memory of a life-in-common, the tectonic plates resting one on the other, deeply inform the present so that its actions are never wholly separable from that past. Even the memory-maker lives under the dispensation according to which "the past is an immense body of which the present is the eye."

But the view that our past is something given, a fate or datum, and not a piece of artifice also captures an important dimension of our relationship to it. We give voice to the past, dispute it, forget it as something not made by us but that rather calls us, seeks to impose a duty on us. The past "wants to be remembered."[97] In invoking it, and giving it voice and remembrance, we answer its call. We do not make, or construct, this past. It is there, remembered or submerged, here and present or awaiting a triggering event to bring it back: a witness's voice, a bearer of memory. Observe again that the past matters so much because it is ours, indeed, it just is us; malleable, to be sure, but nevertheless something important and independent.[98] We therefore know why, for instance, the "revisionist" approach to the Holocaust is fundamentally flawed: not only because it seeks to advance evil in the here and now, because its construction of the past is hurtful in the present, but also because it does a grievous wrong to the past, a past that, in one sense, lies within its grasp, available for distortion or suppression, but that in another sense (moral and ontological) lies beyond its powers of artifice and reinterpretation. We understand why Pierre Vidal-Naquet calls the practitioners of this art "the assassins of memory."[99] To rob us of our memory is to destroy something that is a part of us, something essential to who we are, something arguably as crucial to our identity as our physical person: our enduringness across time, and with that our manifold ties (of responsibility and other kinds) to those before and after us. It is something more as well: writing about the relationship between readers and authors, Charles Péguy speaks of the "terrible responsibility" that weighs on readers to do justice to authors, to preserve the "common memory of common humanity" bequeathed to us in their works.[100] Negationists are the "assassins of memory" because they violate that trust, that "quasi-contract," as Péguy calls it, between past, present, and future. Memory work in relation to the past is, in short, burdened by the bonds and debts incurred in an enduring life-in-common.

Consider, then, what it would mean to adopt the proposition, in its full-blooded form, that political identity could be fashioned anew in one fell (constitutional) swoop. We would then have to say that we have freed the "who we are" of identity from its long roots in the past. A public space constructed in the image of a constitutional patriotism, with universal-democratic principles at its center, almost seems to invite a shedding of the past.[101] And we might be tempted to see this as emancipatory, freeing us from the "syndrome," as Henry Rousso calls it, of the past. Yet, as the Vél' d'Hiv incident suggests, there is a profound moral uncertainty at the center of this emancipation, for in shedding the past, we also thereby free ourselves of responsibility for it. We are, politically speaking, a new "self" which can then treat the deeds and debts of the regimes in power before this rupture as those of another "self." But the conjunction of the post-national or constitutional identity and the ethics of remembrance debates invites us to consider how difficult, or impossible, it is to escape our embeddedness in the community extended through time, the community of remembrance (and anticipation) that is the basic temporal fabric of a common life and shared identity. For that reason, among others, there are limits to the level of abstraction from the particularity of memory-identity. It understates those limits to describe them as a cultural matrix with heuristic implications through which an overarching set of universal principles may be filtered and interpreted. They are rather limits that claim an obligation to past and future, a duty to remember and to correct. They also lay claim to the center of our identity: absent this memory, we would not be what we are. They are, then, *our* collective memories, and so not substitutable; *our* obligations, past and future: these give the past and our memory of it their characteristic particularity.

"We in the land of the perpetrators" ("wir, im Lande der Täter"): Habermas's phrase points to a community in which the past is a living moral presence.[102] It acknowledges that the public space of any community more enduring than a neighborhood of passersby is saturated by the past and the memory of it. It is saturated not in some incidental manner but essentially, because to be a political community, a people, a family, a religious community, or a profession involves a tie between past, present, and future. They are not embedded simply in the sense of having a temporal-spatial nexus, a genealogical tie of some kind. Rather, they are rooted in the manifold forms of a shared past and in an anticipation of a future in common, all prefaced by the particularizing pronoun "our."[103] That "our" also constitutes its members as a subject of attribution, not in the full-blooded sense of author and action but as bearing responsibility. The historical burden that Habermas says Germans share in even today, and the duty to remember that flows from it, point to the centrality of both of these to their common and public identity. "We are," in Walser's words, "the continuation."[104]

I have used the example of Habermas's constitutional patriotism and memory in post–World War II Germany to draw out a number of points. First, it suggests the persistence of memory, identity, and responsibility even across such radical regime change as Germany experienced in the years 1945–1949. Caesura of this magnitude may lead us to imagine that the regime has been fashioned anew, and so profoundly that it marks the beginning of a new (political) self: the Jacobin conceit that the Republic had broken utterly with the *ancien régime,* or the new Germany of the 1949 Basic Law with the Germany of the Hitler years. Nor is this notion of a radical break with the past the sole property of constitutional democratic foundings: the Soviet revolution of October 1917 called on its sympathizers to "erase the past clean" ("Du passé faisons table rase"). The German case intimates that, on the contrary, the memory of a community, the past that it shares as part of its life-in-common, and the responsibility that this bequeaths are not exhausted by constitutional or other political-institutional forms of persistence, nor disrupted by their alteration.[105] In that sense, it calls into question notions of constitutional identity, whether Habermas's or the limited type presented in Aristotle's discussion of debt and regime change in the *Politics*. Second, it hints at the difficulties involved in a purely constitutional vision of citizen belonging, one that seeks to abstract from all identity markers so as to create a space for a strictly rights-based, egalitarian, open mode of belonging. The largely atemporal character of such a conception, as we have seen, makes the attribution of responsibility across time anomalous, and it works against or is indifferent to the collective memory-identities that pervade society. Perhaps, as I suggested earlier, it is that indifference which in part has helped generate the flourishing interest in group histories, the patrimonial fervor in Europe, and the demands for political recognition, group representation, and so on. The political identity that draws from the well of a shared past and its narratives, from its culture, its struggles and injustices, sees little of itself in the cold strictures of a rights regime. Let me leave these observations as markers and revisit some of the issues of memory and democracy in the conclusion to this book.

What I have sought to do here is to advance the claim that memory is central to the identity, individual and collective, of beings who are temporal, whose boundaries, persistence, and relations with one another are in time and are sustained in this duration by memory. I suggested that one part of memory's work is the struggle to secure the wholeness of a life or community, subject as these are to dispersion and erosion across time. Earlier, we saw Jankélévitch writing that "the incessant flux of the years renders this relationship [between the earlier and later person] more and more doubtful, as if unreal." He goes on to say that "memory is nothing other than man's moral protest against this ambiguity. It implies a sort of ethical responsibility, like a moral devotion which obliges me to tie the tangible, physical present to things past, absent, and invisible."[106] A central part of the wholeness that memory works to preserve and restore is ethical in character, meaning both (narrow) responsibility for past and future and a more diffuse but nevertheless vital embeddedness in a past that is not mine in the authorial sense but that is very much a part of identity, individual and collective. I have also tried to move the notion of memory beyond its customary locale in acts of explicit recollection—autobiographies, archives, memorials, and so on—in order to draw out its "thicker" and non-intentional facets, and the many ways in which it thereby enters into identity. Running through both aspects of memory has been the argument that memory-identity is central to the possibility of relationships of accountability for the past, that it stands at the core of our ethical life and of the possibility of doing justice and creating a just community. The migrant farmers of Steinbeck's *Grapes of Wrath* struggle to preserve what they can of their past, its traces, in full awareness that without their past they will become ciphers, characterless as individuals and as families, lacking the wholeness of a lived life. The things they try to bring with them are to testify to that life. So too Steinbeck, in writing of them, bears witness to their fate, gives them an enduringness, and in so doing engages in one form of memory work.

We saw that part of the way in which our life-in-common is constituted and sustained is through the thick memory of habits, mores, and prejudices (unexamined values) that are at the same time the rich deposit, the fruit of human relationships enduring through time and their defining core, the heart of what it means to share a community. It is in no small part the often unnoticed sharing in these things of our everyday life-world, the habits of the heart, that makes us a community, and not a mere agglomeration of strangers passing by one another. Such thick, habit-like memory shapes the ways in which we see and act without itself necessarily being visible to us, except perhaps in times of crisis or loss. "It is memory," Péguy writes, "which constitutes all the depth of man." But beside this "so powerful" memory there is, as I suggested, another kind, "so precarious," the low flame of remembrance, always at the edge of being extinguished.[107] This memory is sometimes autonomous in the sense that it seems to return unsought, to impose itself on us, and at other (perhaps most) times it must be secured by the labors of memory and resistance. The will to remember also belongs to the continuity of a community, to its identity, and despite the theoretical distinction between it and habit-memory, the two are in fact closely related.

In the next chapter I discuss one form of this fragile memory, that of bearing witness. Bearing witness, in its many kinds, is at the center of doing justice, of the continuity of a community over time and of its recognition of itself as accountable. It is also (unlike habit-memory) work done at the intersection of the passing of time, absences (of persons, of justice, and so forth), and traces. Bearing witness, whether in testimony, memorials, or sites, seeks to overcome absence, and it is a central and fragile labor of humans and their relationships in time. It is to that cluster of topics that I now turn.

CHAPTER THREE

Bearing Witness

"I loved you," Paul Celan writes in "Corona," "like poppies and remembrance."[1] With these words, we are pointed to a relationship between memory and those things or people that do the work of reminding us. What kind of love is there between poppies and remembrance? One is that poppies (the "poppy of forgetting" in Celan's phrase), like that other flower of forgetfulness, the lotus of the *Odyssey* (9.8off.), offer amnesia and dreams, a sort of relief from the sleeplessness of too much memory.[2] Another way to think of the relation between poppies and remembrance, perhaps one more familiar in the Anglo-American world, is of the poppy as a symbol of memory, associated with the commemoration of the war dead. But it is more than a symbol; it is a command: "Remember this!" The red poppy has been worn as an appeal to remember and honor the citizen dead, to bear witness to their sacrifice "lest we forget." It is a statement that the person wearing the poppy has remembered and a call to others to remember, an imperative invoking a shared responsibility and debt and insisting on its acknowledgment. The poppy is then both a *pharmakon*, an antidote to the haunting presence of the past in memory, and a "friend of memory," a call to memory. Further on, I will look at the healing powers of forgetting, but first I want to use its gesturing evocativeness to introduce a discussion of the idea of witnesses, bearing witness, and memory-identity.

A witness carries memory and calls on others to hear him and, through him, the past he bears. In its ordinary sense, the witness is the eyewitness, the person who has firsthand experience of an event and who reports what she has seen. The witness testifies to what she can recall from experiences stored in her memory. But witnessing has a more extensive sense as well: it can be bearing witness, which may be the person's own recollection, or a received memory passed on to others, illuminated and interpreted. Those who, like Primo Levi, Eli Wiesel, Jean Améry, or Germaine Tillion, have experienced what needs to be carried to others bear witness to it in their memoirs, poems, or conversations. But those who, for example, on November 11 (Remembrance Day or Veterans' Day) wear red poppies in their lapels also testify, inasmuch as they transform themselves into living reminders of a past and in so doing appeal to others to remember. That the wearing of a small red flower, or its paper imitation, expresses memory and calls on others to do the same is also a useful reminder that bearing witness, the carrying forward of the past, can be the work of places and things, of the world around us, on which are inscribed the traces of the past: a signifier, pointing to a past event, and sometimes also a call to remember, latent and awaiting a witness's voice to cast light on it. To bear witness, then, is to remember, to be a living memory, to guard the past, to ask others to do likewise, and to illuminate the traces of the past and their meaning.

3.1. THE SILENCE OF MEMORY

The act of bearing witness is also a gesture of defiance and resistance: against the flow of time which distances us from what went before, against an absorption in the present, and against the desire to forget or conceal. It is an act of resistance related to an absence, a silence, and therefore to a certain kind of vulnerability: that what is absent will be forever lost. In Kafka's words, "There is a coming and a going, a separation and often no meeting again."[3] In that respect it is something different from the enduring deposit that is the memory of body and habit, memories that scarcely yield anything to the passage of time. It is also quite different from our obtrusive and omnipresent memorial practices. This obtrusiveness is the visible presence of memory, its jutting out, so to speak: the redness of the poppy; memory's at times almost physical imposition in our cities, landscapes, and cultures; monuments that are meant to be unavoidable; days of remembrance and seemingly endless references to our duty to recall. It is almost as if we live ("obsessively" perhaps) amidst a surfeit, and not a deficit, of memory. The presence of the past in its various memorial forms is tangible, apparent to the senses, and seemingly very stable. This may conceal from us that the impulse to bear witness is intimately related to fragility, to a silence of memory and of the past, a silence that fuels the witness's sense of the need to bring that past before his contemporaries. "Silence" plainly cannot be absolute or a total absence, for in that case, whatever this person or event was would simply not have a place in the world. Rather, one might better think of these silences or absences as a sort of topography: hollows or indentations left by the past, unannounced and mute but awaiting memory's voice, a witness, a poet, an orator, or a monument. They wait for their witnesses, yet at the same time these absences or silences are like the hollows of our experience in that even in their absence they shape what is present and experienced.

This last is a perplexing but important notion and one that I want to explore before proceeding. I begin by briefly considering two novels centered on absence and experience: Georges Perec's *La disparition* (translated as *A Void*) and Vassilis Alexakis's *La langue maternelle*.[4] Both are in different ways stories of something missing and its continued presence. On the one hand, *La disparition* is composed entirely without the letter *e*. (This was a device of the Oulipo literary movement, of which Perec was a part.) A coherent story is told, but the absent *e* shapes it and its language. And even where the choice of words is not obviously constrained by the missing vowel, its absence is something felt, rather like the hollows on a path along which one is walking. The absent letter runs like a filament throughout the story, never mentioned but always there, the missing presence of which is almost palpable; absent, yet not entirely so (not quite a void, therefore, but more a disappearance). Alexakis's novel, on the other hand, makes the meaning of a silent and solitary epsilon inscribed on the entrance to Apollo's temple into its central and explicit puzzle.[5] The ignorance of the meaning of the epsilon is tied to other absences or losses: the loss and muteness of the narrator's mother; the narrator's distance from his native country, Greece; and the question of the relationship between that country's ancient and modern histories. The epsilon is here too associated with loss and a void. But this absence, unlike that of the *e* in Perec's novel, is a puzzle and a quest, an aporia that draws the narrator and the reader into the hollows left by the past in the present. The silent epsilon and the speechlessness of the narrator's mother become a sort of guiding thread back into Athens, Greek nationalism, and his family's history. It seems as much a trace as an absence. Perec tells us that even in its silence, the missing letter is there, shaping the present by means of its hollows. Alexakis makes us aware of the seductive, compelling power of these voids, of their ability to lead us into a world whose traces they are.

Silence, then, does not mean the absence altogether of the things, persons, or deeds which are there, mute, in our world. It is not a simple void and utter disappearance. Rather, in their voiceless way they remain like impressions on our landscape, informing it if only by the empty places that mark out their odd presence. They are absences that shape our world by pointing to its incompleteness, to the co-presence in it of the seen and unseen. It is this aspect of the silence of memory that is so central to (the struggle for) the persistence of bearing witness, of appeals to remember, and thus for the return of the past. Pascal Quignard observes that books conserve the past and shelter the dead in their pages. He adds that the "book is a bit of silence in the reader's hands."[6] Out of that fragile sheltering and silence, and the reader's relationship to them, emerges the act of bearing witness. For these almost palpable absences seem to announce an incompleteness that beckons us to make the world whole (or to the extent that it, incompletely, can be made whole), to save the phenomena through memory from their in-between existence, their exile in the absences and hollows of our world, and to do this by giving them a voice in remembrance. They are, in short, something quite different from a mere emptiness. They are a silence that urges its missing presence on us, not unlike the absent *e* in *A Void* or the epsilon of *La langue maternelle,* which draw us to listen, and to dispel that peculiar silence that marks out their exile. Memory, in that sense, might be said to depend on the void.[7] The hollows in which the silence of memory dwells are, then, the obverse of the intrusive presence of the memory sites (memorials, museums, archives) that dot our world.

The sources of these hollows or impressions in our experience of the world are many: effacement, erosion, silence; in other words, forgetting, voluntary or involuntary.[8] Some are the result of an almost nature-like erosion, as if the passage of time washed away the traces of the past, leaving only an indentation in their place. Others are much more deliberate and motivated, as when memory is silenced out of interest, fear, or shame. Effacement: the physical locales of memory may be destroyed to such an extent that they are no longer recognizable, even to those individuals or communities whose past is tied to these places. Housing developments can be built over aboriginal gravesites, amusement parks over national battlefields, tennis courts beside former concentration camps. City neighborhoods can be rebuilt so that the physical traces of their former inhabitants are made to disappear. So too, as in the ancient Greek and Roman practice, effacement can reach not only to the houses, landscapes, and so forth of the persons being banished from the city, but also to the memory of their very names, a type of civic effacement.[9] Just as effective in erasing these sites is the erosion that time brings in its wake: erosion not only physical but also in the minds of those who return to places they hope or expect to be locales of memory. Places change, and so does their import for visitors. One of Perec's projects, never brought to completion, was called *Lieux* (places or locales). Perec planned to visit twelve locales in his native Paris—streets, buildings, and the like bound up with important moments in his life—record his observations and thoughts, and seal them in an envelope, and to do this repeatedly over the years. He expected that at the end of this series of visits, he would be able to reflect on his interaction with these sites, and to see the changes both in them and in his recollection of them.[10]

Silence: some persons, deeds, places find no poet or statesman, no artist or photographer, no visiting pilgrim to record or recall their existence, and thus dwell in the netherworld of silence. Great deeds of valor, Pindar writes, "remain in deep darkness when they lack hymns."[11] Locales of memory, its physical traces, buildings, countryside, and so on, remain just so many spaces in the absence of someone or something to bear witness to their character as sites of memory. Of course, this silence is often not merely the unintended absence of evocation but a more deliberate act of censure or selection. Remembrance, especially in its civic or political form, is closely bound up with power and authority. The memory of the past is often at the mercy of the "official story." As Havel, Solzhenitsyn, Kundera, Milosz, and others have observed, this past century, with its proliferation of totalitarian regimes, has been rife with just such efforts to control memory through fabrication and erasure. But one does not even have to look to such extremes to see a willed silencing. We encounter it in our museums and libraries, and in our various canons, all of which are, in part, exercises in determining what will be left in silence and what will occupy a place in our collective memory.[12] Forgetting or amnesia of a therapeutic kind: a void is created as individuals or societies forget, or choose to forget. Often what is repressed is a trauma, or crimes and misdeeds that would bring shame or divide the community and invite conflict. Forgetting is here not principally an instrument of power or domination but a *pharmakon*, a medicine, a way for a society (or individual) to free itself from a past that threatens to visit either shame or strife on it should it be kept alive in memory.

Lost names: we are told in Isaiah (56:5) that "I shall give them an everlasting name," and inscribed on Commonwealth military cemeteries are the words, "Their names liveth forevermore."[13] Names do not always live on, though, and these statements are best read as a call to remember. Names can be forgotten, never remembered in the first place, or changed. In these ways they become one of memory's hollows. Why does this particular silence of memory matter so? Why does the passing of names into oblivion leave one of those concave impressions, as an imperfection in our experience of the world? Plainly, names individuate us by identifying our family lineage and by giving us individually an identity within that lineage. They are the markers that separate us out, that help to preserve us from a faceless, unindividuated existence. At the same time, they serve as placeholders for our biographies, for the wholeness of our lives.[14] Names are the icons, symbolic of the unity of a life that bears responsibility for these deeds, and so are colored by the shame or pride associated with them. In brief, they are emblematic of our identity, of our persistence and boundedness (separateness). Names, as I said, also link us to our family history: they bind us to generations past and those to come. In that way they represent to the world our identity, not just our present but our identity across time, biographically and intergenerationally in a community. The annihilation of the physical person destroys one seat of his unity and wholeness; the forgetting of his name condemns him to a deathlike absence.[15]

In ancient Greece, Hades was seen as a place for humans without names.[16] This was, in that society, perhaps first and foremost a concern for those who were worthy of *kleos*, of glory or renown. Silence, for them, would be a denial of their rightful due, of the reputation that should live on in their names. Their names together with their deeds would lie in "deep darkness." The silence of the name here carries with it both the second death of effacement and the fall into the crowd of those without names.[17] The effacement, the silence of the name is the obliteration of the person's great deeds, and the denial of the glory and gratitude that is his just desert. For others, that silence, the swallowing up of their names, is a loss not so much of recognition owed, but simply of acknowledgment of their having existed. It is not the loss of *kleos* that threatens the disappeared in Argentina's "dirty war" or the victims of the Holocaust. Rather, until their names are restored to them, until those names live again in the light of memory, these people remain among the lost, in nothingness. Here the void that the silence of their names leaves is not one of great deeds vanished, but that of their existence, and of the wholeness of the world of which they were a part. And where it is a crime, genocide for example, that has erased their names, that void is also a silencing of justice.

The loss or silence of a name is more than the passing into oblivion of a person and his biography, of her deeds, glorious or quotidian. For as I remarked, people's names are part of a filament that reaches out into a lineage across time, a family lineage to be sure, but also more than that, a bond to a community of which they are a part.[18] The absence of a name thus creates a void, an incompleteness in those other communities as well. Even in such seemingly minor events as changing one's name, a small rupture is created. The past of one's original name, its ties to places, to communities, and to earlier generations of one's family, is dissolved, or at least suspended in the night of forgetting. In *Le silence de la mémoire*, Nicole Lapierre writes of her family's changing their name from the Yiddish Lip-steyn to its French equivalent, Lapierre. That change of name, in a sense, severed or obscured their tie to the world of Jewish Poland, and to their town of origin, Płock. It marked an assimilation into their adopted coun-try, and with that a certain muteness, a silence about, indeed even a rup-ture with, their past.[19] Forced or allowed to pass into the silence of mem-ory, names are effaced, and the individuals, places, and communities of which they were reminders enter into a sort of exile.

Places. Maurice Halbwachs writes that memories must be tied to physi-cal objects, to a presence in the world, a locale or space, for example, or a monument.[20] The spaces, the locales of our pasts, private and social, can, like names, become voids too, their ties to us eroded, transformed, or ef-faced. The places of our birth, the houses and towns we have lived in, can be altered or destroyed. So too can the sites that are the locales of mem-ory for our communities, religious for example, or political. And with their separation from us, from our memory and identity, something of us is lost.[21] The changes that transform beyond all recognition the physical spaces of our existence create a silence of memory as still as that left by the erasure of names. Lapierre set out to find what signs remained of the Jewish community of Płock. What she discovered there was that the long-standing presence of the Jewish community had been erased. It was invis-ible, and nothing remained of the homes, businesses, and synagogues of the former inhabitants, as if the very streets and neighborhoods had lapsed into a forgetfulness and silence about the community that once in-habited them. The geography of this community now no longer has a lo-cale, a bounded spatial definition.[22]

In a smaller compass, names of streets can be changed so as to lessen the hold of the past on that part of a city's urban geography. Govern-ments restoring order in the wake of revolutionary unrest sometimes at-tempt to remake insurgent neighborhoods.[23] And on occasion, efforts to reduce these locales of memory to silence are effected through a super-imposition on the (to-be-silenced) landscape. Memory sites themselves can be instruments of silencing just as they can be places of preservation. Museums and libraries, those central institutions and locales for the in-gathering of memory, are also places of selection and power, and so can leave in silence, distort, or preserve as the custodians of memory see fit. The silence of the landscapes of memory and the voids that it leaves can be found not only in the rubble left by physical effacement but also in the triumph of one memory over another.

Sites of memory, then, can yield silence by replacing one memory with another. Halbwachs describes early Christian attempts to refashion in a new guise the Middle Eastern landmarks of Jewish memory, especially those of Jerusalem, and he discusses similar efforts by Roman officials to transform Christian locales of memory.[24] Consider the centrality of the concentration camp system in the recollection of European Jewish life in the twentieth century. This rescues the hour of their destruction from the silence of the rustic settings that might have shrouded Auschwitz and other killing centers. Auschwitz, as a locale of memory, breaks through the silence and oblivion that the perpetrators sought. At the same time, however, it leaves in its shadow the civilization that the victims had created in the centuries prior to their destruction: their faith and culture. Through Auschwitz we come to know them in the moment of their death, their former existence and ways of life poorly conveyed to us by piles of shoes and suitcases.[25] The locales, the dwellings, the synagogues, theaters, businesses, and fields in which they prayed, enjoyed life, and earned their living have long been effaced. The space of their lives now resides in the silence of memory. Only the locales of their deaths have been given, however imperfectly, a presence in the light of remembrance.

3.2. WORDS, SILENCE, AND REMEMBRANCE

Words, spoken or inscribed, are intimately bound up with the memory of communities, political and personal. They transmit memories and leave a testament. But they are more than the vehicles of memory. Language is rather part of the fabric of a life-in-common. And so the silence of words and of languages leaves a void, a space or impression in our experience of things. Alexakis's novel *La langue maternelle* (The Mother Tongue), referred to earlier, points to some of the dimensions of this. It is his mother's silence (to which the title alludes), signaled by the perplexing Delphic epsilon, which leaves its mark on the account of his return to Athens.[26] The title also refers to the author's national language and to its ties to the language of classical Greece. Both the speech of his mother and that of the no longer living language of ancient Greece are in a way lost: the one entirely, the other as a lived presence. Their absence marks a rupture, an empty space or, better, an absence, something lost, a missing continuity perhaps.

Lapierre points to something similar in *Le silence de la mémoire*. There she tells the story of the only Jew remaining in Płock. He is mute, and with his silence the effacement of his community is complete. A silence envelops not only the physical traces of the former Jewish community, its homes, synagogues, and so forth, but also the voice of its sole surviving witness: mute language, silenced voices, absent places.[27] Voices stilled by annihilation or by the passage of time create an absence of witnesses and a rupture in continuity, an empty space in a community's life. They shape one of the silences of memory. Sometimes, however, the muteness of speech is the loss not of an individual's voice but of the language of a community. Alexakis's (skeptical) recounting of modern Greek attempts to keep alive the ancient mother tongue suggests a desire to dispel the silence and rupture that the loss of a shared language entails. And Michel Ragon sketches the loss of his mother's (and earlier generations') Vendéen dialect and his joy at rediscovering it in French Canada. The dialect is here the mark of continuity with a Vendée of the past, before it was absorbed into the French Republican account of it as the essential locale of counterrevolution.[28] The silencing of the patois thus represents a break or discontinuity, and so a threat to the identity of the community as a continuous project arrayed over time and generations.[29]

In other cases, such as that of the fate of Yiddish, the language survives, but as the "language of no one," of a community effectively destroyed or dispersed. It remains a language, to be sure, but one whose soil has been rendered largely barren; a language that therefore bears the stigma of uprooting, death, and annihilation. The poet Jérôme Rothenberg writes, "My mother's language only empty."[30] The remainders of the language, its presence in a world in which the community that was its soil has been destroyed, assume the nature of a rite or memorial. Isaac Bashevis Singer remarks that "for the Yiddish writer who comes from there [Poland] the very ground from which he derived literary sustenance has been destroyed along with Jewish Poland. His characters are dead. Their language has been silenced. All that he has to draw from are memories."[31] As a memorial, it gestures to an absence, something missing, the living community that was once its soil. This language is, of course, not itself silence, but its continued presence points to that silence and, in its capacity as memorial, is based squarely on that silence and absence. Even dead languages, Quignard remarks, continue to watch over their lost peoples.[32]

"The language of my mother, but empty." In that emptiness and silence there is a loss of a heritage, of a bond with the past. "We have already lost all our words . . . our heritage is empty."[33] The lines of identity, of filiation, of the continuity of a community, its names, its locales, and its language are broken or radically transformed. This is the silence of a missing community. Perec writes that his parents' memories were not transmitted to him. Their language, their traditions and hopes, and those of the Jewish Polish community from which they had migrated to France were lost in the silence that followed upon their deaths in World War II. The past of his childhood, of his parents, and of their community, a past that remains his soil, something that belongs to him, is lost in their silence. Their silence envelops those who come after, and in a way makes them part of this silence too.[34]

Woven into their identity, then, into what they are as part of a filiation across time, is this rupture that leaves its mark, an absence that impresses a hollow upon the world that follows it. The loss of the physical locales of the community, the forgetfulness of space, and of languages, names, and stories is also a loss of part of the community. It is, in short, a rupture which transforms the continuity that a society or individuals live in and that gives them their specificity and identity. Being a Jew, Perec writes, is for him "a silence, an absence, a question . . . a disquiet" that comes from the dispossession of memory, language, and community. His name, he says, sounds "almost French . . . almost Breton," but is in fact Polish.[35] And only a tenuous thread ties him to his family's place of origin, the one place where he could not have been born: "I could have been born . . . in Haifa, Baltimore, Vancouver / I could have been Argentinean, Australian, English or Swedish / but in the almost unlimited range of possibilities, / only one thing was simply forbidden: / that of being born in the country of my ancestors, in Lubartov or Warsaw, / and to grow up there in the continuity of a tradition, / of a language, of a community."[36] Name, language, place, and transmitted memories: the loss makes Perec an outsider to something that is his own.

This rupture, this silence or void left by a lost community, creates a distance between people whose soil that community is, but who yet can have only an oblique access to it, one that passes through and is transformed by that silence. The murdered world of European Jewry haunts me, Alain Finkielkraut writes, but precisely because he is excluded from it. His parents' history, their memories, and their ways of being members of their community are absent to him, as they are to Perec.[37] The loss itself is unrecoverable, but as I observed, it is not therefore a nullity. "Exile" is the word Finkielkraut uses for the relationship to this past. But one can only be exiled from one's own, and the term resonates not with utter and complete absence but with the loss of something that once belonged to one. At the same time, however, for Perec the loss of a direct memory of a community makes one a stranger to something, not of others but of one's own: "I am a stranger in relation to something of me. . . . I am 'different,' but not / different from others, different [rather] from what is mine [from my people]: I / do not speak the language my parents spoke, / I do not share the memories they might have had / something which was theirs, which made / them what they were, their history, their culture, / their hope was not transmitted to me."[38] And in being a stranger to this past, in the rupture created by the silence of memory, one's relationship to it comes to border on objectivity, the outsider's standpoint, almost as if it were someone else's story being told. Perec tells us that what he says is "neutral and white" and that the deaths of his parents have become almost a matter of fact, have entered into the "order of things."[39] Yet he also says that his writing is a trace of them, an answer to the "scandal of their silence and of my silence."[40] The ambiguities evident here reside in the phenomena themselves, and not in Perec's telling of them. The silence of memory leaves a hollow, an imprint, a concave sort of presence. That silence also marks out a boundary or rupture, and the deeper the void, the greater the distance between the person or community and the lost. The silence of memory constantly threatens to make us strangers to our past, to render it something objective and apart from us. And so we struggle against this, attempting to preserve the past in the light of remembrance, to keep it among the unlost. We obstinately bear witness.

I have discussed various forms of the silence of memory. And I have remarked that these silences are not mere voids or empty spaces but are rather like hollows or impressions in our experience of the world. They are part of our identity, either as a present absence or in remembrance's response to that absence. Silence is the "exile of the word."[41] But just as the absence of an exile leaves an imprint on the community, a missing something, a distance or diminution, so the exile of the word does not mean its oblivion. And what is more, that absence almost seems to call out for a return, for a rectification of the hollow created by exile, for a sort of restoration, the (always incomplete) making whole again of the world. Traces are the "signs" of this absence, signs that bear "witness to the past presence of an object from now on disappeared."[42] They can point to what is missing, or simply be the markers of absence, of a hollow or impression. Above all, they call us back to what is lost, seeking to ensure that effacement or concealment does not transform the silence of memory into an abyss of permanent forgetfulness. "To investigate," Quignard remarks, has its root in the Latin word for trace.[43]

The silence of memory, the silence that runs even through the trace itself, beckons for a witness, almost as if that silence or absence demands to be redeemed, to have what is lost made unlost. Silence, Quignard says, introduces the invisible into the visible.[44] The desire to bring to light what languishes in obscurity seems to be at the heart of memory's struggle to break the silence of forgetfulness, the silence that envelops the lost. This desire, the search for the invisible in the visible, can be the expression of a life once shared, lived in common, and in particular it can be the result of a moral imperative, a debt to the victims whose existence and fate have been shrouded in obscurity.[45] "How could they be left without trace, those who . . . do not even have a tomb? Silence would be an act of impiety, a scandal that would redouble that of their annihilation, and would complete the assassins' work."[46] Something like this motivates both Claude Lanzmann's *Shoah* and Lapierre's *Le silence de la mémoire*: the effort to evoke traces from a mute physical space in which both crime and its victims have been enveloped by silence. The voids that are the silence of memory draw in memory work.

Traces, then, are those markers that point to or bring to light, however incompletely, a past that dwells in the hollows of the forgotten. They can be family names that gesture, if only obliquely, toward another homeland, and so to exile and rupture. Traces can be part of a landscape: the remnants of Nazi-era architecture that catch the eye of someone passing by, a piece of barbed wire protruding from the ground in rural France, or a gentle depression in the earth that once was a sharp-angled trench. It can be simply that presence of an absence, where the observer is aware of what happened there, or who once lived there, even though no physical trace remains. Language can be a trace too: Ragon's mother's Vendéen accent, or the remainders of the regional dialect, which he hears again among the French Canadians of Acadia.[47] The language of poetry can act as a trace, seeking to keep alive the memory of a now defunct language and the community that spoke it. Rokhl Auerbach writes of post–World War II Yiddish poetry that it was to be the "only cemetery to guard the traces of their [central European Jewry's] passage on this earth."[48] And finally, a trace can be the willed effort to induce remembrance: memorials, museums, the preservation of battle sites, the Somme or Antietam, or the killing camps of Europe. These are traces that set out to evoke memory and to tell the story of the place or person.

Some traces are just there, the detritus of the past whose only remaining work is to hail passersby: an accent, a building's unusual architecture, a depression in the ground. Some stand in need of an act or gesture in order to bring out their trace quality: a writer's narrative, an orator's speech, the lens of a camera and the seeing eye behind it. Even these last, though plainly the result of a willed gesture of resistance against the silence of memory, seem nevertheless to be more an act of discovery than of creation. That is, they bring to light, or give words to, something there but concealed from us by the erosion wrought by time or human efface-ment. They denote something missing and in exile. Without those traces being made manifest, the events and persons of which they are the tokens would lie dormant among the lost, entombed in the silence of memory. It is the witnesses, the image makers, and the writers who do the work of calling memory into the exile of silence and bringing what had been lost into the light of day. It is characteristic of their work that it reveals, draws our attention to, points us to the hollows of memory. Those hollows, in a sense, call out for witnesses, draw them in, and yet, at the same time, they need the makers of words and images to disclose them to us.

Traces are the markers of, the pointers to, what has been shrouded in the silence of memory. They do not, however, bridge that exile fully. The trace points us to the absence, and in so doing awakens in us the desire to remember, to make the past present, to overcome what cannot in fact be fully overcome, namely, that absence itself.[49] Perec's vocation as a writer, he tells us, was born at the same time as his desire to write his own history. And that history has at its core a void, the absence of his parents and the community of which they were a part, an absence that informs his life and work. It is this silence that calls upon him to write, to leave a trace: "I write: I write because we lived together, because I was one among them, shadow in the midst of their shadows, body next to their bodies; I write be-cause they left in me their indelible mark, and the trace of that is what is written: their memory is dead to writing; writing is the memory of their death and the affirmation of my life."[50] Michel de Certeau argues that loss, a vanished presence and a trace, creates an obligation to write ("I will not forget you"), for writing, he states, is memory.[51] Agata Tuszynska cap-tures this in her study of Isaac Bashevis Singer's Poland. I was too late, she says, and therefore she can describe only the "shapes of absence," some-thing missing and beyond recovery, yet still having form and an almost tactile presence. Finkielkraut observes that the remembrance of Euro-pean Jewish life before the Holocaust serves to underscore the rupture and loss that those events produced. Memory does not completely abolish distance, but in its way and at one and the same time brings to light (brings closer) and deepens absence and exile.[52] Traces are vitally impor-tant because they mark out both a connection and a rupture, a presence and an absence.

This complex cluster of relationships between the absences that are the silence of memory, the traces that point to (and, in a way, contain) them and call them to our attention, and the incompleteness that haunts them tell us that whether discovered or the work of artifice, traces gesture to-ward what is absent, and are tied to a will to keep the persons, deeds, or events from passing into the permanent oblivion of the forgotten. They signify something, without causing it to appear.[53] The desire to find or leave a trace illuminates the relations between memory and the void, captured in Anne Carson's remark that memory depends on the void, as longing does for that which is longed after. Traces, as memory objects, are the markers of that longing and, at the same time, of its essential incompleteness, of its often bittersweet quality. The passage in Homer's *Iliad* where the dead Patroklos appears to Achilles beautifully expresses this bittersweetness of memory in its always incomplete holding present of the past. Achilles says to Patroklos, "Stand closer to me, and let us, if only for a little, embrace. . . . So he spoke, and with his own arms reached for him, but could not take him, but the spirit went underground, like vapour."[54] As in Alexakis's story of an expatriate returning to Athens to decipher the epsilon and his mother's muteness, we are drawn by these silences to remember. The person who remembers is always hungry.[55] Traces signal to us, and sometimes we ourselves lay down traces so as to preserve these sites/persons/deeds against erasure. The trace then exists in a world of the near (but not complete) silence of memory and awakens a longing or desire that is emblematic of our resistance to that silence. Traces have a fugitive character, Paul Ricoeur remarks, and are vulnerable to erasure or forgetting, something that explains the often dramatic struggle of bearing witness.[56]

I began these observations by commenting on the obtrusiveness of memory in its many public forms: archives, trials, museums, monuments, and so forth. Here memory's claims are made so insistently that resistance to them mounts. What I have sought to understand in these pages is something different: the silence, the fragility of memory, its mostly concealed, almost lurking presence, where the passage of time and our orientation to the future, or deliberate erasure, have all but razed its landscapes: the physical destruction of the neighborhoods of a once flourishing community, and of the sites of its annihilation; the rupture in the continuity of a family; the loss or warping of a nation's recollection of itself. The now barren landscapes are rarely, however, the end of memory, but rather the locales where it lurks, where it waits to emerge, beckoning us with its traces, unexpected recognition, the sense of absence, questioning. In *Invisible Man*, Ellison describes this as looking "around a corner."[57] The past is there but hidden, around a corner, so to speak, waiting to be seen. I have written that in its absence, memory leaves a hollow, an impression, an almost palpable gap or void. We might then better understand the silence of memory as its exile. As with an exile's absence, there is a gap left in the community that he is expelled from, and often too some trace, an evidence to jar memory, to call it back into that empty space and recover it from the waters of forgetting. These traces, as I said, sometimes need the words of a witness, a poet or filmmaker or the chisel of a sculptor to be drawn fully out of their hollows into the daylight of our remembrance in common. Yet traces are also pointers to something that is there. They evoke or discover more than they create. We might better say that they evoke enough to call our attention to these places/persons/deeds of memory's exile, and in so doing to awaken the desire to remember. Absence, longing, and fragile presence intersect at the site of the trace. Consider again Perec's *A Void*. This story, as I said, is recounted entirely without the use of the letter *e*. The missing vowel is (like the dead) both an absence and a question, and a beckoning absence/presence, intimately linked. The presence of that absence, once recognized, draws us into its hollows, makes us want the light of remembrance. Even the coming of memory, though, cannot entirely dispel the absence that beckons it in the first place. The longing to make present what is lost, to transform the trace into the fullness of remembrance and so to make the lost unlost, is never fully quieted. In that sense, remembrance does not overcome exile but deepens it.

There is, then, a bond between witnesses, silence, and traces. The witness brings to light and evokes the sense of the trace. The trace and the witness together restore (as much as this can be done) what is absent. That is, they overcome the distance, the temporal distance that separates the present from what is being given in the act of witnessing. We could say that the witness seeks to repair and make whole again, as much as can be achieved by human hands and memory, that which is fractured and distant from us. "The angel [looking toward the past] would like to stay, awaken the dead, and make whole what has been smashed."[58] Witnessing, to borrow Elizabeth Spelman's phrase, is a kind of repair work, a restorative labor.[59] Labor: "bearing witness" points to a weight being carried as a duty perhaps but by no means joyously, or even with the bittersweet pleasures of nostalgia. What is borne or carried by the witness is a remembrance, often one without which her life would be better. This suggests that there is something dutiful, even heroic, about the witness. It is not just the trying circumstances and obstacles that stand in her way, but her determination, despite all, to shoulder and move forward with her burden. Perhaps this toilsome quality elicits the love between poppies and remembrance that Celan referred to, a love based on the easing of that often troubling burden promised by a poppy-induced forgetting.

To be a witness, a bearer of memory, is to be related in certain ways to the subjects of that remembrance and to whatever traces they left in the world. But to carry memory is also to bring it to someone. Witnessing is not, or not only, a tie of a certain kind to what is borne in memory, but is also a tie to those to whom it is brought. It is a memory act within the framework of an enduring community. As we shall see, debt and gratitude form part of that framework, as do the present and future of the community. To be a witness, within the manifold dimensions of the community through time, is to bring it the gift of memory. Sometimes, however, that gift is unwelcome, more a source of shame, guilt, or remorse than something welcome. And then the witness may find no hearers for his words but rather amnesia or an edifying, salve-like narrative. Under such circumstances, to witness is to struggle, not against the erosion caused by time but rather in opposition to the seductive power of forgetting. And so we encounter one last turn in Celan's words on the love of poppies and remembrance: it is not only the bearer of memory who may gratefully welcome the solace of forgetfulness and dreams but the people to whom his gifts of memory are given. We bear witness because of a felt moral obligation, because of justice, and because, in our bonds of filiation, we love and desire remembrance. Yet, as I also have suggested, it is a difficult intimacy between witnessing and memory: a burden, a struggle, an often unhappy union that invites us to think about that other sense of the tie between poppies and remembrance, that of a therapeutic *pharmakon* for the witness himself, or perhaps for those to whom his words are directed. Gratitude mixed with the burden of debt; justice, revenge, and lessons for the future: these are among the reasons for bearing witness.

3.3. TRACES AND WITNESSES

In Homer's *Iliad* (22.255), Hektor calls on the gods to be "witnesses . . . and guardians" ("marturoi. . . . kai episkopoi") to his pact with Achilles. The gods are often invoked as guardians of the names of the dead.[60] Grave markers of the unidentified dead in British Commonwealth military cemeteries are inscribed "Known unto God," with God being the last sanctuary, the only witness or guardian of who they were. Witnessing, indeed memory generally, and guarding have a close relationship. All involve a keeping, a preserving of something, and often a preserving of something vulnerable, something threatened by oblivion of one kind or another.[61] To bear witness is to guard something absent, for were it present and plain to see, then the work of testimony about it would not be necessary. It is to keep something in memory, to ensure its persistence through time, and to bring it to others in the present and future. Witnessing as the guarding activity of memory attempts to keep near the absent whose distance from us is, critically, a separation in time. To keep it near means, here, to seek its presence and persistence, to struggle for the "prolongation of the past into the present."[62] This struggle for persistence is the witness's response to absence or silence. The silence of the destroyed Jewish community in Płock, and therefore its twofold absence, is resisted by those whom Lapierre calls the "sentinels of memory," those who testify to its past presence and in so doing attempt to make it present once again.[63] Witnesses are guardians, and bearing witness is centrally the act of guarding in memory and giving this memory to others. This can be, for example, a witness in a courtroom whose testimony reconstructs and represents the crime; it can be the voice of a Wiesel, Antelme, Levi, or Améry bearing witness to the absent dead. Or it can be simply a calling to mind of the common and ordinary things, now forgotten, of a past time, the "little pieces of daily life," as Perec names them. Perec's own *Je me souviens* is (as I remarked earlier) one example of this: a listing of the shared memories of quotidian places, experiences, and objects of one era. And it too, in its very ordinary way, is an *appel à la mémoire*, a bearing of witness, a guarding of the past.[64] The passage of time and the changes it brings with it have made many of these cultural moments absent and foreign to the present. But, Perec says, they can "miraculously" be "rediscovered" and "pulled from [their] insignificance." Witnessing resists the work of time and (here, in Perec's *Je me souviens*) the innocent work of human hands by making the absent present again, after a fashion and incompletely, given the irreversibility of time. To bear witness, in short, is to resist the path of becoming by guarding the past and seeking to ensure its persistence into the present and future.

To bear witness is typically not, however, to construct a unified narrative about the past but rather to guard and convey the traces of that past.[65] But the relationship between witnessing and the trace is more complex than that. For the witness is sometimes called to his memory work by the trace, and writes to bear it and its meaning to others. Witnesses depend in multiple ways on the residues of the past left in the world. At the same time, for the traces to come to light as traces, to emerge fully in the world and not to remain mute and hidden, a bearer or witness is often necessary. Traces are reminders. They are not (principally) the reminders that we create for ourselves, a note, for example, pointers to something to do in the future (though as we shall see, some do have that quality), but a reminder of, a pointer to, people and things past.[66] Traces, we might say by way of an analogy, are themselves incomplete witnesses to, bearers of, that past, and as the presence of something absent, they participate in a cluster of perplexities as ancient as Plato's *Sophist* (240bff.) and *Theaetetus* (194aff.): the possibility and meaning of the *eikōn*, the icon, the presence of an absence.[67] The trace evokes the absent thing, reminds us of it and of its absence. It is not, generally speaking, that the absent past can be read off the trace, but that the trace has the effect of making present or calling on us to make present that absence.

The narrator of *Invisible Man* gives us an example of what traces do: the smell of cooking cabbage draws his memory to the poverty of his childhood, and the odor of a street vendor's baking yams awakens in him a nostalgia for the South.[68] They are, Proust says, like that Japanese game of dipping nondescript pieces of paper into a porcelain bowl of water, which when they touch the water unfold into flowers, houses, and persons.[69] Other traces are silent not because the past to which they point is an internal memory only, but because they await a witness to disclose their presence as traces and not simply bric-a-brac. The pen on Sarah Kofman's writing table is all that she has left of her father, who was deported to Auschwitz and murdered there.[70] This pen would have little or no meaning for a passerby. It would not visibly bear the imprint of the past and would not evoke the particular history of which it is a trace. Once Kofman bore witness to it, however, that pen lost its muteness and became a sign of her father and of the crime of which he was one of the victims. (Recall my earlier reference to Chateaubriand's observations on the power of remembrance held by material things.) Still other things are evidences or traces that belong to a collective memory, the "common things," Perec calls them, the sense of which would be apparent to people who shared in them. The witness simply points to something there, something the meaning of which is already present, if only latently, in the cultural collective memory of a community. In speaking about these things, Perec reminds his generation, that is, he offers it a remembrance of a shared past.[71] Other traces can be in themselves insignificant artifacts which nevertheless point to a silent past, and in so doing help to dispel the night of forgetting. The novelist Patrick Modiano happened to come across an old (1941) issue of *Paris-Soir* in which there was a notice from the parents of a missing teenager, Dora Bruder, requesting information concerning her whereabouts.[72] Dora Bruder and her parents would all perish in Nazi concentration camps. But this trace, and whatever chance it was that led Modiano to stumble across it, yielded a search, and thus the story of this Paris teenager in the 1940s was saved from oblivion. And last, there are traces which themselves are closer to absences than to concrete reminders, but which despite that nevertheless do the work of disclosing a past to us. The discoloration left on a Polish doorframe by the missing mezuzah of its former owners; Wim Wenders's images (in *Wings of Desire*) of the vacant lots, now modern business buildings, in Berlin where once there was Potsdamer Platz; the absent World Trade Center towers on the disfigured New York City skyline; the silence of Perec's parents; the absent Jewish communities of Płock (Poland) and Salonica (Greece) borne witness to by Nicole Lapierre and Pierre Vidal-Naquet. These absences are traces in as much as they signal a gap, a disorder in the world, something to be looked into and perhaps repaired, if only in memory, by bearing witness to them.

Things, words, names, landscapes: all can be traces, inscriptions (in Perec's words, "the insertion of space into time") that carry the past into the present. In that way they are reminders, calls to remember. Often not intentionally left as traces, they are nevertheless central to human resistance to the erosion caused by the passage of the years and by the work of human hands.[73] The notion of a trace suggests that they (and the people and events they point to) are in a sense already there, waiting to be discovered. Traces stand in a relation of (at least partial) independence from those who disclose them, from the witnesses who bring them to light and announce their meaning.[74] This independence is an expression of the fact that they are icons or representatives of something absent. Yet, as I said, traces without witnesses remain mute and languish in the shadows of forgetting. They therefore need witnesses to fulfill their character as inscriptions of a past that persists, if only in the shadows of our world. Traces have need of a Claude Lanzmann to turn his camera lens on the Polish countryside, the now verdant site of former atrocities; of a novelist, Patrick Modiano, to tell us of the fate of a wartime Parisian teenager; of a Solzhenitsyn or Grossman to bring the world of the Soviet Union out of the shadows. Traces, in short, do not typically speak for themselves—do not, that is, force themselves on us—but stand in need of witnesses.[75] Solzhenitsyn writes: "And as I stand here today, accompanied by the shadows of the fallen, with bowed head allowing others who were worthy before to pass ahead of me to this place, as I stand here, how am I to divine and to express what THEY would have wished to say? This obligation has long weighed upon us, and we have understood it."[76] Those witnesses, the bearers of the inscriptions/traces, not only disclose the fact of a trace, its existence, but also attempt to speak its meaning. Yet traces, vulnerable as they and the pasts inscribed on them are to erasure and reinterpretation, do bear the incomplete and revisable marks of the past they carry forward and so have a resisting obstinacy about them. Rather than merely conforming to the narratives of those who seek to master and appropriate them, they are often dislocating, offering themselves to other, better witnesses.

3.4. WITNESSING, IDENTITY, AND JUSTICE

To bear witness, then, is to illuminate, preserve, and transmit the trace, to resist the solvent-like powers of time and becoming, to attempt to ensure the persistence of a truth, of justice, of a person, and to work, as Perec suggests, against death by denying its capacity to reduce all to utter silence and unending absence.[77] I want to turn briefly to a discussion of witnessing's ambition to truth. Witnessing as a truth-preserving resistance to forgetting, falsification, and erasure is perhaps most visible in the writing of history and in judicial settings, though in its role as a bearer of memory, witnessing is often ill at ease with the norms of both these practices.[78] This tension (to which I shall return further on) stems from the manifold purposes that stand at the heart of bearing witness, purposes that drive it in directions sometimes contrary to the practices of historical or judicial inquiry. It is those imperatives of memory that form a guiding thread for my discussion.

Here are the words of witnesses themselves. In a diary recording his life as a Jew in Dresden under the Nazis, Victor Klemperer said: "I will continue to write. That is my heroism. I will leave a testimony, an exact testimony." Anna Akhmatova, writing in Stalin's Russia (1940), says: "Once more the day of remembrance draws near. / I see, I hear, I feel you.... I'd like to name them all by name, / But the list has been confiscated and is nowhere to / be found. / I have woven a wide mantle for them / From their meager, overheard words. / I will remember them always and everywhere, / I will never forget them no matter what comes." So also Germaine Tillion says of her time in Ravensbrück concentration camp that she sought to record as much as possible of what she saw or heard so that the truth would escape the camp and survive efforts to efface the deeds done there. And Primo Levi described his desire, while in Auschwitz, to keep a record of what he witnessed.[79] "An exact testimony": the witness is (in part) a living archive, a repository of the facts and the memory of them.[80] The fidelity, the piety one might almost say, of the witness is here at least in part a fidelity to the truth and its transmission. The gesture of witnessing seems to carry with it the notion of a threat to be resisted, a witnessing *against* as well as a witnessing about. Its opponent is the erasure or erosion to which the absent past is always vulnerable. The witness and her testimony stand as barriers to the "assassins of memory" and to the obliv-

ion of forgetfulness that the passing of time seems to bring about naturally in its wake.[81] Witnesses preserve what happened, but they are more
than just living depositories or archives, ensembles of traces of the past.
Rather, in addition to safeguarding the past, to seeing to the persistence
of the truth, they also transmit it. They are, in that sense, both the
guardians of the past, educators of the collective memory of a community,
and sometimes pointers to its future. Bearing witness, we might say, is the
action that follows from the imperative to see that the truth persists. Yet
the limited reliability of the witness is something remarked on by observers as early as Thucydides: "Those who were eye-witnesses of the several events did not give the same reports about the same things, but reports varying according to their championship of one side or the other, or
according to their recollection."[82]

Witnessing itself is of course subject to inaccuracy and distortion. In
part, this is due to the passage of time and the fading of detail in the witness's memory. In part, too, it is due to the first-person perspective of the
survivor witness and the difficulty in transmitting those memories,
whether in a courtroom or other setting. Human memory, Levi writes, is a
marvelous but flawed instrument, often unreliable and partial.[83] Discussing his own bearing witness to Auschwitz, Levi remarks that those
who, like himself, survived to bear witness never experienced the depths
of the extermination camps.[84] The three editions of Germaine Tillion's
Ravensbrück vary substantially, not so much in regard to the facts she presents as to the interpretation she gives them. Gone in the later editions are
the markedly anti-German references of the 1946 version.[85] And there is
this also: that the witness's memories may be framed in, and shaped by, a
wider context of remembrances. Thus, for example, Jonathan Boyarin
writes that the memorial books of survivors of the vanished Jewish communities in central and eastern Europe are profoundly shaped (and distorted, he says) by the fact that their authors reconstruct their memories
of village life, seeing it through the experience of the Holocaust and the
destruction that it brought to them.[86]

The idea of the witness as a living and flawed vector of truth about the
past, an archive transmitting its contents to others, only touches the surface of the act of bearing witness and its relationship to truth-telling. Consider this observation by Annette Wieviorka: "The mission given to the
witness is not to render an account of events but to keep them present."[87]
The witness, she argues, is not a mere repository of facts, an amateur historian and author of a narrative of causally related series of events, des-
tined to yield objective, explanatory, quasi-scientific knowledge of the
past. To bear witness is to do something different than to write history, de-

spite the fact that both are concerned with guarding the past. The distinction implied here between memory in bearing witness and the writing of history can help us make sense of the calling of the witness, often in the face of the greatest peril, as the keeper of truth against the effacement wrought by time and falsehood, and the partiality and incompleteness of the past they bring to us. If history was once the recounting of (in Hartog's words) "the interval—measured in generations—" between an injustice and its avenging or reparation, we could say that even if it is less confident in setting out the past "wie es eigentlich gewesen" (as it actually was), it nevertheless now aspires to explain and transmit the truth of the past so far as it can be discerned.[88] It is (or seeks to be) detached, critical, and in principle universal rather than being bound up with attachment to the narrative of one community. "I love France," Fernand Braudel writes in *L'identité de la France*, "with the same passion . . . as Jules Michelet. But this passion hardly enters at all into the pages of this work. . . . I must speak of France as if it were another country, another *patrie*, another nation . . . [the historian] an 'observer' as detached as possible."[89] The past here is kept at a distance from the "mineness" of memory-identity: "The once living organization of a society," writes Certeau, "is transformed into a past capable of being studied . . . an object that . . . we are to render thinkable."[90]

Historiography aspires to move alongside the event, outside and parallel to it. It is linear, chronological, and oriented toward the explanation of change. Memory, by contrast, seeks a fusion with the past, seeks to make the past present as its own, as part of an identity, of the persistence of the same.[91] Memory seeks immobility and a "tableau of resemblances," not change. It is not linear, nor causally coherent, but is structured by constellations of morally or politically salient events. Memory, in short, is a unifying ingathering of experiences that are decisive in some way or other for an individual or a community, for its sense of justice and its identity. The history of historians, which is (aspiring to be) distanced, objective, critical, and causal/chronological, is thus often scarcely recognizable to the witnesses, to the bearers of the memory.[92] Jean Améry, who survived Auschwitz, writes in a rebuke to Hannah Arendt that in the concentration camps there was nothing ordinary-looking about Nazi officials, however pathetic they may have appeared decades after the fact, standing as old men in a prisoner's dock.[93] And Germaine Tillion recounts the enormous gulf between the past as she experienced it, and for which she was a witness, and the history of it as presented in the course of the 1947 trial of the Ravensbrück concentration camp authorities. Indeed, she describes her book on Ravensbrück as a confluence of witnessing and history.[94] And so it is: the work is a combination of personal memory, witnessing, and empirically grounded history. It opens with a picture of her mother, beneath which, in longhand, is written: "Madame Emilie Tillion, my mother, arrested August 13, 1942 for resistance [activity], gassed at Ravensbrück, March 2, 1945," and ends with a history (written in a detached voice) of documents related to Nazi deportations from France, and with appendices on the practice of extermination by gas in the camp. Bearing witness to her mother's death and analyzing the organization of the concentration camp are two different comportments to the past, two different but partially overlapping ways of speaking the truth about that past. Tillion wanted to preserve the truth about Ravensbrück and to honor the dead, including her own mother.[95]

Testifying in order to transmit the truth, and in order to fulfill other obligations associated with bearing witness, is also present in Isaac Lewendel's *Un hiver en Provence,* an account of his return to France in search of an understanding of his mother's fate. (She was deported from France to Auschwitz and was killed there.)[96] Part of Lewendel's book belongs to investigative history writing: the bureaucratic forms recording his mother's presence in a transit camp in France and another form listing her possessions; the Marseilles accent of the officials who arrested her; interviews with former local officials; and so on. Discovering and testifying to these facts are embedded in a work that is intended as a hymn to his mother's life and a condemnation of those in France who were complicit in the deportation of Jews from French soil. Even the white and neutral testimony to the facts, of a Perec or a Kofman, say, belongs to a bearing of witness as the imperative to give a silenced mother or father his or her due.[97] In such acts of bearing witness, we see the uneasy intertwining of the transmission of memory as the work of history writing, a fidelity to the truth and its persistence through time, and memory as a bearing of witness, as an act of fidelity of a different kind, one saturated by the memory of a life-in-common in a particular community and laden with ethical burdens of debt and gratitude.[98] To bear witness is, to be sure, to seek to guard, speak, and transmit the truth; indeed, as we have seen, it seeks to guard the truth against effacement or oblivion. But it is a relationship to the truth about the past that is part of a mesh of identity, justice, and debt. Its governing imperative is a mix of debt to the now voiceless past, to preserve the voice of justice against forgetting or falsehood, and to the needs of continuity in identity. Lanzmann's *Shoah* is one such expression of memory and testimony.[99] Not a history, it presents no causal explanation and does not seek systematically to lay out a collection of facts. It is rather an act of remembrance, of witnessing, of making the past present. The particularity of bearing witness, then, consists not in its degree of reliability or unreliability for the purposes of explaining the past but rather in its being a carrier of a past whose actions are bound up with ethics, identity, and justice. In that light, we can understand Wieviorka's effort to write about Auschwitz as a historian, searching to understand "what it was" amidst the welter of memorial controversies that surround the site and, she says, make it near to unreadable.[100] The work of the historian and memory work are both of the past, and are its guardians, but in very different ways.

As I said earlier, the past, and the inscriptions or traces it has left, stand in need of witnesses, a need that is often expressed as an obligation, one that is in our power (in the present) not to answer. They stand in need because being absent, they are mute and unfound. This muteness can be the "scandalous silence" of the victims of the Holocaust or other mass crimes, the muteness of the dead, or of those silent landscapes that await a witness to translate their existence into a human, memory-laden geography. That silence and the resulting need to be heard again are part of a mesh of obligation, the "terrible responsibility," the "quasi-contract" that stands at the heart of the act of bearing witness. In the ancient Greek world, Herodotus wrote his *History* so that the great deeds of Greeks and foreigners would not be lost for all time. Pindar's comment in "For Sogenes" (quoted earlier) on the "deep darkness" of the unsung hero and his exploits describes the threat of oblivion, the promise of memory, and the bearer of that remembrance. The hymns or etchings on a *stēlē* assure the person and his deeds a remembrance, giving him (as Jean-Pierre Vernant points out) a persistence beyond that of his bodily presence in the world. The forgotten warrior or athlete, the one whose renown does not find a poet-witness to bear it in memory into the future, suffers another death.[101]

Pindar writes of memory and its poets as holding "a mirror up to fine deeds." The mirror, here the poem, reflects, carries the image from one place and person to another. It is the deed and its author that are reflected in the mirror of the poet's words and are carried by it to other times and places. The witness testifies, Lévinas says, to what has been said through him."[102] He is the living mirror, the vehicle for a reality beyond himself. The autonomous, external quality of what is borne in memory by the person testifying does not lessen its neediness, its utter dependence on the witness and that witness's audience. The inscription at Thermopylae, "Go tell the Spartans, stranger passing by, that here obedient to their words we lie," is an imperative.[103] It says: "Bear witness to us and carry the remembrance of us to our city so that they will recall us." Modern locales of memory are often marked by similar appeals to remember: "Passant, souviens-toi," (Passerby, remember!), "When you go home tell them of us and say for your tomorrow we gave our today" (Commonwealth military cemetery, Kohima, India).[104] Such words, written in the present, of course, capture an important part of the need of the past for witnesses, and of the work that witnesses are called upon to do, that is, to carry the remembrance home. Without witnesses, the deeds and sacrifices of the dead would languish in the shadows of forgetting. The persistence of their names, their actions, and their sacrifices, or the recognition of the injustices that they suffered: all would perish without a poet, a memorialist, or simply a passerby to bear witness to them. Forgetting is a second death.[105] Being forgotten in relation to the memory of a person and being without a sepulcher in relation to the body are felt as profound wrongs. Remembrance, however, confers another life, a duration, upon the person. Elie Wiesel writes that Roman Vishniac's late 1930s photographs of the doomed Jewish communities of central and eastern Europe allow them to live still.[106] The need for a witness, then, is a need not simply to be remembered, but through remembrance to be granted a new kind of life and an enduring presence in one's community. "People are what we remember about them. With death [the patchwork of life] . . . gets unstitched. . . . Once one realizes how much somebody's life is a hostage of one's own memory, one balks at the jaws of the past tense. . . . Keep that tense at bay."[107]

So the traces, the inscriptions of the past in the present that the person bearing witness carries with him, disclosing and sometimes interpreting them, have an existence independent of the witness and yet needful of him. Now as Ricoeur observes, some traces are pure returns to the past in its pastness, morally neutral and not seeking the persistence of the thing or event, except perhaps as an item of knowledge, as a fact.[108] Such traces, for example, the discovered ephemera of an epoch's everyday life catalogued in Perec's *Je me souviens*, have their independence of the witness too. One could say that traces of this type also need a witness in that the truth they point to needs to be revealed. But the traces I have been discussing seem to be of a different type. They are debt-carrying, and point not just to a fact about the past (though the desire to bring the light of truth to them is central here as well) but to a relationship between the witness and the past, the present, and the future which includes but is more than one of factual transmission. When I said that they were "debt-carrying," I meant that the language of their independence, of their weight to be borne, and of their neediness is to be understood within the context of an ethics of responsibility.[109] Remember Sarah Kofman writing that the only souvenir she has left of her father is his pen. She continues: "It is before my eyes on my work table and *it compels me to write, to write.*"[110] Recall too Perec saying: "I write: I write because we lived together, because I was one among them, shadow in the midst of their shadows, body next to their bodies, because they left on me their indelible mark, the trace of which is writing. . . . [W]riting is the memory of their death and the affirmation of my life." To write is "to try meticulously to retain something, to make something survive: to extract a few precise fragments from the oblivion that envelops them, to leave somewhere a furrow, a trace, a mark, or a few signs."[111] The responsibility to bear witness is here given its particular cast by the scandalous silence of the victims and their intimacy (born of the community they share) with the witnesses. It is to the silent that we have a responsibility.[112]

Bearing witness to those silent human beings is not just a recounting of something about them, but is rather the result of assuming a responsibility to bring them and their fates to light and to a sort of continued presence. This responsibility is owed particularly (as Perec's remark suggests) to those with whom one has shared a life-in-common, within a family or as citizens. Or, in somewhat different terms, it is owed where caring seems most proper: the embrace of, the holding on to, the "tethering" of what is cared for in the world of shared histories and futures that are enduring communities.[113] We owe it as "shadow among their shadows, body next to their bodies," to bear witness to them. In that way, Wiesel is right, I think, to describe Vishniac's photographic testimony to the destroyed world of central and eastern European Jews as a work of love and fidelity.[114] The compulsion to write that Kofman's father's pen produces, the indelible mark that Perec carries from his life with his parents and that is the basis of his writing/witnessing, suggests that a life-in-common, remembrance, and debt are closely related. In the case of sacrifice for the city or community, this bearing witness can be explicitly what is owed, a "recompense," as Pindar calls it, and perhaps a mark of gratitude as well.[115] I now want to look more closely at this responsibility to bear witness, especially to the dead. I will then consider bearing witness as a matter of doing justice, in the sense of seeing that the victims of injustice have their day before the law, even if they themselves are no longer present.

3.5. BEARING WITNESS TO THE DEAD

In *The Reawakening*, Primo Levi writes of the death at Auschwitz of a Hungarian child, known to us only as Hurbinek, the name given to him by other camp inmates, and only through the mirror of Levi's testimony. "He bears witness," Levi says, "through these words of mine."[116] Jorge Semprún recounts the death at Buchenwald of the great theorist of memory and society, Maurice Halbwachs. The account of the circumstances of his death are a way of bearing witness, a passing on to others of the truth of his death, not as in a mystery to be solved or a bringing of evidence to a trial, but as a debt to be paid to Halbwachs.[117] Sometimes, however, the testimony is not the fruit of such intimate familial bonds or immediate experience. Serge Klarsfeld's compilation of the names of Jewish children deported from France to their deaths in the concentration camps of eastern Europe, *Le mémorial des enfants juifs déportés de France*, Modiano's *Dora Bruder*, and Lanzmann's *Shoah* all, in their different ways, give testimony to the dead and make them, if only for a moment, present again in their communities. In these and a myriad other ways (e.g., grave markers, days of remembrance, museums, memorials) and in the privacy of our individual remembrances we bear witness to the dead, to our family members, to those who shared our faith or our political community.

Bearing witness and death seem intimately related. Every death leaves a void, a vacant place. Perec remarks that "all writing is done in relation to something which is no more, which can be captured for an instant in writing, but which has disappeared." Rescuing from the past is "the act by which man wrests something from death."[118] That absence, as I said, is not a nullity but a trace, a "visible shadow." Like the missing letter *e* in Perec's *La Disparition* which by its absence leaves its mark throughout the story, so the dead are shadows or traces in our world. And we are bound to them in a relation of responsibility.[119] But what sort of responsibility, and why? I suggested earlier in these pages that this responsibility can be expressed as the debt of recognition (or shame and pride, a sort of co-responsibility) we owe to those who have shared a community with us (familial, religious, or political). Because the community endures, in its various ways, their absence through death does not sever once and for all the ties of mutuality with them, any more than the absence of the future members of these communities absolves those in the present of all responsibility to them. Identity is the continuity of a community (or person) across time in a number of ways, one of which is as an accountable agent capable of making commitments to its future. These ties, on occasion, are those of justice, and in such cases what we are called on to do is to ensure that the memory of the injury they suffered persists until justice is done and the victim of the crime is acknowledged as such.[120]

I will return to a more detailed discussion of this further on, but for the moment I want to reflect on what is involved in being, as Aeschylus says, a "witness for the dead."[121] The need to inscribe, to etch on a gravestone, to commemorate in words or in the many other ways that this sort of memory work is done is in a very basic sense to resist death and the passage of time. It is not, of course, to resist the brute fact of death, but rather to resist the rupture, the separation and absence that death leaves. Here is the designer's description of the project selected in 2003 for the World Trade Center site memorial: "This design proposes a space that resonates with the feelings of loss and absence that were generated by the death and destruction at the World Trade Center. A pair of reflective pools marks the location of the towers' footprints. The surface of these pools is broken by large voids. These voids can be read as containers of loss, being close-by yet inaccessible."[122] The inscription of names, stories, fates, and so on renders the absence less complete. It restores the dead, after a fashion, to their communities. Forgetting, conversely, radicalizes their absence. To bear witness, in this basic sense, is to struggle against the manifold absence death creates, and against the forgetting that the passage of time brings in its wake, a forgetting that widens the distance between the living and dead members of the community and ruptures its continuity. Memory as witnessing holds together, as best they can be held together, the bonds of a community arrayed vulnerably across time, the bonds that are the heart of our lives-in-common: "shadow among their shadows, body next to their bodies." When the absence created by death is the result of crime, witnessing becomes a duty both of filiation and of resisting the power of violence to destroy the person and erase the memory of him. Levi's testimony about Hurbinek, Klarsfeld's book *Le mémorial des enfants juifs déportés de France*, and Perec's writing about his mother involve witnessing both as a duty of filiation and as a response to a "scandalous silence," that is, to an absence that is both loss and crime. Witnessing here is an act of resistance against absence and injustice, and a duty intertwined with the responsibilities of a shared life.

The burial site is a place of memorialization for the dead, giving them a kind of presence more enduring than that of their frail and transient bodies.[123] But for those who have disappeared in death, who are in that sense homeless and have no fixed abode on this earth to speak to and acknowledge their existence, words and images must serve as their tomb. Perec's statement that the written word is the trace of his mother's absence says that this is so because his mother has no tomb. For Perec, as for Elie Wiesel, and for the authors of the *Yizker Bikher*, bearing witness and writing are a burial and a tomb for those denied such a place.[124] The tomb gives the absent dead a duration, and for that reason it, and the words spoken around it, are part of the care owed to those with whom one has shared a life. The absent who have been given no such memorial stand in need of a witness to create for them a persistence that their persecutors sought to destroy. The witness, Semprún writes, must speak on behalf of those who disappeared and give them words and a tomb.[125] The tomb maker also speaks (perhaps principally) to passersby, and reminds them of the person who lies there.[126] In giving them a permanence not in stone and soil but in words and memory, the witness, then, addresses passersby, those who also shared a life-in-common that once included those now absent. And in so doing she reminds them, she bears witness to them, of their shared bonds with the dead, their filiation, and of the gap in justice that the cause of their deaths created. When Tillion dedicates *Ravensbrück* to the "martyrs without a tomb" and provides a memorial in words for those who died in the camp, she bears witness in both senses: she gives them a name and a sepulcher, and she reminds us of them.[127] Malraux, in his 1964 Panthéon oration, asks, "Without today's ceremony, how many French children would know his [Moulin's] name?" Malraux speaks as if this man, then dead twenty years, were present among them: "Enter here . . . ," he tells Moulin, addressing him in the familiar form as "tu," and reunites him with the great figures of French history: "by the side of . . . the soldiers of Year II, of Victor Hugo . . . Jaurés . . ." Finally, addressing the youth of France, the "16 million children" born there after Moulin's death, Malraux appeals to them to think of Moulin as "they approach his tortured face with their hands."[128] In this gesture of commemoration and witnessing, Moulin is given a second life, now an immortal one in the Panthéon, and is brought before the youth of France. The speech fulfills a debt to Jean Moulin, restores him to a presence in his community, and addresses the present, urging the unity of the nation.

As Malraux's oration suggests, bearing witness to the dead can also be thought of as conferring a new form of enduringness on them, almost a new life. Consider the conclusion of Margarete Buber-Neumann's *Milena*, a book that bears witness to Milena Jesenská, who was interned in Ravensbrück with Buber-Neumann and perished there in May 1944. She says: "I . . . executed Milena's testament. I wrote *our* book on the concentration camp. One day, shortly before her death, she said to me: 'I know that you at least will not forget me. Thanks to you, I can continue to live. You will say to men who I was.' "[129] Buber-Neumann also says that she undertook the task of writing this book "because a profound friendship bound me to her." This last thought expresses something I noted earlier: the embeddedness of bearing witness in the relations of a community's life-in-common, and not just as a background condition of having a past-in-common but rather as part of an ethics of responsibility within the framework of a community across time. Here, however, I want to call attention to Milena Jesenská's statement that "you will say to men who I was" and "thanks to you, I can continue to live." Buber-Neumann will tell them who Milena was, will bear witness to her existence, and she will in that way endure. Anticipating the absence of death, an absence in relation both to her friend and to the community to which Buber-Neumann is asked to bring a remembrance of her, Milena states that if remembered she will continue to live, if only in a mirror, as an icon, in the sense of the presence of an absence. The absent can be made present again, in a new form, if they are remembered. Forgetting, however, ratifies and completes their absence. The language of continued life or rebirth is often found in the words of those bearing this kind of witness, and it conveys the notion that their testimony transforms utter absence into an enduring presence, a continued existence, if of a radically transformed type, in the memory of one's intimates.[130]

3.5.1. *The Citizen Dead*

I now want to turn to the special place that the citizen dead hold in the world of bearing witness. As I wrote earlier, it was Herodotus who handed down to us one of the most celebrated civic appeals to bear witness, the inscription at Thermopylae: "Go tell the Spartans, stranger passing by, that here obedient to their words we lie." The war dead call for witnesses, for those who pass by their place of sacrifice, to bear a message to their community saying where they lie (far from their city) and why (in obedience to its laws). Herodotus himself, of course, is one such witness, and he has carried their words into two millennia of posterity.[131] He has thus succeeded admirably in seeing through to completion the purpose he announces at the beginning of his *History*, "that time may not draw the color from what man has brought into being, nor those great and wonderful deeds, manifested by both Greeks and barbarians, fail of their report."[132] Herodotus here fashions himself a witness, a chronicler of *kleos*, of memory-glory. The appeal to bear witness, inscribed at Thermopylae, however, is certainly not just a call to carry the tale of heroism forward against the operations of time. Rather, it is an appeal to the members of one's community, one's fellow citizens, to remember the sacrifice, and the distant place of this sacrifice. In archaic Greece, the warrior's desire seems to have been more to win individual renown, to die a "beautiful death" in exchange for eternal glory, and in so doing to escape the "crowd of those without names."[133] Here again, the unmarked death, the one shrouded in silence, is tantamount to a complete disappearance, and thus the epitaph, Anne Carson writes, is concerned with having us see what is not there, and so with restoring the absent from their nameless oblivion. Nor is this simply an artifact of an archaic society. Avishai Margalit recalls the severe criticism of an Israeli army officer who forgot the names of the fallen soldiers of his unit. Forgetting the names of the citizen dead seems to suggest great ingratitude, or even the violence of a second death, a deepening of the oblivion begun by the destruction of the life.[134] Jan C. Scruggs writes of his efforts to have a Vietnam war memorial built: "No one remembered the names of the people killed in the war. I wanted a memorial engraved with all the names. The nation would see the names and would remember the men and women who went to Vietnam, and who died there."[135]

Bearing witness to the war dead confirms their common citizenship. They died fulfilling their citizen duty, and they are remembered and thanked for that in their collectivity. As was the case with the celebration of individual heroic virtue in the archaic world, the act of bearing witness to these dead aims to create a lasting "remnant" against the corrosive powers of the passage of time.[136] The poet's or statesman's words may of course serve to celebrate the regime and to educate the living in their civic virtues.[137] The civic epitaph aims to bear enduring witness to dead citizens, and the idea of debt is frequently part of such remembrances.[138] In the Thermopylae inscription, the stranger passing by is asked to go and tell the Spartans, maybe because they have forgotten, with their dead now absent. But to tell them what? That the fallen died in obedience to their laws and to the duties of citizenship. "They were your *witnesses*," Malraux tells his audience at the dedication of a monument to the "Martyrs of the Resistance" while at the same time urging them, in fulfillment of the debt of reciprocity, to be witnesses themselves by reminding France of those who died in her cause.[139] As I noted earlier, the epitaph at one and the same moment seeks out witnesses, those who will carry the word, while it implies the ever-present threat of being forgotten in some unmarked or distant place far from home. That distance and separation almost demand to be closed. The epitaph calls upon passersby to bear the memory of the fallen from the distant places of their death to their cities, and it asks those hearing of them from witnesses to bear in mind the debts of remembrance that issue from the reason for their having participated in the battle.[140] Here, two millennia after the battle at Thermopylae, is a similar appeal, quoted earlier, from the Commonwealth War Cemetery in Kohima, India: "When you go home / Tell them of us, and say / For your tomorrow / we gave our today." Once again, the passerby is asked to be a witness, to carry home word of the fallen's presence, and here again the underlying fear seems to be that of being forgotten. "Tell them of us," as if oblivion might swallow the memory of them. Not simply tell them of us, but remind them of their debt, tell them of the exchange we made: our future for theirs.[141] On French war memorials, the officially authorized phrase "Mort pour la France" expresses a bond of indebtedness, and in the text of the law prescribing this phrase, it was said to establish "a clear and undying title to the gratitude and respect of all Frenchmen."[142] As with Malraux's invocation of Jean Moulin, the Thermopylae and Kohima epitaphs beseech the witness, the stranger or passerby, to bring them back, in speech, to their homes, to make them present once more as if in repayment for the sacrifice they made. Conversely, the German World War II military cemetery at La Cambe in Normandy could offer no such conception of justice (or of debt) as a way of memorializing and redeeming the deaths of the soldiers buried there. Instead the inscription on its central monument ends with the religious consolation that "God has the final word."[143]

These inscriptions and invocations give a meaning to the sacrifice of the citizen dead. It is the survivors and the living who craft such phrases.[144] But is it therefore accurate to conclude that memorials and commemorations inform us principally about the present?[145] Undoubtedly power over these points of contact between generations of the ongoing life of a political community is the privilege of those in the present. But those locales can also be understood as places where the present is called upon to assume the responsibilities inherent in an enduring community, the "terrible responsibility" of preserving memory. It is this call to recognize the bonds that are a central part of citizenship which makes the inscribing power of the present community not a free-floating, aesthetic power but one framed by the responsibilities that belong to a life-in-common. In memorializing and bearing witness, citizens give words to the silent and attempt to capture the sense of debt and reciprocity involved in the life and death of the citizen soldier. In that sense, bearing witness can be understood as a "reciprocal obligation" between generations of a community and an affirmation of their deep identity.[146]

3.6. MEMORY, PLACE, AND POLITICS

I have spoken about the bearing of witness as (in its varied ways) the preserving and carrying forward of a trace. In its most familiar form, it is living witnesses who are carriers of this testimony. Yet, as I have suggested, places too can be traces.[147] Human communities, as I said, have a space, a locale as well as a time, or better: both interwoven. This is not an empty site, a mere receptacle to be filled by objects, a space interchangeable with any other, but a place, a locale intimately bound up with a lived time, narrative, and identities. Such spaces can be a nation's borders, its land-marks and monuments; they can be a family's home, and the place mem-ories of one's youth; or they can be a temple or church, or the holy sites of one's faith.[148] They are, as I just said, not simply abstract spaces or func-tional sites, but places inseparably intertwined with the story and charac-ter of the community that inhabits them.

Now some spaces are what Pierre Nora has termed *lieux de mémoire*, spaces intentionally marked out as sites of memory. These can be li-braries, archives, the physical depositories of memory, for example, or monuments inscribed with appeals to remember.[149] They are places that conserve, either literally, by storing, or by etching in stone what otherwise might disappear from memories of passersby. In their intentional quality, they are a physical-spatial imprint of the narrative of a community, and in that capacity exercise explicitly the guarding or retaining function of re-membrance generally. As the material emplacement of a community's memory, these depository and commemorative sites seek in a way to stabi-lize collective memory, to "thicken" it and render it as immune as it can be to the vicissitudes that afflict memory.[150] When the landscape is altered in this way, the physical space is brought into, and transformed by, the history and memory of the community. And that history and memory are changed too by being given a locale. This willed appropriation of the physical has among its purposes to keep alive a past in the present, in a physical point of exchange between past and present.[151] That exchange can be one of knowledge, the archaeology of a community assembled in its museums and archives, or an appeal for the granting of that memorial recognition that I discussed in the preceding pages. As such, places of memory are ways of bearing witness, of testifying to a life-in-common en-during through time, an endurance whose sediment is gathered in archives and museums.

These locales are appropriations, spaces transformed. "The day these memories are placed on certain locales, they have transfigured them. . . . It is like a witnessing of the senses. . . . [T]he past becomes part of the present: we touch it, we are in direct contact with it."[152] We create these sites in order to have them serve as witnesses, traces, and reminders, and in fulfillment of debts of remembrance. Thus, for example, de Gaulle took the ruined town of Oradour, site of a 1944 Nazi massacre of French civilians, and had it frozen in time, so to speak, turned into a vast museum and reminder of the brutality of the Occupation years.[153] Likewise, a num-

ber of concentration camps, including the ones at Auschwitz, Buchenwald, and Dachau, have been preserved as memorials to those who were
murdered there. Paris alone has over six hundred memorial plaques
commemorating events during the Occupation; Civil War memorials dot
the American landscape. Such sites point to the importance of places and
things as locales of memorial exchange between the moments of an enduring community.

At the same time, their character, and who is included in or excluded
from this binding of space and memory, are very much contested. It is we,
in the present, who decide which dead, which injuries and traumas, are to
be remembered and how. Once they have been created, others in the future will be free to take up the task of assigning meaning to the monuments, museums, and so on that we bequeath to them.[154] The Auschwitz
site and its museum have been contested and transformed by communist
authorities, the Catholic Church, including the Carmelite order, and various Jewish groups. The evolution of the Dachau concentration camp as a
place of memory has been profoundly shaped by postwar German politics.[155] French memorials were often silent about the role of the Vichy
state in wartime repressions, and some are associated with particular political currents, for instance, the Mur des Fédérés at Père-Lachaise cemetery with the French Communist Party. Even the choice of memorial sym-
bols is political: the Revolutionary bonnet or Marianne preferred by the
communists and the Croix de Lorraine by Gaullists.[156] On other occasions, fundamental political change can lead to a wholesale removal or
erasure of previous public memory sites. After the fall of the German Democratic Republic, the Berlin Chamber of Deputies stated, "When a system of government dissolves or is overthrown, its monuments . . . no
longer have a reason to exist."[157] And so memorials associated with the
former GDR were dismantled by the new German republic. Debates in
the United States over Civil War monuments, the Vietnam Veterans
Memorial, and a fitting memorial at the World Trade Center site suggest
a similar politics of memory.[158]

These illustrations could easily be multiplied, but what we learn from
them, I think, is straightforward enough: that the transformation of a
landscape into a memorial site is a political and contested act.[159] The fact
that some are commemorated and others not, that some group memories
are inscribed on a landscape while others do not have a place,[160] that sites
of remembrance may be attached to specific political currents and so on
does not begin to explain what it is or why it is such a contested good. This
duality of memory can be seen in two pieces that appeared in the September 15, 2003, issue of the *New Yorker* magazine. On one page is an ad-

vertisement from the Port Authority of New York and New Jersey showing a boy at a blackboard drawing outlines of the two World Trade Center towers destroyed in the September 11, 2001, terrorist attack. The advertisement carries this text: "9.11.01 Honoring the past / Envisioning the future / Rebuilding, together." In the same issue of the magazine is an article recounting the politics of designing a fitting memorial for the site.[161] What is needed to get to that background, to understand the impulse to draw the towers, and of Americans to commemorate those events, is an understanding of the importance of the sites, an importance that rests on the role they play in the exchange across generations of a community, in the debts they express, the injustices they recognize, and the identities of which they are such a central part. We can glimpse this centrality, if only obliquely, when we consider our response to the absence or defilement of memory-spaces. That Dachau might return, as some of its citizens likely wanted, to being just another city, cleansed of its past; that Katyn, a site of mass murder and burial, might remain disguised as a simple forest; that Auschwitz could revert to being Oswiecm, another Polish town; that the places in Europe inhabited by Jews before the Holocaust would leave no physical reminders of their former inhabitants, their common fate, or their neighbors' behavior; that soldiers' cemeteries would no longer be emblazoned with those words calling on us, the living, to remember them: all these seem unjust, a wrongful forgetting of a deep injury or debt. A community without memorials and places of memory, one that had willfully allowed its wounds and debts to be denied their space in the city, would be a community that acquiesced in the hiding of the memory of injustices and the gifts of sacrifice: an injustice, a deformation of its human habitation in time, and a severing of the fabric of its identity. Lewis Mumford's vision of modern cities as post-memorial seems neither to have come true nor, more important here, to be consistent with the very human ambition to transform mere space into an inhabited place, to make a landscape a locale of memory, of doing justice and repaying the debt of gratitude.[162] The space we occupy is, as I suggested, something more than a functional site: it is also a home, a foyer, a canvas of remembrance. When we answer that imperative to inscribe memory onto our landscapes, we respond to the injury that forgetting threatens to do to us and to the place in which we live. We keep that shared space from a sterilizing forgetfulness.

These stone memorials, plaques, and museums that transform our common space into locales of remembrance are the fruit of our decisions and narratives, with all that entails about the presence of power and forgetting. But they are devices that inscribe our wounds, injustices, and debts in the world. They mark our spaces and, in Robert Lowell's words, "stick like a fishbone in the city's throat."[163] That is, they force upon us, passersby in the course of our daily lives, an exchange, if only a fleeting one, with our community's past. These memory artifices are, in other words, a deliberate transformation of space into a lived place, a place for remembrance and bearing witness. And they arise in part from a rejection of forgetting, of a pristine space unmarked by memory. A felt duty to remember and the unacceptability of forgetting converge in these alterations of our living spaces into witnesses. But the relationship between memorial space and remembrance is still more complicated than this. Consider Maurice Blanchot's remark that words wear out the very memories they express: to speak is to forget.[164] Perhaps the very act of inscription in the landscapes around us also relieves us of the burden of bearing witness. Perhaps it displaces memory, giving it a permanence in stone rather than in the hearts and minds of citizens. "The most remarkable thing about monuments," Robert Musil wrote, "is that no one notices them."[165] Memorializing, on this account, is less an antidote to forgetting than its very agent, and that concern has inspired a counter-memorial movement. In Hamburg, for example, a Holocaust memorial was built with a lead column that gradually sank into the ground, leaving behind only an empty space where once the memorial had been.[166] This design would eventually remove the site of the (physical) placement of memory, leaving it to the memory of citizens to act as a locale of remembrance. Memorial sites, then, can be devices by which we escape our debts and find the shelter of forgetting.[167] Monuments, memorials, words inscribed on granite can transform the landscape of a community not as a trace and a spur to ongoing remembrance but rather as a sequestration of the labors of remembrance. These created locales of memory, in short, can be (to use Lowell's image once more) bones in the throats of passersby, places that disrupt a forgetful absorption in the present, in the "Today [in which] the air is clear of everything. / It has no knowledge except of nothingness," and in so doing draw us to remember.[168] Or they may be instruments of forgetting, of settling accounts with the past rather than being a point of exchange with it.

The landscapes that we make and plan as sites of memory are the most apparent places in which space and remembrance intertwine. There is, however, another, more natural (for want of a better word) locale of memory: the places that carry the imprint of a part of a community's past, a trace that can bear witness (or move us to do so) to what occurred there. The landscape around Auschwitz, and "especially the trees" that were there during the camp's functioning, were the "silent witnesses of the

Holocaust," says Wieviorka.[169] These are places where, in Cynthia Ozick's words, an "uncanny ache . . . cries out from the silence of solid things."[170] The pastoral scene in Poland that opens Lanzmann's *Shoah* points to some of the dimensions of these locales of memory. That scene shows an unblemished countryside, without any trace of crime.[171] Something terrible did occur there, and that stream and forest, now pristine, are a link, a point of exchange between past and present. But what sort of point of exchange? The past lurks here "humbly," not with words etched in stone or bronze, and with no evidence of the events which bloodied that soil. Yet, as Lanzmann writes, the wounds are inscribed there, as if such places retained an imprint of those who were there and their deeds and fates.[172] Alan Cohen's photographs of European sites of violence convey much the same sense. Like the first minutes of *Shoah*, these photographs are of places not immediately recognizable as sites of violence and crime. Unlike, say, the frozen violence and destruction displayed in the village-museum of Oradour, the trenches of the Somme are now mere grassy undulations in the French countryside. Yet they, like the concentration camp images (in Cohen's work, always of the ground), hide within themselves "the material memory of the past." His photographs are the "bearers" of the "traumatic traces" of that past.[173]

Sometimes the relationship between the witness and the place is first-person: Simon Srebnik and Chelmno in *Shoah* or Isaac Lewendel returning to find the cherry orchard in Provence where he last saw his mother before her arrest and deportation to Auschwitz.[174] It can also be more remote: the changed presence of rue Ornano in Paris for Patrick Modiano, who hears Dora Bruder's echo in the neighborhood, as if the road she lived on before her deportation bore an imprint of her. Or it can be a "jolt of recognition" at seeing everyday Nazi architecture in the streets of Berlin, the Lorraine Motel in Memphis or Dealey Plaza in Dallas, even for those of us who have no firsthand experience of those times. That sometimes startling moment of recognition takes place at a point of exchange midway between past and present. Traces, Lévinas writes, upset the (absorbed in the present) order of the world.[175] It is as if the past, the person, or the events are there, latently, so to speak making that space not just any empty vessel but theirs, or better, a space that stands in a sort of continuum between us and them.[176] On the one side, it bears their imprint, without which it would be just an empty space. On the other, it needs us to recognize this imprint, and that requires a voice, a narrator or witness. In *Shoah*, the words of the survivor Simon Srebnik and the visual scene of the countryside are juxtaposed.[177] His words are needed to make that landscape a place of memory. Similarly, rue Ornano would be simply another street without Modiano to illuminate its history and its missing inhabitant; the Lorraine Motel just another building in Memphis without its museum and its narrators. Theodore Dalrymple needs to hear his mother-in-law recount the story told to her by a Jewish woman who, during the war, had hidden in an apartment across from a German command center in Paris in order to feel a jarring recognition when walking past it: "She [his mother-in-law] helped a lady even older than herself, burdened with several shopping bags, onto a bus. They fell to talking, and the older lady asked my mother-in-law where she lived. She told her the apartment block, and the old lady asked what number. My mother-in-law told her, and the older lady began to cry. It was there that she, who was Jewish, had hidden throughout the war years, keeping away from the windows. The windows of the apartment overlook the commissariat de police that during the war was the local Kommandatur. Even now, the old lady could not pass it without a frisson of fear. Oddly enough, ever since I heard the story, I have not been able to look at the commissariat in quite the same way either, though I was born after the end of the war. We inherit the ghosts of the past—even the ghosts of the ghosts."[178] The street and apartment are bearers of an imprint, a trace, but a latent one that needs the good fortune of a chance encounter to bring it to light. Once seen, the locale becomes a place of memory. To read space, as Perec argues, is to read something opaque and not evident. Where this reading is of a geography of memory in which all has been effaced, the witness is called upon to bear witness to a place that once was: thus Pierre Vidal-Naquet's remembrance of the once Jewish quarters of Salonica; the work of Jewish memory books in recreating in words the authors' lost home villages in central and eastern Europe; photographs to compensate for the physical effacement of a landscape.[179] The authors of those interventions are best understood not as writing their words on a neutral, blank canvas of landscape but rather as witnesses using words and images "to cause the trace to emerge," to bring it to light. "Memory," Valéry writes, "awaits the intervention of the present."[180]

Earlier I said (echoing Halbwachs) that inscription in space has a stabilizing effect on memory: that it gives remembrance an objective, indeed physical presence that promises a permanence that the sanctuary of hearts and minds seems unable to offer. As we have also seen, however, space is often more opaque than transparent. A part of the explanation for this is that places of memory are either narrative spaces strictly (e.g., memorials, archives, or museums) or places where recognition of some present imprint and a witnessing narrative are conjoined (e.g., the opening moments of *Shoah*). In both, whatever physical fixity the site possesses becomes intermingled with the power, weaknesses, and purposes of those who give voice to the traces inscribed in these locales.[181] Which sites will receive their memorials, and which will languish in silence; which land-scapes will find a Lowell, Srebnik, or Cohen, a Lapierre or Vishniac, and which will be allowed to conceal what happened on their ground: all these are open matters, open to contest and instability. We are, in that sense, geographers, writers of the world. Places as sites of memory are vul-nerable in another, and more basic, sense. "My spaces," Perec says, "are fragile: time will wear them, destroy them. . . . [F]orgetting invades my memory. . . . Space melts like sand flows between one's fingers. . . . To write: to try meticulously to retain something, to make something survive: to extract a few precise fragments from the oblivion which envelops them, to leave somewhere a furrow, a trace, a mark, or a few signs."[182]

Geographers of memory, those who write words of remembrance on our shared space or narrate and record what they find there, work on traces, on sites that are locales of something absent, markers both of what was and of our distance from it. Locales of memory are places of ex-change, exchange between absence and presence. To bear witness, in all its forms, is (I have said) to struggle to make present, to bring to the light of day, to restore something missing. It is a struggle precisely because (like Robinson Crusoe seeing the footprints in the sand) it is, so to speak, midway between a complete emptiness and a presence. It is, in other words, always an absence, which is not a nullity but an imprint, a trace, the presence of something absent. Places of memory bear the mark of that ab-sence and its related threat of a lapsing into nothingness. Even in the re-membrances inscribed on them, they remind us of (and depend on) ab-sence. Remembrance as a making present or restoration and absence are, as I noted earlier, intimately bound together. It is Dora Bruder's absence that Modiano senses when he passes through her neighborhood. The cherry orchard where Isaac Lewendel last saw his mother, and his coming upon her name engraved on a plaque outside a synagogue, make her present in memory and underscore her absence. Cohen's photographs of the violent ground of Europe are also a reminder of the distance between us and the events that left their mark on that soil. The first few minutes of *Shoah*, writes Marie-France Osterero, suggest the absence of traces in that Polish landscape. Sites of remembrance are at the same time, and essen-tially, locales of absence. But this absence, far from deflecting memory, is the wind in its sails: to remember is to re-call and so to sense and be moved by a distance.[183]

The space we inhabit bears witness. It is a geography of the small things of our daily lives, a source of nostalgia and melancholy. It is also the geog-

raphy of justice and injustice, of crime and loss, and of debt: of the sur-
roundings of our life-in-common, inseparably attached to who we are as a
community. It is geography, in part, because we write it on the face of the
world we inhabit. It is the geography of memorial sites and archives, and
of place-names (and sometimes family or community names tied to them)
which all bear witness to our shared fate across time. And it is a geography
of a humbler and more basic kind: landscapes absorb and retain their
connection to an enduring community and become one of its traces, its
places of exchange with the past. In all of these ways, duration and the
space we dwell in form the locale of our history. This space has the quality
of being inhabited, and thus intertwined with the community's story.[184]
Here I have wanted to map out one dimension of that intertwining: the
way in which (as Sebald suggests) places are witnesses, locales of memory
that we mark out or that simply are there waiting, traces that serve to remind us of those things that need remembering, for which there is a duty
of one kind or another for us to bear witness.[185]

CHAPTER FOUR

Witnessing and Justice

T he silence of memory, Nelly Sachs argues, is the victim's dwelling place. This absence is a silence and a gap in the unity of a family or community, and especially in the completeness, the integrity or wholeness, of its justice. It is the sense of something left undone, of justice's work left incomplete. The silence of memory is here the silence of justice and the absence of retribution. It is an incompleteness both in relation to victim and perpetrator and with respect to the wholeness of justice in the world, and therefore a rupture or incompleteness in the community. Remembrance is called for not so much in order to restore and make something mine again, some part of my identity-shaping past that now lies among the absences of memory, as something foreign to me or to us. Rather, remembrance now appears as an effort to restore the wholeness of justice in the world, as if justice not done leaves an unacceptable void, a hollow, in the order of things. This silence of memory amounts to the exile of the word of justice. And it too beckons us to remember and thus to restore the world to the wholeness of justice. It beckons us, that is, with the disquiet to which this incompleteness gives rise, an unease bound up with an as yet unfulfilled imperative to see justice done. Justice can never make whole again what was broken; it cannot fully restore the world to its status quo ante, if only because of the irreversibility of time and the impossibility of retroactive causality. But the desire for wholeness and restoration is the wind in its sails.

In this chapter I explore the relationship between doing justice in the judicial or quasi-judicial sense and memory as bearing witness. I want to urge that doing justice and bearing witness are at their heart an expression of our memory-laden moral relation to the past, and not simply a useful adjunct of present and future, something merely at hand and tool-like. This is not of course to deny that there are powerful future-oriented stakes in a mastering of the past. Rather it is to suggest that there is something intrinsic to doing justice, as a working on the past, that is not adequately captured in the language of instrumentality and interest, a language that seems to overlook the past-tense dimension of communities of obligation. That incomplete and "distorted [utilitarian] account," as Joel Feinberg calls it, forgets that "the betrayed party is the person now dead as he was in his trusting state antemortem" and not some "diffuse public" good.[1] The felt duty to see to the persistence of the memory of the crime, its perpetrators, and victims, especially in its relationship to witnessing, memory, and justice, is what I will discuss in the pages that follow.

The experience of the past generally, and not in its moral signification alone, is, as I have said, the experience of something absent. History is a writing about the absent, about the voiceless: in Michel de Certeau's words, "L'écriture met en scène une population des morts."[2] Remembering, in the writing of history and in commemoration in its many forms, is a response to absence, and depends precisely on that void. It presupposes the disappearance of the voice and of the living unity of the absent. All, in their sometimes very different ways, seek to make that past present, to bring it to light and make it visible in the present, in short to bring disclosing truth (and more) to it. Driven by its ambition toward truth, the writing of history looks for those hollows in our experience of the world, finds traces, and restores the absent through its causal, explanatory narratives. In de Certeau's image, historiography is rather like Robinson Crusoe finding a footprint in the sand on his island and fearfully wondering about its absent maker.[3] The historian takes that trace of the absent and gives it a voice in the present. Like Crusoe, who sees in that footprint a sign of the boundary between his world and the person who left the imprint, between the visible and present and the absent, so the historian is also at a boundary between past and present, visible and invisible, marked and signaled by the trace.

Injustice leaves its footprint too, and, as Jean-Yves Lacoste observes, part of the moral experience of time is that of the past of the wrong, of the (moral) experience of absence.[4] The pastness of the wrong, here of an injustice, is a consequence of the passage of time, of becoming and irreversibility. The practice of doing justice is concerned with the absent past of persons and deeds. Likewise, it sees in the traces of material evidence or witnessing (mute and vocal bearers of remembrance) the sign of that absence. And again, like the historian, the court, an actor in the present seeks to give a convincing account of that absence. The historian and the court depend equally on absence: a particular void, of what is no longer present but calls out to be made so. Writing history and doing justice, the labor of historians and of courts, are both forms of memory work, for memory is centered on an absence, tries to make it present, and in this effort answers the call of the trace. In its everyday activities, but more visible perhaps in its memorialization efforts, in its monuments, speeches, and epitaphs, memory creates a "place of exchange . . . between present and past."[5] In historiography, it is the text or narrative that is this bridge between past and present, invisible and visible. In doing justice, it is the trial that serves as the meeting place for the absent past and the present.[6]

The judge, the historian, and the memorialist all work at the border between past and present, at that place where a trace can be encountered that calls them back to the absent. These comportments overlap in a way that authorizes us to call them forms of memory work. But this congruence notwithstanding, there are deep and important differences between them, differences that are sometimes vividly on display in the same set of events. Here I want to pick out one core line of demarcation. To begin, we might think about de Certeau's illustration of Crusoe coming upon the footprint in the sand, seeing a trace of something (someone) not there. Why would such a discovery provoke an effort to bridge the distance between the present and the absent? In Crusoe's case, fear or desire for help might be the cause, since the source of the footprint could in fact appear, unlike the sources of the traces of an irreversible past.[7] What then of the historian, the court, or the memorialist? I leave the historian aside here (having briefly discussed her vocation earlier), and ask after the judge and the memorialist.[8] And I turn to their activities with the thought that doing justice generally and remembering, in many of its undertakings, belong among the moral experiences of time. For the struggle to build a bridge between past and present, to overcome absence, is driven primarily not by the desire to construct an explanatory narrative so much as by the imperative to do justice, broadly understood, to the absent past. The labors of memory-justice are at their core forms of resistance to the counter-moral course of time, to a force that constantly threatens to erase the events and persons of the past and to wash away whatever traces, whatever footprints in the sand they have left. It is, in Jean Améry's words, the "moral inversion of time [*Zeitumkehrung*]."[9]

We could say that justice is the "inversion" of time because it is retrospective, whereas the course or flow of time is that of becoming, of a leaving behind of the past. The trial is the "retrospective moment."[10] But clearly this inversion is not simply perspectival, as if justice were a matter simply of looking back. Rather, it is a more radical inversion inasmuch as it seeks to act on the past by making it present. This acting on the past attempts to overcome the void or absence created by the crime by abolishing, after a fashion, the moral indifference inherent in the irreversibility of time, which the passage of time and often human effort seem to seal. So into the darkness of the shadows that can envelop what has slipped away into the distance of the past, the act of doing justice casts its light. But more than that, it seeks to restore, and not just to allow the crime and its perpetrators and victims to be seen (and known) in the light of day, though that certainly is a necessary prelude to the work of repair and restoration. In casting its light, by making visible the facts, justice restores the "moral truth" of the past. And into the refuge of irreversibility, seemingly offered to the crime and the criminal by the forward flow of time, the work of justice enters: literally "*recalling* the facts," calling them back into the present from their refuge in the past and, where possible, bringing perpetrator and victim (or her representative) together and, at the same time, to hear a reenacting of the crime, only now under the gaze of the law. With the material traces of evidence and the humans who bear witness, a bridge is constructed between time present and past, not only so as to permit us to see more clearly what happened but also, and in so doing, to make it present, to act on it, and so to restore justice to the parties, present or absent. In this light we can better understand Améry's phrase, the "inversion of time." But this inversion is also, as I remarked, moral in character. The footprint on this beach, the traces, the evidence and witnessing: all this memory work is a moral response, meaning an attempt to purge the past of its injustices.[11]

We see suggested here a number of points that are gestured toward by the language often associated with doing justice: ending the abandonment of the victims, denying the perpetrators a sanctuary, and bringing the truth to light. All reflect a moral response to the passage of time. (1) The doing of justice answers to an imperative to rectify, at least in so far as this can be done by human hands. The traces, the victim's face, name, or even her nameless impression on the world, are not just inducements to fill gaps in our knowledge but imperatives, traces that call on us, and even in their muteness appeal to the present not to abandon those who have suffered wrong, but rather to fill in a morally unacceptable void. Doing justice searches the past for the truth of things, but the morally relevant one to which we are hailed by the traces of injustice and not that needed for purposes of explanation alone. While the retrospective practices of justice can be given an instrumental interpretation, one that casts their attempts to act justly on the past in the present and future tenses, we would be missing something fundamental about doing justice if we did not see in it a struggle to invert, for moral purposes, the course of time. (2) Relatedly, this language suggests a sometimes overlooked but nevertheless vital background condition for a reading of doing justice as script or narrative writing. This reading has drawn our attention to the role of power in the shaping of judicial and quasi-judicial memory work, the power to decide what is a crime, whose injuries will be recognized, and how their sufferings will be addressed.[12] At a still more fundamental level, this mode of interpretation reminds us that the law is a "regime of temporality," that is, it decides what crimes will remain forever actionable (imprescriptable), which injustices will fall outside the sphere of legal action altogether, and which (through the action of the political sphere) will be the subject of amnesty or judicial forgetting.[13] When we speak, then, of justice as the moral inversion of time, we mean by this (also) that doing justice is the creation of a kind of regime of temporality, the relevant moral horizon of time, and the determination of the relevant norms to select out actionable faults from the panoply of deeds. We are thus led to recognize that which traces of crime are selected for a judicial inversion of time is something that law and politics decide. So, for example, the trial of Maurice Papon, a Vichy official, presupposed a legal definition of crimes against humanity and a determination to apply it to events that predated the trial by a half century or more, as likewise did the trials of military officers in Argentina and of officials of the former German Democratic Republic. In short, we could say that the regime of time, the definition of the relevant voids and absences and their traces, is the work of the present, always selective and shaped by power and contestation.

Yet an account of memory-justice would be radically incomplete if we stopped with an analysis of its various (power) regimes of temporality. For it leaves unsaid why *this* is the terrain, the locale of such bitter contests; and, more basically still, it neglects the dimension of these traces which seem independent of our will and power, so that they seem almost to call on us with their demand for recognition. Phrased differently, we recognize an obligation to do justice to the past, an obligation that obstinately returns if we try to pass it by. The trace, material or human, acts as the representative of the silent victims and their unending appeal for justice. We in the present are the authors of the judicial regime of temporality, but the trace signals to us the ongoing moral reality of the past and its claims. (3) Finally, doing justice is closely (though, as we shall see, often conflictually) related to memory work. Their relationship is not just analogical, but rather doing justice is, in key parts of its practice, memory work. Looking to the past and seeking to act on it by making it present, in a morally grounded manner, is a central part of the way we are as remembering animals. So likewise the resistance to absence signaled by a trace, and the reluctance to consign that absence to the absolute separateness of the "it happened" or to forgetting, are all shared properties of memory (in its many forms) and justice. The doing of justice, then, can be understood in some measure by the utility it provides, but something more is needed as well: an understanding of justice as the effort to secure persistence, as a community's struggle via memory against the effects of the erosion caused by the passage of the years and by the effort of human hands: to restore justice to the world by undertaking a moral inversion of time, through truth-telling and punishment. "Memory is the ultimate form of justice."[14]

Recall Martin Heidegger's remark that memory is the "gathering of thinking . . . preserving, conserving. . . . Keeping is the fundamental nature and essence of memory."[15] From the vantage point of the keeper or guard, an absence or void is a loss; hence the restorative impulse of memory-justice that I shall explore further in the following pages. But to speak of memory as the guardian is also to be directed to still another facet of memory-justice, its kindredness to the spirit of resentment and revenge, and to the tethering embrace of remembrance as part of the concern of members of a community for one another. Heidegger, reading Nietzsche, picks out just this dimension. Revenge, Nietzsche argued, is the "will's ill will against time," against the "it was," against the will's powerlessness "against what has been done."[16] One need not accept Nietzsche's valuation or genealogy of resentment, revenge, and justice to see the accuracy of his account of the relationship between time and revenge.[17] What he is suggesting is that, for example, Améry's notion of justice as the moral inversion of time can be thought of as the will's resistance to (or revulsion at) the pastness of the past, of the will's being "chained to this 'It was,' " chained that is to what cannot be changed, because irreversible, and bound in revulsion (masquerading, according to Nietzsche, as justice) against this impotence, and always in the spirit of revenge. In brief, on Nietzsche's reading, justice is the moral inversion of time, but that means that it is a source of unfreedom, of a restless, sleep-denying, and futilely bitter absorption in the past, in the world of the dead. This thought, which ties the doing of justice to a destructive obsession with the past, advances a case for reining in a poisonous absorption that threatens to destroy life.

In looking at memory work as the core of doing justice, we will keep in mind Nietzsche's observation about time, revulsion, and revenge. We will consider justice in its work of remembering, grounded in a debt to the past, and resistance to that memory work made in the name of the present and future. In focusing on the centrality of remembrance to justice, we see that this argument moves against a very familiar account of practical reason and judgment, moral and judicial. On that view, the coupling of memory and doing justice is an odd one. This is so because such judgments are at their core prescriptive, and so are aimed at the present or future, and their subjects must be living or future beings who have, or will have, interests and so can suffer harm, or will be so affected by our actions.[18] Deliberation, as Aristotle pointed out, is concerned with those matters that can be altered by human action.[19] But what has happened in the past is strictly irreversible, and it therefore lies beyond will ("The will cannot will backwards," Nietzsche writes),[20] beyond the performative character of practical reason. Seen from this vantage point, doing justice must be understood in an instrumental manner, as a practice undertaken and directed by some present or future concern. So, for example, doing justice by putting the perpetrators of mass violations of human rights on trial can be understood as creating the foundations of legitimacy for a successor regime, solidifying the new regime's identity, or deterring other criminals. In this manner an otherwise incomprehensible, or even deplorable, voyage into the irreversible past is transformed into a future-oriented exercise of practical reason. "It is the living, and not the dead, that are to be accommodated."[21]

We who pride ourselves on our post-traditional condition, on our (in Habermas's phrase) "radical openness" to the future, may be especially drawn to this view, more so perhaps than the ancients, who saw both the ethical and obsessional sides of memory-justice. These latter warn us against an all-consuming absorption in the past. Yet they tell us of something else too: that the remembrance of past wrongs is not wholly a trifling and fruitless or destructive "[laboring] in past matters,"[22] but rather is a face of justice itself. Justice is, in one of its key dimensions, the persistence in memory of evil past. The Furies, Daughters of the Night, who "hold the memory of evil," labor mightily to see that the evil they remember does not pass into oblivion. In their undying search for those tainted by guilt, the Furies are the handmaidens of justice. They are its memory, ensuring that the passage of time does not overwhelm the work of justice.[23] Surely the divine Furies and the mortal Electra are driven, and just as surely that costs them (and others) dearly, but still their imperatives to remember and punish evil, and not to let go, belong centrally to justice. As Michèle Simondon writes: "The triad of Zeus, the Erinyes, and Justice maintain the moral order of the world."[24] Their actions, and those of

Electra, are driven by justice, by its remembering eye cast back on the past, not abandoning its work until retribution is made. This is a valuable reminder, as is also the counsel that forgetting is an antidote to the dangers of too much memory, and I shall return to both.

4.1. THE WORK OF MEMORY-JUSTICE

I want to look now at the work of memory-justice as it bears witness, confronts absence, and struggles to answer it with a guarding response, seeking the persistence of what was done. Let me begin with a contemporary example of memory-justice at work in three registers: institutionalized, its diffuse counterpart, and the opposed claims of a restorative forgetting. After some thirty years of conflict in Northern Ireland, a sometimes faltering transition is under way designed to introduce a fuller democratic life in that province and to bring an end to its civil strife.

(1) As part of that transition, Prime Minister Tony Blair created an inquiry (the Saville Inquiry) into the circumstances surrounding the killing of thirteen unarmed Catholic civilians by British soldiers in Derry on January 30, 1972 (Bloody Sunday). Prime Minister Blair reaffirmed the victims' innocence, and spoke of the importance of remembering the dead. He also set the inquiry in the context of his government's peace initiative: "I believe that it is in everyone's interests that the truth [about Bloody Sunday] be established and told. That is also the way forward to the necessary reconciliation that will be such an important part of building a secure future for the people of Northern Ireland."[25] Justice as the institutionalized remembrance of the past is seen here, as in other truth commissions, both as a duty to the dead and as a condition of reconciliation.

(2) At the sites of the Bloody Sunday killings in Derry, the nationalist community mounted wall-sized photographic murals of some of the thirteen civilians in the moment of their deaths.[26] This too was an act of memory-justice, though not of the institutionalized kind. Rather, the community paid a debt of remembrance to its own dead, called to mind the injustice that had been inflicted on both these individuals and their community, and made the dead present once more. Such memory is unlikely to be fully assuaged by the results of the legal proceedings. Justice's memory can keep the bitter well open, and for a very long time indeed. Consider another wall mural in a Catholic neighborhood in Belfast. Titled (in Gaelic) "an Gorta Mór" (the Great Famine), it depicts bodies being carted out of a field in Ireland during the mid-nineteenth-century famine. On the mural is a line from a poem by Seamus Heaney: "They

buried us without shroud nor coffin." That also is a memory of justice, a giving of remembrance and dignity to those who were not granted it in their time, and a part of the community's long memory and identity, linked no doubt to the fresher wounds depicted on the Bloody Sunday murals. And, arguably, it is a manipulated and distorted one.[27]

(3) But justice's memories, institutionalized or informal, of long or brief duration, can also be seen as a destructive wallowing in the past and so be challenged by the call to forget for the sake of peace. Winston Churchill wrote derisively of Ulster: "But as the deluge subsides and the waters fall short we see the dreary steeples of Fermanagh and Tyrone emerging once again. The integrity of their quarrel is one of the few institutions that has been unaltered in the cataclysm [World War I] which has swept the world."[28] Against this apparent absorption in the injustices of the past, Blair urged the parties "to put our histories behind us, try to forgive and forget," and he appealed for "a Northern Ireland free from . . . the battles of the past. Offering the children here the future they deserve."[29]

These are not simply separate paths of memory and resistance to it. Rather, they often coexist and conflict with one another: judicially institutionalized memory-justice seeking to address and sometimes limit the effects of the informal, bitter memories of injustice; that latter pressing upon the institutions of justice its often unanswerable demands; and justice as forgetting, attempting to still the voice of memory in the name of the future. As Archbishop Desmond Tutu put it: "We could not make the journey from a past marked by conflict, injustice, oppression, and exploitation to a new and democratic dispensation characterized by a culture of respect for human rights without coming face to face with our recent history. No one has disputed that. The differences of opinion have been about how we should deal with that past; how we should go about coming to terms with it."[30]

I will return to the informal and diffuse presence of memory-justice. Here I want to focus on three of the judicial or quasi-judicial faces of memory-justice as it deals with the past: trial and punishment; illumination and acknowledgment; forgetting for the sake of a future in common. (1) Criminal charges: These have been brought against the perpetrators or some subset of them in, for example, Nuremberg, the Eichmann trial, the proceedings against the Greek junta leaders, against those responsible for the Argentinean "dirty war," and against the erstwhile head of the East German *Stasi*, Erich Mielke. (2) Truth commissions: Here the strategy is not prosecution or punishment but disclosure and, perhaps more important, acknowledgment of the evils committed, and of its victims.[31] Illustrations include the Truth and Reconciliation Commission (TRC) in South Africa, the various official and unofficial "Nunca Más" (Never Again) efforts in Latin America, the Saville Inquiry, and the Study Commission for the Assessment of the History and Consequences of the SED Dictatorship in Germany.[32] (3) Amnesty: If the end result of criminal justice proceedings against accused perpetrators is sanction, and knowledge/acknowledgment the result of truth commissions, then amnesty we might say is a form of political-judicial forgetting that puts the past out of sight. The past is here placed beyond the reach of justice and into the shadows of civic-judicial forgetting. The objective of such amnesties is almost always the keeping of civil peace, born of the need to protect the young and vulnerable democracy from being torn apart by an absorption in the past and in its attendant spirit of revenge. Democracy and its future must, on this view, take precedence over the past and its demands that justice be done. In the pages that follow, I consider each of these ways of engaging in the moral inversion of time.

4.1.1. Retribution

Aharon Appelfeld's novel *The Iron Tracks* portrays a son's unceasing hunt for his parents' Nazi murderers. The "iron tracks" are the memory of the crime, and they suggest both the rectitude of his memory work and the compulsion, the life-sapping absorption in the past, that drives him: "My memory is my downfall. It is a sealed well that doesn't lose a drop. . . . Were it not for my memory, my life would be different—better, I assume."[33] We recognize in him, as in other more ancient bearers of memory, Electra for example, what Nietzsche called the "sleeplessness," the destructive compulsiveness of too much bitter memory. Might it not be better, we ask, to let go of the past, to invest our energy and time in building a future rather than dwelling on the evils of an irreversible past? Perhaps the price of our future is that we allow the poisonous memory of the past, of its victims and perpetrators, to pass into oblivion. Our orientation in the world seems to take its bearings from the future or present. From that vantage point, justice as the duty to remember is archaic, useless like other passions of memory such as remorse or regret, irrational, or even dangerous. And so we look with suspicion on those mired in the past: on those in the former Yugoslavia, for example, riven by ancient animosities and squandering the potential of an open future for the sake of settling old accounts.[34] We wonder at the waste of three thousand lives lost in a conflict governed, it seems, by the memory of the Battle of the Boyne and the Easter 1916 Uprising. To sacrifice the present and future on the altar of grievances, whether of the recent or long-distant past, appears deeply irrational and wrong. Our reaction to Achilles, driven by the memory of the death of his comrade Patroklos, or to Electra, who lives in the shadow of her murdered father, are likely of a piece with our views of these more modern conflicts. It is not the quantity of the time passed between the motivating event and the present response that puzzles or repels us, though the greater the temporal distance, the more likely we are to be perplexed at the long duration of the wound's presence in people's lives. Rather, we see it as life-destroying, as the "gravedigger of the present,"[35] negative, divisive, and irrational precisely because these individuals and peoples have lost the use of their future-oriented compass. Justice as memory work seems in need of an apology precisely because, in what Heidegger termed its keeping or guarding character, memory-justice keeps alive the passion for revenge and retribution, fuels an inextinguishable resentment, chains the will to the "it was."

Persistence, retribution, and resentment seem to find expression in the application of the law and the enduringness of its work. All are the voices of memory seeking to address, as Nicole Loraux puts it, a "loss which creates a gap in our present that nothing can fill."[36] That void can be the loss of individuals, of their lives, or of their civil status, the loss of a regime of rights, or, more basically still, the destruction of a law-governed condition. To demand reparation, to insist on the punishment of the perpetrators and on recognition for the loss of the victims, is to seek repair in so far as that is possible. The exactions here are those of justice, not of a raw rejection of the irreversible "it was." Justice's revulsion, bound up with its unrelenting memory, is directed not at becoming, at the passage of time, but at the way in which the absences thereby created tend to erase the crime, shelter the perpetrators, and deny the victims their due measure of retribution. The preservative function of memory here is the work of justice against that process of obliteration, whether the latter is the result of the flow of time or of human action. The past and the void it leaves are the mark of our non-possession, of loss or absence. The past of crime and the void it creates of incomplete justice are what justice as memory struggles against. To bring the perpetrator, the victim, and the (represented) political community together in court is to "annul time . . . to deny time its [power of] moral erosion."[37]

Memory's guarding of moral outrage, the core of resentment and of the thirst for vengeance or retribution, is at the heart of doing justice. Crime as the absence of justice calls for memory to keep it present against the forces of erosion arrayed against the work of justice. Memory helps to ensure that time does not prematurely heal all wounds, because healing of that kind would deny justice its due. And it tries to ensure that those wounds, left by a gross violation against human beings, are answered by justice and not by forgetting or other salves. The trial, seen as the institutionalization and civic domestication of vengeance, is the public voice of the need to ensure that the crime will continue to have a moral reality or presence, to be certain that the truth of the injury is not lost and that the absence of the crime, separated from us by the passage of time, does not become a natural force exonerating the perpetrators.[38]

Perhaps this is how we should understand Martha Minow when she writes that to respond to mass atrocity with legal prosecution is to embrace the rule of law.[39] To embrace the "rule of law" is to put oneself in opposition to the lawlessness and violence of dictatorship. But it is to do something more: it is to embrace the enduring rule of law over the erosion caused by the passage of time and by forgetting. The fear for memory-justice is that the memory of the injury will not endure, that the crime will be allowed to slip into oblivion, into the forgotten; that the passage of time will, like a natural solvent or a willed forgetting, free the perpetrators and loosen the already weak hold of the hands of justice in the world. The trial is one forum of resistance to this, seeking the victory of the memory of justice over the becoming of time and the will to forget; seeking, in that sense, the "rule of law." Justice and memory resist the passage of time, and deny to it any power of moral/legal absolution. Faced with the power of the process of becoming, and of a concernful comportment toward the future, memory-justice, as the voice insisting on keeping the past present, must seek to prevent the effacement of the memory of the crime. Justice thus becomes the memory of injury, and it fights against the forgetfulness that must always threaten to engulf it, to give sanctuary to the perpetrators and a victory to injustice.[40] Expressed in this manner, what at first sight appears as a straightforward conflict between the vengeful, all-remembering Furies and the demands of legal justice becomes, in the light of memory, more nuanced. For all of the real tension between their pursuit of those polluted by guilt and the requirements of the world of a law-governed civic order, the Furies are, at least in part, simply doing the work of justice. Their ferocity is directed equally against the criminals and against the forgetting that shields them from retribution, and their refusal to let go of the past expresses one of the core demands of the "rule of law" understood as justice's memory work. Their work may be (to borrow Bacon's term) "Wilde," but in its determined insistence on preserving the memory of crime, it is justice too.

Retribution, then, is restorative of a just or lawful condition. The Furies, Simondon writes, belong to a universe ruled by justice, and in awakening us, in calling us back from our forgetfulness, they serve justice and restore or bring to light again its presence in the world.[41] Retribution answers not only to the call to see justice or the rule of law embraced, but to the appeal of the victims as well. "Those who have been hurt need a response," writes Bernard Williams.[42] The absence that justice seeks to overcome is also that of the victims, especially those rendered silent by the crime. When I said that the co-presence of accuser and accused in the courtroom abolishes the time that has passed between the trial and the crime, I could have added that the trial gives voice to the victims, makes them present, if only through the intermediary of the court, its evidence and testimony. The response that the law seeks, it seeks in part with and for them. In the brutal language of Greek tragedy, a language that conveys both the justice of persistent memory and its attendant dangers, the "dead are killing the living."[43] The imperative to answer the needs of the victims for a response can be understood as a duty to the wronged, including the dead, something that their absence and whatever traces remain of them and their fate call us to fulfill. Memory-justice's tenacious clinging to the remembrance of the crime and its victims is something owed to them, rather than being in the first instance something valuable to the living, or to the future. The face of justice is here at least turned entirely toward the past, and the rightness of its present actions is understood squarely in light of a debt to the dead. We find striking the idea of indebtedness to those with whom we have no contract or bargain, nor even any tangible community except perhaps the communion created by memory itself. Is the idea of a debt grounded in the imperatives of fidelity so very odd? Perhaps Sophocles' understanding that Orestes and Electra owe it to their dead father, Agamemnon, to see that his murderers do not escape punishment captures a dimension of memory-justice that is still at work among us. Remarking on the various efforts to deal with the past in the course of South Africa's transition to majority rule, Arieh Neier said that the motivation was to recognize the dignity of the victims.[44] To do otherwise, he concluded, would be to acknowledge that only the future has value. Related sentiments of the morality of memory lie behind our practice of public and private commemoration, of monument-building, and so forth. That too is surely also among the lessons of the Furies, Electra, and Achilles: their absorption in their debts to the dead costs them (and others) mightily, but those costs, and the obliviousness to the future that helps bring them about, are at least partially justified and seen as good in light of the commitment to a just fidelity, to keeping faith with the victims.[45] We may be tempted to see in the logic of the Furies an obsessional immersion in the past, or an illustration of the need for a law-governed political order to vanquish their "Wilde" and private vengeance.[46] Here I have chosen to look at another of their faces: as memory-justice giving voice to the past and its victims, and insisting on the restoration of justice in the world against the oblivion of forgetting.

I have thus far considered the doing of justice as the work of memory-justice. Memory seizes the crime, keeps it among the unforgotten, and insists on retribution. No other good or end to be achieved is invoked to justify this process. Nor, by the same token, are countervailing considerations, the unhappy effects of the relentless pursuit of justice, to be entertained. The language here is not that of healing, nor of sustaining the reemergence of democracy, nor of identity, but rather of the imperative to do what justice demands.[47] I have emphasized this point as a counterweight to our tendency to instrumentalize memory as the doing of justice, to see it exclusively as a tool in the service of some present and future good, and so to leave unstated its struggle to invert, morally, the flow of time. Yet in the panoply of human passions and interests that inform such present-tense encounters with the absence of the past, we need also to give due weight to that present and its agents (and, by proxy, the future as well) in these retributive judicial proceedings (and other, non-retributive processes such as the Truth and Reconciliation Commission [TRC] in South Africa), especially those that occur in the wake of regime changes or after mass violations of human rights.[48] In general terms, we could say with Václav Havel that societies, especially those that have experienced the trauma of dictatorship or state-led mass crime, have a need to deal with the past.[49] This need is not for therapy but for a foundation for the new regime, for a national identity, for lessons for the future, and for "lay[ing] a foundation for an enduring peace."[50] It should be observed (and I will return to this issue further on) that besides the politics, the conflicting principles and play of interests that are inherent in any process managed by human beings, the introduction of the concerns of the present and future sets the stage for a tension between the demands of doing justice to the past and attending to the needs of present and future.[51] Or, more exactly, it is a matter of attending not simply to their needs but to the sometimes conflicting claims to justice of past, present, and future and thus to the different uses to which memory-justice can be put.

Undoubtedly one such need is to delegitimize or root out the former non-democratic elites. Other purposes include reintegrating the victims, and enhancing the credibility and legitimacy of the new regime by underscoring its break with the past. Retroactive justice, Carlos Nino argued, was essential to democratic transitions, whether in Argentina (where he was one of the leading figures in efforts to bring to justice those responsi-

ble for the conduct of the "dirty war"), in Greece after the fall of the
junta, or in the 1991 Czech lustration law.[52] Other judicial practices, such
as the TRC in South Africa, are aimed not at punishment but at reconciliation as the basis for the establishment of trust and ongoing social cooperation, seen as a prerequisite for democratic flourishing.[53] Now the work
of trials and other judicial processes as acts of memory-justice in the wake
of massive state crimes and the transition to democracy can be framed by
drawing on other languages. Preventative and didactic purposes are examples of those other justificatory idioms. Both are future-oriented, and
their claims rest squarely on the accuracy of their empirical assumptions
about the long-term effects of such measures. The preventative rationale
is perhaps most familiar to us from the "Nunca Más" process in Argentina,
El Salvador, Guatemala, and elsewhere after the end of their "dirty wars."
In his prologue to the *Report of the Argentine National Commission on the Disappeared*, Ernesto Sabato writes that "great catastrophes are always instruc-
tive. Only with democracy will we be certain that NEVER AGAIN will events
such as these . . . be repeated in our nation." The purpose of the Argen-
tinian trials related to the "dirty war" was, as Raúl Alfonsín (the former
president of Argentina) says, not so much to punish as to prevent. A similar hope is expressed in the Guatemalan *Nunca Más* report, under the aus-
pices of the Catholic Archdiocese of Guatemala.[54] Trials and other actions
against the perpetrators can serve as a warning, and thus even if they do
not wholly uproot the personnel and institutions responsible for state
crimes and dictatorship, they nevertheless put those forces on notice that
there is no sanctuary from justice, and in so doing (it is hoped) help prevent the recurrence of injustice. Something like this motivation was no
doubt part of the rationale for the war crimes trials at Nuremberg and the
trials that followed the collapse of military juntas in Greece and Argentina. It is also part of the underpinning of the work of the TRC and
similar devices.[55]

Another, and no less powerful reason (related to the preventative function just discussed) for the public deployment of memory-justice in the
form of trials and truth commissions is didactic and identity-forming: the
way we remember shapes what we are and what we will become.[56] Trials
can be used for didactic purposes not so much in the sense of warnings
for the future but rather as contributions to the shaping of the collective
memory of a community and to the instruction of future citizens in their
history and struggles for justice.[57] The ingathering of the past, here carried out through institutionalized memory-justice, allows these societies
to cement their political-legal identity in the aftermath of trauma and dis-
ruption.[58] Courts, then, can be seen as locales in which an account of re-

sponsibility is given, and placed on the wider canvas of the community's political identity, of what was lost and what needs to be restored. Here the restoration is of a (partial) status quo ante, a former version of the community: Republican France prior to Vichy; Greece before the military coup d'état, or Chile before Pinochet's seizure of power. And the narrative of remembrance takes its bearing precisely from that earlier condition. On other occasions, there is no past democratic and law-governed regime to serve as the focal point of a restorative narrative. Restoration there means the recovery of a law-governed condition not from the community's own past but, one might say, from justice itself. This is the memory of justice not in an empirical or historical sense, but rather as an almost Platonic recollection of justice: a reminder to the community of how it had strayed, not from its own past but from justice. The courtroom then becomes the locale of a rupture, in which the past, acknowledged and condemned, is seen not as a regrettable interregnum, as if it were the work of criminal interlopers, but as the past of the community simply. A trial serves, under these conditions, as a call to remember the claims of justice on us, and to repudiate one's former self in the light of those claims.[59]

Whether by restoring integrity to a community that has strayed from justice or by condemning a deviation from its own core values, these applications of memory-justice are arguably of special importance to the restoration or creation of democratic regimes after the defeat of dictatorship. This is so because properly conducted (i.e., not as show trials involving gross violations of the basic norms of a constitutional, law-governed society), they reinforce the constitutional-judicial foundation of society. In other words, they demonstrate in practice the difference between a lawless regime and a mode of governance restrained by law. In its legal form, memory-justice holds on to the past for the sake of retribution and restoration of the rule of law and thus of a law-ordered moral/political universe. In so doing, it can also restore a political identity, announce a rupture, and help induce a new birth, and it can be a part of the rejection of the old self or regime and as such a (partial) response to the pollution bequeathed by its predecessor.[60]

In the preceding paragraphs I have treated doing justice as fulfilling a debt to the past, as preventative, didactic, and identity-shaping, as if these were clear and separate undertakings. I did this for analytical purposes, but it is important to note that they tend to be intermingled and are in fact often inseparable (and frequently in conflict, too). Consider the 1961 Eichmann trial in Jerusalem. That trial bore witness to the injustices suffered by the victims of the Holocaust, and in that sense corrected the near silence that enveloped the fact of the European judeocide at the Nuremberg trial. At the same time, it made the Shoah an explicit part of Israeli national consciousness and was seen as a didactic device by means of which to educate Israeli youth. And finally (as Haïm Gouri suggests in his anecdote about an Israeli schoolgirl who, learning of the victims of the Holocaust, asks why didn't our army help them?), the trial served to remind Israelis and the Jewish community generally of their vulnerability without a state of their own. In all of these, memory was at work, as the duty of bearing witness to the absence of the victims and insisting on the persistence of the (recognition of) the injury, but also in the service of other goods, present and future.[61]

4.1.2. *Justice and the Memory of Truth*

We have just seen how closely entangled are memory and retribution. Grief, remorse, revenge, and retribution all participate in memory and so as well in the resistance to forgetting. They therefore cling to the past and fight against the erosion of memory brought about by the becoming of time, its unceasing movement toward the openness of the future. But the "memory of evil" that the Furies hold, that central part of memory-justice, is not bound up with retribution alone. Once more, the ancient Greeks offer us insight. They named truth *alētheia*, the "unforgotten" (from the root *lēthē*, or "forgetting"). Forgetting rather than falsity is the antonym of truth/*alētheia*: "Truth is always about something forgotten, which it retrieves from its non-remembered condition."[62] Remembrance is thus, as we saw Plato writing in the *Philebus* (34a), the guardian or savior (*sōtāria*) of appearances. It is not surprising, then, that truth as the unforgotten on the one side and justice as memory-justice on the other are closely linked. Justice seeks the truth, we might say, though concealed beneath that commonplace is the deeper observation that justice wants truth the way memory desires that the phenomena remain (or become) unforgotten. It is the work of justice to bring the truth to light, to secure the deeds, the victims, and the perpetrators, in *alētheia*, in the unforgotten, in the realm of memory; hence the often (though, as we shall see, not exclusively) negative valuation attached to forgetting in the classical literature. Forgetting is opposed to both memory and justice. Or better: forgetting is opposed to that core of justice which lies in the guarding work of truth/memory.[63] In our time, this connection between memory-truth-justice has become, if anything, even more compelling. For one of the goals of the perpetrators of mass crime in this past century has been the obliteration of the memory of the victims.[64] To erase the memory of the crimes and their victims is, of course, a device used by criminals, great and small. But here it is something more: by effacing their names, histories, and fates, it was hoped that the fact, the truth, of their existence would also disappear. Thus, the Nazis planned to transform a Prague synagogue into a "Museum of a Vanished Race" once the annihilation of the Jewish communities of Europe was complete. They would then have been able to destroy that community twice over: the first time in its existence, the second time in the remembrance of it.[65]

In preserving the memory of the crimes, we bear in mind the words of the Polish poet Zbigniew Herbert: only "a fatal defect in our tools / or a sin of memory" could leave the disappeared in the shadows of forgetting. "Ignorance about the disappeared / undermines the reality of the world."[66] "Undermines the reality of the world . . .": these individuals, the victims of mass crime, are left faceless and nameless; the hour, manner, and place of their last moments unknown, outside the light of truth, lost to forgetting. And so the world is incomplete, its integrity broken, its reality undermined. The very incompleteness, the absences, that such efacement creates command memory's attempt to recover these persons. The need for precision that Herbert refers to in the title of this poem ("Mr. Cogito on the Need for Precision") is precisely the need to restore the truth against forgetting or effacement, whether willed or simply the consequence of the passage of time. What is missing and in need of restoration is not just a fragment of a now incomplete whole, a shard to be restored to a shattered vase. Rather, justice in a life-in-common is missing: "we are despite everything / the guardians of our brothers," Herbert writes in the lines immediately preceding the one that tells us that ignorance about the disappeared disrupts the reality of the world. To be their guardians is to keep them in the sanctuary of truth-memory, which at the same time preserves the (just) reality of the world. It is in this spirit that the (unofficial) Guatemalan *Nunca Más* report called for "the restitution of truth and the collective memory of the victims."[67]

Earlier, I set out a general account of witnessing and memory. Here I return to some of those themes and put them to work in looking at doing justice as truth-telling. Now, bearing witness, I argued, plays a central part in the struggles of memory to save absences from a final oblivion. As I also suggested, the act of bearing witness, despite its association with the courtroom, has many other forms. Although they are different from and by no means subject to the same strictures as courtroom testimony, these other types of witnessing are worth noting for the light they cast on the sort of testimony that I am discussing. Consider, for example, an issue of the literary journal *Leopard* devoted to bearing witness.[68] Among its contributions is a memorial tribute to Leopold Labedz, an essay on the silence surrounding the persecution of Kosovar Albanians, a collection of photographs of democratic opposition leader San Suu Kyi and of daily life in Burma taken over a six-year period, and a poem written in memory of two Northern Irish policemen assassinated by the IRA. One thing that these otherwise disparate pieces have in common is a silence or absence: of the dead and of peoples silenced through repression. A second common trait is that all, in essays, poems, or images, carry testimony to us in the present about these absences. The writer or photographer is here a bearer of things absent, though the absence that the witness seeks to overcome need not always be that of times past. And finally, in certain defining moments, bearing witness, making visible the truth about the absent, is a matter of justice as the bringing to light of the moral truth of things not visible.

The witness, in the context of the trial, is also the living power of conservation in memory, the mirror of what has been, and so is key to making present the truth about the past.[69] As a conserver of memory, the person who bears witness has a certain obstinacy, a stubbornness and a willingness to resist. Like that other guardian óf memory, the man of resentment and revenge, he answers the crime with the enduringness of the will to remember, to testify, and to see that justice does not forget. The phrase "bearing witness" suggests a weight to be carried from a place of absence to another, that of the present, and it savors of a determination: *Ich will Zeugnis ablegen bis zum letzten* (I Will Bear Witness to the End), the title of Victor Klemperer's war diaries. What the witness carries from the past is, as I said, the moral truth of that past, of its victims, of its perpetrators, and of the crime. Pause for a moment to reflect further on that notion. The witness in the courtroom is an agent of memory called on to give a true account of the facts as he knows them. Like the historian, the court looks to the witness for evidence. Yet the witness as a vector of memory testifies to matters already placed within a legal horizon saturated with moral judgments, with notions of responsibility, agency, and fault.[70] She is thus more than a living archive, though the witness as a trace of the past does have something important in common with those inanimate witnesses.[71] As a crucial part of the work of memory-justice, the witness brings the past to the light of moral truth, and in his testimony he already straddles the role of giving evidence, telling the truth, and doing justice. The recognition of the facts about wrongs done is itself inseparable, in the context of a trial, from justice.[72] One final thought on bearing witness: the witness's action carries with it an implied imperative or plea to his listeners: "Believe me!"[73] At the same time, the witness herself is under an imperative, to be the porter for things past, to be faithful to "invisible things," to those who by their silence or absence cannot tell of their own fates, and who therefore depend on witnesses to do this on their behalf.

The victims, especially the voiceless dead, are there, writes Jorge Semprún, in "the immensity of historic memory, constantly menaced by an unacceptable forgetting."[74] The dead, of course, cannot be menaced, cannot suffer the fate of a "second death" announced in that most common of metaphors about them. They are a handful of dust, without interests, and beyond harm and injustice. The moral intuition that this metaphor captures is rather this: it is to them as once living persons with whom we shared an enduring community that harm is possible even after they are dead.[75] It is because (in Perec's words), "we lived together, because I was one among them, shadow in the midst of their shadows, body next to their bodies," in other words, because we shared and continue to share a relationship, that forgetting is a wrong, even a second death. Remembering, then, bringing into the light of truth, restores a kind of life to the victims of mass crime. Memory is a sepulcher, giving survival to what is remembered: "In spite of them [the Nazis], the souls of your brothers and sisters will live on, the martyrs whom they sought to destroy. For no one can annihilate letters. They have wings, and they fly around in the heights . . . into eternity."[76] In the words of S. Y. Agnon's short story "The Sign": "If my town has been wiped out of the world, it remains alive in the poem that the poet wrote as a sign for my city. . . . [T]he poem sings itself in the heavens above."[77] Remembering, and here bearing witness, is to make what is past present, to rescue it from the status of what-had-happened, or, more radically still, from the oblivion of forgetting. It connects what is lost to what is here. Not to bring the dead into the sanctuary of truth-memory-justice is to fail to bear witness to them, to annihilate them a second time. It is a second death because it would ratify and deepen the oblivion to which the initial crime had sought to consign them. Adam Michnik writes, "After they [the murdered Jews of Jedwabne, Poland] died they were murdered again, denied a decent burial, denied tears, denied truth about this hideous crime, and . . . for decades a lie was repeated."[78]

Bringing the victims into memory/truth saves them from being forever lost among the forgotten. Memory is the truth of things, of victims, perpetrators, and crimes, because it preserves the deeds and persons. What is left in silence dies and languishes among the lost. What we do not remember is as if it never happened; it is effaced from the memory of the world. Out of this sense of menace to those who have already suffered comes an imperative of justice to remember, to be a mirror, a witness, and thereby to restore the truth. Illustrations of this abound. Nicole Lapierre, writing of the extermination of the Jews of Płock, says that "the efface-ment was total. . . . [W]hat was left was my rage to write and to describe." In a similar vein, Germaine Tillion said that her will to survive in Ravens-brück was fueled by the desire to bear witness and to bring the truth out from the catastrophe of the camps. But perhaps it is Patrick Modiano, in his *Dora Bruder*, who best captures the imperative at the heart of truth-memory-justice. Modiano says of Dora that "if I were not here to write it, there would be no trace."[79]

The language of truth-memory-justice is not, at its core, that of the "truth will set us free" or of the truth-as-healing kind.[80] Although it may be vital to reconciliation, what principally justifies this pursuit of truth through the various public and private institutions of memory is the lan-guage of fidelity, of what is owed to the dead. Here is Czeslaw Milosz in his Nobel lecture: "Those who are alive receive a mandate from those who are dead and silent forever: to preserve the truth about the past."[81] This mandate demands of those who come after the crimes that they act as wit-nesses to the truth of what happened, witnesses who speak on behalf of those who cannot. Theirs is a responsibility to the truth and it is an act of fidelity, of faithfulness to the victims. Silent deeds die, whether those of greatness and heroism, celebrated by a Homer or a Pindar, or those of abominable crime preserved in memory by a Levi or an Améry. All are in need of words, letters, monuments, of us as witnesses and makers of words, to preserve them among the unlost.[82] In that sense there is an elec-tiveness about this aspect of memory-justice: it is up to us, in the present, to give or withhold voice. As Alain Finkielkraut argues, posteriority con-fers "mastery (but not supremacy)": the power to misread or to allow to fall into forgetting, to set aside the "terrible responsibility" of remem-brance.[83] But the fact of its voluntariness, far from diminishing its moral weight, rather strengthens the mandate to remain faithful to the victims of mass crime by not completing the perpetrators' work of effacement. The impetus that draws us to the work of truth-memory-justice is at once both palpable and perplexing. Palpable is the moral claim that we owe them the light of truth/remembrance; that silent though they are, they call on us to be witnesses to the fact of their having existed and to their fate. We know and are familiar with the hold of truth-memory-justice over us. We see it in the "memory books" composed by the survivors of the de-stroyed Jewish communities of Europe. We see it in the work of Serge Klarsfeld: a nearly two-thousand-page memorial composed of the names, photographs, addresses, and convoys of Jewish children deported from France to Nazi concentration camps. At the legal-political level, we see it in the work of truth commissions and similar processes that have accompanied transitions to democracy in South Africa, Chile, and El Salvador as well as in post-reunification Germany. Yet it can seem difficult to articulate the basis for the intuition and practice of our sense that we have a bond across time to which we must remain faithful, a bond never stated or articulated but that nevertheless denies us the right to be silent.[84] That thought goes beyond our customary understanding of obligation and its sources, as does its consequence: the weight that it attaches to this duty over our present and future concerns.

Is this preservation in the light of remembrance sufficient for justice to be said to have been done? For Sophocles, Electra and her brother are not simply the living truth and memory of the crimes committed against their father. They are also the instruments of retribution, and the justice they embody is complete in the unity of truth, remembrance, and a corrective. It is not surprising, then, that some have judged truth commissions and similar memorial strategies for dealing with the past to be inadequate. They are found wanting both (and relatedly) because their focus is on disclosure and not on punishing the perpetrators, and because they are sometimes accompanied by amnesties, needed to heal divisions and to encourage the perpetrators to come forward. As Wole Soyinka puts it, referring to the TRC in South Africa: "Truth as a prelude to reconciliation, that seems logical enough; but Truth as the sole exaction or condition for Reconciliation? That is what constitutes a stumbling block in the South African proceedings."[85] Truth alone, he says, the mere opening of police files, for example, cannot substitute for the vindication that only the appearance of the oppressor before a court of law can bring to his victims. Some measure of restitution is necessary, Soyinka concludes.[86] While Soyinka discusses this vindication in terms of healing and catharsis, another, less psychological way to phrase it would be to say that justice-truth-memory and justice-retribution-memory are two faces of justice and its relation to the past. Remembrance, as preserving the truth of the past, of the victims and perpetrators, is at once the saving of the phenomena and the fulfillment of a debt of fidelity to the dead. But as Electra's life makes clear, the light of truth does not exhaust the entirety of justice. We want crime not simply to stand exposed in the light of truthful remembrance but to be punished as well.

4.2. MEMORY, IDENTITY, AND THE LIMITS OF THE LAW

Now I want to ask about the limits of the legal expressions of memory-justice, to ask if they exhaust the work of bearing witness that memory-justice seems to demand of us. Or do they rather leave a sense of incompleteness, as if law's empire could not reach as far as memory-justice requires, could not hold up a mirror to all that needs to be remembered? According to one interpretation, it is from the standpoint of revenge, or "Wilde Justice," that the work of the law in dealing with the past is judged frustratingly incomplete in wiping "the slate clean."[87] I want to suggest that this incompleteness is the recognition, from the vantage point of memory-justice, of a premature closure, and of something important left undone. This can be seen even where legal action has been taken against the perpetrators, for example, in Europe after World War II. This may simply reflect the memory of incomplete legal action: in considering how to deal with officials of the former German Democratic Republic, the concern that many Nazis escaped justice altogether or were dealt with too leniently as Germany went from being a defeated enemy to an ally in the cold war.[88] Similarly, in France, one of the factors explaining the longevity of the "Vichy syndrome" is the concern that some French officials, collaborators with the Germans in the persecution of Jews and of the Resistance, were never called to answer for their actions. Yet the persistence of something like the "Vichy syndrome" not only in France but also in postcommunist eastern Europe and Germany suggests that the legal expression of memory-justice does not exhaust the claims of the past on us, any more than does the historian's grasp of it.[89]

(1) The persistent politics of memory can be accounted for, at least partially, by the fear that the completion of the trials will become an occasion for closure, on the pretext that all that can be done has been done. I have discussed the doing of legal justice in these pages as the making present of the absent past. And so it is, but it has a double role: at once to do the work of memory and restoration and, through its definitive decision, to close off that past once and for all. In this latter facet, doing justice differs both from memory work and from that other venture into the past, the work of the historian.[90] Claude Lanzmann argues that the trial marks a rupture and allows the past to become historic in character rather than present or, worse, creates a sort of quasi-amnesia about it.[91] To see this more clearly, consider how similar concerns have been raised over the building of monuments and museums to the victims of mass state crime. The worry here is that the object, the monument or inscription, becomes in effect the final testimony and gesture of compliance with the demands of memory-justice, and thus the latter is transformed into history, the past perfect, and ceases to be part of the lived world of justice.[92] Remembrance itself, in other words, can sometimes be used to quit the debt once and for all, to throw off the weight of the past. Henri Raczymow writes of Mathieu

(a central character in his novel, *Un cri sans voix*) and his efforts to be done with the memory of his sister, Esther, who committed suicide years earlier: "My son [Mathieu says] will be saved from the past. He will carry no stigma from it. I will never speak to him of Esther. . . . My book will have effaced her. Strangely, it required words for that. Words, and not silence, . . . Esther is buried. Good and buried. . . . Her name is on the tomb, and her body inside it. Localized. Esther is no longer in me. I expelled her."[93] The memoir and the tomb are ways not of preserving the memory of Esther but of freeing her brother (and his son) from her. So too trials, monuments, and days of remembrance can free their communities from a burdensome past. De Certeau argues (too sharply, perhaps) that "writing only speaks about the past in order to bury it. It is a tomb in this double sense that, in one and the same text, it honors and eliminates."[94] The doing of legal justice is both the moral inversion of time, characterized by the labors of memory, and the search to overcome the haunting presence of that past in memory, to affirm the pastness of the past once justice is done, to draw a thick line between past and present. Writing about the 1963–1965 Frankfurt Auschwitz trial, Martin Walser says that many want their peace and quiet, and that putting Nazi officials on trial promises to bring peace under the "beautiful name of justice."[95] Yet precisely that therapeutic closure, which is its political value, makes it seem flawed and unsatisfactory to memory-justice, which struggles against the final consigning of the crime, perpetrator, and victim to the pastness of the past.

(2) As I have just suggested, law's empire, even while doing memory work, nevertheless does not reach as far as memory-justice and witnessing, and brings a closure that the latter resists. Consider once more the trial as the retributive face of memory-justice. From the standpoint of the law, criminal trials of former regime officials can have their own difficulties, for example, retroactivity, statutes of limitation, and so forth. Seen, however, from the vantage point of memory-justice, trials are hobbled by two related restrictions: (a) their focus on guilt, and (b) their definitiveness. They may be focal points for shaping collective memory, and it may well be that the public face they give to memory-justice is essential to the work of justice.[96] But there is at once an incompleteness and an excessive definitiveness about them, properties that help to mark out their limits.

(a) As legal events involving criminal charges, trials of the perpetrators of state crimes must inevitably look to individual accountability in their proceedings.[97] The trial, Walser says, can only focus on deeds for which there is a perpetrator. In regimes where there was a gray area of collaboration and passive acquiescence or even support, that creates a very nar-

row focus, shifting the weight of responsibility entirely onto those held to
be directly the authors of the crimes.[98] The co-responsibility of a people
and state does not readily fit into the horizon of a courtroom proceeding,
which looks for bloody hands that no one except the direct perpetrators
will have. Such proceedings, then, tend to free gray-area occupants from a
full reckoning with their own involvement, via a life-in-common, with the
perpetrators.[99] That part of the past selected out by legal processes as the
locale of accountability may, in other words, only partially overlap with
the sphere of responsibility as understood in memory-justice.[100] As we saw,
the concern with guilt, understood as a clear line and "threshold" concept, emphasizes the discrete actions of an individual rather than a responsibility more diffuse (but perhaps also more important, politically
speaking) than direct authorship. Memory-justice, in its ingathering of
the past, seems to need something else, a testimony to and a recognition
of a responsibility that, although it includes individual accountability,
reaches beyond it to something not reducible to guilt. As Bernhard
Schlink writes, in the post–World War II German context, "Pointing at
the guilty parties [in trials] did not free us from shame."[101] What is wanted
is a self-understanding on the part of the members of a political community as co-responsible even if not legally accountable. This we could call,
in the aftermath of mass crimes, a sense of shame that emerges not from
direct authorship of actions but from membership in a community implicated in these deeds.[102] Consider this illustration: Albie Sachs, a South
African anti-apartheid activist severely wounded by a security service
bomb, was approached by an Afrikaner who asked him for forgiveness.
Sachs was perplexed: since we do not accept collective responsibility, why
should this man feel guilt and apologize? Perhaps, as Stanley Cohen suggests, what he was expressing was a quite appropriate shame, not guilt.
Memory as shame, then, seems to be part of the demand of memory-
justice, and it ranges far beyond the issue of guilt that is at play in criminal
trials. The absence of such a sense of shame, of the recognition of the responsibility of a community, is one of the things that struck Hannah
Arendt during her 1950 visit to Germany.[103] It also, one suspects, lies behind the critical reaction to President Mitterrand's reluctance in 1992 to
acknowledge any French co-responsibility for the deportation of Jews
from France during World War II.

   For our purposes, shame and guilt differ, as do the kinds of responsibility conferred by membership in a community versus individual authorship; by the unity of a community's (or person's) existence across time
versus the discreteness of the actionable deed; by shame's enduringness
as opposed to the closure that legal action and the punishment of the

guilty provide. Trials and retribution, no matter how thoroughgoing they are in the prosecution of those accused of crimes, in doing their part of the work of memory-justice, do not bear witness to that recognition of broad and enduring responsibility, the "tectonic plates" of a community's life-in-common over time. Not only can a trial not attain to that wider form of responsibility, but it also (and therefore) offers another type of premature closure as well: as if by seeing the guilty leaders punished, we have freed ourselves of the burden of responsibility for these crimes. As I suggested earlier, this may partially explain why the legacy of World War II lives on and disturbs Europe, even where there were trials and purges of those most directly accountable. What motivates that sense of incompleteness is not principally that there are Nazis, collaborators, or dictators still unpunished but rather that legal action weaves the past into the national biography, into the memory of a community, in only a limited way.

(b) We saw earlier that a second (and related) way for the memory-justice of law to secure the past is through truth-telling, saving the deeds, victims, and perpetrators from the darkness of oblivion and falsehood. But the truth and memory of the witness, and of the collective memory of the community that it informs, may only partially overlap with the truth sought in legal or quasi-legal proceedings.[104] Some of this difference is suggested to us in Germaine Tillion's remarks on the postwar trial of her former Ravensbrück persecutors, where she writes about the distance between her experience of the camp and the descriptions she heard during the course of the trial.[105] Similarly, viewers of Lanzmann's *Shoah* will readily discern the differences between the testimony/memory of witnesses and the voice of the sole historian to appear in the film, Raul Hilberg. As Tillion herself observed, part of this is the difference between first-person memory and the transmitted, objectified past of the courtroom or the historian. At one level, of course, we can describe these differences in terms of the intimacy of the remembered event for the (first-person) witness, and therefore likely also its emotion-laden presence in his or her life. (In *Shoah*, Lanzmann had to wrest the words from some of his witnesses.) Some might also suspect such memory of being partial and not always accurate. The memory-truth of the courtroom is an act of witnessing and fidelity, of bearing the truth about the past and saving it from the oblivion of forgetting, and so of doing justice. Yet it also aspires to a certain detachment, and its drive for truth is directed by the desire to assign guilt.

But the differences are more than those expressed in the opposition of intimacy over against detached objectivity. There are two related dimensions that are of special importance. I have already remarked that an essential part of witnessing is the keeping of the victims in the light of truth.

The bearing of truth-memory is, in this sense, an act of fidelity, and typically fidelity (or its opposite, forgetfulness as infidelity) to members of one's own community who have been lost. Memory-truth is not a gesture of fidelity to just anyone. Rather, it is a faithfulness in the context of a community: a marriage, a religion, or a political life-in-common. The truth of remembrance differs, then, from the truth of history in that its core is fidelity (here to the victim), a fidelity that occurs within the context of a shared something, a life-in-common across generations. Doing justice straddles both.[106] Remembrance not only takes place within the context of a community and its relations of fidelity, but also serves to reintegrate the victims into their community, to restore that community and ensure its survival after the rupture induced by crime. Bearing witness as an act of faithfulness, of obligation to the lost, and the (re)integration of the community are two sides of the same phenomenon. This obligation to the absent, as I said, is not to the handful of dust that the dead have become, nor necessarily to any religious conception of their endurance, but to the living members of our community that they once were. As Patrick Baudry writes, the living "transform their previously established relationships, the ties that bound them to their [dead], by sheltering them from forgetting."[107]

That latter face of memory-truth further distinguishes it from what is sought in the courtroom. Here memory serves not so much to establish that such-and-such took place, that x was its perpetrator and y its victim, but rather to give a voice to those rendered silent and absent, to reintegrate the lost into the unity of the community, and to reincorporate them into its justice. In this role, memory-justice-truth is the ingathering of the past in fulfillment of an obligation to the dead and for the sake of the continuity of the community across time. What is sought is not a (historical) explanation or a (legal) determination of responsibility, so much as to do right by the absent and to restore the unity of a broken community.[108] The truth here is the truth of that obligation and the unity or identity in which it is embedded. Memory's truth, as it appears in such contexts, is tied to the obligations incurred in a life-in-common across time. This is to suggest that memory-justice and memory-identity are deeply intertwined. The ingathering of the past of justice and injustice is part of both doing justice and affirming the continuity or identity (or rupture and new identity) of a community. The witness fulfills an obligation to the absent of her community, protests against the effacement of their past, and in so doing affirms the continuity of the community and its core identity.[109]

When bearing witness as the labor of a broad memory-justice enters the courtroom, the locale of doing justice in a narrower judicial sense, we can see memory and justice at work in both registers, the legal and that of the memory-justice of a community, and observe their overlapping but differentiated characters, and their sometimes conflictual relationship. Some of this overlap and tension was apparent in the Eichmann trial, where the prosecutor, Gideon Hausner, took on the role of a protector of memory and of the victims' voices against the strictures of the trial form, saying that by his side in the courtroom were the "six million accusers. . . . Their blood cries out, but their voice is not heard. Therefore I will be their spokesman and in their name I will unfold the awesome indictment."[110] Witnessing here was not attesting to facts directly relevant to the trial. Rather it was the bearing the voices of the lost, carrying them to the community in the present. Consider, in a similar vein, the trial of Klaus Barbie, former head of the SS in Lyon. In one way, the arrest of Barbie and the testimony against him belonged foursquare to the world of law. But when Serge Klarsfeld, in his testimony, read out the names, ages, and some of the correspondence of the Jewish children of Izieu, deported (under Barbie's command) to Auschwitz and murdered there, he went beyond a legal presentation of evidence. His words about the children of Izieu were of course, in part, evidence of one of the most tragic of Barbie's wartime crimes in France. Yet its substance was not, Klarsfeld said, a lawyer's speech, that is, directed to the verification of facts and determination of culpability, but an "introduction." "It seemed important to me to have all these children enter into the court," he said. In his address to the court, Klarsfeld described the proceeding as an act of justice bound up with an act of memory, and said that the purpose is "as much to remember, in actions, as it is to deny a pleasant old age to the executioner of the children of Izieu." It was to introduce and name these children, lest "the winds of forgetting extinguish the names." Claude Lanzmann captured this facet of Klarsfeld's speech to the court: "It was the act of naming. He restored their proper name to each child of Izieu."[111]

The naming of the victims, so that they will not be lost to this oblivion of forgetting, is at the heart of memory-justice fulfilling its obligation to the dead. "After April 23, 1945," wrote Tillion, referring to the date of her liberation from Ravensbrück, "I used this vast assembly of memories [in the recovery camp] to gather that which they retained about all those whom we had lost. At least their names, their only sepulchers."[112] The act of naming is the "most archaic and simplest form of commemoration."[113] We have seen the importance of the name in a number of contexts. Here are two principal reasons for this, evident in Klarsfeld's words. (1) It individuates the person and is part of his permanence. To take away his name, to erase its presence in the world, is to de-individuate him and to destroy his continuity and ties. In Ellison's *Invisible Man*, the radicalness of the dispossession suffered by African Americans is signaled to us by the namelessness of its narrator. And so to restore the name to a person is to return to him a part of the unity of his life that was taken from him by the crime. (2) But a name is also a social fact: to be sure, it individuates us, but at the same time it points to our family lineage; it conveys who we are to others and is a marker of our place in a community. Witnessing as naming is an act, done in public, here a courtroom but also through war memorials, grave markers, and other such locales. This act is the making present of the absent in their individuality and as members of the group to which the testimony is given. It is a way of restoring a lost individuality to the person and of bringing her back, via the trace of her name, to her community and in so doing restoring a kind of imperfect wholeness to it.[114] One of the design proposals for the World Trade Center memorial captured this dimension of naming: "On glass and stone, the names are revealed. Here, as stories are shared, they become part of our collective. A final resting place for the unidentified remains embraces a private area for family members and loved ones. This space, at bedrock, becomes the most sacred."[115] And remembering the names in public is also, as the passage quoted from Tillion's *Ravensbrück* suggests, a sepulcher for those who have none. Arno Klarsfeld described his father's work as bringing the innocent dead into the light of day, restoring their civil status and dignity, in short making them human beings and citizens again.[116]

"It seemed important to me to have all these children enter into the court": to make the dead present. Klarsfeld's language here draws on another important dimension of memory-justice apparent in both the classical world, in, for example, the dead Clytemnestra's appearance in the *Eumenides,* and in the modern, as when Malraux addresses Jean Moulin in the present tense as his ashes are interred in the Panthéon. Memory-justice in this role collapses the distance between past and present. It is an "incarnation"; "language is the *only resurrection* for that which has disappeared"; "in a few words to make alive again . . . these martyrs."[117] The victims are restored, if only in memory and speech, to their place in the community. And the living of that community are reminded of their continuity with the past: "Remembrance is the proof itself of filiation," writes Rachel Ertel, or in the words of the Guatemalan *Nunca Más* report, they are given "a memory of solidarity."[118] Naming and incarnation: just to characterize Klarsfeld's words in this way is to make plain a second register at work in them. The memory work being done in his speech has less to do with demonstrating Barbie's guilt than with the observance of a commitment to the victims, and an evocation of their presence that affirms the community's identity across time, and even through such violent traumas. Consider this observation of Halbwachs's: "The dead retreat into the past . . . because there remains nothing of the group in which they lived . . . and their names little by little are forgotten."[119] A community that endures as a community preserves these ties and does not forget the names of its dead. Only the absence of a community could explain such a disappearance into the forgotten past. At the same time, however, the court was not merely a platform for a speech entirely foreign to its purposes. It is not a trivial fact that this speech was delivered in a court of law, for Klarsfeld's courtroom gesture speaks to the proximity of memory-justice in its capacity as law and as bound up with bearing witness and identity. Through remembrance, both do the work of restoring the absent victim and repairing justice undone. The Barbie trial, Finkielkraut writes, was an attempt to wrest that past from the "shroud" of history, of the past perfect, by drawing his crimes (via the memory of justice and injustice) into the "judicial present."[120] Klarsfeld's speech belongs to that attempt. In its naming and its restoring of the dead to their community (and of the living community to its own past), however, it is among the other tasks of memory-justice. It is therefore at once evidence, a part of a judicial exercise of ascertaining an individual's responsibility, the carrying out of a debt, the bringing into the light of truth, and the assertion of a community's identity through time.

Allow me, finally, to turn to some of these overlapping and conflicting dimensions of memory work and doing justice, drawing now on the story of the 1997 trial of Maurice Papon. This trial was part of what has been called the second wave of Vichy-related purges in France, of legal actions against officials of that regime. It took place against the background of the troubled place of Vichy in modern French history, of the fraying of the Gaullist story of one nation in arms against the German occupier, with the dark years of Vichy as a mere parenthesis, of the role of Frenchmen in the deportation of Jews from France to Nazi concentration camps, and of President Georges Pompidou's granting of a pardon to Paul Touvier. Important too in the story of this trial was the emergence in the years preceding it of memory militants determined to dispel what they saw as the national amnesia that enveloped France's role in the persecution of some of its own citizens (and resident aliens), especially the Jewish minority. As I remarked earlier, acts of remembrance require actors, people who have contexts, interests, conflicts, and so on. The background to the Papon trial shows the importance of the politics of memory, of power, contest, silence, and voice. Yet however useful the power politics approach in explaining the dynamics of an event such as this one, we need (as I said before) something else to understand why memory was the contested good here and why it was contested in a court of law. For that we need to see doing justice as memory/identity work of a particular sort.

To begin this sketch, really a coda to the preceding analysis, we might observe that the Papon trial took place a full fifty-three years after the events it was concerned with. The trial, in a sense, annihilated that distance and with it the "regularization" that the passage of time seemed to have won for Papon.[121] But was this even a trial of Papon? Or was he a proxy for the Vichy regime, or for the complacency of the French about their own role in the persecutions carried out during the dark years? Was the trial a stage on which to end the silence of the victims? The trial was in fact enmeshed in all of these, and its didactic and memorial aspects rested uneasily with the norms of a legal memory, for which the only relevant issue was Papon's culpability or innocence.[122] Perhaps the clearest expression of the uneasy co-presence of the manifold faces of memory-justice can be seen in some of the acts of bearing witness that occurred during the trial. Witnessing, normally a device for helping to ascertain facts, became something quite different here. The names of Jews deported from Bordeaux were read out by witnesses in the court (and outside the courthouse as well). Photographs of the dead were exhibited, in Arno Klarsfeld's words, "as if these names wanted to show one more time the face that was theirs." One witness requested that a photograph of her murdered parents be displayed, saying that she expected the trial to become a sepulcher for them. When another witness asked to read to the court the names of members of a convoy of deportees, the judge answered that the court was not a "monument to the dead."[123]

The judge's response to this sort of bearing witness was echoed in the observations of some commentators. Antoine Garapon referred to justice becoming here an auxiliary to memory, and Éric Conan remarked on what he saw as the contempt of memory activists for legal justice and its rules. For Conan, the appeal to justice of some of these witnesses and of memory militants such as the Klarsfelds stood in manifest contradiction to their use of the courtroom for memorial and didactic purposes remote from the doing of legal justice.[124] These observations, I think, are both correct and incorrect. The use of a court proceeding (primarily) to put an epoch, or current indifference and amnesia, on trial is likely at odds with the norms of justice in a liberal society. Less menacing, perhaps, but equally at odds with the strictures of the legal forum is the use of the court as a locale for bearing witness in a memorial/identity way. Arno Klarsfeld, at the trial of Papon, spoke of conviction as important for the memory of the children and other victims whose murder Papon had a hand in, for the collective memory of France, and for the present and future.[125] Doing justice is itself a kind of memory work, and the intrusion into it of other dimensions of memory-justice is the entry not of something foreign but rather of a kindred practice. Doing justice to the absent seems to demand more than its legal expression can provide, and thus out of their shared enterprise but different horizons (different moral regimes of time and memory) we see both why the court was sought for this bearing of witness and why the latter exceeded the boundaries of that institutional setting.

The memory of justice works in a number of ways. Within the orbit of law, it can have the face of retribution and punishment, of exposure and truth-telling, or of public amnesia (amnesty). Varied (and overlapping) too are the imperatives driving these phenomena: to fulfill a debt to the dead by punishing the perpetrators; to preserve justice and the truth of things; to save the dead from the second death of forgetting. All of these, in their different ways, display the intimate yet conflictual bond between memory and justice. At the same time, they point to the limits of law's reach. For memory-justice demands more than a court or truth commission can provide. Freed from the constraints of determining individual guilt, memory-justice finds the conviction of only the direct perpetrators and/or their political masters to be too narrow an understanding of co-responsibility in an enduring (identical) community. Concerned lest trials draw so thick and final a concluding line between past and present that we are thereafter absolved of the work of remembrance, memory-justice refuses to let the trial seal the well of memory, to let this past become simply the historical past, the past perfect. And finally, looking for the truth about the past not for its evidentiary or explanatory value, memory-justice seeks instead to make the past present, to bring the lost back into our midst, and in so doing to do justice to the dead and to affirm the reality and enduringness of the community we share with them. The demand for a recognition of wide co-responsibility across generations, of shame; for the imprescriptible character of these sorts of crimes, with the result that condemnation does not end with the conviction of one or many perpetrators; for memory-justice as the core of identity across time and even through the most radical ruptures in a community's life: these faces of memory-justice mark out the limits of a legal overcoming of the past.

4.3. THE FORGETTING OF JUSTICE

Where there is a radical deficiency of memory and commemoration, or of doing justice, there is also, in Herbert's phrase, an "ignorance about the disappeared / [that] undermines the reality of the world," a void, something incomplete, that seems almost to demand correction. "The pyramid of martyrs obsesses the earth."[126] Consider the breach left by the largely uncommemorated victims and crimes (absent, but still a lingering presence) of the Soviet era. To be sure, the torments of the former Soviet Union have had their great literary chroniclers and witnesses: Aleksandr Solzhenitsyn, Anna Akhmatova, and Vassili Grossman, for example. But, as Anne Applebaum observes, post-Soviet Russia has seen little public recognition or memorialization of the millions of victims of the Gulag and other instruments of state-led terror, much less any thorough doing of justice through trials or truth commissions.[127] And that silence is more than an emptiness; it is a gap in the moral architecture of the world, an incompleteness of justice. It is also a demand: bearing witness responds to the moral/political imperative, "Do not forget!"[128]

From that perspective, forgetting seems at first glance to be little more than a default on our ethical duties. I have set out this failure in a variety of contexts. (1) The preserving of truth, especially the truth about crime and injustice. If truth is *alētheia*, the unforgotten, then it would appear that what is forgotten is a deficit in the domain of truth and particularly of truth/justice. (2) Forgetting is a rupture in the continuity and hence the identity of the community, in the bonds that, stretched across time, give it its life-in-common and create debts and responsibilities that extend beyond the present. (3) To forget the victims of injustice is to deny them (and justice too) their due recognition, and to consign them to the "waters of death" of a forgetful oblivion.[129] Because memory, justice, and political identity are so intimately related, the issue of remembrance becomes one with the sense of who we are as members of a political community, including our shared perception of justice. The invocation of the duties of remembrance involves a person whose fate, whether oblivion or a second life in the memory of his fellow citizens, is in the community's hands to decide. By contrast, forgetting seems to disrupt the continuity of identity and debt that is the fabric woven of collective memory. It is a forgetting typically of past injustices and strife, and so a forgetting of what we are as a body-accountable. It frees the community of the debts it owes the past, to the individuals who form those earlier moments of what it is as a civic body. Forgetting, then, can be seen as a flight from responsibility, from the weight of memory and its duties, or, as Plato says in the *Republic* (621a), a sort of respite by the "river of no cares [or forgetfulness]." Remembrance, we might therefore conclude, occupies a privileged ethical position in relation to forgetting.

Just as memory work required a defense because of its nurturing of a passion for revenge and retribution, so too forgetting stands in need of an apology, of a defense before the seemingly overwhelming demands of memory, witnesses, and their presumptive virtue.[130] Although I doubt that the case for forgetting can be defended in an unqualified manner, I do want to look at the claims made on its behalf: that far from being a mere tactical expedient, supported on instrumental grounds alone, it has rather its own moral justificatory language. That we can, in short, speak of a duty to forget, to heal ourselves, and to allow a rebirth or a strengthening of our civic ties. Let me begin this defense of forgetting with Cicero. He tells us that a learned man once offered Themistocles, an Athenian "endowed with wisdom and genius on a scale surpassing belief," a science that would allow him to remember everything. "Themistocles replied that he would be doing him a greater kindness if he taught him to forget what he wanted than if he taught him to remember."[131] But what sort of kindness or good would this be? One kind is therapeutic. Forgetting can sometimes be a necessary therapy, a way to minimize the aftershocks of trauma. Jorge Semprún, who emerged alive from Buchenwald in 1945, tells us that memory was deadly for him and that consequently "I chose forgetting. I put in place, without too much concern for the good of my own identity . . . the strategy of voluntary amnesia, cruelly systematic."[132] He gave up his vocation as a writer, and the "adventure of witnessing," so that he might live. Giving a voice to the past would have resulted in his death. Only by a willful forgetting could he prevent the past from becoming, in Nietzsche's words, the "gravedigger" of the present. Resentment "nails each of us firmly to the cross of our destroyed past."[133]

In the ancient view, *Mnēmosynē*, memory, is also the healer who allows us to forget our ills.[134] I spoke earlier about a French soldier of the First World War, Anthelme Mangin, who survived, but with a total loss of memory. One might say that his amnesia spared him the all-absorbing, nightmarish memories of those who, like Louis Aragon or Jean Giono, retained their recollections of the war years and, frozen in that moment, lived in it for their remaining time. Giono writes: "I cannot forget the war. I would like to. . . . [T]wenty years have passed . . . and I have not cleansed myself of the war. . . . I bear [its] mark. All survivors bear [its] mark."[135] Forgetting permits us to live in the present, and to be open to the future; resentment, however, is without future. It is the permanent past. Memory, in the absence of this salve, can chain us to the past, and, where it is memory of crime or injustice, to bitterness and resentment: the man of ressentiment, Nietzsche says, knows "how not to forget."[136] We can see this clearly in the case of Electra and Orestes. They are the embodiment of memory-justice. Precisely because of that they are bound hand and foot to the past. They are not creatures of the present and future, and the "iron tracks" of their absorption in the past bar them from those human times and their associated joys. Broadly speaking, this is the familiar view that a surfeit of memory is destructive of life. Remembrance draws us to what is dead and to the irreversible. It is nostalgia, bitterness, or the thirst for revenge. All of these dwell in what is beyond human agency to modify; all irrationally resist the becoming of time. Worse, all therefore sacrifice the present and future for the sake of the past. Perhaps forgetting, the letting go of the past, is a necessary adaptation to the present and something essential to life, to the possibility of "new things."[137]

I have suggested that bearing witness is often an obstinate act of resistance: against the corrosive effects of the passage of time, the frailty of human remembrance, and the always present desire to be done with the past. But there is another, very different kind of resistance rooted in part in what I have just discussed; one that, as Nietzsche reminds us, struggles in the opposite direction, against the weight of the remembered past. Resistance to bearing witness sometimes comes from the witnesses, who want to divest themselves of a tormenting past. Being a witness can be extraordinarily hard: because of the trauma and because there may be a reluctance to be marked as a witness, as a bearer of that particular past, to being made to carry that status as one's identity.[138] In its *Final Report*, the South African Truth and Reconciliation Commission stated that "many . . . were able to reach towards healing by telling the painful stories of their past." The report added, however, that "not all storytelling heals. Not everyone wanted to tell his or her story."[139] Many times, those who know of these traces of the past, and who can bring them to light, want to rid themselves of the burden of the past so as to be able to live in the present and future.

I remarked earlier that in acts of bearing witness, the role of others is central. They are the ones who receive the (often burdensome) gifts of memory; they are often the ones implicitly (or explicitly) accused, and always those who are called upon to believe what is brought to them in testimony. Perec, in his essay on Robert Antelme, writes of the difficulties and failures in communicating the reality of the concentration camps encountered by those returning from them to bear witness, difficulties not all internal to those who had suffered injustice and wanted to testify to it.[140] Those to whom these remembrances are offered may themselves be a less than welcoming audience, and thus the apparent absence of witnessing may be (to paraphrase the title of an article by Annette Wieviorka on this issue in France) more the result of its being inaudible than unspeakable. Clearly one reason for resistance to the bearers of memory is that what they bring back is a past that inculpates the community, or substantial parts of it, or causes them to feel shame. In a short story titled "The Spoilsport," Siegfried Lenz describes a man who forgets nothing, neither his own past nor that of others. He quickly becomes unpopular because of this extraordinary memory. People want to forget, Lenz writes, and would prefer not to spend their lives before a mirror.[141] Perhaps something like this accounts for the preference for forgetfulness that greeted concentration camp survivors upon their return to France.[142] It may also help us to understand the hostile response in the 1970s to such films as *The Sorrow and the Pity,* which called attention to Vichy, collaboration, and anti-Semitism in France. Witnesses can be living reminders, bearers of a past that they make present through their testimony, and as such act as mirrors, reminding others of their flaws or worse.

The passage of time might also be said to stiffen resistance to witnessing. This is so, I think, because of the (almost Parfitian) sense, discussed earlier, in which the changes brought about in the passage of time are seen as effectively rendering the body politic a different self, one entitled therefore to a distance from the deeds of earlier generations. Just as, in the Parfitian account of different selves over time, time ought to end pains and old quarrels because one is no longer the same person, so too in the life of a political community the years might be expected to bring a different self, an absolution, and a forgetting (as, for example, in the case of the German firm Degussa, mentioned earlier). It is that expectation which is challenged by the persistence of the witness, a challenge (often) resented by contemporaries. This calls attention to still another facet of witnessing, one that presumably becomes more pronounced and visible with the passage of time: the witnesses' absorption in the past, and their determination to force it into the present. The thought that there is no consigning of deeds to a historical past, to the closure of "what happened, happened," but only a testifying to them, a making present of them, seems to make the witness into the "gravedigger" of the present. Consider Henri Raczymow's description of Esther, who, though born after World War II, never left it and lived out her life in the borrowed memory horizon of wartime Warsaw. It was necessary, he writes, to "turn the page," to abandon Esther and the war to which she bore witness. Bearing witness to the past, refusing the cup of forgetting, making oneself the instrument of the iron compulsion to justice and vengeance: all this seems too much, too destructive of present and future, the locales of hope, of the possible, and of human action.[143] Perhaps bearing witness as the commitment to doing justice to the past is more than can be expected of individuals or political communities. And thus the obstinacy of the witness, the resistance to becoming and to turning the page, appears deeply destructive, the "iron tracks," an obsession. The wish to forget can also be motivated by the suspicion that remembrance is not only obsessional but also in a way useless: that the iron tracks never arrive at a terminus but only mark out a bitter and endless path. The challenge that awaits the memory of bearing witness, or of remorse, regret, or nostalgia, is that time is irreversible and hence nothing can be undone, not even by recalling it into the present.[144] Memory's making present is thus always radically incomplete and so a "jaded idling," a "useless passion," an anachronism. Its very orientation to an irretrievable past and its limited capacity to restore give memory its particular jaded aura, but unlike its kindred forms of nostalgia and regret, the character of bearing witness is more bitter than sweet, and so more likely to be met with the resistance of forgetting.

Forgetting is also sustained by a set of political justifications. In the classical Greek world, we can, I think, find one of the more thoughtful cases for Renan's position (as Raymond Aron reads him) that forgetting is among the principal virtues needed for politics.[145] There, memory and forgetting were a pair. Forgetting is portrayed by Hesiod as one of the Daughters of the Night, and her powers are by no means simply those of an unjust forgetting. *Lēthē* is, of course, the forgetting of the past, and the "waters of death," but it is also the therapy by which we free ourselves from our ills. It is a *pharmakon*, the remedy that quiets pain and brings calm and peace, the drug that Helen puts in the wine so as to wash away the memories of Odysseus and of his absence. But the *Odyssey* also sets out the politically curative power of forgetting. After Odysseus has returned to Ithaka and slain Penelope's suitors, Zeus calls on Athena to urge the combatants to forget the bloodshed and live as friends.[146] Perhaps this beneficent forgetting is possible only once justice has been done. Still, the radicalness of it is striking: the relatives of the dead are to forget their kin, to consign them to the second death of forgetfulness. What could possibly justify such a neglect? Homer's answer here, which is a response to Athena's query as to whether Zeus intends to inflict faction and strife on the parties, is that only through forgetting will peace come to Ithaka. The obligation with respect to the dead is put aside; the soil is allowed to conceal their blood so that it will not be repaid by still more violence. Forgetting for peace, remembering for strife: forgetfulness is necessary for peace, just as the memory of death was necessary, in the *Iliad*, for Achilles' combat. Avenging Patroklos, doing justice to him, requires memory; but when the time comes for the bloodshed and strife to end, Zeus ordains that the living shall forget their dead.[147]

Forgetting, memory, and justice, then, stand in an uncertain and perplexing relationship. To do justice is to remember, to preserve and guard in memory the injury, the victim, and the perpetrator. Yet peace and a life-in-common, the foundation of a civic community, make their claims on us, one of which is that we allow the forgetting of past evils. For Zeus to have the families of the dead forget is to interrupt the relations of justice between living and dead, and it is also in a way to erase the truth, the *alētheia* (the unforgotten quality) of that past, to put it in the "shadow of forgetting" rather than the light of disclosure. At the same time, it is the core of another good: the openness to a future in common. Still, forgetting for the sake of peace is embedded in an overarching story of remembrance that opens with an appeal to the Muse, and is woven of Odysseus' memory of his household, his *oikos*, and of his resistance to the forgetting offered in the world of the lotus-eaters. Memory and forgetting both make claims on us. The poet, the Muse, and Odysseus' own recollection of his native Ithaka do memory work, but not without reminding us that forgetting is sometimes a good.

Forgetfulness then is the remedy for the bitter strife induced by too much memory. In Aeschylus' *Eumenides* the confrontation between the needs of the present and the demands of the past is also made political. Here the Furies, awakened by the murdered Clytemnestra, pursue Orestes. Their desire for vengeance is taken up in an Athenian court, where Orestes is, with Athena's help, acquitted. And the Furies themselves are tamed, renouncing vengeful slaughter as contrary to the interests of the city. Vengeance, and the memory that is its tinder, are shown in a way to be unpolitical. Not defeated, Athena reassures them, but honored in their new role as the spirit of blessings, the insistent voices of the past and of revenge have been put aside by the city which will henceforth legislate over them, if not a forgetting, then at least a setting aside of the crimes.[148] Nor was this erasure of the past the work of the theater alone, for democratic Athens itself commanded the forgetting of some of the deeds of the Thirty. This is a civic forgetting, one intended to preserve the community against the present ills of strife. It is the antidote to the aching desire for vengeance, a desire that afflicts both individuals and cities. Forgetting is, however, more than a therapeutic balm for a spirit seething with resentment: for what it expunges is not merely a psychological state but the presence and the reality of the past, the persistence of injury, and so the possibility of doing justice. The Furies in Aeschylus' *Eumenides* are not placeholders for Orestes' distress, nor for Athens's discomfiture over its turmoil, but rather they are the past and its claims to justice operative in the present. And that is what gives this reflection on forgetting its poignant dimension: it is a putting aside or moderating of the needs of justice and debt.

Forgetting for the sake of peace and of a political life-in-common is what is at issue here. Renan instructs us in the value of forgetting when he says that citizens have much to remember, and much to forget.[149] The citizens of France, he writes, should forget the Saint Bartholomew's Day massacre. Such memories can only divide the body politic. Years after Renan's essay, de Gaulle showed just how useful such a forgetting could be, as he reduced the Vichy period to a mere parenthesis and shrouded the France of collaboration and apathy under the story of one nation in resistance to the Occupation. This public forgetting, he understood, was necessary to put an end to the civil strife threatening France at the end of the war, and to the bitter desire for vengeance against the occupier's French allies. So too in Latin America, Spain, and eastern Europe, arguments for forgetting and amnesty in the wake of democratization have been powerful forces.[150] Forgetting is called upon in order to shield the community from divisive conflicts over the past.

It also serves another purpose central to a life-in-common: the forgetting of difference. The citizens of Plato's *Republic* (414d) bathed in these waters, but such amnesia would seem especially important in a liberal democratic polity, where justice is in part the openness and equality of a diverse community of citizens. Memory, individual or collective (the idea of the historical community, the community of memory), is deeply particularistic. It confers a sense of "mineness," that we are bounded subjects constituted by these memories. Human beings, Vladimir Jankélévitch writes, distinguish themselves from one another more by their pasts and memories than by their aspirations for the future.[151] Not only is memory-identity profoundly at odds with universalism or indeed any kind of impersonal vantage point, but also it tends to invoke autochthonous modes of belonging over the long duration, often grounding itself in the memory markers of shared ethnicity, language, or religion. In short, it defines the we-group by sharp and near-to-impermeable boundary lines, and thereby cultivates a foundation for particularism and self-preference, and often draws on attributes other than political ones in establishing that identity.[152] A form of political life that rejects such a notion of identity and in its stead establishes a set of (roughly) universal-democratic norms must institute a type of forgetting (or a counter-memory), at least for its public space. The critique of a memory-based politics, and the "duty to forget," dethrone memory, as Todorov writes, "not in the interests of forget-ting . . . but of certain universal principles and the 'general will.' "[153] So as a public matter, then, we forget this memory-identity: all are citizens, and endowed with identical rights by virtue of that citizenship. The *longue durée* does not figure here, or at most it is a cultural residue.

This cleansing of the public domain of the (identity) claims of memory and the long duration is perhaps most evident in social contract theories. Consider Locke's use of the idea of a state of nature and of membership by consent, tacit or express. The unit of consent is the person understood as a bearer of rights. In the mutual political engagements of such persons, the only relevant criteria are the active consent of citizens or the tacit con-sent given by those who enjoy the fruits of the community.[154] Seen from that standpoint, the weight of the past, a strong memory-identity, is not germane: sharing in a long-rooted collective memory does not trump the common status of rights-bearers and so it does not figure in Locke's ac-count. Not only does it not figure, but Locke can be read as supplanting it with an egalitarian, rights-based, and non-particularistic counter-memory.[155] Contemporary social contract theory is of a piece with this. Robert Nozick, for example, sets out a historical account of justice. But for him the relevant history is not that of the thick memory of a commu-nity. Rather, it is justice in a linked series of transactions. Rawls's veil of ig-norance is in part a way of ensuring a forgetting of those particularizing roots that would distort the creation of a framework of justice. Striking, too, is that even in the non-contraction literature of liberal modernity, the regulative principles governing the public sphere are cast so as to achieve a level of forgetting. Thus Bruce Ackerman's *Justice in the Liberal State* looks at membership in terms of a dialogical competence in which the claims of particularity and memory-identity are rendered moot.[156] Or con-sider again Habermas's idea of a constitutional patriotism. Here attach-ment is defined strictly in terms of adherence to a set of public norms, broadly universal-democratic in character. The burdens of the past, of the long roots of memory, are here put to one side, made a cultural tradition, and denied a place in the norms of governance and in the civic dimen-sions of a life-in-common.

At the risk of some smudging of the edges between these varied classes of arguments, we might say that they have in common a lessening of the weight of the past and of memory, and the refashioning of citizenship into a condition where the possession of the past is (mostly) irrelevant. This political forgetting is meant to allow for an identity that nurtures im-partiality, a neutrality as between citizens, a condition in which the only relevant fact about their status is that of their shared citizenship. Such a forgetting attaches citizens to their political belonging and gives them a common status. At the same time, it defines the boundaries of the community in porous and political terms, thereby making them consistent with its (in principle) universal-democratic values. A related achievement of this forgetting is that it makes possible an accommodation between membership and diversity. The conflicting memories of various groups and the reflex of self-preference of the "founding peoples" here give way (as in Lincoln's 1858 speech) to a common political memory, that of the regime, its construction, constitution, and values. On the one hand, it rejects the idea that a community is, as Stuart Hampshire says, "in the grip of particular and distinguishing memories and of particular and distinguishing local passions" and that its political identity must therefore include a common history and memory, a "community of recollections," as John Stuart Mill called it, a partnership with the dead and the yet-to-be born.[157] A community, on the other hand, that for public purposes has let go of these memories would seem to be able to achieve the equality and openness of the liberal or constitutional-patriotic regime.

I now want to turn to the issue of amnesty, one particularly salient intersection of the claims of justice and civic forgetting. Recall René Char's remark that the dead martyrs obsess the earth. We have seen the sometimes obsessional character of the pursuit of justice. Justice and retribution, I have said, stand in an uneasy relationship with other comportments, even virtues, that seek to moderate or season memory-justice. Pardon, mercy, and forgiveness are three of these, and all calm vengeful memory without the need for forgetting. The first two lessen or annul the (justly deserved) punishment; the third changes our attitude, how we feel, about the perpetrator.[158] Pardon and mercy belong to the doing of justice; forgiveness is subjective, and sometimes a matter of faith. It is the overcoming, on moral grounds, of resentment, and it is especially important in allowing human relations to continue that otherwise would be disrupted.[159] In that light, my earlier reading of Susan Wolf's observation that relationships take time could be amended so as to say that not only is remembered time vital to them but the forgotten hours of conflict and division as well. Because of its restorative power, forgiveness is a virtue, even (in Archbishop Tutu's phrase) a "civic sacrament," often advocated in times of regime transition. "True forgiveness deals with the past . . . to make the future possible."[160] Yet there is a tension in the relationship of pardon, mercy, and forgiveness to justice, a tension that comes from the fact that though all are counted virtues, the work that forgiveness, pardon, and mercy strive to do is to lessen or moderate the full measure of the rightful claims of justice.[161] Although neither pardon nor forgiveness directly involves forgetting, and indeed in a crucial way both depend precisely on the memory of the crime, they accomplish something quite similar to the work of forgetting, namely, loosening the bitter grasp of memory which holds the event in a permanent present.[162] Some such concern may have motivated this comment by the daughter of a Polish officer murdered by Soviet officials during the 1940 Katyn massacre: "We must not pardon, we cannot forget. In my opinion, hatred sustains memory. . . . On the other hand, a pardon does not settle anything. If we pardon, the whole matter will be forgotten."[163]

Forgiveness and clemency, then, stay the severity of justice's sword but are only indirectly related to the temporal dimension of doing justice as the work of memory.[164] Amnesty is another uneasy way in which justice may be seasoned, one that shares much in common with forgiveness and clemency but that is more explicitly bound up with (and in opposition to) the moral "inversion of time" that is the task of memory-justice. I wrote earlier that keeping deeds and persons in memory is in one sense an elective matter, indeed almost a matter of resistance against the natural course of things, of fighting against the corrosive quality of the passage of time and of our concernful preoccupation with the future. We are called upon (in classical tragedy) to reflect on what it would mean for children to forget the murder of their father, to live untroubled in the presence of his killers and their unanswered crime, as if no injustice had been done. That would be to undermine the "[just] reality of the world." Antagonistically related to this retrospective glance of memory-justice and its efforts to ensure the persistence of the memory of the wrong is an attempt to overcome the hold of the unforgotten, of remembrance, on us. This is a rejection of memory, and being grounded in that refusal, intimately connected to the object of its refusal. Let me begin, as before, with a classical account of this. We saw that after Odysseus has killed Penelope's suitors, Zeus tells Athena, "Let us make them forget the death of their brothers and sons, and let them be friends with each other, as in the time past, and let them have prosperity and peace in abundance."[165] Forgetting (a sort of amnesty) is here the precondition not of individual well-being (as in Semprún's account), but of a return to peace. So too in the *Eumenides*, when Orestes is acquitted and Clytemnestra's Furies, anxious for revenge against her son and killer Orestes, rage against the great dishonor and ills that they feel they have received at the hands of Athena and the jury.[166] Athena, in what Pierre Vidal-Naquet calls the West's first argument for a statute of limitations, persuades the Furies (who are motivated both by anger over the acquittal and by shame at being bested) to lay down their threat to inflict strife and death on the city.[167] The putting aside or forgetting of past crimes for the sake of peace and civic unity was not just a device of ancient epic and tragedy. As part of the Athenian reconciliation agreement of 403–402 BC which restored democracy after the dictatorship of the Thirty, an amnesty was proclaimed, "not to remember evil [*mē mnēsikakein*]," here the evils of the Thirty.[168] It was clear that civic peace could not be restored without a public forgetting. Memory-justice as retribution divides and poisons; it impedes renewal. It would seem therefore that, as the Athenian democrats recognized, forgetting is an essential part of politics because it is an ally of peace and unity, just as the Furies, vengeance, and memory-justice are antithetical to it.[169]

Amnesty is, as Carl Schmitt puts it, a "mutual forgetting" that effectively precludes the evocation of the perpetrators' deeds.[170] Because it effects a rupture with the past (locale of injury; source of the desire for revenge), political-judicial forgetting can be seen as a therapy for the desire for revenge and through that as an instrument of peace. It seeks to draw a thick line between past and present, and to debar memory-justice "from keeping . . . [the] Wounds greene," from forcing the present to drink from the bitter, polluted cup of the past, in brief, from sacrificing renewal to revenge. For the authors of the Athenian reconciliation agreement, peace and unity were great goods, and more to be attended to than the search for full retribution. Note that the justice of the demands for retribution is not in dispute here, but rather a choice (to put it rather too starkly) between peace and justice when, as is often the case, the two lead us in quite different directions. Forgetting responds to one vital need of a community, and especially so after deeply divisive political strife: the need to allow an end, a final point, to strife. Hence the political importance of amnesties following the defeat of the Paris Commune, in Germany and formerly occupied Europe after World War II, and in France in the wake of the Algerian war of independence.[171] Of course, the process of forgetting extends beyond such legal-political actions as amnesty. Amnesia, a sort of informal collective forgetting, and the crafting of conciliatory counter-narratives of the past have also played an important role. Hans Enzensberger observes that following the Second World War, Europeans took shelter behind a great amnesia, generally, but especially in Germany (where the National Socialist period was left in silence) and in France, where de Gaulle managed to weave a tale of Vichy as a parenthesis in French history and of a nation in arms in opposition to German occupation.[172]

No doubt this combination of formal amnesty and informal amnesia served present interests: the desire of the perpetrators to escape justice, of the collaborators not to be stained by their acts of betrayal, and of passive bystanders to find redemption in an edifying story of courage and moral uprightness. Equally certain is that they have been instruments of political actors in the present seeking to install one memory or expunge another. But here again, we should not stop with the motivating presence of current interests in the politics of amnesty and amnesia. Rather, memory and forgetting speak to something more elemental than the opportunism of those seeking to save themselves or to profit from a regime change. Amnesty overturns the moral imperative of memory-justice for the sake of other goods: so that we may be oriented to the present and future, and not (or not solely) to the fulfillment of a debt to the victims or to the carrying out of the demands of justice for its own sake. It asks, "What is the practical importance now of a judgment that injustice occurred in the past?" For, as Raúl Alfonsín argues, the consequences of punishing for the past must be weighed against the present and future, and too high a cost there rejected.[173] The "thick line" between past and present that amnesty permits should be seen not (necessarily) as the avoidance of moral judgment, but as an expression of the view that justice needs to be seasoned not so much by compassion for its own sake as by a concern for the future, the goods of which might be lost in a too strict adherence to the demands of the "iron tracks" of memory-justice. Hence the decision (in Uruguay) "to give [via amnesty] priority to the possibility of a future of agreement over a past of division."[174]

It may be that amnesty, and in general a displacement of the grievances of the past, is of particular importance in transitions to (or restorations of) democracy.[175] The degree of civility, trust, and tolerance necessary for a democracy to flourish would be jeopardized, it is argued, by memory-justice's too zealous pursuit of either prosecutions or disclosures. The memory-justice of retribution, Ackerman suggests, is absorbed in the past, and divides a people into the guilty and the innocent, collaborators and resisters. It is a negative device, focused on culpability rather than (future-regarding) constitution-framing and institutional reform. In his account, it is not just prosecutions that are wrongheaded but policies of disclosure as well: the secret police files should be burned, he urges, and not as in the post-unification German policy made available to the public.[176] The well of bitterness and division must be drained. On this view, amnesty, political-judicial forgetting, is an answer to the Furies, to the vengeful face of memory-justice.[177] Here, as in the *Eumenides*, the claims of retributive justice are not so much disputed as seasoned or moderated. An amnesty says not that doing justice and meting out punishment are wrong as such, but rather that pursuing justice would ill serve other and equally (or more) important purposes (e.g., reconciliation). Thus the Furies are tamed, or better, brought into the city's institutions and their claims moderated by other imperatives, one of which requires us to ask of such measures what their impact is on the present and future. This means that the demands of the victims to see justice done must be weighed against the claims of the present and future, precisely because as humans we live in all these temporal registers, and all call to us, telling us of their dependence on us and insisting that we attend to their just claims.

What is wrong then, we might ask, with such a solution, with bringing an end to the burden of the past, letting the dead bury their dead, binding the hands of justice and keeping its Furies from contaminating the present and future with bitter resentment? In a way, it seems almost the natural course of action: time and forgetting begin the work on which judicial forgetting merely puts the capstone. Not only is forgetting an ally of time and community, but also its victory and remembrance's defeat seem equally inevitable since time is essentially becoming: an "oceanic forgetting" submerges all, and remembrance therefore always tends towards nullity.[178] Memory and resentment, the aching longing for a rectification of past injustice, must always appear, from the standpoint of the flow of time, as the voices of the impossible, of those wanting to reverse the irreversible. When combined with an unquenchable thirst for punishment, it is poisonous and, in a political community, deeply divisive. Forgetting, then, seems the natural ally of time as becoming, of civic harmony, and of a certain kind of moral/political life-in-common. For justice-memory, however, a putting aside of the past in the name of present and future needs is unacceptable: that would be to do the work of the flow of time, of the erosion that accompanies time, and to complete or ratify the efforts of the perpetrators to erase their victims from the face of the earth. Amnesty and amnesia, in general forgetting, seen from the vantage point of this face of memory-justice, are not positions that take their bearing from the strictures of morality and justice, but rather are so many ways of yielding to the logic of present interests or to the extra-moral course of becoming. Lévinas writes that "forgetting is the law, the happiness, and the condition of life. But here [in the trial of the Struthof concentration camp guards], life is wrong."[179] And Ralph Ellison says of race in the United States, "Perhaps more than any other people, Americans have been locked in a deadly struggle with time, with history. We've fled the past and trained ourselves to suppress, if not forget, troublesome details of the national memory, and a great part of our optimism . . . has been bought at the cost of ignoring the processes through which we've arrived at any given moment of our national existence." And, "by pushing significant details of our experience into the underground of unwritten history, we not only overlook much of what is positive, but we blur our conceptions of where and who we are. Not only do we confuse our moral identity, . . . we misconceive our cultural identity."[180] As agents whose capacity for responsibility (and future commitment) depends on the identity of the acting subject across time, we resist forgetting.

Memory-justice, as we have seen, speaks with the voice of the silenced victims. It is the vehicle of their presence, a second life that witnessing and doing justice breathe into them. Their continued presence depends on us, as bearers of testimony, and it is a test of our fidelity whether we answer their need. Conversely, and since the time of the ancient Greeks, it has been thought that to be forgotten is a second death, an extinction in a sea of forgetting. To be forgotten, whether through the passage of time, through weariness over the labors demanded by remembrance, or by legislative or judicial fiat, is to suffer a disappearance, another vanishing: the first, the physical disappearance brought about by death and crime; the second, the vanishing from memory. Doing justice, then, with its privileging of the voices of the victims and of the reality of their fate, seems to be morally at odds with judicial forgetting.[181] Amnesties are also subject to a second objection: "Do not forget truly it is not in your power / to forgive in the name of those betrayed at dawn," writes Herbert.[182] "Not in your power": how can anyone other than the victims extend the gesture of reconciliation that is amnesty? Samuel Pisar's questions about pardoning apply to amnesty as well: "Who will pardon? Who could pardon? The dead? The survivors? The rest of humanity? No one."[183] And since forgetting is typically a forgetting of the victims and the crimes committed against them, amnesties may outrage our moral sensibilities both because they raise the question "Who can forgive and forget?" and also because they seem to violate our debt of fidelity to the victims, a debt that is redeemed through remembrance. Amnesty, in short, is an obstructing or forbidding of the logic of doing memory-justice, and therefore would seem to require an extra-judicial will in order to be achieved.[184]

Such strategies of willed forgetting, expressed in injunctions of the type "not to remember evil," may put crimes into the civic shadows, beyond judicial evocation, but they are (like memory) vulnerable. They cannot undo the fact of the crime having been done. And forgetting is no certain solution for life, personal or political, since the past has a way of coming back into the present. The "event," as Jankélévitch says, "wants to be remembered."[185] The irreversibility of time means both that past injustices cannot be directly undone (or repaired) and also that it is difficult if not impossible to have their traces disappear entirely.[186] These traces, in their many forms, are likely to remain, awaiting a witness of one kind or another to bring them to light. In Aeschylus' words, "Whoever sins, as this man has, and hides his blood-stained hands, as avengers of bloodshed we appear against him to the end, presenting ourselves as upright witnesses [*martures*] for the dead."[187] The passage of time increases our distance from the past, but in its irreversibility it conserves it, leaving traces that threaten the complacency of forgetting. And so the Furies sleep, but they can be awakened.[188] Jorge Semprún, whom I quoted earlier on the need to forget for the sake of life, also said that "despite the detours, the deliberate or involuntary censoring, the strategy of forgetting . . . despite all the pages written to exorcise this experience . . . despite all this, the past preserved the shattering power of the smoke and snow [of Buchenwald], just as on the first day."[189] So too de Gaulle's strategy of amnesia (Vichy as a parenthesis) overlaid with a tale of heroic national resistance unraveled when the true character of Vichy and of the extent of collaboration and passivity during the "dark years" was restored from the shadows by films such as *The Sorrow and the Pity*. Nor did the Vichy-related amnesty laws promulgated in France in the early 1950s put an end to the demands of memory-justice.[190] No society can live forever in amnesia, Benjamin Stora writes in relation to the French war in Algeria. The past of injustice lingers like a gangrene.[191] Thus, in Argentina, a series of amnesties and pardons for the perpetrators of crimes during the 1976–1983 dictatorship has failed to put to rest demands that justice be done. Nestor Kirchner, elected president of Argentina in 2003, some twenty years after the end of the military dictatorship, made the issue of justice for the victims of the "dirty war" central to his presidency, seeking, he said, to "exercise power 'without rancor but with memory.' "[192] Our memory of the past, of its victims and perpetrators, has the ability to return almost unbidden. The Furies are always there waiting to rouse us from our sleep, should we become oblivious to the demands of memory-justice.[193] "The past," says, Archbishop Tutu, "far from disappearing . . . has an embarrassing and persistent way of returning and haunting us unless it has in fact been dealt with adequately."[194] As Ellison puts it, "In the underground of unwritten history, much of that which is ignored defies our inattention by continuing to grow and have consequences."[195]

Since forgetting cannot completely erase what has been done and its traces, amnesty and amnesia are at best provisional means to deal with the past.[196] At the same time, however, justice as memory work is itself vulnerable to the passage of time and to the waning of the passions that sustain the obstinacy of justice in its resistance to forgetting. Even imprescriptibility, the attempt to make timeless certain classes of actionable crimes, lasts only as long as the lives of the perpetrators. The call for an unforgetting resentment is both life-destroying and doomed to failure.[197] Amnesty and memory-justice are fragile, and both therefore are obstinate and in conflict as each seeks to preserve the goods that reside in their respective moral/temporal registers. My concern here, however, is with the precariousness of forgetting. Although the direction of time as becoming is unchangeable, the fact of what happened is therefore irreversible as well. Time, then, may neutralize the effect of the crime, but not the fact of its having happened. In that sense, the crimes are a stain, a sort of pollution, ensuring the instability of forgetting and of the victory of the present and future over the past. This is already apparent in the *Eumenides*: the Furies need only to be stirred, to be reawakened, and the remembrance of the past blows like a wind over the present. The past, thought to have disappeared (at last!), always seems to "catch up with us," Günter Grass says.[198] It is always there, adamantine in its having occurred. The deeds of the past are there, not just in the ineradicable past-perfect sense, but also in their aorist form that is, never completely past and gone, in the forefront or background, but never permanently erased. No deed can be erased once and for all. "What we have forgotten does not forget us. . . . In societies (more than in individual men or women) the past always tends to resurface." "And so they are ever returning to us the dead."[199] What will trigger their return in memory is manifold: the fiftieth anniversary of the end of World War II in Europe, Bitburg, the trial of Klaus Barbie, or the Touvier affair. Speaking about the German case, Eberhard Jäckel remarks that the further in the past the Nazi period is, the closer or more present it seems to become. And so "the glimmer of remembrance never ceases to illuminate the night of forgetting."[200]

In brief, the claims of memory-justice, vulnerable though they are to our pressing current needs and concerns for the future, can always transgress those boundaries that we erect in the vain attempt to be done with the past. But it will be apparent from this discussion of bearing witness and of amnesty that memory's case against forgetting rests on more than the instability of the latter. Our (partial) embeddedness in the present and future, and their just claims on us, are not exhaustive of the universe of justice. Perhaps this also helps to account for the precariousness of forgetting: attempts to allow only a past-less community of interests and expectations and not a community of memory, and so among other things to draw a "thick line" between past and present through amnesty and amnesia, only serve to awaken the Furies, justice, and in so doing show just how futile is the attempt to draw such a line. Be that as it may, I want to begin this part of the critique of forgetting with the observation that the antonym of forgetting is not memory but justice.[201] In other words, the imperative to remember is not the leaden voice of what has gone before, but rather it is the call of justice insisting on the irreversibility and persistence of what has been done, its claims on us which are neither diminished nor augmented by the extra-moral passing of time, and which call on us to bear these injustices in mind.[202] Reflect back on the Furies, the Daughters of the Night, in the *Eumenides*. Awakened by Clytemnestra, they are urged by her to pursue her son and killer, Orestes. Although their mission is made deeply ambiguous by the fact that Clytemnestra murdered her husband, and that Orestes was moved by Apollo to kill her, the murder of his kin and the resulting blood politics nevertheless do seem to demand an accounting before justice. The challenge that they lay down— "What is there here that anyone shall call just?"—is by no means empty.[203] How can it be that Orestes should escape justice, and that the status quo ante should in a sense be restored, as if the deed had not occurred, and the bloodstain washed away, unexpiated? Their question is a good one, in part because we do not believe that injustice's escape into the flow of passing time, here because of the Furies' having fallen asleep, puts to rest the issue of justice. The Furies can always be reawakened, a fact that reflects the incorrigible character of the past, its relation to justice, and the latter's drive to ensure the persistence of the memory of the wrong, at least till justice is done.

That the past slips into the oblivion of forgetting does not change its moral nature. The passage of time may dull our recollection of events, but it does not erase the (morally weighty) fact of their having happened nor the wrong involved in them. The passing of the years does not absolve us of moral accountability for our actions. We owe it to those who suffered injustice to keep alive the memory of them, for if we do not, we become complicit in the original wrong done them, indeed, help to complete it by assisting in the effort to erase the trace.[204] Memory therefore wages a defensive struggle: it seeks to halt both the natural process of erosion and willed forgetting. Memory here acts not in resistance to the becoming of time as such but to the moral consequences that this can have, and in particular to the forgetting of justice that may result from the relentless distancing of the past. In that sense, it seeks to bring the past before us, to make it present, not so as to reverse the irreversible, nor from a nostalgic desire to restore some status quo ante, but rather as a memory of justice. Like Clytemnestra arousing the Furies, memory reawakens the past and the vengefulness that accompanies it. Its efforts must seem therefore to be at the very heart of resentment, of a vengeful bondage to the past that denies us a future. Perhaps there is such a malaise, a hostility that will not let go what needs to be allowed to slip away, for the sake of life and community. But what is being discussed here is something different: the memory of justice resists the corrosive effect of forgetting not because it is in the obsessive grip of the past, but because the call to remember is the appeal of the principles of justice and morality themselves.[205] In the end, while there may be a deep difference between resentment and the memory of justice, both do, for their not entirely separate reasons, draw us to the past.

Finally, let me return to the issue of identity, forgetting, and justice. Earlier, I discussed the notion that liberal political thought confers on citizens a similar situatedness, a commonalty of position with respect to deliberation about justice. I also suggested there that forgetting covers over the scars left by political traumas, and thus allows the community to live, if only precariously, without vengeful strife. This last point could be rephrased to say that forgetting the divisiveness of the past permits the community to retain, or better construct, a sort of coherence and continuity against the threatening divisions that come in memory's wake. Forgetting in this sense preserves community, a paradoxical conclusion since, as I argued earlier, memory is the core of identity over time, and amnesia creates multiple selves (or, most radically, abolishes the self altogether). But this sort of forgetting, even if fully feasible, has political/moral consequences. Now one key thing that identity does is, as I said, to mark out an individual or a community as an enduring subject of attribution. It is only on this assumption of the identity of the person across time that we can hold an individual to account for her past actions; and it is only on that same assumption of identity that we consider political communities responsible for their pasts. Forgetting, then, would disrupt the sameness or identity of the regime through time, and it would also, and for just that reason, break the thread of accountability, the thread that ties us to a past that is ours, and in so doing would absolve us of responsibility for it. Who we were, and what we did: both would be submerged in the lake of oblivion. Something like this was at work in the attempt to "bracket" Vichy. In the words of François Mitterrand quoted earlier: "The Republic, across all its history, has constantly adopted a totally open attitude" with regard to the rights of all its citizens. "Thus, do not demand an accounting of this Republic" for the deportation of French Jews during the Occupation. In Germany, the efforts to "normalize" the country's history had a similar effect. Although the Federal Republic was not seeking to disown the National Socialist years, as was done in East Germany, the thrust of this attempted normalization was to de-center the National Socialist period, with the Holocaust at its core, both by embedding it in the wider, long duration of German history, and by seeing it in a comparative perspective.

Such a de-centering of the period of fascism and of the Holocaust would also have been a way of relieving the community of the burden of past injustice: not quite the forgetting of evil, but like amnesia in its consequences. The balm of forgetting, then, used therapeutically to heal the wounds of a divisive past and to restore or create something like a "normal" identity, one not obsessively burdened with the past, disrupts the continuity of a political community over time, and as a result undermines the coherence of that community as a subject of attribution. In brief, it erodes both identity and justice.

Insomnia, the sleeplessness of too much memory: an obsessive, injurious, and divisive absorption in the past seems to call out for the *pharmakon* of forgetting. Lévinas, however, tells us that the central meaning of insomnia is the "rectitude of responsibility."[206] To be responsible is to acknowledge the past as one's own, as an encumbrance, a debt, a burden. It is to bear witness to one's past, and to guard it in memory, private or public. "Like poppies for remembrance," so the witness's words for memory. Memory is a kind of love.[207] It is a love for, even a devotion to, the past, not time past as such (the past perfect), but the inhabited past of relationships, civic and other, which is continuous with and still present among us.[208] Perhaps, then, it is the love or filiation of a life-in-common and the debts incurred in such a life, and therefore foreign to the seductions of forgetfulness. It is also a call to act. By its vivid redness, the poppy hails passersby to remember; so too the witness, in her testimony, thrusts the past into an often forgetful present. And it is the will to call the living back from their comfortable amnesia. This appeal to remember is also an affirmation of the continuity of the community across time, of the unity of past and present, not in some abstract or universal sense, but for a particular group of persons and their locales. Relatedly, the call to remembrance is an imperative of identity, a way of insisting on a certain moral topography of the community's past. And finally, I remarked that this intrusion of the past into the present is often a form of judgment, the appeal of justice on behalf of the past, the Furies reminding us that time does not wash away crime.

Devotion, community, and judgment: the witness is engaged in all these. She transmits and preserves the names, deeds, and fates of those past, calls the present to a communion with its past, and offers herself as the voice of justice. In all these dimensions of witnessing, the *summum malum* most to be avoided is forgetting. Most obviously, this is the evil to be resisted when forgetting or erasure was the intent of the perpetrators. Then the appeal to remember is bound up with overcoming their injustice. But more generally the evil of forgetting tracks the ethical imperatives at work in that complex relationship between the poppy and remembrance, between witnessing and memory. It severs the bond to the enduring community, and in so doing violates the devotion, and the debt, owed to it. For the victims and the lost, forgetting is a "second death." It breaks the unity across time of the community and leaves a part of its identity lost to amnesia; forgetting silences the claims of justice and leaves the victim voiceless.

Against that background, the ethical underpinning of witnessing emerges more clearly. It is above all an ethics of debt. Of a debt to the dead: sometimes personal, as in the case of Primo Levi and the Hungarian child Hurbinek, Germaine Tillion and her mother, Buber-Neumann and Milena; and at other times more generally to a lost community, their places effaced and the dead without sepulcher. Of a debt to the community in its present form: to bind its current members with past ones; to provide a lesson, a warning. It is also a debt owed to justice: to ensure that its voice and claims will not be overwhelmed by the passing of the years, or by the deliberate effacement of the perpetrators. And in the end, the witness expresses a truth-preserving ethic as well, to be a living archive, though as we have seen, only within the horizon of a universe of memory shaped by the particularity of the community and individual, and of the uneven moral topography of their pasts. The witness is, then, the bearer of the past, but in manifold ways, a manifold that mirrors the temporal nexus in which her wider community is also bound up, and which we term identity: a time of fidelity, judgment, indebtedness, of the mutuality of an ongoing project.

CHAPTER FIVE

Democratic Memory

I have argued in these pages that there is an element of enduringness through time, our common "remembering, forgetting, and recalling," in Gadamer's words, that belongs to communities (and individuals), whether political, religious, family, or vocational, and that this is central to what we mean by their identity.[1] Political (and other) communities are meshes of relationships, ways of living together, of habits acquired in the commerce of everyday life, relations of trust and suspicion, of expectation and commitment. Such relationships take time and are a way of being together in time. Time here is not an empty vessel, nor is it the abstract, homogeneous time of calendar days and years; rather it is the past, present, and future inseparably bound up with the jagged topography of a memory-borne life-in-common. This is the time that grounds identity, a sameness sufficient to make of the present community a life-in-common and the responsible bearer of its past, the locus of trust and continuity and the promise-maker committing itself to future projects.[2] Memory, the ingathering and guarding of the past, raises us, individually and collectively, above the point-like existence of creatures of the moment by giving us a duration as an accountable community (or individual). It is via memory, both explicit and enacted, and thick, or habit-like, that we have an identity, a commonality with the past and recognition of it as ours, and it is through promises, projects, and commitments that we show our will to continue into the future as responsible agents. Debts, commitments, and responsibility need an enduring subject. Memory is one of the ways in which that enduringness is protected against the changes wrought by the passing of time, and the "memory of the will" is the foundation of the persistence needed for commitments into the future.

All societies, writes Claude Lefort, "communicate with [their] past and find [themselves] informed in some way by it." Informed *and* obliged, but in different ways: what we also need is an account of what François Hartog calls "regimes of historicity."[3] One could read this idea of the plural regimes of time as beginning with the claim that temporality and enduringness (orders of time) are essential to all associations, including the political one, insofar as they have an identity as responsible agents capable of action, and that this depends in no small part on memory. At the same time, however, the character of the association, itself shaped by the past, also involves particular ways of remembering. The sacred calendar of the Catholic Church, the lineage narratives of monarchies, the autochthonous and ethno-historical scripts of some nationalist movements, the constitutional history of republican regimes, the canons of scholarly or artistic communities, the family photo album and its stories: all these are so many ways in which the life of the group and its particular relationships shape its appropriation of the past through memory, just as they in turn are shaped in their specificity by that memory. That character, as I have suggested, is not itself a free-floating moment. Rather, it is, in part, the presence of the past and the anticipation of the future. The embeddedness of human relations in time, the enduringness of their identity, their forms of responsibility and commitment are not of a single type but vary according to the epoch and the character of the association, which is itself an efflux of the past.

It is not surprising therefore that liberal democratic modernity has given its own cast to the face of memory and politics. While the recent period has witnessed a proliferation of memory work and its kindred identity politics, it remains broadly true that modernity, and liberal modernity in particular, is suspicious of the social role of memory.[4] This can be traced, in part, to the beginnings of the modern period in the West: to the fact that memory and tradition were seen as the handmaidens of the *ancien régime,* and as bulwarks against progress. The revolutionary beginnings of democracy in the West were in no small measure battles against the legitimacy-conferring weight of the past. Burke's response to English republicanism, accusing its proponents and their French tutors of a boundless and dangerous thirst for present novelties, and Thomas Paine's critique of Burke's anti-revolutionary use of tradition are early displays of the contest over that characteristically modern effort to unseat the past, and memory as its bearer, from their place at the fountainhead of legitimacy. In more general terms, modernity can be said to have created a moral/political distance from the past, a post-traditional world in which memory, the past, and its bequeathed traditions are reflexively and critically appropriated and displaced from the commanding heights of political identity.[5] I mentioned earlier that this distancing from memory in favor of the more abstract universe of reason and rights gave the revolutionary, early modern period its taste for museums and archives as a substitute, a mausoleum, for what it was seeking to undermine. That distance and those locales for its storage, Pierre Nora argues, radically transform the social place of memory. It is no longer a source of legitimacy and memory, as the lived presence of the past has been transformed into a "locale" (*lieu*) rather than a "milieu" of memory, a "mémoire de papier" (a "paper memory").[6] In Nora's account, the multiplication of memory sites, of archives, museums, and memorials, the interest in genealogy and patrimony, and so forth, are the swan songs of a memory that no longer lives among us. The collection of the surface, material remnants of the past seems almost to consign it to the past perfect, locales "on the shores of the living" that are "consecrated to the conservation of the dead."[7]

On one reading (not Nora's own), his multivolume collaborative effort, *Lieux de mémoire*, shows precisely the malaise of a society lost in the "empire of the perpetual present," lost "in the making present of the 'today.' "[8] As Sebald writes, we "keep throwing ballast overboard, forgetting everything that we might otherwise remember. . . . [L]eaving a present without memory, in the face of a future that no individual mind can now envisage, in the end we shall ourselves relinquish life without feeling any need to linger at least for a while."[9] Yet a pure "presentism," the thought that there is such a freestanding present moment, one not enmeshed in the extension of past and future, of experience and expectation, seems fundamentally flawed. If the idea of a dwelling in the pure present is difficult to accept, so too is a narrow reading of the observation according to which modernity is characterized by a "radical openness" to the future. For the openness to the future of an agent capable of action and responsibility, and of making commitments, rests, as we have seen, on a certain view of sameness and enduringness, tied to the duration of an accountable agent in the past and the memory of his will in the future. That, as I have suggested, is the insight underlying Burke's remark that "people will not look forward to posterity, who never look backward to their ancestors."[10]

Resistance to memory comes not just from a certain presentism but also, in a number of ways, from the modern liberal dispensation. To advance a conception of justice is not something that can be done by reference to the past, or to the (once) unproblematic and uncontested traditions of the life-world of our society. Rather, such claims are sustained by reference to reason and rights, to (for example) an original position, the historylessness of which is assured by the veil of ignorance. In that sense, as I said, modernity defines itself in opposition to the traditionalist, or weight-of-the-past, view. The remembered past as a source of authority and legitimacy has yielded to a justification framed in terms of reason, free will, and contract.[11] This reading, it seems to me, is unsurprising and generally accurate; but in any case a further exploration of the historical background of the reasons underlying it, including the tradition-based self-definition of the *ancien régime*, is not within the scope of this study. Perhaps, then, we could better express the changing place of collective memory by going beyond the observation that it is no longer the uncritically accepted foundation of legitimate power, beyond the question, that is, of the intertwining of memory, the past, and legitimacy. There are still other and, I think, more basic sources of a liberal democratic suspicion of memory, and it is to those that I want to turn.

Let us begin with something already implicit in the discussion of justification, framed by (contractual) acts of the will. What that sort of justification highlights is the centrality of choice, of the willed construction, to the liberal ethos. As I noted earlier, Nietzsche remarked on the modern antipathy to tradition and institutions: the latter were sources of disquiet because they conveyed fatality, the power of something unchosen, "a kind of will . . . which is anti-liberal to the point of malice: the will to tradition, to authority, to responsibility for centuries to come, to the solidarity of chains of generations, forward and backward."[12] In the most basic sense, the past in its irreversibility has an anchor-like quality: it cannot be undone. Unlike the present and future, the past is a sealed well, cut off from action and deliberation, and while our recollection and interpretations of it may in some measure be variable and willed, it nevertheless has an autonomy, a power (it seems) to impose itself. In a fundamental way, the irreversibility of time puts the past beyond the reach of choice. And even where choice is viable, the memorial making present of the past is already invested with a thick or implicit memory which has a considerable measure of independence vis-à-vis our will.[13] And it has something more than an autonomy, too, for it acts as a steering mechanism, informing our decisions and actions. It is of course true that civic education is aimed in no small part at the cultivation of those habits needed for good citizenship, and that relatedly they can decay and be corrupted. Nevertheless, habit-memory is something that we do not choose and could scarcely dispose of by an act of the will. It is the deeply ingrained pattern of a way of life, acquired in a myriad of small ways, most often invisible in their pedagogy and unchosen by us. Burke's idea of "just prejudice" as the stock of untaught political wisdom inherited from ages past captures some of this, as does his (related) opposition to the "civic education" of "enlightened self-interest."[14]

We are not free to choose our past. Its irreversibility and autonomy, its presence in thick memory, and its character as a testament, an inheritance, bequeathed to us in our habits, traditions, and stories: all these make it something that lies mostly beyond our control.[15] One way to think about this would be to reflect on the idea of inheritance as a form of transmitting the past, and the issues it raises. We inherit values and habits, faith, and property from our families, and in an important way some of these are the often unsought, and obligation-carrying, "gifts of death," as Anne Gotman calls them. Whether in the explicit instructions of a testament or in the "quasi-contract" between past and present, they convey the will of the giver to the recipient, of the past to the present and future. They are gifts, but also the "exercise of the will" and the "weapon of the dead," "the most ridiculous and insolent of all tyrannies."[16] Hence the desire of the narrator of Raczymow's *Un cri sans voix* to be done with the ghost of Esther (herself haunted by World War II), to "turn the page . . . of the past," saying: "My son will be saved from the past. . . . He will truly be a child of the after."[17] Sometimes these obligations are explicit, the terms of a will or an endowment, for example. They can also be implicit, say, a sense of responsibility by virtue of one's family name. Responsibilities, both chosen and received, seem to come with relationships, whether those of family members or of the citizens of a political community. Collective memory can be understood (in part) as a type of inheritance, manifold in its forms, and it shares some of the same ambiguities just mentioned. In particular, though both memory and inheritance are associated with the deepest attachments, familial and political, they nevertheless carry with them a sense of the autonomy-denying power of the dead over the living, of a constraining bond between generations. Not surprisingly, those committed to a voluntaristic account of human agency tend, as Samuel Scheffler observes, to be hostile to the idea of unchosen responsibilities: "It would be unfair, they believe, if people could be saddled with such burdens against their wills, and so it would be unfair if special responsibilities could be ascribed to people who had done nothing voluntarily to incur them."[18]

Yet this too does not seem to be a complete and sufficient explanation for the sense that memory is a sort of yoke to be thrown off. We can bring more focus to the difficulty of an unchosen force in our midst by looking at the idea of a bequeathed identity, conferred on us, so to speak, by memory and inherited by individuals and communities, that is, the notion that the identity, the "we," of a political community is something inherited by us from our history, with memory as a principal vector.[19] The idea that who we are, our identity as members of a political community and as individuals, is something given to us from our past via (collective or individual) memory is central here; that the political community is in Burke's words "a partnership . . . between those who are living, those who are dead, and those who are to be born."[20] Now, as I suggested earlier, the reasons for modernity's suspicion of the notion of an unchosen burden of the past as the core of political identity are many. Despite powerful arguments that democracy cannot survive without some such "community of recollections," the idea of a chosen, elective or contractual political community, one governed by reasons and not memory and tradition, remains a central and informing vision of liberalism, even when it allows (as Rawls does) that much of what we are and the way we understand our place in the world comes to us unchosen from our society and culture.[21] Historically accurate or not, sustainable as the groundwork for an enduring regime or not, the "choosiness" of liberalism is a central moment in its conception of both individuals and political communities. And so it is drawn to what Anthony D. Smith terms a "gastronomic" language. By the same token, this understanding of the sources of political identity is one of the wellsprings of the rejection of nationalist conceptions of a non-political and unchosen ("geological") identity.[22] The key thought here is that there is something radically unfree about having political identity determined by the past and thus beyond our control.[23] Nationalism is perhaps the leading modern proponent of that view, and thus theorists of "liberal nationalism," such as Yael Tamir, while acknowledging the importance of the (cultural) past made present in collective memory, must nevertheless attempt to find a middle path between the discovery (inherited) and choice models of identity.[24]

We can see this more clearly at the micro-level, by looking at the role of family names as "tenacious [signs] of identification."[25] Our family names, ours from birth in most cases, confer on us an identity bound up with the past (and future) of that family line, and sometimes with place as well. "You have a name that you have not chosen, and throughout your life, you are the prey of this name."[26] Earlier, I mentioned some illustrative, if atypical, examples of this sort of burden: for example, German children who bear the names of their infamous war criminal fathers. The family name gives them, without their ever willing it to be so, a tie to a history that, though not of their making, nevertheless becomes (through family names and the identity they signal) theirs to bear. But this is also true, if less dramatically so, of those whose family names mercifully carry less horrific inheritances with them. My name is central to identity, and it affirms my belonging to a community enduring through time. It confers on me a continuity with others without my volition being engaged at all. A name, in short, is an identity marker that denotes a past, and determines a central part of who I am.[27] On the one hand, then, we might interpret the ability to change names as a sort of emancipation from an unchosen identity conferred by birth into a family and made visible in the trace of the name.[28] To change one's name seems to be to break with the weight of the past that the family name carries and confers on its holders, to shed the burden of memory by erasing its traces, and in so doing to allow for the free creation of one's own ties.[29] Or, on the other hand, it might be seen as a loss of a defining part of oneself, a rejection of an inheritance and, in a way, a betrayal. And so on a larger political stage, membership in a continuous political community confers a heritage on citizens, making our predecessors as much us as we ourselves are, and it engages us in a co-responsibility with them, one icon, sign, or evidence of which is the community's name: American, German and so on.

Perhaps our ability to be nomadic, to experience identity "less as a heritage than as a construction and as a mystery: [to be] 'in a foreign country in my country itself,' " to reject what is sedentary and anchor-like (a rootedness in memory and space), and to move between political communities is a welcome liberation from these memory fetters, a way to "untie the knot a little."[30] Speaking of these "stateless . . . nomads," Ugrešić says: " 'We insist on our dislocation, rootlessness. . . . We have not been given an identity. . . . Our forebears are not what determines us, we choose our forebears, . . . We build our own identity . . . building our archaeology of the civil society.' " Their achievement, she says, is "personal freedom."[31] Or then again, perhaps like the loss of family names and memories, it is a part of us that vanishes in exile: "Exile deprives one of the points of reference that helped us to make projects, choose our goals, to organize our activities. . . . [W]e have been catapulted out of history . . . and we have to cope with, to use the expression of an exile writer, 'the unbearable lightness of being.' "[32] The palpable sense of loss of the farmers in Steinbeck's *Grapes of Wrath*, as they leave the traces of their past behind them; Tocqueville's description of the African American slave who has "lost even the memory of his homeland; he no longer understands the language his fathers spoke; he has abjured their religion and forgotten their mores"; Perec's parents' memories, language, and traditions vanished in the silence that followed on their deaths during World War II. All these suggest the centrality of memory to our identity, and the gravity of its loss. In having an identity, family, political, religious, and so forth, we inherit something without choosing to do so: a name and the past it bears, a nation's history, a legacy of faith and deeds. That inheritance, conveyed and guarded by memory in its many forms, we experience both as a burden and as a part of who we are.

I have argued that the defining commitment of liberalism to the "choosiness" of identity and community makes memory, as the bearer of an unchosen past and identity, an uncomfortable basis for political community. I now want to push that thought one step further. Memory and identity are problematic for liberal modernity not simply because of the fated, often almost involuntary character of the presence of the past, but also because memory (as a core part of identity) is deeply particularizing, and in a manner that liberals find difficult to accept. In collective memory, as Halbwachs noted, it is the unifying similarities of the group that matter, similarities expressed in the habits acquired over the course of a life led in common, in civic histories and memorials, canons, liturgies, and so on.[33] I have just spoken about the unchosen burdensomeness of family names. Names also individuate groups large and small. Names, habits, shared memories and narratives mark out the sometimes near-to-impenetrable boundaries of a community. Memory, whether ingrained, habit-like, in a people or explicitly recounted in their narratives, is the "guardian of difference." It helps draw a line between those who belong and those who do not, and can readily come to glorify belonging.[34] As I said at the beginning of this book, to identify is to distinguish. It is the past, then, guarded in memory that constitutes the *differentia specifica* of a community. And these differences, preserved in collective memory, are a core part of the group's identity and make it and its members non-substitutable with others.[35] One consequence of the rootedness that memory-identity offers is the related sharpening of lines of differentiation with others. This "mineness" of memory-identity (if it is more than something merely folkloric and detached from its life in common) is in tension with the universally justified norms of a liberal democratic society.[36] In other words, core liberal notions of the universal scope of its past-less basic principles (rights, the equal status of persons, and so on) are at odds with the individuating quality of an identity centered on memory and inheritance. The result is that if it is to install itself as the definitive public way of life of a community, liberalism must (in Todorov's words, quoted earlier) dethrone memory "not in the interests of forgetting . . . but of certain universal principles and the 'general will.' " In Todorov's argument, forgetting is needed to install both universalism (as against an exclusionary particularism) and a general will (as against the inheritance or tectonic plates model).

Here is a small, symbolic illustration of the universalist dimension of this claim. In 1996 a competition was held to develop designs for the new Euro banknotes, which were about to be introduced. Traditionally, national currencies had carried images of celebrated historical figures or places with which the community identified. But these memory emblems were not to appear on the new supranational currency. "For his central motif, reported the *International Herald Tribune*, the designer, Robert Kalina, "chose a bridge—not Pont Neuf in Paris or Venice's Bridge of Sighs. Mr. Kalina's was a bridge that no European had ever crossed. The ground rules for the design strictly prohibited displaying any recognizable national monuments or heroes that risked giving greater prominence to one country over another. So Mr. Kalina took bits and pieces of Europe's great bridges and with the help of his computer melded them into a neutered bridge presumably acceptable to all. 'Hopefully,' Mr. Kalina said with a grin, 'no one will recognize the old places' incorporated in the design."[37] Here the particularities of place and history are washed away. An "abstract modern theme" is how the European Central Bank described the designs, which were said by their designer to stand for the "new and the open" in Europe.[38] The hope for a peaceful European union based on a rejection of communities of memory is not a new one. Jean Giraudoux's novel *Siegfried et le Limousin* (1922), for example, described an amnesiac French soldier who, having lost his memories of France, easily adapts to life in Germany and assumes a German identity.[39] The lesson was meant to be that arriving at a new and open Europe, no longer mired in the particularisms which had bedeviled its history, depended squarely on abstraction from memory. It is important, though, to observe how even this vision of a memory-less Europe rests on the tectonic plates and the memory of its own past. The new Europe, writes Annette Wieviorka, "is founded on an emptiness. Six million—perhaps a little less, perhaps a little more—Jews were murdered, of whom one million were killed at Auschwitz. The Jews absent from then on from most European countries are the phantom limb of Europe . . . the presence of which is always sensed. . . . [T]he memory of this absence and that of the crime launched the construction of Europe."[40]

Once more, nationalism provides a useful illustration of the tension between memory and democracy. On one account, national communities are dense meshes of a common past, shared through narratives ("ways of recounting the past"), language, mores, and the many habits acquired and transmitted through the various informal mechanisms of a stable, enduring community. It is this thick memory, more than shared blood, that makes the community what it is. Although a shared memory may be the cornerstone of this sort of national identity, the focus on the enduring character of the community across time and change readily melds with autochthony. There, continuity is established through a genealogy, narrating common descent with or without a story of a continuous life-in-common, or the habits of such a life.[41] Both the autochthonous notion of continuity with the past and the memory (continuous history and ways of life) variants tend to produce largely unshareable, often exclusionary practices of membership, and in that way both create equally strong barriers to outsiders and to liberal democratic universalist norms. More generally, from a liberal standpoint, these forms of continuity privilege morally irrelevant factors in the political life of the community.[42] One's embeddedness in a shared past, whether secured through memory in its various forms or autochthonously, is not a factor that ought to carry civic weight. It is not surprising therefore that liberal defenses of the political/normative importance of culture and continuity tend to recast these in terms drawn from the lexicon of culture, choice, and will: for example, Kymlicka's liberal defense of the importance of culture as a "context of choice," or Tamir's notion of nationalism as partially elective and (as a form of deep mutuality) important to the sustainability of a caring welfare state.[43]

For those who see identity-as-continuity as crucial to the possibility of an enduring community and its debts and projects, such communities and the skein of relations that constitute them just are pervasively temporal-historical in character (in the manifold ways I have discussed). That is, they have an extension across time which is the heart of their identity, an identity that in certain respects may be different from the norms of citizenship.[44] This does not mean, of course, that the presence of the past is to be understood necessarily in terms of origins. The idea of an unchosen membership in an enduring community of memory does not have a unique political expression. Consider again Abraham Lincoln's 1858 speech, which ties identity and enduringness not to ethnicity or origins, but to core political values and the Constitution, to the memory of freedom.[45] Still, even the detachment of this view of identity from autochthonous, lineage types of accounts of continuity with the past does not mean that they are any less bounded. Memory-identity must always be bounded and essentially local in character, circumscribing a group able to preface the collective memory with the possessive pronoun "our." The function of identity is to set boundary conditions as well as those that describe duration. Indeed, the idea of a commonality based on universal values, or of a global or even supranational regional memory seems wrongheaded.[46] Definitions of this cement of society which were unbounded would not do the work that identity does, that is, would not individuate the community, for, as I said, identification requires differentiation. Abstract doctrines of rights do not fulfill the boundary-setting function of identity.[47] On the contrary, they can, in their abstraction from the dense connections of collective memory, be shared even with nonmembers.

Yet on one account, the particularity of memory is challenged not only by the principles of liberal modernity but by globalism as well, a development that (literally) dislocates the moral weight of the past from its traditional temporal-spatial and political locales. This challenge does capture something important about memory: that it can reach beyond the boundaries of the community in which it is interwoven with identity and responsibility. For example, Emmanuel Lévinas, and Daniel Levy and Natan Sznaider, see in the Jewish experience of diaspora and of the Holocaust a particular resonance extending beyond the boundaries of that community.[48] The memory of the Holocaust, Levy and Sznaider argue, has moved beyond the communities of the victims and perpetrators to become global.[49] This globalization of memory was apparent in the writing of Robert Antelme. His account of what he had experienced and learned in Buchenwald, Gandersheim, and Dachau was titled *L'espèce humaine* (The Human Species). In that book, as Maurice Blanchot says, Antelme "guarded the human truth," a truth that Sarah Kofman tells us was that "of the indestructible unity" of the human species.[50] Germaine Tillion and Pierre Vidal-Naquet drew on the memory of their wartime experiences and losses to develop a critique of the French war in Algeria and the use of torture there. All drew wider, more universal lessons from particular memories of suffering and loss. This stepping outside the boundaries of the memory community can also be seen in the French National Assembly's 1998 declaration concerning the recognition of the Armenian genocide: "Our country, and democracies [generally], have an imperative duty to remember. This memory should not be limited to the history of each nation. It should also be extended to include the memory of humanity tragically effected by the several genocides of this century."[51] In these and other ways, the memory of a particular community moves beyond its original frontiers.

The memory of the Holocaust, Levy and Sznaider argue, belongs no longer only to Jews and Germans, or to others directly involved in those crimes, but also globally to humankind.[52] We might, however, better think of this as a translation of memory into metaphor so as to allow for its transmission and use outside of the community to whose past it belongs. "By turning the concrete memory of slavery into a universalizing metaphor of reciprocity, the [ancient Jewish] ex-slaves discover a way to convert imagination into a serious moral instrument," writes Cynthia Ozick. "Metaphor is . . . universalizing: it makes possible the power to envision the stranger's heart."[53] The debate over the treatment of the Anne Frank story brings to light the distinction between a globalizing (as a future-oriented memory-symbol or metaphor for all) and a particularistic memory, rooted in a community, its identity, and its fate. For some critics, the "Americanization" of Anne Frank involved a distorting commercialization: the glossing over of those parts of her diary that were particularly Jewish in order to make her accessible to a wider, non-Jewish audience. The singularity of the Holocaust and of Anne Frank's fate as a Jew are lost in this globalization. For others, this was the memory of Anne Frank breaking free of its boundaries and in this manner becoming available to the future and to the world, and not only to her community and its past.[54] Globalization, Levy and Sznaider maintain, does not abolish memory but displaces it, frees it from the bonds of the past, identity, and geography. This is not, however, a part of the owned and accountable past of memory-identity, but rather a future-oriented, pedagogical, cosmopolitan memory, and it is something quite different from memory-identity. "There is no universal memory," writes Halbwachs. "All collective memory is grounded in a group limited in space and time."[55]

If memory-identity is at odds with a globalism and with a liberal modernity that hold particularizing identity claims under a heightened scrutiny, it is also in a different way in tension with multiculturalism. The axis of this conflict is not (as before) memory-identity as against some more universal set of identity-conferring principles; rather, it is to be found in the debate over a hegemonic, "nationalized" collective memory. The key notion here is that the political memory-identity of a nation-state tends to "nationalize" collective memory and banishes the group's memories of minorities, immigrants, and the powerless generally.[56] Lincoln's optimism notwithstanding, diversity, whether class or ethnic, indigenous or via immigration, in a democratic context makes a single homogeneous national memory difficult to justify and sustain.[57]

An essential part of the politics of plural societies, whether longstanding democracies or ones only recently emerging from dictatorship, is the flourishing of group memories as they seek to recover and win recognition for a past submerged by an overarching national or state-imposed collective memory. In other words, there is an insurgent politics of memory-identity, the purpose of which is not to dethrone memory but to disrupt a unitary, all-absorbing official story of the past. If some state memory work, for example, Pericles' funeral oration, Lincoln's 1858 address or his speech at Gettysburg, Malraux's oration at the Panthéonization of Jean Moulin, and so on, clings to and reinforces the view of a single community united in a common memory, the most recent period has witnessed a fragmentation of memory-identity, a kaleidoscope of revisions of these unitary memories. This is evident in eastern and central Europe and in the republics of the former Soviet Union, where memory imposed from above has yielded to a proliferation of national and group memories.[58] In France, the dominance of a centralized Republican memory, with its emphasis on the unity of the country, faced an explosion of regional memories.[59] The integration of immigrants and their particular collective memories has gènerated tensions and challenges to traditional national memories. And in the United States, African Americans, women, and immigrant communities have struggled for a place in the national memory narrative, and for a recognition of their specific histories and memories.[60] What I want to highlight in these various political debates is the centrality both of contestation and of the fact that identity is bound up with memory. To struggle to restore a collective memory suppressed under dictatorship (in eastern Europe, for example, or as in the Argentinean film *The Official Story*) or to insist on the plurality of memory groups as against a homogenizing national narrative is to do both of these. Marc Augé's study (discussed earlier) of the Paris Métro system as a topography of memory captures this point nicely. The Métro station names themselves are, in many instances, remembrances of the great figures and events of French history. But beneath those official memories, so to speak, there is the multitude of other memories: those of the immigrant suburbs, of the communities and individuals who make up the city and whose particular memories have their own topography and narratives. Is "our" past also their present and future? Levy and Sznaider ask.[61] These memories jostle against one another in an effort to conserve (aspects of) identity.

On the one side, then, is the case that liberal modernity has unseated memory and in so doing has cleared the ground for a regime of rights and made for an open and plural society. The view that memory-identity is strictly a product of power, a confection, and that the business of critical reflection is to provide, as Nietzsche did in another context, a genealogy that will undermine the foundations of identity and reveal not a continuous story but fissures and fault lines is a powerful ally in this dethroning.[62] On the other side, as I have just shown, the proliferation of memories in formerly invisible groups can be seen to undermine the unified memorial identity of the political community as a whole. Here critiques of immigration and multiculturalism focus on the fragmentation of national/civic memory narratives with the resulting loss of unity and sense of shared membership. The flourishing of memory and narrative writing in formerly marginal groups, the recasting of national memory in the wake of large-scale immigration, and the concern over the possibility of retaining a common citizen memory-identity in the face of both the universalizing rights-type challenges and those coming from minority and historically marginalized groups: all of these point once again to the centrality of memory to identity. The reason for this was already suggested in the passage from *The Grapes of Wrath* quoted at the beginning of this book: "How will we know it's us without our past?" Individuals and communities have identities, that is, continuities of a particular kind across time, in as much as through memory (habit and volitional) they preserve a sameness with that past (and future). The memorial passion and identity politics do go hand in hand, then, though as I remarked, their relationship has been only incompletely theorized. This passion can be seen as arising in opposition to rapid technological change and globalizing currents (economic, cultural, and/or rights) or as a form of resistance of the excluded to a hegemonic memory narrative.[63] Or it can be an attempt to reaffirm a united national community against the twin challenges of globalization and group politics. What all of these currents have in common, however, is the concern for the loss of memory-identity and relatedly the absence of recognition.

Yet at the same time, this politics of memory also shows a very modern contest, along a number of axes, over memory and identity. Can complex societies even have identities? Habermas asks. That is, can identity withstand the forces of differentiation combined with a disposition to view inheritances and memory critically and in a detached manner? And perhaps the focus on identity (and memory-identity in particular) reveals the fundamental boundedness, self-preference, and group (rather than individual) orientation, that is, the anti-liberalism, of the passion for identity. For Todorov, the memorial obsession of the recent period is one symptom of this thirst, a thirst that in his view is a basic threat to liberal democratic politics. The ills that memory-identity brings in its train are many, and surely it is the case that in the past century we have been the witnesses to many of these. The capacity of collective memory to keep alive ancient hatreds, or to be used to cloak newly manufactured ones in the guise of something old, has fueled conflict around the globe. Memory keeps the "wounds greene" and the embers of conflict glowing. There also can be little doubt that communities bound together in deep memories, particularly of the ethnic/autochthonous kinds, are capable of great insularity, if not open xenophobia and intolerance. And finally, there is surely something right in the "iron tracks" view of memory-identity. It can seem too much of an anchor, even an obsession, and thus life-denying. So perhaps we need to balance the question of Steinbeck's Dust Bowl–era farmers ("How will we know it's us without our past?") with the meaning of Zygmunt Rogalla's burning down of the local museum in Siegfried Lenz's novel *Heimatmuseum* (*The Heritage*).[64] Whereas the Steinbeck passage invites us to reflect on the centrality of the past and memory for identity, Lenz wants us to think about the ways in which they can become the instruments of exclusion and violence. Rogalla's incendiary dethroning of the past has as its principal purpose an end to the particularism of memory-identity, a force that can readily fan the flames of violence and injustice. Ugrešić writes that "the terror of remembering is, of course, also a war strategy of setting up frontiers, establishing differences: we [Croatians] are different from them (the Serbs), our history, faith, customs . . . we are better."[65] It reminds us that in the wholeness of the historicality of human beings and their communities, their "remembering, forgetting, and recalling" (in Gadamer's phrase), forgetting too has a place, if an unstable and sometimes problematic one.

In this book I have assumed that these lines of criticism are in their various forms familiar to us and that they stand in less need of detailed articulation. Why, then, in the light of the concerns I have sketched here, does identity as enduringness matter? A general answer would be that where memory is dead, there is no longer an identical subject.[66] The analysis I have set out offers at least some further, if partial, responses. Recognition of ourselves (and recognition by others) as accountable, responsible subjects, the literal integrity of our lives, seems in a way primordial.[67] The person without a memory is radically deficient, and that intuition is likely why the farmers of *The Grapes of Wrath* are so anxious to preserve the traces of their past, and why exiles, according to Milosz, always look back.[68] This deficiency can be expressed as something lacking in the unity or (literal) integrity of a life, its wholeness and what makes persons of us. We see intimations of this in cases of Alzheimer's and other profound forms of amnesia. The loss may involve many things, both functional and moral, but at root what is undermined is something quite primitive: it is the loss of human wholeness and the responsibility that it sustains. The loss of memory also diminishes the capacity for relationships because those relationships are pervasively historical in character, that is, they are imbued with remembering, forgetting, and recalling. As I said at the beginning of this book, relationships take time, which means in part that they have a past, though as I also noted they do not (except in pathological cases, perhaps) dwell in that past. Rather, the past dwells in them, guarded in memory and memory-habit, and in a way too in their anticipations of the future. It is the thread that binds these persons in a shared past, in their relations of affection and anger, trust and suspicion, and expectation. A political community without memory would be radically deficient in similar ways. Yawning gaps in collective memory disrupt the continuity of the community as an association across time and can be pathological, a hole or a "gangrene" (to use Benjamin Stora's term) in their midst: Germany and Austria in the postwar period, France after the Algerian war of independence, the United States with its history of slavery and discrimination. A deep, often unnoticed memory is at the same time the stuff of civil mores, the political habits of the hearts of citizens and of their relations of trust and commitment: "The citizen . . . thinks and acts in responsibility, and thus in the duration."[69] For individuals, families, and political communities, the voice of memory can also sometimes be explicit. It can be found in autobiographies, family stories and souvenirs, commemorative days, and so on. In political communities it can take the form of civic history or national days of commemoration. Memory seeks, transmits, and guards these pasts; a heritage, we might say, but not one that resides, museum-like, outside of us but rather one that is present in the fabric of who we are and of the relationships we share.

Once more I want to underline the moral/practical sense in which memory, and the identity that it grounds, is central. This can be expressed in the first instance as the continuity of the subject, understood as a person capable of responsibility, of owning (so to speak) the actions on her ledger, and relatedly of having the capacity to engage in commitments to the future. To be a subject capable of imputation is to be capable of having a past, in the way that having a past is a part of identity, that is, through memory. Likewise, because societies have a past (in the sense just stated), they too are the subjects of imputation and agents of promise-making. Memory matters for doing justice. In its most basic signification, this means that doing justice involves the holding in memory of the wrong. Bearing witness (that act of keeping in memory and transmitting) is therefore a fundamental comportment of justice, guarding the relevant past and making it present. Relatedly, memory is bound up with the preservation and carrying out of obligations to the past, with the bonds of fidelity and of debt that are part of ongoing relationships, personal or political. Some of these are obligations to the victims, to see justice done. Others are between those who sacrificed for their community and those who live in and have received the benefits of that society: "What have we done with the society they bequeathed to us? What have we done with their ideal of solidarity? What significance have we given to their death?"[70] On other occasions, debts can be implicit and unspoken: a felt obligation to conserve and transmit, an obligation that has both a retrospective and a future-oriented time. Both the articulated and the silent obligations call on us to remember and so preserve as part of the relations of fidelity, continuity, and justice that make a political community something more than the project of the moment, that make it an (imperfect) whole and give it integrity.

Memory-identity, in its role as the underpinning of the continuity of the community, its justice, and its habits of the heart, also burdens through its legacies, creates boundaries, and keeps wounds fresh. And this is a deep and not a contingent relationship. The ills and the benefits that the gifts of memory provide are not readily separable. One could imagine a society where (in the words of Wallace Stevens's poem "A Clear Day and No Memories") "the air is clear of everything. / It has no knowledge except of nothingness / And it flows over us without meanings, / As if none of us had ever been here before / And are not now: in this shallow spectacle, / This invisible activity, this sense."[71] Such a society might be, as Stevens calls it, a "shallow spectacle," but it might well also be peaceful, open, and without resentment or a thirst for revenge. Yet I think we recognize that it would lack the shared relations immersed in a common past, present, and future, their justice and their ties to debt and commitment. Indeed, it would be like people who have spent no time together, and therefore have nothing in common, no past and no future, indeed scarcely any society or fabric of relationships at all.

While Todorov and others stress that a preoccupation with particularizing identity (memory) erodes core values (universal/voluntarist, liberal), it is also essential to underline the thought that justice and community require memory-identity.[72] Without it, as I just said, there would be no political community, not because it would lack shared cultural traditions but because it would be missing duration, habits of the heart, and justice, which is (to extend Aristotle's observations on the relationship between justice and the just man) the persistence of norms of a certain kind through time. To have a duration means to inherit, own, and be shaped by a history in the sense of the rich deposit left by the actions, mores, and memorials of a life led in common and across time. It also means to affirm that duration through forward-reaching promises and commitments. Democracy as a regime of time does not alter those brute facts of duration. It is not given to us, any more than to other societies or ages, to choose our cradle (our past, our inheritance, and the memories that make them present for us). But our present dispensation allows us a space in which we decide whether and in what manner we acknowledge that duration, past and future. The significance of this possibility is perhaps most apparent in issues of the recognition of responsibility for past injustices. Inheritance in the life of a community arrayed across time is the receiving of traditions and culture but also of the enduring weight of injustices. Communities exist in time and are responsible in time, and not through choice alone. In other words, communities have special burdens given to them by the fact of their being enduring bodies of a certain (morally accountable) kind.[73] And those burdens form part of their (unchosen) identity. Yet how that ledger is addressed is up to us, and that answer (or silence) too becomes part of who we are. Thus, in the German case, the struggle to recognize the persistence of the weight of the Holocaust has been a central part of establishing a postwar democratic German identity. Ownership and responsibility belong to the time of individuals and communities, but recognition is where we have a choice.[74] Not to recognize the fullness of our ledger, its debts and injustices, is itself a wrong of a special kind, a wrong by virtue of not bearing in mind one's responsibility to the victims or of gratitude to one's benefactors. It also, by attacking the bases of moral identity (the enduringness of the accountable/promising self), undermines the possibility of trust by refusing to recognize the connection between past and present wills, which in turn weakens faith in the forward-directed power of the will to commit my/our future self.

Political communities possess a kind of continuity, which we term their identity, and on that foundation they are capable of having experience, and expectation, of relations of trust, accountability, and commitment. Identity as enduringness in time, we might say, is essential to relationships in general and to the body of special relationships that make up a political community. Central to this continuity are the manifold ways in which memory binds together the moments of our lives, and of our lives together, into a certain wholeness or unity. This can be in part the community of a thick, autonomous memory of the habits of the heart which seems to particularize and (largely) to escape choice. In fact, that memory deeply informs the vision guiding the very choices we make. These thick memories might, for example, be the egalitarian habits ingrained in democratic societies. Or they might be more specific: the haunting presence of racial injustice in American political life, a presence that Tocqueville thought would endure (with color as its visible reminder: "Race perpetuates memories of slavery") long after the institutions of slavery had been abolished.[75] Judith Shklar, as I noted earlier, saw this continued presence in the importance attached to voting and employment status among citizens. Memory of this kind is not only something called up, invoked, or imagined; rather it almost appears to infiltrate, reflex-like, our present life-in-common. But memory can also be in certain respects within our power. Liberal democracy in particular opens before us the prospect that we have some measure of choice in addressing the ties of memory-identity. Enabled by what reflective distance from the past we are capable of securing, and by the commitment (in principle) of liberal societies to a certain set of universal norms, we determine how our understanding of the past will be shaped, and how we will do justice to it, and to the present and future. Democracy in this sense is the (partial) civic control of responsibility (in the duration, both its past and future registers), partial because we deliberate and decide these and other matters within a horizon already saturated by memory.[76]

Whether the issue is the Holocaust, the truth about Bloody Sunday, an apology to Japanese Americans interned during World War II, reparations for slavery, the fate of the personnel of the former apartheid regime in South Africa or of the leaders of the "dirty war" in Argentina and elsewhere, democracies old and new have a choice with respect to how to assume responsibility for their past.[77] The particular inheritances which are ours, and which are the stuff of these democratic choices, are not themselves matters of choice (any more than are the habits of the heart which inform them). Rather, they are the givens of a community's condition. And as I have observed, those pasts which never are erased have a way of resisting oblivion and forgetfulness, of returning unbidden even as we try to consign them to the forgotten. The event (Jankélévitch says) "wants to be remembered."[78] Yet it remains true that we are free to assume this past which is ours in any case, that is, to recognize it as ours, and to take responsibility for it in the varied ways of memory-justice, to bear witness to it. The choice we have here is that of whether and how we bear witness to the past which is ours. The integrity, meaning the ethical wholeness, of our community across time as a responsible agent, able to assume responsibility for the past and bind itself through commitments to the future, seems to demand the recognition that is the meaning of bearing witness. Liberal democracies, deeply embedded in memory but also constituted in part by a resistance to the particularism of a too robust politics of memory-identity and by the capacity for choice as to whether and in what manner to acknowledge the burdens and gifts of their duration, have as their particular fate, their inheritance, that this universalism and "choosiness" must interact, often uneasily, with their existence as communities of memory.

Notes

Preface

1. Saint Augustine, *Confessions*, trans. Henry Chadwick (Oxford: Oxford University Press, 1991), 10.8.12, 14; Marcel Proust, *À la recherche du temps perdu (Du côté de chez Swann)*, ed. Jean-Yves Tadié (Paris: Gallimard Bibliothèque de la Pléiade, 1987), 46–47; Charles Péguy, *Clio* (Paris: Gallimard, 1932), 35.

2. Aristotle, "De memoria et reminiscentia," in *Aristotle on Memory*, ed. Richard Sorabji (Providence: Brown University Press, 1972), 449a9.

3. Marc Bloch, *Apologie pour l'histoire ou Métier d'historien* (Paris: Armand Colin, 2002), 49 and note.

4. Pascal Quignard, *Petits traités II* (Paris: Gallimard, 1990), 87–88.

5. Joseph Brodsky, "In a Room and a Half," in *Less Than One: Selected Essays* (New York: Farrar, Straus and Giroux, 1986), 447–501; Gaston Bachelard, *La poétique de l'espace* (Paris: Presses Universitaires de France, 1957), 24, 26–27, 65; Joëlle Bahloul, *La maison de mémoire. Ethnologie d'une demeure judéo-arabe en Algérie (1937–1961)* (Paris: Éditions Métailié, 1992), 9–10; Frances A. Yates, *The Art of Memory* (London: Routledge and Kegan Paul, 1966), 3–4.

6. On the photo album as a conservatory of a family's memories and an affirmation of its unity, see Anne-Marie Garat, *Photos de familles* (Paris: Seuil, 1994), 7, 22; Anne Muxel, *Individu et mémoire familiale* (Paris: Nathan, 2002), 150, 176–77; Pierre Bourdieu and Luc Boltanski, *Un art moyen: essai sur les usages sociaux de la photographie* (Paris: Éditions de Minuit, 1965), 53–54.

7. Vladimir Jankélévitch, *L'irréversible et la nostalgie* (Paris: Flammarion, 1974), 294.

8. Robert Pinsky, "Poetry and American Memory," *Atlantic Monthly* (October 1999): 70.

1. Identity and Memory

1. Dubravka Ugrešić writes in similar terms of refugees from another catastrophe half a century later, the collapse of Yugoslavia into civil war: "Nameless ex-Yugoslav refugees scattered over all the countries and continents of the world have taken with

them in their refugee bundles senseless souvenirs which nobody needs . . . In the same bundle of memory jostle fragments of past reality, which can never be put back together, and scenes of war horrors." Dubravka Ugrešić, *The Culture of Lies*, trans. Celia Hawkesworth (University Park: Pennsylvania State University Press, 1998), 231.

2. John Steinbeck, *The Grapes of Wrath* (New York: Penguin, 1992), 120.

3. Wallace Stevens, "A Clear Day and No Memories," in *The Palm at the End of the Mind*, ed. Holly Stevens (New York: Vintage, 1990), 397.

4. Hans-Georg Gadamer, *Truth and Method*, ed. Garrett Barden and John Cumming (New York: Crossroad, 1982), 16.

5. Ralph Ellison, *Invisible Man* (New York: Vintage, 1995), 259, 508.

6. Jean Améry, *Jenseits von Schuld und Sühne. Bewältigungsversuche eines Überwältigen* (Stuttgart: Klett-Cotta, 1977), 96; Georges Poulet, *L'espace proustien* (Paris: Gallimard, 1982), 40.

7. Ellison, *Invisible Man*, 272–73.

8. The embeddedness of some forms of memory in things and places suggests that "remembering is more than a matter of mind alone." This underlines the "worldliness" of memory. Edward S. Casey, *Remembering: A Phenomenological Study*, 2nd ed. (Bloomington: Indiana University Press, 2000), 85, 243, 289; Maurice Halbwachs, *La mémoire collective* (Paris: Presses Universitaires de France, 1968), 130ff. Chateaubriand writes of the power of remembrance held by material things and the powerlessness of speech. This, as much as or more than (cultural) property rights, may help explain the drive to repatriate the past of national art and archaeological treasures from their exile in foreign museums and collections. See François-René Chateaubriand, *Mémoires d'outre-tombe*, vol. 1 (Paris: Gallimard, 1997), 132; Katherine Verdery, *The Political Lives of Dead Bodies: Reburial and Postsocialist Change* (New York: Columbia University Press, 1999), 48–49. It needs to be remarked that as notoriously open-ended as the concept of collective or social memory is, it is not necessary to read it as an attribution to a collective subject of the memory activities of individuals. Such a concern can be found in Bloch's critical review of Halbwachs's *Les cadres sociaux de la mémoire*. Marc Bloch, "Mémoire collective, tradition et coutume," *Revue de synthèse historique* 14 (1925): 78.

9. Will Kymlicka, *Liberalism, Community, and Culture* (Oxford: Clarendon Press, 1991), 165. Dienstag correctly points to the odd omission of this temporal dimension from much of the recent political philosophical consideration of identity. Joshua F. Dienstag, *Dancing in Chains: Narrative and Memory in Political Theory* (Stanford: Stanford University Press, 1997), 1–2. This is less true of the European literature than of contemporary English-language studies. Even in that latter group, however, there are exceptions, e.g., writings on narrative identity, which will be discussed in the course of this book. Laitin, Fearon, and Brubaker and Cooper set out some of the difficulties in the contemporary social scientific and political philosophy identity literature. David D. Laitin, *Identity in Formation: The Russian Speaking Populations in the Near Abroad* (Ithaca: Cornell University Press, 1998); James D. Fearon, *What Is Identity (as We Now Use the Word)?*, November 3, 1999, <http://www.wcfia.harvard.edu/misc/initiative/identity/ activities/confpapers/fearon2.pdf>; Rogers Brubaker and Frederick Cooper, "Beyond 'Identity,'" *Theory and Society* 29, no. 1 (February 2000): 1–47.

10. David Wiggins, *Sameness and Substance* (Cambridge: Harvard University Press, 1980), 70; Paul Ricoeur, *Parcours de la reconnaissance. Trois études* (Paris: Stock, 2004), 45, 63.

11. Susan Wolf, "Self-interest and Interest in Selves," *Ethics* 96 (July 1986): 709.

12. Casey, *Remembering*, 181.

13. Christine M. Korsgaard, "Personal Identity and the Unity of Agency: A Kantian Response to Parfit," *Philosophy and Public Affairs* 18, no. 2 (spring 1989): 121n.

14. Iris M. Young, *Justice and the Politics of Difference* (Princeton: Princeton University Press, 1990), 43–48.

15. David Hume, *A Treatise of Human Nature* (1739), ed. L. A. Selby-Bigge (Oxford: Oxford University Press, 1973), 252.

16. Ibid., 260, 254–55.

17. Derek Parfit, "Later Selves and Moral Principles," in *Philosophy and Personal Relations*, ed. Alan Montefiore (Montreal: McGill-Queen's University Press, 1973), 137–39, 141–42; Parfit, *Reasons and Persons* (Oxford: Oxford University Press, 1984), 211, 215–17, 239, 241, 275, 445; Sydney Shoemaker, "Parfit on Identity," in *Reading Parfit*, ed. Jonathan Dancy (Oxford: Basil Blackwell, 1997), 137, 139.

18. Parfit, "Later Selves and Moral Principles," 151; Parfit, *Reasons and Persons*, 191.

19. Parfit allows that both reductionist and non-reductionist theories of desert are defensible. Parfit, *Reasons and Persons*, 323ff.; Vinit Haksar, *Individual Selves and Moral Practice* (Edinburgh: Edinburgh University Press, 1991), 188, 196.

20. Paul Ricoeur, *Temps et récit*, vol. 3, *Le temps raconté* (Paris: Seuil, 1985), 442; Ricoeur, *Parcours de la reconnaissance*, 165, 187, 191–92.

21. Friedrich Nietzsche, *On the Genealogy of Morals*, trans. Walter Kaufmann and R. J. Hollingdale, ed. Kaufmann (New York: Vintage, 1969), 57–58.

22. We have expectations about the future, and the possibility of making commitments. Yet the future has an openness, an abstractness or emptiness, that cannot secure identity in the way that the particularizing past does. Steinbeck's tenants can find no anchor for their identity, no security for who they are, in the indeterminacy of the California that awaits them in the future, but only in the things that bear the traces of their past. The future, Kundera writes, "is only an indifferent void no one cares about, but the past is filled with life." Milan Kundera, *The Book of Laughter and Forgetting*, trans. Aaron Asher (New York: HarperCollins, 1996), 30. See also Charles Taylor, *Sources of the Self: The Making of the Modern Identity* (Cambridge: Harvard University Press, 1989), 50–51.

23. Hume, *A Treatise of Human Nature*, 261; Haksar, *Individual Selves and Moral Practice*, xiv, 3, 12–13.

24. John Locke, *An Essay Concerning Human Understanding*, vol. 1 (1690; New York: Dover, 1959), 459.

25. Ibid., 467.

26. Casey, *Remembering*, 39–40; Wiggins, *Sameness and Substance*, 15, 62, 64–65, 67–69, 92–93, 151.

27. Korsgaard, "Personal Identity and the Unity of Agency," 104.

28. Ibid.

29. Locke, *An Essay Concerning Human Understanding*, 444, 448, 458, 460, 467.

30. Paul Ricoeur, *Soi-même comme un autre* (Paris: Seuil, 1990), 143, 146–47, 164–65, 343–44; Robert Merrihew Adams, "Should Ethics Be More Impersonal?" in Dancy, *Reading Parfit*, 265–68.

31. Korsgaard, "Personal Identity and the Unity of Agency," 110–11, 113–15, 120, 121n, 127; Mark Johnston, "Human Concerns without Superlative Selves," in Dancy, *Reading Parfit*, 162.

32. Simon Blackburn, "Has Kant Refuted Parfit?" in Dancy, *Reading Parfit*, 189, 191; Shoemaker, "Parfit on Identity," 138–39; Korsgaard, "Personal Identity and the Unity of Agency," 128.

33. Korsgaard, "Personal Identity and the Unity of Agency," 103, 120.

34. Wiggins, *Sameness and Substance*, 151; Korsgaard, "Personal Identity and the Unity of Agency," 119.

35. Locke, *An Essay Concerning Human Understanding*, 444, 449, 458, 460.

36. See Norman Malcolm, *Knowledge and Certainty* (Englewood Cliffs, N J.: Prentice Hall, 1964), 187–92; Thomas Reid, "Of Identity," in *Personal Identity*, ed. John Perry (Berkeley: University of California Press, 1975), 114.

37. Joseph Butler, "Of Personal Identity," in Perry, *Personal Identity*, 100; Reid, "Of Identity," 115; Sydney Shoemaker, "Personal Identity and Memory," in Perry, *Personal Identity*, 120; Parfit, *Reasons and Persons*, 204–5, 223; Jean-Yves Tadié and Marc Tadié, *Le sens de la mémoire* (Paris: Gallimard, 1999), 49.

38. Wiggins, *Sameness and Substance*, 176; John McDowell, "Reductionism and the First Person," in Dancy, *Reading Parfit*, 233, 237.

39. Paul Valéry, *Cahiers*, ed. Judith Robinson-Valéry, vol. 1 (Paris: Gallimard/Bibliothèque de la Pléiade, 1973), 1222.

40. Jonathan F. Bennett, *Kant's Analytic* (Cambridge: Cambridge University Press, 1966), 117; Immanuel Kant, *Critique of Pure Reason* (1787), trans. Norman Kemp Smith (New York: St. Martin's Press, 1970), A101ff., B133. The Kantian notion of historicality and identity is not the dense, particularizing memory associated with character and community but something transcendental. That is especially evident in his account of moral action, where the particularizing time of a person's life and character is explicitly removed from the core of moral judgment. Kant, *Critique of Pure Reason*, A554–55, B582–83. Particularizing time, for Kant, belonged to empirical psychology or anthropology.

41. Pascal Quignard, *Petits traités II* (Paris: Gallimard, 1990), 48.

42. Alasdair MacIntyre, *After Virtue* (Notre Dame, Ind.: University of Notre Dame Press, 1984), 204ff., 212, 218; Michael Oakeshott, "The Tower of Babel," in *Rationalism in Politics and Other Essays* (Indianapolis: Liberty Press, 1991), 467ff. Pinsky writes that "the source of wholeness is in memory." Robert Pinsky, "Poetry and American Memory," *Atlantic Monthly* (October 1999): 70.

43. Casey, *Remembering*, 181.

44. Vladimir Jankélévitch, *L'irréversible et la nostalgie* (Paris: Flammarion, 1974), 62, 152, 256, 338.

45. In the political philosophical literature, the narrative account of identity and of the relationship to the past has been influentially developed by Hannah Arendt, Paul Ricoeur, and Alasdair MacIntyre. See Hannah Arendt, *The Human Condition* (Chicago: University of Chicago Press, 1958), 178ff.; MacIntyre, *After Virtue*, 205, 211–25; Paul Ricoeur, *Temps et récit*, 3 vols. (Paris: Seuil, 1984); also Jacques Le Goff, *History and Memory*, trans. Steven Rendell and Elizabeth Claman (New York: Columbia University Press, 1992), 52. On Arendt and narrative, see Seyla Benhabib, "Hannah Arendt and the Redemptive Power of Narrative," *Social Research* 57 (spring 1990): 167–96. See Taylor, *Sources of the Self*, 47ff. But see also Galen Strawson's critique of narrativity, discussed later on in this book.

46. Christa Wolf, *Ein Tag im Jahr. 1960–2000* (Munich: Luchterhand, 2003), 5.

47. Oliver Sacks, *The Man Who Mistook His Wife for a Hat and Other Clinical Tales* (New York: Simon & Schuster, 1970), 111

48. Dieter Henrich, *Der Gang des Andenkens. Beobachtungen und Gedanken zu Hölderlins Gedicht* (Stuttgart: Klett-Cotta, 1986), 141–42; Mary Warnock, *Memory* (London: Faber and Faber, 1987), 2, 56–57, 132.

49. Martin Heidegger, *Being and Time*, trans. John Macquarrie and Edward Robinson (Oxford: Basil Blackwell, 1973), 376. The phrase "sanctuary of [our] having been" is from Jankélévitch, *L'irréversible et la nostalgie*, 338.

50. Halbwachs, *La mémoire collective*, 128; Edmond Jabès, *Le Seuil. Le Sable. Poésies complètes, 1943–1988* (Paris: Gallimard, 2001), frontispiece. Halbwachs's work has not received the attention it deserves in the English-speaking political philosophical world.

Lewis A. Coser's introduction to his translation of selections from Halbwachs's writings is very good. Maurice Halbwachs, *On Collective Memory*, ed. and trans. Lewis A. Coser (Chicago: University of Chicago Press, 1992). In French, Paul Ricoeur has written extensively on Halbwachs from a philosophical perspective. Gérard Namer, *Mémoire et société* (Paris: Méridiens Klincksieck, 1987), is probably the best overview of his work. For a biography of Halbwachs, see Annette Becker, *Maurice Halbwachs. Un intellectual en guerres mondiales, 1914–1945* (Paris: Agnès Viénot Éditions, 2003).

51. *Plato: In Twelve Volumes*, vol. 3, *Philebus*, trans. Harold North Fowler, Loeb Classical Library (Cambridge: Harvard University Press, 1925), 21c–d.

52. Hume, *A Treatise of Human Nature*, 261.

53. Parfit, *Reasons and Persons*, 211–12, 275, 472; Parfit, "Later Selves and Moral Principles," 140, 142.

54. Parfit, *Reasons and Persons*, 316.

55. Marcel Proust, *À la recherche du temps perdu. (Le Côté de Guermantes)*, ed. Jean-Yves Tadié (Paris: Gallimard/Bibliothèque de la Pléiade, 1987), 439; Wolf, "Self-interest and Interest in Selves," 709.

56. Wim Wenders and Peter Handke, *Der Himmel über Berlin. Ein Filmbuch* (Frankfurt am Main: Suhrkamp, 1987), 168.

57. Jürgen Habermas, *Theory of Communicative Action*, vol. 1, trans. Thomas McCarthy (Boston: Beacon Press, 1984), 70, 82.

58. Pierre Bourdieu and Luc Boltanski, *Un art moyen: essai sur les usages sociaux de la photographie* (Paris: Éditions de Minuit, 1965), 53–54.

59. Edmund Burke, *Reflections on the Revolution in France* (1790; Indianapolis: Library of Liberal Arts, 1955), 38–39, 98; Jean-Louis Déotte, *Oubliez! Les ruines, l'Europe, le Musée* (Paris: L'Harmattan, 1994), 58, 70–71.

60. Adams, "Should Ethics Be More Impersonal?" 268.

61. Aristotle, *The Politics*, trans. Harris Rackham, Loeb Classical Library (Cambridge: William Heinemann, 1932), 1276a20–40.

62. Adams, "Should Ethics Be More Impersonal?" 271.

63. Aristotle, *The Politics*, 1276A18–20. Note that the question of identity here emerges in the context of promise keeping in relations between one city and another. Aristotle's analysis of relations within the city (especially in his critique of Plato's *Republic*) gives much more scope to differentiation and disunity. Yan Thomas observes that in the Roman case, the issue of the identity and persistence of the city arose not domestically but in relation to contracts and treaties with other cities, and that Roman legal-political thought rejected the Aristotelian theory of the persistence of constitutional forms as the basis of continuity. Yan Thomas, "L'institution civile de la cité," *Le Débat* 74 (March–April 1993): 24, 29, 36–38. Identity as the foundation of imputability and commitment seems especially visible in relations between states (or persons), but it is clearly also a part of a community's relation to itself and its members over time.

64. See Peter A. French, *Responsibility Matters* (Lawrence: University of Kansas Press, 1992), 65–66; W. H. Walsh, "Pride, Shame, and Responsibility," *Philosophical Quarterly* 20, no. 78 (January 1970): 13.

65. Bernhard Schlink, "Recht-Schuld-Zukunft," ed. Jörg Calließ, in *Loccumer Protokolle*, vol. 66 (Rehburg: Evangelische Akademie Loccum, 1988), 58.

66. As Joel Feinberg remarks: "There can be no such thing as vicarious guilt. Guilt consists in the intentional transgression of a prohibition." Joel Feinberg, "Collective Responsibility," in *Individual and Collective Responsibility*, ed. Peter A. French (Rochester, Vt.: Schenkman Books, 1998), 59. See also H. D. Lewis, "The Non-moral Notion of Collective Responsibility," ibid., 167.

67. French, *Responsibility Matters*, 66.

68. Peter A. French, *Collective and Corporate Responsibility* (New York: Columbia University Press, 1984), 5, 10–11, 13; Peter A. French, "Types of Collectivities," in French, *Individual and Collective Responsibility*, 37–50. For an analysis of corporate and political responsibility, see also Jude Dougherty, "Collective Guilt," *American Journal of Jurisprudence* 35 (1990): 1–14.

69. Peter A. French, "The Responsibility of Monsters and Their Makers," in French, *Individual and Collective Responsibility*, 4; French, *Collective and Corporate Responsibility*, 13.

70. French, *Responsibility Matters*, 138–40.

71. But consider the controversy over this case: In 2003, a German chemical firm, Degussa, was barred from participating in the construction of the Memorial to the Murdered Jews of Europe in Berlin because, during World War II, a sister company had manufactured Zyklon B, the chemical used in the Nazi gas chambers. Since the war, the firm has apparently had an exemplary record, acknowledging its past and contributing to the work of remembrance and atonement in Germany. "At what point, especially 60 years later, has a company earned exoneration for its past behavior? [One principle at work here is] of a sort of forgiveness for a company that has taken real action to atone for its past. The people who work at Degussa are not the same people who worked for it 60 years ago. According to this principle, it is wrong to penalize them for something that they had nothing to do with." In the words of a spokesman for the Foundation for Remembrance, Responsibility, and the Future, "The Degussa of today is not the Degussa of 60 or 70 years ago." Richard Bernstein, "Holocaust Legacy: Germans and Jews Debate Redemption," *New York Times*, October 29, 2003, <http://www. nytimes.com/2003/10/29/international/europe/29GERM.html?hp>. Michael Naumann, writing in *Die Zeit*, drew out the analogy between the judgment of this firm and the question of the continuity of the state: "Germany, including its companies, is no longer identical with that state the Jewish victims of which are remembered in the [Holocaust] memorial." Michael Naumann, "Hygiene am Bau. Schuldig für immer? Degussa und das Berliner Holocaust-Mahnmal," *Die Zeit*, October 30, 2003, <http://www.zeit.de/2003/45/Leiter_]2_45>.

72. "The unity of memory accompanies the Church from generation to generation as history runs its course." Pope John Paul II, *Memory and Identity: Conversations at the Dawn of a New Millennium* (New York: Rizzoli, 2005), 150. He is speaking of the memory of faith, but the apology over Constantinope suggests an institutional memory as well, "the divine-human identity of the Church."

73. Walsh, "Pride, Shame, and Responsibility," 8; French, *Collective and Corporate Responsibility*, 11.

74. See Roger Scruton and John Finnis, "Corporate Persons," in *Proceedings of the Aristotelian Society* 63 (London: Aristotelian Society, 1989), 239–66; Dominique Schnapper, *La communauté des citoyens. Sur l'idée moderne de nation* (Paris: Gallimard, 1994), 117–18.

75. Nicole Loraux, *La cité divisée. L'oubli dans la mémoire d' Athènes* (Paris: Payot, 1997), 267.

76. Aristotle, *The Nicomachean Ethics*, trans. Harris Rackham, Loeb Classical Library (Cambridge: William Heinemann, 1932), 1103a5–10, 1103b3ff., 1105b19ff., 1179b23ff.; Aristotle, *The Politics*, 1276b25–7b30, 1334a12ff.

77. This does not necessarily commit us to the strong narrative view of the unity of a life. Even those explicit memory narratives themselves (individual or social) can be jagged, uneven, and marked by substantial gaps. The underlying unity of the subject as a person or society having a ledger and thus being accountable for its past is the key here, and that unity is powerfully informed by memory in its many guises. This unity is not weakened by the sometimes episodic character of memory, nor by a failure to see

myself in the present as identical with myself in the past. See Galen Strawson, "Against Narrativity," *Ratio* 17, no. 4 (December 2004): 428–52.

78. It is worth bearing in mind Ricoeur's caution that too wide a theory of imputability loses its power because it dilutes the "mineness" of the event. Bernhard Schlink writes that for the current generation of Germans, memory and a sense of co-responsibility for the events of World War II have become more historical in character, because universal, and have relatedly lost their biographical-identity salience. Ricoeur, *Parcours de la reconnaissance*, 163; Bernhard Schlink, *Vergangenheitsschuld und gegenwärtiges Recht* (Frankfurt am Main: Suhrkamp, 2002), 155.

79. Ernest Renan, *Qu'est-ce qu'une nation* (Paris: Agora, 1992), 54.

80. Jacques Le Goff, preface to *À l'Est, la mémoire retrouvée*, ed. Alain Brossat (Paris: La Découverte, 1990), 8; Anthony D. Smith, *Myths and Memories of the Nation* (Oxford: Oxford University Press, 1999), 10, 208; Maurizio Viroli, *For Love of Country: An Essay on Patriotism and Nationalism* (Oxford: Oxford University Press, 1995), 9, 174; Stuart Hampshire, *Morality and Conflict* (Oxford: Basil Blackwell, 1983), 135.

81. See Tzvetan Todorov, *Nous et les autres* (Paris: Seuil, 1989), 254; Halbwachs, *La mémoire collective*, 40, 42.

82. Renan, *Qu'est-ce qu'une nation*, 54–55; Schnapper, *La communauté des citoyens*, 168.

83. John Stuart Mill, *Considerations on Representative Government* (South Bend, Ind.: Gateway, 1962), 307.

84. On homogeneous time, see Benedict Anderson, *Imagined Communities* (London: Verso, 1991), 24, 33. Péguy writes that homogeneous time renders into a common calculus the "innumerable varieties" of human experience. Charles Péguy, *Clio* (Paris: Gallimard, 1932), 51. Evans-Pritchard says of the Nuer that time in their society is measured and valued according to the activities that fill it. Edward Evan Evans-Pritchard, *The Nuer* (Oxford: Oxford University Press, 1940), 102–3.

85. Françoise Zonabend, *La mémoire longue: temps et histoires au village* (Paris: Jean-Michel Place, 1999), 283; Lucien Aschieri, *Le passé recomposé. Mémoire d'une communauté provençale* (Marseilles: Tacussel, 1985), 65ff., 116. On the unevenness and lapses of remembered common time, see Péguy, *Clio*, 265.

86. Brassaï, *Marcel Proust sous l'emprise de la photographie* (Paris: Gallimard, 1997), 20; Anne-Marie Garat, *Photos de familles* (Paris: Seuil, 1994).

87. Brassaï, *Marcel Proust sous l'emprise de la photographie*, 24.

88. Yves Bonnefoy, *Ce qui fut sans lumière* (Paris: Gallimard, 1987), 69.

89. Valéry, *Cahiers*, 1222.

90. André Malraux, "Transfert des cendres de Jean Moulin au Panthéon (19 Décembre 1964)," in *André Malraux. Oeuvres complètes* (Paris: Gallimard/Bibliothèque de la Pléiade, 1996), 948–55. Moulin was de Gaulle's emissary, sent to France to unite the resistance to the German occupation. In 1943 he was betrayed to the Germans and arrested. Tortured, he revealed nothing, and died of his injuries. Daniel Cordier notes that when Malraux gave his funeral oration, the French public knew very little of Moulin. Daniel Cordier, *Jean Moulin. La République des catacombes* (Paris: Gallimard, 1999), 15.

91. Halbwachs, *La mémoire collective*, 77.

92. See Jeremy Waldron, "When Justice Replaces Affection: The Need for Rights," *Harvard Journal of Law and Public Policy* 11, no. 3 (summer 1988): 630, quoting MacIntyre. Identity in this sense is often defined in opposition to some other community or way of life. Halbwachs, *La mémoire collective*, 79; Schnapper, *La communauté des citoyens*, 106.

93. Ancient Greek passage, source unknown, quoted in Quignard, *Petits traités II*, 450.

94. Jabès, *Le Seuil. Le Sable. Poésies complètes 1943–1988*, frontispiece.

95. Halbwachs, *La mémoire collective*, 37; Namer, *Mémoire et société*, 226; Schnapper, *La communauté des citoyens*, 117–18.

96. See Mary Douglas, *How Institutions Think* (Syracuse: Syracuse University Press, 1986), 69–80. Bloch remarked on the "inertia" of institutions, preserving ways of life long past the circumstances that originally gave birth to them. Marc Bloch, *Apologie pour l'histoire ou Métier d'historien* (Paris: Armand Colin, 2002), 61.

97. Friedrich Nietzsche, *Twilight of the Idols*, in *The Portable Nietzsche*, ed. and trans. Walter Kaufmann (New York: Penguin, 1954), 543; Friedrich Nietzsche, *The Will to Power*, trans. Walter Kaufmann and R. J. Hollingdale (New York: Vintage, 1968), 43; Martin Heidegger, *What Is Called Thinking?* trans. Fred D. Wieck and J. Glenn Gray (New York: Harper and Row, 1968), 67.

98. Jean-Jacques Rousseau, *Considerations on the Government of Poland*, in *The Social Contract and Other Later Political Writings*, ed. and trans. Victor Gourevitch (Cambridge: Cambridge University Press, 1997), 179, 181, 185, 189. See also Aristotle, *Nicomachean Ethics*, 1103b4–5; Aristotle, *The Politics*, 1334b15ff.

99. Casey, *Remembering*, 265, 304–5.

100. Ibid., 150.

101. See Henri Bergson, *Matière et mémoire* (Paris: Presses Universitaires de France, 1993), 162; but note also 168. Pierre Nora, "Entre mémoire et histoire," in *Les lieux de mémoire*, ed. Nora, vol. 1, *La République* (Paris: Gallimard, 1984), xxv; Halbwachs, *La mémoire collective*, 68. The sentence "to walk is to remember" is from Valéry, *Cahiers*, 1219.

102. Bergson, *Matière et mémoire*, 82, 85, 87; Casey, *Remembering*, 151.

103. Bergson, *Matière et mémoire*, 167.

104. Halbwachs, *La mémoire collective*, 42, 51.

105. Alexis de Tocqueville, *Democracy in America*, trans. George Lawrence, ed. J. P. Mayer (New York: Anchor, 1969), 287; Tocqueville, *De la démocratie en Amérique*, ed. François Furet, vol. 1 (Paris: Flammarion, 1981), 392.

106. Michael Oakeshott, "Rationalism in Politics," in *Rationalism in Politics and Other Essays* (Indianapolis: Liberty Press, 1991), 5–42; Oakeshott, "Political Education," ibid., 56ff.; MacIntyre, *After Virtue*. On democratic habits of the heart, see relatedly Jeffrey Stout, *Democracy and Tradition* (Princeton: Princeton University Press, 2004). Halbwachs thought that national events were too remote from individuals ever to take root in the collective memory of a people. See Halbwachs, *La mémoire collective*, 66–67.

107. Judith N. Shklar, "The Liberalism of Fear," in *Political Thought and Political Thinkers*, ed. Stanley Hoffmann (Chicago: University of Chicago Press, 1998), 9; Judith N. Shklar, *American Citizenship: The Quest for Inclusion* (Cambridge: Harvard University Press, 1991), 19–20, 85–86.

108. Robert D. Putnam, *Making Democracy Work: Civic Traditions in Modern Italy* (Princeton: Princeton University Press, 1993), 121ff., 167, 179. Bo Rothstein sets out the importance of collective memory in the emergence of trust and cooperation. Bo Rothstein, "Trust, Social Dilemmas, and Collective Memories," *Journal of Theoretical Politics* 12, no. 4 (2000): 493ff. Cases such as the conflict in Northern Ireland suggest that memory can also be the source of suspicion and non-cooperation. The habits of the heart are not always conducive to peace or democracy. See Jowitt's discussion of the legacies of habits acquired in Russia during the course of seventy years of Soviet rule. Ken Jowitt, *New World Disorder: The Leninist Extinction* (Berkeley: University of California Press, 1992), 285ff.

109. Halbwachs, *La mémoire collective*, 124, 132–33, 146, 165.

110. William Faulkner, *Absalom, Absalom!* (New York: Vintage, 1990), 115.

111. Paul Ricoeur, *La mémoire, l'histoire, l'oubli* (Paris: Seuil, 2000), 49, 51; Casey, *Re-*

membering, 198, 202; Gaston Bachelard, *La poétique de l'espace* (Paris: Presses Universitaires de France, 1957), 28; Aleida Assmann, "Erinnerungsorte und Gedächtnislandschaften," in *Erlebnis-Gedächtnis-Sinn*, ed. Hanno Loewy and Bernhard Moltmann (Frankfurt am Main: Campus, 1996), 13.

112. S. Yizhar, quoted in Meron Benvenesti, *Sacred Landscape: The Buried History of the Holy Land since 1948*, trans. Maxine Kaufman-Lacusta (Berkeley: University of California Press, 2000), 6.

113. Casey, *Remembering*, 186,189, 195; Poulet, *L'espace proustien*, 58–59, 69, 73; Bachelard, *La poétique de l'espace*, 24, 27, 32; Améry, *Jenseits von Schuld und Sühne*, 96–97.

114. Alexis de Tocqueville, "Lettre à Marie Mottley, July 1833," in *Oeuvres complètes*, vol. 14, *Correspondance Familiale*, ed. Jean-Louis Benoît and André Jardin (Paris: Gallimard, 1998), 385. See also Tocqueville, "Lettre à Gustave de Beaumont. October 5, 1828," in *Oeuvres complètes*, vol. 8, *Correspondance d'Alexis de Tocqueville et de Gustave de Beaumont (1)*, ed. J.-P. Mayer and André Jardin (Paris: Gallimard, 1967), 49–50.

115. Marc Augé, *Un ethnologue dans le Métro* (Paris: Hachette Littératures, 1986), 7–8.

116. Bachelard, *La poétique de l'espace*, 32.

117. Halbwachs, *La mémoire collective*, 42. See also Smith, *Myths and Memories of the Nation*, 63; Anne Muxel, *Individu et mémoire familiale* (Paris: Nathan, 2002), 45.

118. Niccolò Machiavelli, *Discourses on the First Ten Books of Titus Livy*, trans. Leslie Walker, ed. Bernard Crick (Harmondsworth: Penguin, 1970), 163–64, 385–86; Putnam, *Making Democracy Work*, 132.

119. Charles Baudelaire, "Le cygne," in *Oeuvres complètes*, ed. Claude Pichois, vol. 1 (Paris: Gallimard/Bibliothèque de la Pléiade, 1975), 85. On locale, loss, and memory in "Le cygne," see Jean Starobinski, *La mélancolie au miroir. Trois lectures de Baudelaire* (Paris: Julliard, 1997), 57–58. Brombert captures the fluidity of time in that poem, a fluidity that is central to memory itself. Victor Brombert, "'Le Cygne': The Artifact of Memory," in *The Hidden Reader: Stendhal, Balzac, Hugo, Baudelaire, Flaubert* (Cambridge: Harvard University Press, 1988), 97–102.

120. Proust, *À la recherche du temps perdu*, 420; Poulet, *L'espace proustien*, 23–24.

121. Luis Buñuel, *My Last Sigh*, trans. Abigail Israel (New York: Alfred A. Knopf, 1983), 4–5; Tadié and Tadié, *Le sens de la mémoire*, 297; Daniel L. Schachter, *Searching for Memory: The Brain, the Mind, and the Past* (New York: Basic Books, 1996), 1–2.

122. Patti Davis, "The Faces of Alzheimer's," *Time*, August 26, 2002, 78.

123. Sacks, *The Man Who Mistook His Wife for a Hat*, 35.

124. Quoted in Jean-Yves Le Naour, *Le soldat inconnu vivant* (Paris: Hachette Littératures, 2002), 11, 93. Le Naour adds, "The man that he was before the declaration of war was dead the day he lost his mind and his identity on the battlefield or in the German prisoner of war camp" (189).

125. This underlines the fact that memory and its loss are not simply events in the psychological life of an individual but are deeply social. Where memory vanishes, so do relationships, that is, the communion in a shared past. The movie *Eternal Sunshine of the Spotless Mind*, for example, portrays the unraveling of a relationship as the memories of the couple's shared time vanish. Conversely, forgetting can be important for breaking the hold of pathological and destructive memory on us and our relationships. The Finnish film *The Man Without a Past* depicts a man whose amnesia allows him a new life. Memory and forgetting both have their roles to play.

126. Plato, *Philebus*, 34a.

127. Chateaubriand, *Mémoires d'outre-tombe*, 601.

128. Georges Perec, *Ellis Island* (Paris: P.O.L., 1995), 59.

129. Alain Finkielkraut, *Le Juif imaginaire* (Paris: Seuil, 1980), 138; Rachel Ertel,

Dans la langue de personne. Poésie yiddish de l'anéantissement (Paris: Seuil, 1993); Richard Marienstras, *Être un peuple en diaspora* (Paris: Maspero, 1975), 10–11.

130. Finkielkraut, *Le Juif imaginaire*, 51.

131. Faulkner, *Absalom, Absalom!*, 210; Casey, *Remembering*, 194; Pascal Quignard, *Dernier royaume*, vol. 2, *Sur le jadis* (Paris: Grasset, 2002), 128–31,158, 195, 229. Casey is here discussing body-memory, though his argument applies as well to other forms of habit-memory.

132. Quignard, *Sur le jadis*, 26, 139–40, 240; Casey, *Remembering*, 162, 214, 271–72.

133. Ralph Ellison, "Commencement Address," in *The Collected Essays of Ralph Ellison*, ed. John F. Callahan (New York: The Modern Library, 2003), 417.

134. Quignard, *Sur le jadis*, 43.

135. Bonnefoy, *Ce qui fut sans lumière*, 12, 69; Yves Bonnefoy, *In the Shadow's Light*, trans. John Naughton (Chicago: University of Chicago Press, 1991), 4, 96, 99.

136. Starobinski emphasizes the role of hope in opposition to memory in Bonnefoy's poems, while Hans Jauss discusses their complex account of memory. Jean Starobinski, "La poésie, entre deux mondes," introduction to Yves Bonnefoy, *Poèmes* (Paris: Gallimard, 1982), 15–16; Hans Robert Jauss, "Ein Abschied von der Poesie der Erinnerung—Yves Bonnefoys *Ce qui fut sans lumière*," in *Memoria. Vergessen und Erinnern*, ed. Anselm Haverkamp and Renate Lachmann (Munich: Wilhelm Fink Verlag, 1993), 457, 463, 482.

137. In Erwin Mortier's *Marcel*, a novel concerned with the lingering effects of wartime collaboration in a Flemish family, the grandmother keeps her house as a "temporary annexe to heaven," filled with carefully tended photographs of the dead. But in addition to her still-life memorial, the presence of the past lingers in a daily, lived form in the family's resentment over actions taken against collaborators, and above all in the troubled remembrance of Marcel, a collaborator and volunteer in the German army, killed on the Russian front. Erwin Mortier, *Marcel*, trans. Ina Rilke (London: Harvill, 2001), 2, 32–33, 98–99, 116–18.

138. Pascal Quignard, *Dernier royaume*, vol. 1, *Les ombres errantes* (Paris: Grasset, 2002), 40; Georges Perec, *Espèces d'espaces* (Paris: Galilée, 1974), 122.

139. Georges Perec and Robert Bober, "Interview with Monsieur Chaïm Lipa Rubman," in *Récits d'Ellis Island. Histoires d'errance et d'espoir* (Paris: P.O.L., 1994), 141; Perec, *Ellis Island*, 39, 51, 52 57, 60, 63–64; Georges Perec, *Je suis né* (Paris: Seuil, 1990), 98.

140. Poulet, *L'espace proustien*, 22, 148. Poulet writes of Proust's insight into the fear awakened in people by the sense of being lost or in an unfamiliar place.

141. Czeslaw Milosz, "On Exile," *Parabola* 18, no. 2 (summer 1993): 25–26.

142. Mahmud Darwish, "Chronique de la tristesse ordinaire," trans. Olivier Carré in *Chronique de la tristesse ordinaire. Poèmes palestiniens* (Paris: Cerf, 1989), 13. On the political importance of territory and memory, see Smith, *Myths and Memories of the Nation*, 63, 151–52. Uday Singh Mehta analyzes the curious silence of Anglo-American liberal theorizing on the importance of territory for political identity in *Liberalism and Empire: A Study in Nineteenth-Century British Liberal Thought* (Chicago: University of Chicago Press, 1999), 117ff. For a critique of the particularizing effects of rootedness in a particular locale and for a welcoming of the "de-localization" (*Entortung*) that globalism is said to give modernity, see Emmanuel Lévinas, "Heidegger, Gagarine et nous," in *Difficile liberté. Essais sur le judaïsme* (Paris: Albin Michel, 1976), 324–25; Daniel Levy and Natan Sznaider, *Erinnerung im globalen Zeitalter: Der Holocaust* (Frankfurt am Main: Suhrkamp, 2001), 9, 23, 39.

143. Milosz, "On Exile," 27.

144. Mahmud Darwish, "Ma bien-aimée se lève de son sommeil," trans. Olivier

Carré, in *Chronique de la tristesse ordinaire*, 181; Darwish, "Identité," trans. Olivier Carré, ibid., 79–81.

145. Benvenesti, *Sacred Landscape.*

146. Maurice Halbwachs, *La topographie légendaire des évangiles en terre sainte. Étude de mémoire collective* (Paris: Presses Universitaires de France, 1971), 1, 88, 126. Both Halbwachs and Benvenisti analyze the Middle East as a locale of contested memorylandscapes, the former looking at Judaism and Christianity, the latter at Israelis and Palestinians.

147. Strawson, "Against Narrativity," 432.

148. Bloch, *Apologie pour l'histoire ou Métier d'historien*, 49n; Walter Benjamin, "Theses on the Philosophy of History," trans. Harry Zohn, in *Illuminations*, ed. Hannah Arendt (New York: Schocken, 1968), 261; Jean-Yves Lacoste, *Note sur le temps. Essai sur les raisons de la mémoire et de l'espérance* (Paris: Presses Universitaires de France, 1990), 32; Stéphane Moses, "Eingedenken und Jetztzeit—Geschichtliches Bewußtsein im Spätwerk Walter Benjamins," in *Memoria. Vergessen und Erinnern*, ed. Anselm Haverkamp and Renate Lachmann (Munich: Wilhelm Fink Verlag, 1993), 385–86, 389.

149. Bergson, *Matière et mémoire*, 162.

150. Quignard, *Sur le jadis*, 17, 63.

151. Bergson, *Matière et mémoire*, 147.

152. Emile M. Cioran, *E. M. Cioran: Ein Gespräch. Geführt von Gerd Bergfleth* (Tübingen: Rive Gauche, 1985), 9; Albert Camus, *La peste* (Paris: Gallimard, 1947), 47–51, 60–61; Maurice Halbwachs, *Les cadres sociaux de la mémoire* (Paris: Librairie Félix Alcan, 1935), 111; Georges Balandier, *Le dédale. Pour en finir avec le XXe siècle* (Paris: Fayard, 1994), 67.

153. Quignard, *Sur le jadis*, 123. But his collection of essays *The Name on the Tip of the Tongue* shows that forgetfulness and memory coexist even in something as seemingly stable as our speech. "The name on the tip of the tongue reminds us that language is not a reflex-like act for us; that we are not animals who speak in the same way that they see." Language is eaten away by forgetting and shadows, and thoughts or names on the tip of the tongue are one kind of "memory hole." Pascal Quignard, *Le nom sur le bout de la langue* (Paris: Gallimard, 1993), 57; Quignard, *Petits traités I* (Paris: Gallimard, 1990), 579, 585; Quignard, *Petits traités II*, 75, 366.

154. Lacoste, *Note sur le temps*, 15.

155. Tocqueville, *Democracy in America*, 493–96.

156. Bergson, *Matière et mémoire*, 76.

157. This middle position is also argued for in Smith, *Myths and Memories of the Nation*, 164–65, 167, 171, 175. For a version of the inheritance reading, see MacIntyre, *After Virtue*, 220–21. Instrumentalist/constructivist accounts of memory are much more prolific. As Barry Schwartz puts it, "The most widely accepted approach sees the past as a social construction shaped by the concerns and needs of the present." Barry Schwartz, "Social Change and Collective Memory: The Democratization of George Washington," *American Sociological Review* 56, no. 2 (April 1991): 221. For some illustrations, see Anderson, *Imagined Communities*; Yael Zerubavel, *Recovered Roots: Collective Memory and the Making of Israeli National Tradition* (Chicago: University of Chicago Press, 1995), 147, 214, 232; Marie-Claire Lavabre, "Du poids et du choix du passé. Lecture critique du *Syndrome de Vichy*," in *Histoire politique et sciences sociales*, ed. Denis Peschanski, Michael Pollak, and Henry Rousso, Questions aux XXe Siècle, no. 47 (Brussels: Éditions Complexe, 1991), 269–70, 274, 278.

158. Casey, *Remembering*, 271–72, 274–75.

159. Quignard, *Petits traités II*, 573.

2. Memory, Accountability, and Political Community

1. Bernard Williams, *Shame and Necessity* (Berkeley: University of California Press, 1993), 93–94. This discussion of shame owes a great deal to Williams's account. The differences between shame and guilt discussed here are, of course, not exhaustive. For other lines of demarcation, see, for example, John Rawls, *A Theory of Justice* (Cambridge: Harvard University Press, 1971), 440ff.

2. Gabriele Taylor, *Pride, Shame, and Guilt: Emotions of Self-assessment* (Oxford: Clarendon Press, 1985), 90–91.

3. Taylor, *Pride, Shame, and Guilt*, 58–59, 64, 85, 89, 90–92, 97; Williams, *Shame and Necessity*, 94.

4. Emmánuel Lévinas, *De l'évasion* (Paris: Fata Morgana, 1982), 111.

5. Taylor, *Pride, Shame, and Guilt*, 114, 132.

6. Lévinas, *De l'évasion*, 112.

7. Joel Feinberg, "Collective Responsibility," in *Individual and Collective Responsibility*, ed. Peter A. French (Rochester, Vt.: Schenkman Books, 1998), 63; Herbert Morris, *On Guilt and Innocence* (Berkeley: University of California Press, 1976), 135.

8. Quoted in Yael Tamir, *Liberal Nationalism* (Princeton: Princeton University Press, 1993), 98.

9. Niklas Frank, *Der Vater. Eine Abrechnung* (Munich: Bertelsmann, 1987); Marie Chaix, *Les lauriers du lac de Constance. Chronique d'une collaboration* (Paris: Seuil, 1974).

10. Peter Sichrovsky, *Born Guilty: Children of Nazi Families*, trans. Jean Steinberg (New York: Basic Books, 1988), 154.

11. Christine M. Korsgaard, "Personal Identity and the Unity of Agency: A Kantian Response to Parfit," *Philosophy and Public Affairs* 18, no. 2 (spring 1989): 127.

12. Bernhard Schlink, *The Reader* (1995), trans. Carol Brown Janeway (New York: Pantheon Books, 1997), 217–18. Sichrovsky writes of a postwar generation that "continues to trip . . . over their parents' past." Sichrovsky, *Born Guilty*, 15. It is, I think, not simply their parents' past. They stumble over it, rather than just passing by, because it belongs to them as well, as members of a community arrayed across time.

13. Schlink, *The Reader*, 171.

14. Aleksander Kwasniewski, President of the Republic of Poland, "Official Address at the Jedwabne Ceremony," Jedwabne, Poland, July 10, 2001, <http://www.radzilow .com/jedwabne-ceremony.htm>.

15. Jaspers suggests something like this; see in Karl Jaspers, "Die Schuldfrage," in *Hoffnung und Sorge. Schriften zur deutschen Politik 1945–1965* (Munich: Piper, 1965), 98, 100–101.

16. Charles Montesquieu, *Considerations on the Causes of the Greatness of the Romans and Their Decline*, trans. David Lowenthal (Ithaca: Cornell University Press, 1965), 25. In this light we can understand Nietzsche's thoughts on the antipathy to institutions as "a kind of will . . . which is anti-liberal to the point of malice: the will to tradition, to authority, to responsibility for centuries to come, to the solidarity of chains of generations, forward and backward." Friedrich Nietzsche, *Twilight of the Idols*, in *The Portable Nietzsche*, ed. and trans. Walter Kaufmann (New York: Penguin, 1954), 543; Nietzsche, *The Will to Power*, trans. Walter Kaufmann and R. J. Hollingdale (New York: Vintage, 1968), 43. Bloch writes that humans create institutions of which they subsequently become "more or less voluntarily" the prisoners. Marc Bloch, *Apologie pour l'histoire ou Métier d'historien* (Paris: Armand Colin, 2002), 61.

17. Pierre Nora, "La nation-mémoire," in *Les lieux de mémoire*, ed. Nora, vol. 2, pt. 3, *La nation (L'idéel)* (Paris: Gallimard, 1986), 648.

18. Dubravka Ugrešić, *The Culture of Lies*, trans. Celia Hawkesworth (University

Park: Pennsylvania State University Press, 1998), 100. Much of her book is a commentary on the abuse of remembering and forgetting in the politics of the civil wars in the former Yugoslavia. Power and memory are also evident in the memory dictatorships of the former regimes of central and eastern Europe and the Soviet Union. See Václav Havel, "Letter to Dr. Gustáv Husák," in *Václav Havel: Living in Truth*, ed. Jan Vladislav (London: Faber and Faber, 1986), 25–27.

19. Jean-Louis Déotte, *Oubliez! Les ruines, l'Europe, le musée* (Paris: L'Harmattan, 1994), 18; Christian Jacob, preface to *Le pouvoir des bibliothèques. La mémoire des livres en Occident*, ed. Christian Jacob and Marc Baratin (Paris: Albin Michel, 1996), 11.

20. Pierre Nora, "Entre mémoire et histoire," in *Les lieux de mémoire, ed. Nora*, vol. 1, *La République* (Paris: Gallimard, 1984), xxxi, xxxiii; Philippe Joutard, *Ces voix qui nous viennent du passé* (Paris: Hachette, 1983), 164.

21. Ouriel Reshef, "Une commémoration impossible: l'Holocaust en Israël," in *Les Commémorations*, ed. Philippe Gignoux, Bibliothèque de l'École des Hautes Études, Section des sciences religieuses, vol. 91 (Louvain: Peeters, 1988), 353; Yosef Hayim Yerushalmi, "Réflexions sur l'oubli," in *Colloque de Royaumont: usages de l'oubli* (Paris: Seuil, 1988), 16.

22. Vassilis Alexakis, *La langue maternelle* (Paris: Fayard, 1995), 114–15, 118, 133; Anthony D. Smith, *Myths and Memories of the Nation* (Oxford: Oxford University Press, 1999), 78. The strong Greek nationalist response to Anastasia Karakasidou's study *Fields of Wheat, Hills of Blood* suggests how potent this sort of politics remains. See Roger Just, "'Locals' into Greeks," review of Anastasia N. Karakasidou, *Fields of Wheat, Hills of Blood: Passages to Nationhood in Greek Macedonia, 1870–1990, Times Literary Supplement* (London), February 13, 1998.

23. Nicole Loraux, *The Invention of Athens*, trans. Alan Sheridan (Cambridge: Harvard University Press, 1986), 132, 143; Loraux, *Né de la terre. Mythe et politique à Athènes* (Paris: Seuil, 1996), 50, 63.

24. Lucette Valensi, *Fables de la mémoire. La glorieuse bataille des Trois Rois* (Paris: Seuil, 1992), 257–58; Loraux, *The Invention of Athens*, 19, 182, 185–87. Hence the Socratic hostility to the political funeral oration. Nicole Loraux, "Socrate contrepoison de l'oraison funèbre. Enjeu et signification du Ménexène," *Antiquité Classique* 43 (1974): 172–211; Pierre Vidal-Naquet, *La démocratie grecque vue d'ailleurs: essais d'historiographie ancienne et moderne* (Paris: Flammarion, 1990), 127.

25. Maurice Halbwachs, *La mémoire collective* (Paris: Presses Universitaires de France, 1968), 78; Pierre Nora, "De la République à la Nation," in *Les lieux de mémoire*, 1:652.

26. André Malraux, "Transfert des cendres de Jean Moulin au Panthéon (19 Décembre 1964)," in *Oeuvres complètes* (Paris: Gallimard/Bibliothèque de la Pléiade, 1996), 955.

27. Henry Rousso, *Le syndrome de Vichy de 1944 à nos jours* (Paris: Seuil, 1990), 112.

28. William Faulkner, *Absalom, Absalom!* (New York: Vintage, 1990), 172.

29. Bloch, *Apologie pour l'histoire ou Métier d'historien*, 6off.; Maurice Halbwachs, *Les cadres sociaux de la mémoire* (Paris: Librairie Félix Alcan, 1935), 177, 380–81.

30. Gérard Namer, *Mémoire et société* (Paris: Méridiens Klincksieck, 1987), 39, 225; Halbwachs, *La mémoire collective*, 12–13. Halbwachs distinguished between voluntary historical memory and perspectival collective memory. Freddy Raphaël and Geneviève Herberich-Marx, "Comment les souvenirs rentrent dans le rang," in *Maurice Halbwachs 1877–1945. Colloque de la Faculté des Sciences Sociales de Strasbourg (Mars 1995)*, ed. Christian de Montlibert, vol. 24 (Strasbourg: Collection de la Maison des Sciences de l'Homme de Strasbourg/Presses Universitaires de Strasbourg, 1997), 77.

31. Halbwachs, *La mémoire collective*, 36; Halbwachs, *Les cadres sociaux de la mémoire*, 30, 191, 195, 197, 400–401.

32. Ralph Ellison, *Invisible Man* (New York: Vintage, 1995), 273, 416.

33. Georges Perec, *Je me souviens. Les choses communes* (Paris: Hachette, 1978); Perec, *Je suis né* (Paris: Seuil, 1990), 81–83.

34. Jean Améry, *Jenseits von Schuld und Sühne* (Stuttgart: Klett-Cotta, 1977), 78, 84, 97; Jean-Clément Martin, "La Vendée, Région-Mémoire," in Nora, *Les lieux de mémoire*, 1:611; Michel Ragon, *Enfance vendéenne* (Paris: Albin Michel, 1990), 29, 172; Namer, *Mémoire et société*, 104–5, 109, 223.

35. Améry, *Jenseits von Schuld und Sühne*, 88, 90; Georges Perec, *Ellis Island* (Paris: P.O.L., 1995), 59; Georges Balandier, *Le dédale. Pour en finir avec le XXᵉ siècle* (Paris: Fayard, 1994), 67; Stefan Zweig, *Die Welt von Gestern. Erinnerungen eines Europäers* (Frankfurt am Main: Fischer, 1970), 468. Heidegger argues for the close relationship between home and mother tongue. So too the importance of the regional dialect of his native Vendée for Michel Ragon: the recognition even in remote places of the regional patois (the language of the land, Ragon writes, as opposed to French, the language of modernity) of one's place of origin, a dialect that reminds one of a community's past. Martin Heidegger, "Sprache und Heimat," *Hebbel Jahrbuch* (1960): 27–50; Michel Ragon, *L'accent de ma mère* (Paris: Plon, 1989), 31, 121–22, 210.

36. Halbwachs, *La mémoire collective*, 138.

37. Alexis de Tocqueville, *Democracy in America*, trans. George Lawrence, ed. J.P. Mayer (New York: Anchor, 1969), 317.

38. John Keats, "Ode to a Nightingale," in *Complete Poems*, ed. Jack Stillinger (Cambridge: Harvard University Press, 1978), 281; Yves Bonnefoy, "La maison natale," in *Les planches courbes* (Paris: Mercure de France, 2001), 93.

39. Dieter Henrich, *Der Gang des Andenkens. Beobachtungen und Gedanken zu Hölderlins Gedicht* (Stuttgart: Klett-Cotta, 1986), 141; Vladimir Jankélévitch, *L'irréversible et la nostalgie* (Paris: Flammarion, 1974), 340ff.; Milan Kundera, *l'ignorance* (Paris: Gallimard, 2003); Pascal Quignard, *Dernier royaume*, vol. 3, *Abîmes* (Paris: Grasset, 2002), 41–47.

40. Namer, *Mémoire et société*, 103; Denis Paillard, "URSS. Figures de la mémoire: *Mémorial* et *Pamiat*," in *À l'Est, la mémoire retrouvée*, ed. Alain Brossat (Paris: La Découverte, 1990), 375.

41. Martin Walser, "Auschwitz und kein Ende" (1979), in *Deutsche Sorgen* (Frankfurt am Main: Suhrkamp, 1997), 229; Georg Simmel, "Exkurs über den Fremden," in *Der Gast, der bleibt. Dimensionen von Georg Simmels Analyse des Fremdseins*, ed. Almut Loycke (Frankfurt am Main: Campus, 1992), 11–12; Halbwachs, *La mémoire collective*, 78.

42. Halbwachs, *La mémoire collective*, 5.

43. Paul Ricoeur, *Temps et récit*, vol. 1 (Paris: Seuil, 1984), 344, 349.

44. André Malraux, "Antimémoires," in *Oeuvres complètes* (Paris: Gallimard/Bibliothèque de la Pléiade, 1996), 110; Stuart Hampshire, *Morality and Conflict* (Oxford: Basil Blackwell, 1983), 195.

45. Halbwachs, *La mémoire collective*, 70, 74–75, 79; Smith, *Myths and Memories of the Nation*, 14–15; Michael Walzer, "Nation and Universe," in *The Tanner Lectures on Human Values*, vol. 11 (Salt Lake City: University of Utah Press, 1990), 554; Loraux, *Né de la terre*, 34, 109, 125; Sheldon Wolin, *The Presence of the Past* (Baltimore: Johns Hopkins University Press, 1989), 40.

46. Ugrešić, *The Culture of Lies*, 230n.

47. Halbwachs, *Les cadres sociaux de la mémoire*, 190, 392; Loraux, *The Invention of Athens*, 38, 269.

48. David Miller, *On Nationality* (Oxford: Clarendon Press, 1995), 23, 164; Smith, *Myths and Memories of the Nation*, 10; Nora, "Entre mémoire et histoire," xix, xxxiv.

49. Ragon, *L'accent de ma mère*, 271; Alexakis, *La langue maternelle*, 327. Burke associ-

ated the emergence of the national museum with the attack of the revolutionary Rights of Man on the lived inheritance of the past: "We cherish and cultivate those inbred sentiments. . . . [We are] . . . not . . . like stuffed birds in a museum, with chaff and rags and paltry blurred shreds of paper about the rights of men." Edmund Burke, *Reflections on the Revolution in France* (1790; Indianapolis: Library of Liberal Arts, 1955), 98. On museums as characteristic of modernity, see Andreas Huyssen, *Twilight Memories: Marking Time in a Culture of Amnesia* (New York: Routledge, 1995), 15, 252.

50. Paul Ricoeur, *Le juste*, vol. 1 (Paris: Esprit, 1995), 36; François Bédarida, "La mémoire contra l'histoire," *Esprit* 193 (July 1993): 7.

51. I am grateful to a referee for the *American Political Science Review* (commenting on an earlier version of this discussion) for drawing this international dimension of identity and remembrance to my attention. Another international facet of the issues discussed here is the way in which memory constrains a country's foreign policy behavior, and the manner in which that behavior is perceived by others. Andrei S. Markovits and Simon Reich, *The German Predicament: Memory and Power in the New Europe* (Ithaca: Cornell University Press, 1997); Ian Buruma, *The Wages of Guilt: Memories of War in Germany and Japan* (London: Jonathan Cape, 1994), 14ff.

52. Quoted in Éric Conan and Henry Rousso, *Vichy, un passé qui ne passe pas* (Paris: Gallimard, 1996), 60–61.

53. *Le Monde*, November 15–16, 1992, 6. See also Blandine Kriegel, "Vichy, la République et la France," *Le Monde* (Paris), September 8 1995, 14; Kriegel, "Pardon et crime d'état," *L'Histoire* (November 1995): 78. Kriegel does allow that contemporary France has an obligation to evoke and criticize this past, but her reasons are characteristically Republican: because the Vichy regime issued from a legal vote of the Republican Assembly.

54. "L'autorité de fait dite 'Gouvernement de l'État français' (1940–1944)." Subsequently, in 1995, Jacques Chirac accepted responsibility on behalf of France, a recognition that was reiterated by Prime Minister Lionel Jospin in 1997. Conan and Rousso, *Vichy, un passé qui ne passe pas*, 91. Suggestive of the kind of ambiguities I am discussing here, Chirac's 1995 speech commemorating the Vél' d'Hiv seizure of French Jews speaks sometimes of the responsibility of the "French State" (dropping the "de facto authority called . . ." qualifier) and at others of the "life of a nation" or simply "we." What Chirac calls France's "imprescriptible debt" to the Jews deported from there to Nazi death camps is not made to rest on the question of the constitutionality of the Vichy regime.

55. Jacques Le Goff, "Introduction des Entretiens du Patrimoine," introduction to *Patrimoines et passions identitaire*, ed. Le Goff (Paris: Librairie Arthème Fayard, 1998), 12.

56. Alain Finkielkraut, *La défaite de la pensée* (Paris: Gallimard, 1987), 126–27; Tzvetan Todorov, *Nous et les autres* (Paris: Seuil, 1989), 256; Burke, *Reflections*, 110. Ugrešić speaks of the "untranslatability" of collective memory. Ugrešić, *The Culture of Lies*, 230n.

57. Arthur Ripstein, "Context, Continuity, and Fairness," in *The Morality of Nationalism*, ed. Robert McKim and Jeff McMahan (Oxford: Oxford University Press, 1997), 220–23.

58. The issue of memory and American identity is a contested one. "Imagine, if you can, a society formed from all the nations of the world: English, French, Germans. Everyone having a language, a faith, different opinions, in a word, a society without roots, without memories, without prejudices, without routine, without shared ideas, without national character, a hundred times happier than ours, [but] I doubt more virtuous . . . What makes a people of all this? *Interest*, that is where the secret lies." Alexis

de Tocqueville, "Voyage en Amérique," in *Œuvres*, ed. André Jardin (Paris: Galli-mard/Bibliothèque de la Pléiade, 1991), 29. Of course, Tocqueville's study of the habits of the heart was grounded in the American experience. Ugrešić discusses con-temporary European views of a memory-less America, or rather of the painless nostal-gia of a country that has not experienced loss on the scale Europe has. Ugrešić, *The Culture of Lies*, 222–23. Such a reading of the American polity finds some support in Thomas Paine's *Rights of Man*, which vigorously rejects the idea that the past (and pre-sumably our memory of it) can have any role to play in a democratic rights-governed community. Thomas Paine, "Rights of Man," in *The Complete Writings of Thomas Paine*, ed. Philip S. Foner, vol. 2 (New York: Citadel Press, 1945), 250–51, 255. Barry Schwartz's studies, by contrast, make a very strong case for the political importance of memory in America. Barry Schwartz, "Mourning and the Making of a Sacred Symbol: Durkheim and the Lincoln Assassination," *Social Forces* 70, no. 2 (December 1991): 343–64; Schwartz, "Social Change and Collective Memory: The Democratization of George Washington," *American Sociological Review* 56, no. 2 (April 1991): 221–36; Schwartz, "Memory as a Cultural System: Abraham Lincoln in World War II," *American Sociological Review* 61, no. 5 (October 1996): 908–27; Schwartz, "Postmodernity and Historical Reputation: Abraham Lincoln in Late-Twentieth-Century American Mem-ory," *Social Forces* 77, no. 1 (September 1998): 63–103; Barry Schwartz and Todd Bayma, "Commemoration and the Politics of Recognition: The Korean War Veterans Memorial," *American Behavioral Scientist* 42, no. 6 (March 1999): 946–67. Pinsky de-scribes the notion of a memory-less America as a "national myth or delusion" and ar-gues that in an ethnically diverse country such as the United States, only memory can be the source of identity. Robert Pinsky, "Poetry and American Memory," *Atlantic Monthly* (October 1999): 60–61, 62. See also Alfred F. Young, *The Shoemaker and the Tea Party: Memory and the American Revolution* (Boston: Beacon Press, 1999); Michael Walzer, "What Does It Mean to Be an 'American?'" *Social Research* 57, no. 3 (fall 1990): 594ff.; Michael Kammen, *Mystic Chords of Memory* (New York: Vintage, 1993), 216; Nora, "Entre mémoire et histoire," xxi.

59. Abraham Lincoln, "July 10, 1858 Speech," in *The Complete Lincoln-Douglas De-bates of 1858*, ed. Paul M. Angle (Chicago: University of Chicago Press, 1958), 40–44.

60. Huyssen, *Twilight Memories*, 83.

61. Maurizio Viroli, *For Love of Country: An Essay on Patriotism and Nationalism* (Ox-ford: Oxford University Press, 1995), 9, 13–14, 174.

62. Theodore Dalrymple, "The Specters Haunting Dresden," *City Journal* 15, no. 1 (winter 2005), <http://www.city-journal.org/html/15_1_urbanities-dresden html>.

63. For a survey of the "historians' debate" and Habermas's role in it, see Charles S. Maier, *The Unmasterable Past: History, Holocaust, and German National Identity* (Cam-bridge: Cambridge University Press, 1997); Peter Baldwin, ed., *Reworking the Past* (Boston: Beacon Press, 1990); José Brunner, "Pride and Memory," *History and Memory* 9 (fall 1997): 256–300; Huyssen, *Twilight Memories*, 83; Dan Diner, "On Guilt Discourse and Other Narratives," *History and Memory* 9 (fall 1997): 301–20.

64. Jürgen Habermas, *Between Facts and Norms*, trans. William Rehg (Cambridge: MIT Press, 1996), 492, 495; Habermas, "Können komplexe Gesellschaften eine vernünftige Identität ausbilden?" in *Zur Rekonstruktion des historischen Materialismus* (Frankfurt am Main: Suhrkamp, 1976), 101.

65. Or to make them "sub-tenants" of a community of memory. Ugrešić, *The Culture of Lies*, 250–51.

66. John Rawls, *Political Liberalism* (New York: Columbia University Press, 1993), 277.

67. Habermas, *Between Facts and Norms*, 500, 507; Jürgen Habermas, "Nochmals:

Zur Identität der Deutschen," in *Kleine politische Schriften*, vol. 7, *Die nachholende Revolution* (Frankfurt am Main: Suhrkamp, 1990), 217, 220, 223.

68. Jürgen Habermas, "Die Stunde der nationalen Empfindung. Republikanische Gesinnung oder Nationalbewußtsein?" in *Kleine Politische Schriften*, 7:158–59.

69. Fernand Braudel, *L'identité de la France*, vol. 1 (Paris: Arthaud-Flammarion, 1986), 9; Buruma, *The Wages of Guilt*, 247, 249.

70. Jürgen Habermas, "Burdens of the Double Past," trans. Sidney Rosenfeld and Stella P. Rosenfeld, *Dissent* (fall 1994): 513–17; Joseph Rovan, introduction to *Devant l'histoire. Les documents de la controverse sur la singularité de l'extermination des Juifs par la régime nazi* (Paris: Cerf, 1988), xxii; Jean-Marc Ferry, "Interview with Jürgen Habermas," trans. Stephen K. White, *Philosophy and Social Criticism* 14, no. 3-4 (1988): 433–39.

71. The debate over the "normalization" of German history arose again in the controversy over Martin Walser's 1998 Peace Prize address. Martin Walser, "Erfahrungen beim Verfassen einer Sonntagsrede," in *Friedenspreis des Deutschen Buchandels 1998* (Frankfurt am Main: Börsenverein des Deutschen Buchandels, 1998), 39–51; Jan-Holger Kirsch, "Identität durch Normalität. Der Konflikt um Martin Walsers Friedenspreis Rede," *Leviathan* 27, no. 3 (September 1999): 309–53. Related disputes have occurred over the question of raising, or remaining silent about, the wartime suffering of German civilians. See Winfried Georg Sebald, *On the Natural History of Destruction*, trans. Anthea Bell (New York: Random House, 2004), x, 78–79, 103–4; Jörg Friedrich, *Der Brand. Deutschland im Bombenkrieg 1940–1945* (Munich: Propyläen, 2002). Röhl's polemical account of German civilian suffering ("the forgotten victims") explicitly ties these issues to the normalization of German history and identity. Klaus Rainer Röhl, *Verbotene Trauer. Die vergessenen Opfer* (Munich: Universitas, 2002), 213ff. Günter Grass's *Crabwalk*, which deals with the 1945 sinking of the *Wilhelm Gustloff*, is another foray into this difficult set of issues. These were in plain view in the controversy over the instrumentalization by the German far right of the sixtieth anniversary commemoration of the firebombing of Dresden. See Gerhard Schröder, *Erklärung von Bundeskanzler Gerhard Schröder zum 60. Jahrestag der Zerstörung Dresdens*, February 13, 2005, <http://www.bundeskanzler.de/www.bundeskanzler.de-7698.787177/Erklaerung-von-Bundeskanzler-Gerhard-Schroeder-z htm>.

72. Walser remarks that the drive to explain such crimes can step over into a justification of them. An account of the "why?" of something can easily become a sort of understanding (in the ethical sense) of it. Walser, "Auschwitz und kein Ende," 228.

73. Michael Stürmer, "Geschichte in geschichtslosem Land," in *Historikerstreit. Die Dokumentation der Kontroverse um die Eigenartigkeit der nationalsozialistischen Judenvernichtung* (Munich: Piper, 1987), 36, 38.

74. Jürgen Habermas, "Warum ein 'Demokratiepreis' für Daniel J. Goldhagen? Eine Laudatio," *DieZeit*, March 14 1997, <http://service.ecce-terram.de/zeit-archiv/daten/pages/historie.txt.19970314.html>.

75. Ferry, "Interview with Jürgen Habermas," 438–39.

76. Améry, *Jenseits von Schuld und Sühne*, 122; Walser, "Auschwitz und kein Ende," 229.

77. Péguy quoted in Alain Finkielkraut, *Le mécontemporain. Péguy, lecteur du monde moderne* (Paris: Gallimard, 1991), 88.

78. Jürgen Habermas, "On the Public Use of History," trans. Shierry Weber Nicholsen, in *The New Conservatism* (Cambridge: MIT Press, 1989), 233–34, 236.

79. See Bernard Williams, "Persons, Character, and Morality," in *The Identities of Persons*, ed. Amélie Oksenberg Rorty (Berkeley: University of California Press, 1976), 202–5.

80. Habermas, "Warum ein 'Demokratiepreis' für Daniel J. Goldhagen?"; Jürgen

Habermas, "Historical Consciousness and Post-traditional Identity," trans. Shierry Weber Nicholsen, in *The New Conservatism*, 251; Habermas, "On the Public Use of History," 236.

81. Ferry, "Interview with Jürgen Habermas," 438; Habermas, "Burdens of the Double Past," 514–15. It should be noted here that, despite our "unfettered intuition" that the dead can be wronged and that there are debts and responsibilities to them, there is a substantial literature that debates the issue of how we can (in the present) harm, have obligations to, or correct the wrongs done to a dead person. The core thought here is that only living persons have interests that can be harmed or repaired, and that relatedly even postmortem noncompliance with their (living) wishes or interests can cause them no injury. See, for example, Joel Feinberg, *The Moral Limits of the Criminal Law*, vol. 1, *Harm to Others* (Oxford: Oxford University Press, 1984), 79–95; George Pitcher, "The Misfortunes of the Dead," *American Philosophical Quarterly* 21, no. 2 (April 1984): 183–88; Ernest Partridge, "Posthumous Interests and Posthumous Respect," *Ethics* 91, no. 2 (January 1981): 243–64; Barbara Baum Levenbook, "Harming Someone after His Death," *Ethics* 94, no. 3 (April 1984): 407–19.

82. Jaspers did extend the issue of responsibility beyond the circle of contemporaries. In so doing, he encounters difficulties similar to Habermas's in defining the subject of collective imputation: is it a blood community or a *Gedankenwelt*; a community of fate or a way of thinking? See Karl Jaspers, "Antwort an Sigrid Undset," in *Hoffnung und Sorge*, 47–48; Jaspers, "Die Schuldfrage," 113–14, 130. Rothenpieler offers a survey of the history of jurisprudential reasoning on collective guilt in the Anglo-American and European traditions. See especially Friedrich W. Rothenpieler, *Der Gedanke einer Kollectivschuld in juristischer Sicht* (Berlin: Duncker und Humblot, 1982), 46, 106.

83. See Huyssen, *Twilight Memories*, 83.

84. Habermas, "Können komplexe Gesellschaften eine vernünftige Identität ausbilden?" 119–21.

85. Habermas, "Historical Consciousness and Post-traditional Identity," 252.

86. Améry, *Jenseits von Schuld und Sühne*, 121–22, 124; Siegfried Lenz, *Über das Gedächtnis. Reden und Aufsätze* (Munich: DTV, 1992), 107.

87. Habermas, "Historical Consciousness and Post-traditional Identity," 251; Habermas, "On the Public Use of History," 233, 236; Habermas, "Warum ein 'Demokratiepreis' für Daniel J. Goldhagen?"

88. Christian Meier, "Kein Schlußwort. Zum Streit über die NS–Vergangenheit," in *Historikerstreit. Die Dokumentation der Kontroverse um die Eigenartigkeit der nationalsozialistischen Judenvernichtung* (Munich: Piper, 1987), 272–73.

89. Meier, "Kein Schlußwort," 273; Maier, *The Unmasterable Past*, 55–56, 59–60.

90. Philipp Jenninger, "Rede anlässlich des 50. Jahrestages der Reichskristallnacht (1938) [Speech to the Bundestag on the Fiftieth Anniversary of Kristallnacht, 1938]," November 11, 1988, <http://www.mediasam.de/pdf_bg/jenninger_rede.pdf>. Jenninger resigned in the wake of controversies over this speech, parts of which were seen as offering an excuse (via an explanation) for the Nazi regime. For a brief history of this incident, see Buruma, *The Wages of Guilt*, 239–47, 249.

91. Habermas, "Können komplexe Gesellschaften eine vernünftige Identität ausbilden?"

92. Schwartz, "Social Change and Collective Memory," 221.

93. Variations, philosophical and applied/empirical, on this can be found in Tamir, *Liberal Nationalism*; Benedict Anderson, *Imagined Communities* (London: Verso, 1991); Miller, *On Nationality*; Yael Zerubavel, *Recovered Roots: Collective Memory and the Making of Israeli National Tradition* (Chicago: University of Chicago Press, 1995); Anas-

tasia N. Karakasidou, *Fields of Wheat, Hills of Blood: Passages to Nationhood in Greek Macedonia, 1870–1990* (Chicago: University of Chicago Press, 1997).

94. Karakasidou, *Fields of Wheat, Hills of Blood*, 228–37.

95. Émile Benveniste, "Formes et sens de *mnaomai*," in *Sprachgeschichte und Wortbedeutung. Festschrift Albert Debrunner* (Bern: Francke, 1954), 13.

96. See Michel Foucault, *The Archaeology of Knowledge*, trans. A. M. Sheridan Smith (New York: Pantheon, 1972), 128–31.

97. Jankélévitch, *L'irréversible et la nostalgie*, 294.

98. David Lowenthal, *The Past Is a Foreign Country* (Cambridge: Cambridge University Press, 1985), 365.

99. Pierre Vidal-Naquet, *Les assassins de la mémoire* (Paris: Seuil, 1995); François Bédarida, *Comment est-il possible que le "revisionnisme" existe?*, special issue of *Cahiers* 4 (1993): 21–22.

100. Charles Péguy, *Clio* (Paris: Gallimard, 1932), 35.

101. Schlink, "Recht-Schuld-Zukunft," ed. Jörg Callieβ, *Loccumer Protokolle 66* (Rehburg: Evangelische Akademie Loccum, 1988), 59–60, 67–68.

102. Habermas, "Warum ein 'Demokratiepreis' für Daniel J. Goldhagen?" Michael Gorra observes that contemporary Germany is "marked by a past that seems at once omnipresent and yet impossibly distant." Michael Gorra, *The Bells in Their Silence: Travels through Germany* (Princeton: Princeton University Press, 2004), 100.

103. Le Goff, preface to *À l'Est*, 8; Jacques Le Goff, *History and Memory*, trans. Steven Rendell and Elizabeth Claman *(New York: Columbia University Press, 1992)*, 111. On nation and history, see Miller, *On Nationality*, 23ff., 41–42.

104. Walser, "Auschwitz und kein Ende," 229.

105. Schnapper's remarks on Habermas are in a similar vein. Dominique Schnapper, *La communauté des citoyens. Sur l'idée moderne de nation* (Paris: Gallimard, 1994), 78, 82.

106. Vladimir Jankélévitch and Béatrice Berlowitz, *Quelque part dans l'inachevé* (Paris: Gallimard, 1978), 74.

107. Péguy, *Clio*, 35, 228.

3. Bearing Witness

1. Paul Celan, "Corona," in *Gedichte in zwei Bänden*, ed. Beda Allemann, vol. 1 (Frankfurt am Main: Suhrkamp, 1975), 37.

2. The phrase "poppy of forgetting" is from Paul Celan, "Die Ewigkeit," ibid., 68. See also François Hartog, *Mémoire d'Ulysse. Récits sur la frontière en Grèce ancienne* (Paris: Gallimard, 1996), 37; Otto Pöggeler, *Spur des Worts: Zur Lyrik Paul Celans* (Freiburg: Karl Alber, 1986), 278.

3. Franz Kafka, *Nachgelassene Schriften und Fragmente 1*, in *Schriften. Tagebücher. Kritische Ausgabe*, ed. Jürgen Born et al. (Frankfurt am Main: Fischer, 1993), 7.

4. Georges Perec, *La disparition* (Paris: Gallimard, 1969); in English, *A Void*, trans. Gilbert Adair (1969; reprint, London: Harvill, 1994). Vassilis Alexakis, *La langue maternelle* (Paris: Fayard, 1995).

5. Alexakis, *La langue maternelle*, 32–33.

6. Pascal Quignard, *Petits traités I* (Paris: Gallimard, 1990), 87; Quignard, *Petits traités II* (Paris: Gallimard, 1990), 87.

7. Anne Carson, *Economy of the Unlost: Reading Simonides of Keos with Paul Celan* (Princeton: Princeton University Press, 1999), 38.

8. Régine Robin, *Le roman mémoriel: de l'histoire à l'écriture du hors-lieu* (Montréal: Le Préambule, 1989), 21.

9. On *damnatio memoriae* in the Roman tradition, see Friedrich Vittinghoff, *Der Staatsfeind in der römischen Kaiserzeit. Untersuchungen zur "damnatio memoriae,"* Neuen Deutschen Forschungen (Alte Geschichte), vol. 2 (Speyer: Pilger, 1936), 12ff., 64ff.; John Bodel, "Punishing Piso," *American Journal of Philology* 120, no. 1 (1999): 43–63.

10. Georges Perec, *Je suis né* (Paris: Seuil, 1990), 58–60; Perec, *Espèces d'espaces* (Paris: Galilée, 1974), 76–77.

11. Pindar, "For Sogenes of Aigina: Winner, Boys' Pentathlon," in *Works*, ed. and trans. William H. Race, vol. 2, *Nemean Odes, Isthmian Odes, Fragments*, Loeb Classical Library (Cambridge: Harvard University Press, 1997), ll. 10ff.

12. Alain Resnais made a short film about the Bibliothèque nationale de France, with the wishful title *Toute la mémoire du monde* (All the Memory of the World). Péguy uses the same phrase to describe the responsibility of the living in relation to books and their authors. Charles Péguy, *Clio* (Paris: Gallimard, 1932), 35.

13. These words from Isaiah are also quoted at the beginning of Claude Lanzmann's *Shoah*. The title of the Yad Vashem Holocaust Memorial in Israel comes from the Hebrew for "name" in that passage.

14. "Persons without a name are persons without a history." David Bouvier, *Le sceptyre et la lyre: L'Iliade ou les héros de la mémoire* (Grenoble: Éditions Jérôme Millon, 2002), 357.

15. Marcel Detienne, *Les mâitres de la vérité dans la Grèce archaïque* (Paris: L'Ouverture, 1994), 64, 90, 119.

16. Joël Candau, *Anthropologie de la mémoire* (Paris: Presses Universitaires de France, 1996), 3.

17. Hartog, *Mémoire d'Ulysse*, 42.

18. Françoise Zonabend, "Pourquoi nommer?" in *L'Identité*, ed. Claude Lévi-Strauss (Paris: Presses Universitaires de France, 1995), 260, 263.

19. Nicole Lapierre, *Changer de nom* (Paris: Stock, 1995), 134, 169; Lapierre, *Le silence de la mémoire. À la recherche des Juifs de Płock* (Paris: Plon, 1989), 26–27, 259.

20. Maurice Halbwachs, *La topographie légendaire des évangiles en terre sainte. Étude de mémoire collective* (Paris: Presses Universitaires de France, 1971), 128.

21. Maurice Halbwachs, *La mémoire collective* (Paris: Presses Universitaires de France, 1968), 138.

22. Lapierre, *Le silence de la mémoire*, 225–27, 241; Annette Wieviorka and Itzhok Niborski, eds., *Les livres du souvenir. Mémoriaux juifs de Pologne* (Paris: Gallimard, 1983), 55–57.

23. Dieter Simon, "Verordnetes Vergessen," in *Amnestie oder die Politik der Erinnerung in der Demokratie*, ed. Gary Smith and Avishai Margalit (Frankfurt am Main: Suhrkamp, 1997), 25; Halbwachs, *La topographie légendaire*, 127.

24. Halbwachs, *La topographie légendaire*, 126–27, 137–38.

25. James E. Young, *The Texture of Memory: Holocaust Memorials and Meaning* (New Haven: Yale University Press, 1993), 113, 132–33.

26. Alexakis, *La langue maternelle*, 330, 374.

27. Lapierre, *Le silence de la mémoire*, 9, 241; Henri Raczymow, *Contes d'exil et d'oubli* (Paris: Gallimard, 1979), 85–86; Agata Tuszynska, *Lost Landscapes: In Search of Isaac Bashevis Singer and the Jews of Poland* (New York: William Morrow, 1998), 10, 14.

28. Michel Ragon, *L'accent de ma mère* (Paris: Plon, 1989), 32, 123, 210, 297–369; Jean-Clément Martin, *La Vendée de la mémoire* (Paris: Seuil, 1989), 7.

29. This surely explains in part the importance of the preservation of the French language in Quebec.

30. In Rachel Ertel, *Dans la langue de personne. Poésie yiddish de l'anéantissement* (Paris: Seuil, 1993), 13, 139.

31. Isaac Bashevis Singer, "Concerning Yiddish Literature in Poland" (1943), trans. Robert Wolf, *Prooftexts* 15, no. 2 (May 1995): 127; Ertel, *Dans la langue de personne*, 14, 16–17, 32–33. Singer's 1978 Nobel lecture struck a more optimistic note about the future of Yiddish: "There are some who call Yiddish a dead language, but so was Hebrew called for two thousand years. It has been revived in our time in a most remarkable, almost miraculous way. Aramaic was certainly a dead language for centuries but then it brought to light the Zohar, a work of mysticism of sublime value. It is a fact that the classics of Yiddish literature are also the classics of the modern Hebrew literature. Yiddish has not yet said its last word. It contains treasures that have not been revealed to the eyes of the world. It was the tongue of martyrs and saints, of dreamers and Cabalists—rich in humor and in memories that mankind may never forget. In a figurative way, Yiddish is the wise and humble language of us all, the idiom of frightened and hopeful Humanity." Isaac Bashevis Singer, "Isaac Bashevis Singer: Nobel Lecture," 8 December 1978, <http://nobelprize.org/literature/laureates/1978/singer-lecture.html>.

32. Quignard, *Petits traités II*, 366.

33. Jacob Glatstein quoted in Ertel, *Dans la langue de personne*, 140.

34. Georges Perec, *W ou le souvenir d'enfance* (Paris: Gallimard, 1993), 25, 46–47, 63; Lapierre, *Le silence de la mémoire*, 259. Much of Perec's work is about memory, and clearly much of it is tied to his family's fate and to that of the Jewish community in Europe. Nevertheless, he said that his principal semi-autobiographical work, *W ou le souvenir d'enfance*, was not meant to be a tragic history. Georges Perec, *Ellis Island* (Paris: P.O.L., 1995), 59; Perec, *Je suis né*, 83–84; Claude Burgelin, *Georges Perec* (Paris: Seuil, 1988), 105.

35. Perec, *Ellis Island*, 58–59; Perec, *Je suis né*, 100–101.

36. Perec, *Ellis Island*, 59.

37. Alain Finkielkraut, *Le Juif imaginaire* (Paris: Seuil, 1980), 49, 52, 138.

38. Perec, *Ellis Island*, 59; Perec, *Je suis né*, 100.

39. Perec, *W*, 17, 63.

40. Ibid., 63.

41. André Naher, *L'exil de la parole. Du silence biblique au silence d'Auschwitz* (Paris: Seuil, 1970).

42. Marc Augé, *Les formes de l'oubli* (Paris: Payot et Rivages, 1998), 33. quoting J.-B. Pontalis.

43. Pascal Quignard, *Dernier royaume*, vol. 2, *Sur le jadis* (Paris: Grasset, 2002), 61–62.

44. Quignard, *Petits traités I*, 99; Quignard, *Petits traités II*, 79.

45. Quignard, *Petits traités II*, 573.

46. Ertel, *Dans la langue de personne*, 16.

47. French Acadian society itself has a long history of trying to preserve its identity since its dispersion in the mid-seventeenth century. Perhaps the best-known literary effort to preserve the memory of this community is Antonine Maillet, *Pélagie-la-Charrette* (Quebec: Bibliothèque québécoise, 1990).

48. Quoted in Ertel, *Dans la langue de personne*, 16.

49. Gertrud Koch, "Der Engel des Vergessens und die Black Box der Faktizität," in *Memoria. Vergessen und Erinnern*, ed. Anselm Haverkamp and Renate Lachmann (Munich: Fink Verlag, 1993), 69.

50. Perec, *W*, 63–64.

51. Michel de Certeau, *L'écriture de l'histoire* (Paris: Gallimard, 1975), 385–88.

52. Tuszynska, *Lost Landscapes*, 8, 93; Finkielkraut, *Le Juif imaginaire*, 49–52.

53. Emmanuel Lévinas, *Humanisme de l'autre homme* (Paris: Fata Morgana, 1972), 65.

54. Homer, *The Iliad*, trans. Richmond Lattimore (New York: Harper and Row, 1951), book 23, ll. 65ff., 95ff.

55. Alexakis, *La langue maternelle*, 330, 374; Péguy, *Clio*, 217–18.

56. Paul Ricoeur, *Parcours de la reconnaissance. Trois études* (Paris: Stock, 2004), 168–69.

57. Ralph Ellison, *Invisible Man* (New York: Vintage, 1995), 273, 508.

58. Walter Benjamin, "Theses on the Philosophy of History," trans. Harry Zohn, in *Illuminations*, ed. Hannah Arendt (New York: Schocken, 1968), 257.

59. Elizabeth V. Spelman, *Repair: The Impulse to Restore in a Fragile World* (Boston: Beacon Press, 2002).

60. Avishai Margalit, *Ethik der Erinnerung (Max Horkheimer Vorlesungen)* (Frankfurt am Main: Fischer, 2002), 15.

61. Martin Heidegger, *What Is Called Thinking?* trans. Fred D. Wieck and J. Glenn Gray (New York: Harper and Row, 1968), 151.

62. Edward S. Casey, *Remembering: A Phenomenological Study*, 2nd ed. (Bloomington: Indiana University Press, 2000), 39; Paul Ricoeur, *La mémoire, l'histoire, l'oubli* (Paris: Seuil, 2000), 6.

63. Lapierre, *Le silence de la mémoire*, 10.

64. Georges Perec, *Je me souviens. Les choses communes* (Paris: Hachette, 1978); Perec, *Je suis né*, 81–84.

65. Tzvetan Todorov, "La mémoire devant l'histoire," *Terrain. Carnets du Patrimoine Ethnologique* 25 (September 1995): 103; Todorov, *Mémoire du mal, tentation du bien. Enquête sur le siècle* (Paris: Robert Laffont, 2000), 141.

66. Casey, *Remembering*, 90, 93–94.

67. Aristotle uses the term "icon" in the sense of a copy. It also meant an image or statue. Plato radicalized and made problematic the notion of the icon as something that both is and is not ("though not really existing, really does exist"), that is both visible and not (the "cosmos [is] a perceptible God made in the image of the Intelligible"). Aristotle, *Aristotle: In Twenty-three Volumes*, vols. 17, 18, *The Metaphysics*, trans. Hugh Tredennick, Loeb Classical Library (Cambridge: Harvard University Press, 1989), 991a30, 1079b35; Herodotus, *The History*, trans. David Grene (Chicago: University of Chicago Press, 1987), 7 69; Plato, *Plato: In Twelve Volumes*, vol. 7, *Sophist*, trans. Harold North Fowler, Loeb Classical Library (Cambridge: Harvard University Press, 1989), 240b; Plato, *Plato: In Twelve Volumes*, vol. 9, *Timaeus*, trans. R. G. Bury, Loeb Classical Library (Cambridge: Harvard University Press, 1989), 92c. This calls us back to one of the original, and now lost, meanings of the word "icon" as a sign of something not seen. Saint Paul writes that it is Christ "who is the icon of the invisible God" ("hos estin eikōn tou Theou tou aoratou"). In the Roman Catholic faith, the priest is an "icon" of Christ. *Catechism of the Catholic Church*, 2nd ed. (Vatican City: Libreria Editrice Vaticana, 1997), 1142. Paul Ricoeur has a superb discussion of Plato's presentation of the problems surrounding the idea of the icon. Ricoeur, *La mémoire*, 8ff., 297.

68. Ellison, *Invisible Man*, 262, 296.

69. Marcel Proust, *À la recherche du temps perdu (Du côté de chez Swann)*, ed. Jean-Yves Tadié (Paris: Gallimard/Bibliothèque de la Pléiade, 1987), 46–47.

70. Sarah Kofman, *Rue Ordener, rue Labat* (Paris: Galilée, 1994), 10.

71. Perec, *Je suis né*, 83; Marc Augé, *Un ethnologue dans le métro* (Paris: Hachette Littératures, 1986), 36–37.

72. Patrick Modiano, *Dora Bruder* (Paris: Gallimard, 1999), 7.

73. Perec, *Je suis né*, 87; Lévinas, *Humanisme de l'autre homme*, 66–67.

74. Shoshana Felman and Dori Laub, *Testimony: The Crisis of Witnessing in Literature, Psychoanalysis, and History* (New York: Routledge, 1992), 3.

75. Maurice Merleau-Ponty, *Phénoménologie de la perception* (Paris: Gallimard, 1945), 473.

76. Alexander Solzhenitsyn, *Nobel Lecture in Literature, 1970*. Nobel e-Museum, December 3, 2003, <http://www.nobel.se/literature/laureates/1970/solzhenitsyn-lecture. html>.

77. Perec, *Je suis né*, 87.

78. Ricoeur, *La mémoire*, 201–2.

79. Victor Klemperer, *Ich will Zeugnis ablegen bis zum letzten*, ed. Walter Nowojski and Hadwig Klemperer (Berlin: Aufbau-Verlag, 1995), 99; Anna Akhmatova, "Epilogue II," trans. Judith Hemschemeyer, in *The Complete Poems of Anna Akhmatova*, ed. Roberta Reeder (Boston: Zephyr Press, 1997), 392–93; Germaine Tillion, *Ravensbrück*, 1st ed. (Neuchâtel: Éditions de la Baconnière, 1946), 11, 19, 50; Tillion, *La traversée du mal. Entretien avec Jean Lacouture* (Paris: Arléa, 2000), 86; Primo Levi, *Le devoir de mémoire. Entretien avec Anna Bravo et Federico Cereja*, trans. Joël Gayraud (Paris: Éditions mille et une nuits, 1995), 23, 26.

80. Michèle Simondon, *La mémoire et l'oubli dans la pensée grecque jusq'à la fin du Vᵉ siècle avant J.-C.* (Paris: Les Belles Lettres, 1982), 225.

81. Siegfried Lenz, *Über das Gedächtnis. Reden und Aufsätze* (Munich: DTV, 1992), 17.

82. Thucydides, *The History of the Peloponnesian War: Books I and II*, trans. Charles Forster Smith, Loeb Classical Library (Cambridge: Harvard University Press, 1991), bk. 1, sec. 22; Nicole Loraux, *Né de la terre. Mythe et politique à Athènes* (Paris: Seuil, 1996), 108–9; Simondon, *La mémoire et l'oubli dans la pensée grecque*, 266–68; Bernard Williams, *Truth and Truthfulness: An Essay in Genealogy* (Princeton: Princeton University Press, 2002), 151ff.

83. Primo Levi, *The Drowned and the Saved*, trans. Raymond Rosenthal (New York: Vintage, 1989), 23.

84. Ibid., 17, 19, 23, 83; Georges Perec, "Robert Antelme ou la vérité de la littérature," in *Robert Antelme. Textes inédits. Sur L'Espèce Humaine. Essais et témoignages*, ed. Daniel Dobbels (Paris: Gallimard, 1996), 176–77. There is an important literature on the difficulty, even impossibility, of bearing witness to the Shoah. See, on this and related issues, Felman and Laub, *Testimony*; Dominick Lacapra, *History and Memory after Auschwitz* (Ithaca: Cornell University Press, 1998); Ricoeur, *La mémoire*, 223.

85. Tillion, *Ravensbrück*, 1st ed., 36–37; Germaine Tillion, *Ravensbrück*, 2nd ed. (Paris: Seuil, 1973), 7, 9, 213; Pierre Vidal-Naquet, *Les juifs, la mémoire et le présent*, vol. 3, *Réflexions sur le génocide* (Paris: La Découverte, 1995), 197–99.

86. Jack Kugelmass and Jonathan Boyarin, eds. and trans., *From a Ruined Garden: The Memorial Books of Polish Jewry* (Bloomington: Indiana University Press, 1998), 41.

87. Annette Wieviorka, *Déportation et génocide. Entre la mémoire et l'oubli* (Paris: Plon, 1992), 163.

88. François Hartog, *Régimes d'historicité. Présentisme et expériences du temps* (Paris: Seuil, 2003), 11; Marc Bloch, *Apologie pour l'histoire ou Métier d'historien* (Paris: Armand Colin, 2002), 124. Bloch reads Herodotus' *History* (1.95.1) as sharing in Ranke's ambition to say what actually happened: *ton eonta legein*.

89. Fernand Braudel, *L'identité de la France*, vol. 1 (Paris: Arthaud-Flammarion, 1986), 9.

90. Certeau, *L'écriture de l'histoire*, 55, 60, 74. Certeau observes that history treats death and the absent as objects of study and that the historian's work (like society itself in its relation to past and present) is informed by both the "latencies," the weight of the past, habit-memory generally speaking, and what differentiates its own epoch from those earlier ones. Bloch's essay on the defeat of his country in 1940 is an example of

both a passionate bearing of witness and an analytical effort to understand the events of that time. Marc Bloch, *L'étrange défaite (Témoignage écrit en 1940)* (Paris: Gallimard, 1990), 29–30. Bloch was executed by the German Occupation authorities in 1944.

91. See Jean-François Lyotard, "Anamnèse," in *Hors Cadre 9. Film/Mémoire,* ed. Michèle Lagny, Marie-Claire Ropars, and Pierre Sorbin (Paris: Presses & Publications de l'Université de Paris VIII Vincennes, 1991), 109.

92. Yosef Hayim Yerushalmi, "Réflexions sur l'oubli," in *Colloque de Royaumont: usages de l'oubli* (Paris: Seuil, 1988), 16–17; Gaston Bachelard, *La poétique de l'espace* (Paris: Presses Universitaires de France, 1957), 9, 28; Péguy, *Clio,* 230–31, 237, 265.

93. Jean Améry, *Jenseits von Schuld und Sühne. Bewältigungsversuche eines Überwältigen* (Stuttgart: Klett-Cotta, 1977), 52.

94. Tillion, *Ravensbrück,* 2nd ed., 10–11, 203–4; Germaine Tillion, *Ravensbrück,* 3rd ed. (Paris: Seuil, 1988), 12.

95. Tillion, *Ravensbrück,* 2nd ed., 21, 41; Tillion, *La traversée du mal,* 86.

96. Isaac Lewendel, *Un hiver en Provence* (Le Château: Éditions de l'Aube, 1996).

97. Perec, *W,* 62–63; Burgelin, *Georges Perec,* 146; Sarah Kofman, *Paroles suffoquées* (Paris: Galilée, 1987), 16; Kofman, *Rue Ordener, rue Labat,* 10.

98. See Wieviorka and Niborski, *Les livres du souvenir,* 9–10, 59; Todorov, "La mémoire devant l'histoire," 103, 105; Isaac Lewendel, "Le témoin et sa mémoire face à l'histoire," *La pensée et les hommes* (Brussels) 39 (1998): 41–53.

99. Lanzmann argues that the Holocaust in no way belongs to memory. He means that the Holocaust belongs to the present and not to the what-has-been. Claude Lanzmann, "De l'Holocauste à Holocauste ou comment s'en débarrasser," in *Au sujet de Shoah. Le film de Claude Lanzmann,* ed. Bernard Cuau (Paris: Belin, 1990), 316. "In my writings," the Hungarian novelist Imre Kertész says, "the Holocaust could never be present in the past tense." Imre Kertész, *Nobel Lecture,* 2002, Nobel Foundation, <http://nobelprize.org/literature/laureates/2002/kertesz-lecture-e.html>.

100. Annette Wieviorka, *Auschwitz, 60 ans après* (Paris: Robert Laffont, 2005), 20–21.

101. Jean-Pierre Vernant, *L'individu, la mort, l'amour. Soi-même et l'autre en Grèce ancienne* (Paris: Gallimard, 1989), 53, 55, 70; Detienne, *Les mâitres de la vérité dans la Grèce archaïque,* 65; Simonond, *La mémoire et l'oubli dans la pensée grecque,* 119–20, 124.

102. Quoted in Felman and Laub, *Testimony,* 3. Lévinas's context here is theological, and he argues that such witnessing is not testifying to some fact or other. See Emmanuel Lévinas, "La gloire du témoignage," in *Éthique et infini. Dialogues avec Philippe Nemo,* L'espace intérieur, vol. 26 (Paris: Fayard, 1982), 113–14, 115.

103. Herodotus, *The History,* 7.228.

104. Serge Barcellini and Annette Wieviorka, *Passant, souviens-toi! Les lieux du souvenir de la Seconde Guerre mondiale en France* (Paris: Plon, 1995), 27–28.

105. Detienne, *Les mâitres de la vérité dans la Grèce archaïque,* 23–26; Lenz, *Über das Gedächtnis,* 10. To forget a book, Péguy writes, is to bring death to it. Péguy, *Clio,* 29.

106. Elie Wiesel, foreword to *A Vanished World: Roman Vishniac* (New York: Farrar, Straus and Giroux, 1983); Quignard, *Petits traités II,* 311.

107. Joseph Brodsky, "In Memory of Stephen Spender," in *On Grief and Reason: Essays* (New York: Farrar, Straus, and Giroux, 1995), 480.

108. Ricoeur, *La mémoire,* 497.

109. Earlier, I quoted Péguy writing of the "terrible responsibility" imposed by the "quasi-contract" between past and present, a responsibility to remember and in so doing to guard the "honor," "reputation," and "life" of the dead. Péguy, *Clio,* 35.

110. Kofman, *Rue Ordener, rue Labat,* 10. Emphasis added.

111. Perec, *Espèces d'espaces,* 123.

112. Jorge Semprún, *L'écriture ou la vie* (Paris: Gallimard, 1994), 182. Wyschogrod sees this responsibility to the silent as central to the work of historians. Edith Wyschogrod, *An Ethics of Remembering* (Chicago: University of Chicago Press, 1998), xii. In a similar vein, see Certeau, *L'écriture de l'histoire*, 385, 388.

113. See Casey, *Remembering*, 274.

114. Wiesel, foreword to *A Vanished World*.

115. Pindar, "For Sogenes of Aigina," ll. 15–16; Pindar, "For Melissos of Thebes: Winner, Chariot Race," in *Nemean Odes*, 7ff. Heidegger says that "thankfulness," "thinking," and "memory" share a common root in German. Heidegger, *What Is Called Thinking?* 141, 145.

116. Primo Levi, *The Reawakening*, trans. Stuart Woolf (New York: Simon & Schuster, 1995), 25–26.

117. Jorge Semprún, *Mal et modernité: le travail de l'histoire* (Paris: Climats, 1995), 44ff.; Semprún, *L'écriture ou la vie*, 36–38. Semprún's almost lyrical account of Halbwach's death, a mixture of invention and memory, has been the subject of critical comment. See Annette Becker, *Maurice Halbwachs. Un intellectual en guerres mondiales 1914–1945* (Paris: Agnès Viénot Éditions, 2003), 19, 413–17. Becker's portrait of the reality of Buchenwald, and the contemporary sketches of Halbwachs there, describe a fundamentally brutal, inhuman world.

118. Perec, *Je suis né*, 91; André Malraux, "Pour sauver les monuments de Haute-Égypte," in *Oeuvres complètes* (Paris: Gallimard/Bibliothèque de la Pléiade, 1996), 929; Georges Poulet, *Études sur le temps humain*, vol. 4, *Mesure de l'instant* (Paris: Plon, 1964), 214.

119. Emmanuel Lévinas, *La mort et le temps* (Paris: L'Herne, 1991), 20.

120. See Antoine Garapon, *Des crimes qu'on ne peut ni punir ni pardonner. Pour une justice internationale* (Paris: Odile Jacob, 2002), 161.

121. Aeschylus, *Works in Two Volumes*, ed. and trans. Herbert Weir Smyth, vol. 2, *Eumenides*, Loeb Classical Library (Cambridge: Harvard University Press, 1971), l. 318.

122. Michael Arad, *Reflecting Absence: World Trade Center Site Memorial Competition*. November 19, 2003, Lower Manhattan Development Corporation, <http://www.wtc-sitememorial.org/fin7.html>.

123. Vernant, *L'individu, la mort, l'amour*, 70.

124. Wieviorka and Niborski, *Les livres du souvenir*, 9, 173; Kugelmass and Boyarin, *From a Ruined Garden*, 31; Ricoeur, *La mémoire*, 476.

125. Semprún, *L'écriture ou la vie*, 182.

126. Vassili Grossman, "Repos éternel," trans. Sophie Benech, in *La Madone Sixtine* (Paris: Éditions Interférences, 2002), 59.

127. Tillion, *Ravensbrück*, 1st ed., 165, 167–69, 170–71; Tillion, *Ravensbrück*, 3rd ed., 11.

128. André Malraux, "Transfert des cendres de Jean Moulin au Panthéon (19 Décembre 1964)," in *Oeuvres complètes* (Paris: Gallimard/Bibliothèque de la Pléiade, 1996), 948.

129. Margarete Buber-Neumann, *Milena*, trans. Alain Brossat (Paris: Seuil, 1986), 269.

130. Wieviorka and Niborski, *Les livres du souvenir*, 15, 28–29; Kugelmass and Boyarin, *From a Ruined Garden*, 1. The real presence of the past is a central idea in Catholic theology. "Christian theology not only recalls the events that saved us but actualizes them, makes them present." See *Catechism of the Catholic Church*, §1104; Jean-Yves Lacoste, *Note sur le temps. Essai sur les raisons de la mémoire et de l'espérance* (Paris: Presses Universitaires de France, 1990), 200. According to Yosef Yerushalmi, the Passover Seder is also a making present rather than a thinking back to the flight from

Egypt. Yosef Hayim Yerushalmi, *Zakhor: Jewish History and Jewish Memory* (Seattle: University of Washington Press, 1996), 44; Margalit, *Ethik der Erinnerung*, 46–47; Emmanuel Kattan, *Penser le devoir de mémoire* (Paris: Presses Universitaires de France, 2002), 55.

131. Inaugurating a monument at Glières to Resistance members killed there during World War II, André Malraux quoted the inscription at Thermopylae and called on modern passersby to go tell France of those who fell at this site. André Malraux, "Inauguration du monument à la mémoire des martyrs de la Résistance," in *Oeuvres complètes*, 956–57.

132. Herodotus, *The History*, 1 1.

133. Vernant, *L'individu, la mort, l'amour*, 79; Hartog, *Mémoire d'Ulysse*, 41–42.

134. Carson, *Economy of the Unlost*, 73; Margalit, *Ethik der Erinnerung*, 12–15.

135. Quoted in *Vietnam Wall: The Memorial*, <http://www.vietnamwall.org/memorial.html>.

136. Casey, *Remembering*, 226, 256, 273.

137. Nicole Loraux, *The Invention of Athens*, trans. Alan Sheridan (Cambridge: Harvard University Press, 1986), 122, 132, 144–45, 202. Loraux reads Plato's *Menexenus* as a critique of the seductive falseness of the funeral oration, in other words, as a form of political speech. Nicole Loraux, "Socrate contrepoison de l'oraison funèbre. Enjeu et signification du Ménexène," *L'Antiquité Classique* 43 (1974): 172–211; Loraux, *The Invention of Athens*, 312–14. On the role of commemorations in affirming citizenship in the wake of the First World War, see Jay Winter, *Sites of Memory, Sites of Mourning: The Great War in European Cultural History* (Cambridge: Cambridge University Press, 1995), 80.

138. See Winter, *Sites of Memory*, 95.

139. Malraux, "Inauguration du monument à la mémoire des martyrs de la Résistance," 957. The audience is asked to bear witness in one sense, to carry the story of their fellow citizens, because the dead Resistance fighters were witnesses in another sense, that of having given themselves in evidence of their political community. The term "martyr" in the title of Malraux's address has both of these meanings. In classical Greek, the witness in a legal proceeding was a *martus*, one who attested to something (*marturomai*). The Christian sense of this expanded the meaning of martyr to include those who attested to faith by the forfeit of their lives. *Catechism of the Catholic Church*, 2472–73.

140. Honoring preserves the memory of the honored. Casey, *Remembering*, 226.

141. See Loraux, *The Invention of Athens*, 115–16; Carson, *Economy of the Unlost*, 39. Many of the last letters of Resistance fighters to their families express both the purpose of their sacrifice and the request that they be remembered. Guy Krivopissko and François Marcot, eds., *La vie à en mourir. Lettres de fusillés (1941–1944)* (Paris: Tallandier, 2003).

142. Barcellini and Wieviorka, *Passant, souviens-toi!* 11.

143. On the sixtieth anniversary (2004) of the Normandy invasion, Chancellor Gerhardt Schröder, the first German head of government to attend these commemorative ceremonies, did not visit La Cambe, or any of the six German military cemeteries in the area. In his speech in Caen, Schröder described the German military dead as having been sent into a war aimed at the "murderous oppression of Europe." "Spezial D-Day. Schröeder erinnert an Verbrechen," *Frankfurter Allgemeine Zeitung*, June 7, 2004, <http://www.faznet/s/Rub594835B672714A1DB1A121534F010EE1/Doc~E4AF47915FD23405AAB 36040069B35232~ATpl~Ecommon~Sspezial.html>.

144. Dieter Henrich, "Tod in Flandern und in Stein," in *Konzepte. Essays zur Philosophie in der Zeit* (Frankfurt am Main: Suhrkamp, 1987), 97–102; Reinhart Koselleck,

"Kriegerdenkmale als Identitätsstiftungen der Überlebenden," in *Identität,* ed. Odo Marquard and Karlheinz Stierle (Munich: Wilhelm Fink Verlag, 1979), 255–76.

145. Annette Wieviorka, "1992. Réflexions sur une commémoration," *Annales ESC* 48, no. 3 (May–June 1993): 703.

146. Bouvier, *Le sceptyre et la lyre,* 99. In the Homeric world, this was seen as just such an expression of indebtedness across generations.

147. Anne Muxel, *Individu et mémoire familiale* (Paris: Nathan, 2002), 44.

148. For a typology of places of memory, see Aleida Assmann, "Erinnerungsorte und Gedächtnislandschaften," in *Erlebnis-Gedächtnis-Sinn,* ed. Hanno Loewy and Bernhard Moltmann (Frankfurt am Main: Campus, 1996), 19. Three extensive studies of place and memory are Pierre Nora, ed., *Les lieux de mémoire* (Paris: Gallimard, 1984–1992); Étienne François and Hagen Schulze, eds., *Deutsche Erinnerungsorte* (Munich: C. H. Beck, 2001); Simon Schama, *Landscape and Memory* (New York: Simon & Schuster, 1995).

149. In 1979 Valéry Giscard d'Estaing, then president of France, described the public archives as the "memory of the life of the nation." Valéry Giscard d'Estaing, "La Loi 79–18 du 3 Janvier 1979," <http://www.genenord.tm.fr/gnarc/gnarc79.htm>; Krzysztof Pomian, "Les archives," in Nora, *Les lieux de mémoire,* vol. 3 (pt. 3), *Les France (De L'archive à L'emblème)* (Paris: Gallimard, 1992), 163.

150. Bachelard, *La poétique de l'espace,* 28, 130; Halbwachs, *La topographie légendaire,* 124, 128; Casey, *Remembering,* 93–94, 198, 202–3, 264; Assmann, "Erinnerungsorte und Gedächtnislandschaften," 13.

151. Carson, *Economy of the Unlost,* 73, 85.

152. Halbwachs, *La topographie légendaire,* 1.

153. Sarah Farmer, *Martyred Village: Commemorating the 1944 Massacre at Oradour-sur-Glane* (Berkeley: University of California Press, 1999), 10, 71, 94.

154. Young, *The Texture of Memory,* 3.

155. On memorial sites at Auschwitz and Dachau, see Wieviorka, *Auschwitz, 60 ans après,* 227ff.; Jean-Charles Szurek, "Pologne. Le camp-musée d'Auschwitz," in *À l'Est, la mémoire retrouvée,* ed. Alain Brossat (Paris: La Découverte, 1990), 540, 551–52; Young, *The Texture of Memory,* 130ff., 144; Robert Jan van Pelt and Debórah Dwork, *Auschwitz: 1270 to the Present* (New Haven: Yale University Press, 1996); Pierre Vidal-Naquet, "Des musées et des hommes," in *Les juifs, la mémoire et le présent* (Paris: La Découverte, 1991), 107–8; Geneviève Decrop, *Des camps au génocide: la politique de l'impensable* (Grenoble: Presses Universitaires de Grenoble, 1995), 217, 220–21; Harold Marcuse, *Legacies of Dachau: The Uses and Abuses of a Concentration Camp, 1933–2001* (Cambridge: Cambridge University Press, 2001). Relatedly, see Jenny Edkins, *Trauma and the Memory of Politics* (Cambridge: Cambridge University Press, 2003), 135–49.

156. Mariana Sauber, "Traces fragiles. Les plaques commémoratives dans les rues de Paris," *Annales ESC* 48, no. 3 (May–June 1993): 725–27; Madeleine Rebérioux, "Le Mur des Fédérés," in Nora, *Les lieux de mémoire,* vol. 1, *La République* (Paris: Gallimard, 1984), 619–49; Barcellini and Wieviorka, *Passant, souviens-toi!* 19–20.

157. Quoted in Sophie Calle, *Souvenirs de Berlin-Est* (Paris: Actes Sud, 1999), 7.

158. See, for example, David W. Blight, *Race and Reunion: The Civil War in American Memory* (Cambridge: Harvard University Press, 2001); Sanford Levinson, *Written in Stone: Public Monuments in Changing Societies* (Durham: Duke University Press, 1998).

159. Ugrešić describes the (political utility-driven) transformation of the town of Krin first into a nationalist memorial sight and then into a ghost town. Dubravka Ugrešić, *The Culture of Lies,* trans. Celia Hawkesworth (University Park: Pennsylvania State University Press, 1998), 227n.

160. Gérard Namer, *Mémoire et société* (Paris: Méridiens Klincksieck, 1987), 212.

161. "Generations Will Remember," advertisement, *New Yorker*, September 15, 2003, 43; Paul Goldberger, "Can Daniel Liebeskind Win at Ground Zero?" ibid., 72–81.

162. Discussed in James E. Young, "Écrire le monument: site, mémoire, critique," *Annales ESC* 48, no. 3 (May–June 1993): 734. On cities and the absence of memory, see also Maurice Halbwachs, *Les cadres sociaux de la mémoire* (Paris: Librairie Félix Alcan, 1935), 189; Jean Chesneaux, *Habiter le temps. Présent, passé, futur: esquisse d'un dialogue politique* (Paris: Bayard Éditions, 1996), 67–69. Aleida Assmann remarks on modernity's militating against rootedness in space. Assmann, "Erinnerungsorte und Gedächtnislandschaften," 14.

163. Robert Lowell, "For the Union Dead," in *Life Studies and For the Union Dead* (New York: Farrar, Straus and Giroux, 1999), 71.

164. Maurice Blanchot, *L'attente l'oubli* (Paris: Gallimard, 1962), 15, 49–50.

165. "Das auffallendste an Denkmälern ist nämlich, daß man sie nicht bemerkt." Quoted in Étienne François, "Reconstruction allemande: les monuments de Berlin, de la guerre à la réunification," in *Patrimoines et passions identitaire*, ed. Jacques Le Goff (Paris: Librairie Arthème Fayard, 1998), 319.

166. Esther Gerz-Shalev, "Le Mouvement perpétuel de la mémoire," in *Travail de mémoire 1914–1998: une nécessité dans un siècle de violence*, ed. Jean-Pierre Bacot (Paris: Autrement, 1999), 25; James E. Young, *At Memory's Edge. After-images of the Holocaust in Contemporary Art and Architecture* (New Haven: Yale University Press, 2000), 120ff.; Peter Reichel, *Politik mit der Erinnerung. Gedächtnisorte im Streit um die nationalsozialistische Vergangenheit* (Munich: Carl Hanser, 1995), 87, 120.

167. "There is only one tomb: the heart of a friend." Tacitus, quoted in Quignard, *Petits traités I*, 13. Quignard is arguing here that memory of a kind blocks the past. Pierre Nora offers a related account of the patrimonial/memorial passions of modernity. They are, he suggests, efforts to preserve in physical sites the memory that has ceased to be a living one. See Pierre Nora, "L'ère de la commémoration," in *Les lieux de mémoire*, vol. 3 (pt. 3); Nora, "Entre mémoire et histoire," ibid., vol. 1, xvii, xix, xxvi; Young, *The Texture of Memory*, 5, 127; Yerushalmi, *Zakhor*, 10.

168. Gunter Demnig's project "Hier wohnte 1933–1945" (Here Lived 1933–1945) involves replacing cobblestones in front of homes formerly occupied by victims of Nazi oppression with a small block and plaque (a *Stolperstein* or "stumbling block") inscribed "Here lived" with their names, dates, and fate. Gunter Demnig, *Stolpersteine. Hier wohnte 1933–1945*, June 6, 2004, <http://www.stolpersteine.com>. Passersby literally trip over their past. Recall Sichrovsky's remark that the postwar generation "continues to trip . . . over their parents' past." As I remarked earlier, it is theirs too as members of an enduring community, and not just their parents'.

169. Wieviorka, *Auschwitz, 60 ans après*, 85.

170. Cynthia Ozick, "The Posthumous Sublime," in *Quarrel and Quandary: Essays by Cynthia Ozick* (New York: Vintage, 2000), 29; Georges Poulet, *L'espace proustien* (Paris: Gallimard, 1982), 76, 87, 144, 150. Places are bound up with the identities of persons and communities, with loss and presence, and they are often indissolubly woven together with events and crimes. Ozick is here remarking on the use of photographs and descriptions of places to "freeze time into a poignant immobility." See Quignard, *Sur le jadis*, 192; Brassaï, *Marcel Proust sous l'emprise de la photographie* (Paris: Gallimard, 1997), 24. In the Potsdamer Platz scene in Wim Wenders's *Wings of Desire*, the old man touring the modern-day site can see only what is no longer there. Cassiel, the angel accompanying him, dwells in a timeless condition and sees a wartime vista of the Potsdamer Platz as if it were present. Notice that memory for this angel is not a struggle to recall the past, but happens effortlessly. When another of the film's angels, Damiel, becomes

human at the end of the story he writes, "Now I know what no angel knows." Wim Wenders and Peter Handke, *Der Himmel über Berlin: Ein Filmbuch* (Frankfurt am Main: Suhrkamp, 1987), 168. We saw earlier that one of the things he learns is that (to adapt Susan Wolf's words) relationships take time. Perhaps another is the labor that memory and remembrance, the making present of the past, involves.

171. Marie-France Osterero, "De l'histoire à la mémoire dans Shoah," in *Hors Cadre 9. Film/Mémoire*, ed. Michèle Lagny, Marie-Claire Ropars, and Pierre Sorbin (St. Denis: Presses & Publications de l'Université de Paris VIII Vincennes, 1991), 97.

172. Claude Lanzmann, "J'ai enquêté en Pologne," in *Au sujet de Shoah. Le film de Claude Lanzmann*, ed. Bernard Cuau (Paris: Belin, 1990), 212; Sander L. Gilman, "Alan Cohen's Surfaces of History," in Alan Cohen, *On European Ground* (Chicago: University of Chicago Press, 2001), 6, 10; Modiano, *Dora Bruder*, 7, 28, 141.

173. Cohen, *On European Ground*; Gilman, "Alan Cohen's Surfaces of History," 4; Jonnathan Bordo, "Phantoms," in Cohen, *On European Ground*, 95.

174. Claude Lanzmann, *Shoah* (Paris: Fayard, 1985), 15ff.; Lewendel, *Un hiver en Provence*, 17.

175. Lévinas, *Humanisme de l'autre homme*, 66; Brian Ladd, *The Ghosts of Berlin: Confronting German History in the Urban Landscape* (Chicago: University of Chicago Press, 1997), 141; Georges Poulet, *Études sur le temps humain*, vol. 1, *Études* (Paris: Plon, 1952), 428.

176. Casey, *Remembering*, 189.

177. Osterero, "De l'histoire à la mémoire dans *Shoah*," 99.

178. Theodore Dalrymple, "The Europe of Yesterday," *City Journal*, August 6, 2003, <http://www.city-journal.org/html/eon_8_6_03td.html>.

179. Pierre Vidal-Naquet, "Salonique déjudaïsée," in *Les juifs*, 436; Wieviorka and Niborski, *Les livres du souvenir*, 56–57; Lapierre, *Le silence de la mémoire*, 237–38. Mark Mazower discusses the emergence of modern Salonica, transformed by the fate (the absence) of its Jewish community in World War II, and that of its Muslim minority forced into exile in the early years of the twentieth century. Mark Mazower, *Salonica: City of Ghosts. Christians, Muslims, and Jews, 1430–1950* (London: HarperCollins, 2004).

180. Paul Valéry, *Cahiers*, ed. Judith Robinson-Valéry, vol. 1 (Paris: Gallimard/Bibliothèque de la Pléiade, 1973), 1218.

181. Jacques Le Goff, "Passé et présent de la mémoire," in *Lieux de mémoire et identités nationales*, ed. Prim den Boer and Willem Frijhoff (Amsterdam: Amsterdam University Press, 1993), 34.

182. Perec, *Espèces d'espaces*, 105, 123.

183. Osterero, "De l'histoire à la mémoire dans *Shoah*"; Poulet, *Études sur le temps humain*, 36.

184. Bachelard, *La poétique de l'espace*, 24; Martin Heidegger, *Erläuterungen zu Hölderlins Dichtung* (Frankfurt am Main: Vittorio Klostermann, 1971), 16–17; Casey, *Remembering*, 195.

185. Winfried Georg Sebald, *Austerlitz*, 2001, trans. Anthea Bell (New York: Random House, 2001), 221.

4. Witnessing and Justice

1. Joel Feinberg, *The Moral Limits of the Criminal Law*, vol. 1, *Harm to Others* (Oxford: Oxford University Press, 1984), 95. The utility of justice might, for example, be understood in classical Benthamite terms, or in Posner's wealth-maximization approach. See Richard A. Posner, *The Economics of Justice* (Cambridge: Harvard University Press,

1981), 60–76. The justificatory register, in either case, employs the future tense and makes its occupants the principal object of concern.

2. Michel de Certeau, *L'écriture de l'histoire* (Paris: Gallimard, 1975), 138, 388; Certeau, *L'absent de l'histoire* (Paris: Maison Mame, 1973), 7, 156. It "makes the dead speak." Paul Ricoeur, *La mémoire, l'histoire, l'oubli* (Paris: Seuil, 2000), 479.

3. Certeau, *L'absent de l'histoire*, 9, 158, 174, 179.

4. Jean-Yves Lacoste, *Note sur le temps. Essai sur les raisons de la* mémoire *et de l'espérance* (Paris: Presses Universitaires de France, 1990), 53.

5. Anne Carson, *Economy of the Unlost: Reading Simonides of Keos with Paul Celan* (Princeton: Princeton University Press, 1999), 85.

6. Certeau, *L'absent de l'histoire*, 158, 174; Antoine Garapon, *Des crimes qu'on ne peut ni punir ni pardonner. Pour une justice internationale* (Paris: Odile Jacob, 2002), 261, 264; Carlo Ginzburg, *The Judge and the Historian: Marginal Notes on a Late-Twentieth-Century Miscarriage of Justice*, trans. Anthony Shuggar (London: Verso, 1999).

7. Certeau, *L'absent de l'histoire*, 179.

8. I remarked earlier on the aspiration of history to explain what is not present, and in a manner detached from the possessiveness and attachment of memory. But the not-present is frequently what it is because of injustice and oppression, and so the writing of history can readily merge with the work of justice. Chateaubriand writes, "In the silence of abjection . . . when all trembles before the tyrant . . . the historian appears, carrying the vengeance of peoples." François-René Chateaubriand, *Mémoires d'outre-tombe*, vol. 1 (Paris: Gallimard, 1997), 946. Raphael Samuel observes that for E. P. Thompson, the writing of history was an act of reparation, rescuing the defeated from the condescension of posterity. On Benjamin's view of the importance of history for doing justice to the scorned and defeated, see Raphael Samuel, *Theatres of Memory*, vol. 1, *Past and Present in Contemporary Culture* (London: Verso, 1994), viii; Stéphane Moses, "Eingedenken und Jetztzeit—Geschichtliches Bewußtsein im Spätwerk Walter Benjamins," in *Memoria. Vergessen und Erinnern*, ed. Anselm Haverkamp and Renate Lachmann (Munich: Wilhelm Fink Verlag, 1993), 401.

9. Jean Améry, *Jenseits von Schuld und Sühne. Bewältigungsversuche eines Überwältigen* (Stuttgart: Klett-Cotta, 1977), 116, 123; Vladimir Jankélévitch, *Le pardon* (Paris: Aubier-Montaigne, 1967), 53; Antoine Garapon, "La justice et l'inversion morale du temps," in *Pourquoi se souvenir?* ed. Françoise Barret-Ducrocq (Paris: Grasset, 1998), 113.

10. Garapon, "La justice et l'inversion morale du temps," 117.

11. Garapon, ibid., 116–18, 122; Garapon, *Des crimes qu'on ne peut ni punir ni pardonner*, 58, 199, 255.

12. Excellent in this regard are Jan-Werner Müller, ed., *Memory and Power in Post-war Europe* (Cambridge: Cambridge University Press, 2002); Gary Jonathan Bass, *Stay the Hand of Vengeance: The Politics of War Crimes Tribunals* (Princeton: Princeton University Press, 2000).

13. Paul Martens, "Temps, mémoire, oubli et droit," in *L'accélérations du temps juridique*, ed. Phillipe Gérard, François Ost, and Michel van de Kerchove (Brussels: Facultés universitaires Saint-Louis, 2000), 731; Yan Thomas, "La vérité, le temps, le juge et l'historien," *Le Débat* 102 (November–December 1998): 22, 27–29.

14. Roger Errera in Stephen Schulhofer et al., "Forum: Dilemmas of Justice," *East European Constitutional Review* 1, no. 2 (summer 1992): 22.

15. Martin Heidegger, *What Is Called Thinking?* trans. Fred D. Wieck and J. Glenn Gray (New York: Harper and Row, 1968), 150–51.

16. Friedrich Nietzsche, *Thus Spoke Zarathustra*, in *The Portable Nietzsche*, ed. and trans. Walter Kaufmann (New York: Penguin, 1954), 251–52; Heidegger, *What Is Called Thinking?* 93, 96, 103.

17. Revenge he calls the "tyrannomania of the impotent" and an expression of the will to equality. Nietzsche does, however, distinguish between justice and *ressentiment.* Nietzsche, *Thus Spoke Zarathustra,* 211–12; Friedrich Nietzsche, *On the Genealogy of Morals,* trans. Walter Kaufmann and R. J. Hollingdale, ed. Kaufmann (New York: Vintage, 1969), 73–74.

18. Jeremy Waldron, "Superseding Historic Injustice," *Ethics* 103, no. 1 (October 1992): 4; Ernest Partridge, "Posthumous Interests and Posthumous Respect," *Ethics* 91, no. 2 (January 1981): 243–45, 249.

19. Aristotle did allow that the dead could suffer further misfortune. Aristotle, *The Nicomachean Ethics,* trans. Harris Rackham, Loeb Classical Library (Cambridge: William Heinemann, 1932), 1101b5ff., 1139b7–11.

20. Nietzsche, *Thus Spoke Zarathustra,* 251.

21. Thomas Paine, "Rights of Man," in *The Complete Writings of Thomas Paine,* ed. Philip S. Foner, vol. 2 (New York: Citadel Press, 1945), 251.

22. Francis Bacon, "Of Revenge," in *Francis Bacon,* ed. Arthur Johnston (New York: Schocken, 1965), 104.

23. Aeschylus, *Eumenides,* l. 381; Sophocles, *Works,* ed. and trans. Hugh Lloyd-Jones, vol. 1, *Oedipus Tyrannus,* Loeb Classical Library (Cambridge: Harvard University Press, 1994), l. 870.

24. Michèle Simondon, *La mémoire et l'oubli dans la pensée grecque jusq'à la fin du Ve siècle avant J.-C.* (Paris: Les Belles Lettres, 1982), 223–24, 227; Nicole Loraux, *La cité divisée. L'oubli dans la mémoire d' Athènes* (Paris: Payot, 1997), 275; Clémence Ramnoux, *La nuit et les enfants de la nuit de la tradition grecque* (Paris: Gallimard, 1959), 148.

25. "Prime Minister Blair's Statement to the House of Commons, 29 January 1998," <http://www.bloody-sunday-inquiry.org.uk/index2 asp?p=1>.

26. Martin Melaugh, "Exhibition of Large-Scale Photographs in Situ at Site of Original Events, 18 September 1997," *Photographs Related to "Bloody Sunday," 30 January 1972,* September 18, 1997, CAIN Web Service: The Northern Ireland Conflict (1968 to the Present), <http://cain.ulst.ac.uk/images/photos/bsunday/bs997b.htm>.

27. Bill Rolston, "Republican Tradition: Figure 11. Ardoyne Avenue. Belfast," *Contemporary Murals in Northern Ireland: Republican Tradition* (1997), CAIN Web Service: The Northern Ireland Conflict (1968 to the Present), April 4, 2001, <http://cain.ulst ac.uk/bibdbs/murals/slide11.htm#11>. The line, which actually reads "without shroud *or* coffin," is from Seamus Heaney's "Requiem for the Croppies." The dead in the poem are not victims of the Great Famine but rebels from the 1798 Irish Uprising. I am grateful to Roy K. Gottfried for identifying this passage and placing it in its historical context.

28. Peter Mandelson, MP, speech to Royal Institute for International Affairs/Chicago Council for Foreign Relations, September 18, 2000, Northern Ireland Information Service, <http://www.nio.gov.uk/000919a-nio.htm>.

29. Speech by Prime Minister the Right Honourable Tony Blair MP to the Oireachtas, Dublin, Thursday, November 26, 1998, Northern Ireland Information Service, <http://www.nio.gov.uk/press/981126g-nio.htm>; Remarks by the Prime Minister the Right Honourable Tony Blair MP, April 1, 1999, Northern Ireland Information Service, <http://www.nio.gov.uk/990401dec-nio.htm>.

30. Archbishop Desmond Mpilo Tutu, "Foreword by the Chairperson," in *Truth and Reconciliation Commission Final Report,* vol. 1 (1998), chap. 1, <http://www.chico.mweb. co.za/mg/projects/trc/volume1.htm>.

31. Stanley Cohen, "State Crimes of Previous Regimes: Knowledge, Accountability, and the Policing of the Past," *Law and Social Inquiry* 20, no. 1 (winter 1995): 18.

32. Priscilla B. Hayner, "Fifteen Truth Commissions, 1974–1994: A Comparative

Study," in *Transitional Justice: How Emerging Democracies Reckon with Former Regimes*, ed. Neil J. Kritz, vol. 1, *General Considerations* (Washington, D C.: United States Institute of Peace, 1995), 225–61.

33. Aharon Appelfeld, *The Iron Tracks*, trans. Jeffrey M. Green (New York: Schocken, 1998), 9, 195. Appelfeld's autobiography makes clear both his desire to break free from this memory and the struggle to retain parts of it as he is assimilated into the new world of Israeli society. Aharon Appelfeld, *The Story of a Life*, trans. Aloma Halter (New York: Schocken, 2004), 105, 114.

34. On memory sounding Yugoslavia's death knell, see Ilana R. Bet-El, "Unimagined Communities: The Power of Memory and the Conflict in the Former Yugoslavia," in *Memory and Power in Post-war Europe: Studies in the Presence of the Past*, ed. Jan-Werner Müller (Cambridge: Cambridge University Press, 2002), 206–8.

35. Friedrich Nietzsche, *The Use and Abuse of History*, trans. Adrian Collins (Indianapolis: Library of Liberal Arts, 1957), 7.

36. Nicole Loraux, "Pour quel consensus?" *Le genre humain* 18 (October 1988): 11; Jeffrie G. Murphy, "Forgiveness and Resentment," in *Forgiveness and Mercy*, ed. Jeffrie G. Murphy and Jean Hampton (Cambridge: Cambridge University Press, 1988), 33.

37. Garapon, *Des crimes qu'on ne peut ni punir ni pardonner*, 240, 250.

38. Siegfried Lenz, *Über das Gedächtnis. Reden und Aufsätze* (Munich: DTV, 1992), 14; Améry, *Jenseits von Schuld und Sühne*, 112–13; Nicole Loraux, "De l'amnistie et de son contraire," in *Colloque de Royaumont: usages de l'oubli* (Paris: Seuil, 1988), 38–39.

39. Martha Minow, *Between Vengeance and Forgiveness: Facing History after Genocide and Mass Violence* (Boston: Beacon Press, 1998), 25; Minow, "Memory and Hate: Are There Lessons from Around the World?" in *Breaking the Cycles of Hatred: Memory, Law, and Repair*, ed. Nancy L. Rosenblum (Princeton: Princeton University Press, 2002), 21.

40. Vladimir Jankélévitch, *Le pardon* (Paris: Aubier-Montaigne, 1967), 23, 25, 29–30, 53; Améry, *Jenseits von Schuld und Sühne*, 115–16.

41. Simondon, *La mémoire et l'oubli dans la pensée grecque*, 223, 227.

42. Bernard Williams, *Shame and Necessity* (Berkeley: University of California Press, 1993), 70.

43. Aeschylus, *Works in Two Volumes*, ed. and trans. Herbert Weir Smyth, vol. 2, *Libation-Bearers*, Loeb Classical Library (Cambridge: Harvard University Press, 1971), l. 886. The translator notes the ambiguity of the original Greek text.

44. Arieh Neier, José Zalaquett, and Adam Michnik, "Why Deal with the Past?" in *Dealing with the Past: Truth and Reconciliation in South Africa*, ed. Alex Boraine, Janet Levy, and Ronel Scheffer (Cape Town: Institute for a Democratic Alternative for South Africa, 1997), 3. See also Arno Klarsfeld, *Papon. Un verdict français* (Paris: Éditions Ramsay, 1998), 150. Recall Joel Feinberg's observation that "the betrayed party is the person now dead as he was in his trusting state antemortem" and not some "diffuse public" good.

45. Jankélévitch, *Le pardon*, 73; Vladimir Jankélévitch, *L'imprescriptible. Pardonner? Dans l'honneur et la dignité* (Paris: Seuil, 1986), 60.

46. Judith N. Shklar, *The Faces of Injustice* (New Haven: Yale University Press, 1990), 94–95; Nietzsche, *On the Genealogy of Morals*, 75–76; Paul Ricoeur, *Le juste* 2 (Paris: Esprit, 2001), 257ff. The Furies' conflict with the city in *The Eumenides* can be seen as illustrative of a tension between public and private justice on the model of, say, the ban on dueling as the modern state sought to establish its monopoly on the means of violence. Here I emphasize another facet of their behavior: that it is not so much their private character that needs to be tamed but rather their destructive single-mindedness in light of the multiple goods sought by human beings. Once they are so tamed, their transition to (legal) justice in the city is seamless.

47. Minow, *Between Vengeance and Forgiveness*, 26, 63; Lawrence Weschler, *A Miracle, a Universe: Settling Accounts with Torturers* (New York: Pantheon Books, 1990), 244.

48. An excellent overview of the politics of war crimes trials can be found in Bass, *Stay the Hand of Vengeance*. Archbishop Desmond Tutu, in his foreword to the *South African Truth and Reconciliation Commission Final Report*, makes clear the multiple concerns at work in such proceedings: amnesty so as to induce truth-telling, opposition to the lustration of implicated persons, and so on. Tutu, "Foreword by the Chairperson"; Neier, Zalaquett, and Michnik, "Why Deal with the Past?" 3.

49. Adam Michnik and Václav Havel, "Justice or Revenge?" *Journal of Democracy* 4, no. 1 (January 1993): 25; Havel, "Letter to Dr. Gustáv Husák," in *Václav Havel: Living in Truth*, ed. Jan Vladislav (London: Faber and Faber, 1986), 25ff. Especially good on trauma and memory is Jenny Edkins, *Trauma and the Memory of Politics* (Cambridge: Cambridge University Press, 2003).

50. Judge Richard J. Goldstone, foreword to *Between Vengeance and Forgiveness: Facing History after Genocide and Mass Violence* (Boston: Beacon Press, 1998), x.

51. Amy Gutmann and Dennis Thompson, "The Moral Foundations of Truth Commissions," in *Truth v. Justice: The Morality of Truth Commissions*, ed. Robert I. Rotberg and Dennis Thompson (Princeton: Princeton University Press, 2000), 23, 25, 30; Waldron, "Superseding Historic Injustice," 13; Ruti G. Teitel, *Transitional Justice* (Oxford: Oxford University Press, 2000), 6, 51; Raúl Alfonsín, " 'Never Again' in Argentina," *Journal of Democracy* 4, no. 1 (January 1993): 18.

52. Carlos Santiago Nino, *Radical Evil on Trial* (New Haven: Yale University Press, 1996), x, 19, 21, 33ff.

53. Desmond Mpilo Tutu, *No Future without Forgiveness* (New York: Doubleday, 1999), 31, 35, 165; Teitel, *Transitional Justice*, 88. For a brief history of the democratic uses of judicial instruments, see Samuel P. Huntington, *The Third Wave: Democratization in the Late Twentieth Century* (Norman: University of Oklahoma Press, 1991), 218ff. Williams notes the novelty of the TRC approach to reconciliation via a confrontation with the past rather than through amnesty alone. Bernard Williams, *Truth and Truthfulness: An Essay in Genealogy* (Princeton: Princeton University Press, 2002), 209.

54. Ernesto Sabato, prologue to *Nunca más: The Report of the Argentine National Commission on the Disappeared* (New York: Farrar, Straus and Giroux, 1986), 6; Raúl Alfonsín, " 'Never Again' in Argentina," *Journal of Democracy* 4, no. 1 (January 1993): 16; Archdiocese of Guatemala Human Rights Office, *Guatemala: Never Again! Recovery of Historical Memory Project, Official Report of the Human Rights Office, Archdiocese of Guatemala* (Maryknoll N.Y.: Orbis, 1999), xxxiii.

55. Robert I. Rotberg, "Truth Commissions and the Provision of Truth, Justice, and Reconciliation," in Rotberg and Thompson, *Truth v. Justice*, 3.

56. See Jürgen Habermas, "Die Stunde der nationalen Empfindung. Republikanische Gesinnung oder Nationalbewußtsein?" in *Kleine Politische Schriften*, vol. 7, *Die nachholende Revolution* (Frankfurt am Main: Suhrkamp, 1990), 158. The didactic value of some of the great mass crimes trials of the past century has been questioned. Martin Walser argues that Nuremberg had little impact on Germans, and Ian Buruma discusses the ambiguous legacy in Japan of the postwar Tokyo trials. Desmond Tutu suggests that the shortcomings of the Nuremberg trial influenced democratic South Africa's decision to formulate the truth and reconciliation model. Martin Walser, "Unser Auschwitz" (1965), in *Deutsche Sorgen* (Frankfurt am Main: Suhrkamp, 1997), 193; Ian Buruma, *The Wages of Guilt: Memories of War in Germany and Japan* (London: Jonathan Cape, 1994), 159ff; Tutu, *No Future without Forgiveness*, 19–20.

57. Mark Osiel, *Mass Atrocity, Collective Memory, and the Law* (New Brunswick, N.J.: Transaction, 1997), 3, 6, 18–19; Henry Rousso, *Vichy. L'événement, la mémoire, l'histoire*

(Paris: Gallimard, 1992), 685; Gary Smith, "Ein normatives Niemandsland? Zwischen Gerechtigkeit und Versöhnungspolitik in jungen Demokratien," in *Amnestie oder die Politik der Erinnerung in der Demokratie,* ed. Gary Smith and Avishai Margalit (Frankfurt am Main: Suhrkamp, 1997), 19; Lawrence Douglas, *The Memory of Judgment: Making Law and History in the Trials of the Holocaust* (New Haven: Yale University Press, 2001), 2. A very good overview of the literature on law and memory can be found in Austin Sarat and Thomas R. Kearns, "Writing History and Registering Memory in Legal Decisions and Legal Practices: An Introduction," in *History, Memory, and the Law,* ed. Austin Sarat and Thomas R. Kearns (Ann Arbor: University of Michigan Press, 1999), 1–24.

58. Annette Wieviorka, *L'ère du témoin* (Paris: Plon, 1998), 81, 95; Huntington, *The Third Wave,* 211; Waldron, "Superseding Historic Injustice," 5–6.

59. Plato, *Phaedrus* 249c, e, 254b; Karl Jaspers, "Die Schuldfrage," in *Hoffnung und Sorge. Schriften zur deutschen Politik 1945–1965* (Munich: Piper, 1965), 100; Bernhard Schlink, "Recht-Schuld-Zukunft," ed. Jörg Calließ, in *Loccumer Protokolle,* vol. 66 (Rehburg: Evangelische Akademie Loccum, 1988), 66–67; Schlink, "Die Bewältigung von Vergangenheit durch Recht," in *Leviathan. Zeitschrift für Sozialwissenschaft,* ed. Helmut König, Michael Kohlstruck, and Andreas Wöll, vol. 18, *Vergangenheitsbewältigung am Ende des zwanzigsten Jahrhunderts* (Opladen/Wiesbaden: Westdeutscher Verlag, 1998), 437.

60. Jürgen Habermas, "Warum ein 'Demokratiepreis' für Daniel J. Goldhagen? Eine Laudatio," *Die Zeit,* March 14 1997, <http://service.ecce-terram.de/zeit-archiv/daten/pages/historie.txt.19970314.html>; Alain Brossat et al., introduction to *À l'Est, la mémoire retrouvée,* ed. Alain Brossat (Paris: La Découverte, 1990), 25; Teitel, *Transitional Justice,* 62; Waldron, "Superseding Historic Injustice," 5–6.

61. Recall Feinberg's critique of utilitarian accounts of justice. Brodsky writes that "our belief that we can learn from history, and that it has a purpose, notably ourselves, . . . this assumption is monstrous, since it justifies many an absence as paving the way to our own presences." Joseph Brodsky, "Profile of Clio," in *On Grief and Reason: Essays* (New York: Farrar, Straus, and Giroux, 1995), 119. On the Eichmann trial and its relationship to Nuremberg and to Israeli identity, see Douglas, *The Memory of Judgment,* 57, 73; Hannah Arendt, *Eichmann in Jerusalem: A Report on the Banality of Evil* (New York: Penguin, 1992), 9–11, 257–58; Haïm Gouri, "Facing the Glass Booth," in *Holocaust Remembrance: The Shape of Memory,* ed. Geoffrey H. Hartman (Oxford: Basil Blackwell, 1994), 154; Wieviorka, *L'ère du témoin,* 95; Aharon Appelfeld, "The Awakening," in Hartman, *Holocaust Remembrance,* 149–52; Tom Segev, *The Seventh Million: The Israelis and the Holocaust,* trans. Haim Watzman (New York: Hill and Wang, 1993); Gouri, *Face à la cage de verre. Le procès Eichmann, Jérusalem 1961,* trans. R. Cidor (Paris: Tirésias, 1995), 7, 9, 12, 26.

62. Pascal Quignard, *Sur le jadis,* vol. 2 of *Dernier royaume* (Paris: Grasset, 2002), 57, 220–21; Loraux, "De l'amnistie et de son contraire," 37; Harald Weinrich, *Lethe: Kunst und Kritik des Vergessens* (Munich: C. H. Beck, 1997), 16.

63. Yosef Hayim Yerushalmi, "Réflexions sur l'oubli," in *Colloque de Royaumont. Usages de l'oubli* (Paris: Seuil, 1988), 20; Marcel Detienne, *Les maîtres de la vérité dans la Grèce archaïque* (Paris: L'Ouverture, 1994), 6, 69–70, 76.

64. Minow, *Between Vengeance and Forgiveness,* 1; Hélène Piralian, "Maintenir les morts hors du néant," in *Travail de mémoire 1914–1998: une nécessité dans un siècle de violence,* ed. Jean-Pierre Bacot (Paris: Autrement, 1999), 64.

65. Elisabeth Kiderlen, "Le musée juif de Prague," in Brossat, *À l'Est,* 312–17.

66. Zbigniew Herbert, *Report from the Besieged City and Other Poems,* trans. John Carpenter and Bogdana Carpenter (New York: Ecco Press, 1985), 65, 67.

67. Human Rights Office, *Guatemala: Never Again!* 313.

68. "Bearing Witness," *Leopard* 4 (London: Harvill, 1999).

69. Simondon, *La mémoire et l'oubli dans la pensée grecque*, 225; Garapon, *Des crimes qu'on ne peut ni punir ni pardonner*, 255; Garapon, "La justice et l'inversion morale du temps," 122.

70. Thomas, "La vérité," 30, 35.

71. See Ricoeur, *La mémoire*, 209; Paul Ricoeur, "Définition de la mémoire d'un point de vue philosophique," in *Pourquoi se souvenir?* ed. Françoise Barret-Ducrocq (Paris: Grasset, 1998), 30–31.

72. Garapon, *Des crimes qu'on ne peut ni punir ni pardonner*, 218.

73. Ricoeur, *La mémoire*, 204–05; Edward S. Casey, *Remembering: A Phenomenological Study* 2nd ed. (Bloomington: Indiana University Press, 2000), 216. Both future-oriented promise-making and bearing witness to the past draw on credibility and trust, which in turn rests on the continuity (the identity) of the responsible agent. See Paul Ricoeur, *Parcours de la reconnaissance. Trois études* (Paris: Stock, 2004), 192, 194.

74. Jorge Semprún, *Mal et modernité: le travail de l'histoire* (Paris: Climats, 1995), 91.

75. Here I draw on and adapt Feinberg's argument about posthumous harm and Pitcher's essay on that same theme. Joel Feinberg, *Harm to Others*, vol. 1 of *The Moral Limits of the Criminal Law* (Oxford: Oxford University Press, 1984), 83–93; George Pitcher, "The Misfortunes of the Dead," *American Philosophical Quarterly* 21, no. 2 (April 1984): 184ff. For a critique of that position, see Ernest Partridge, "Posthumous Interests and Posthumous Respect," *Ethics* 91, no. 2 (January 1981): 244, 248. See relatedly the observations on a spouse's sense of the importance of remembering her dead husband, and the fear that forgetting would be to inflict another death on him, in Patrick Baudry, *La place des morts. Enjeux et rites* (Paris: Armand Colin, 1999), 159–60. Anthony Minghella's film *Truly, Madly, Deeply* (1991) captures some of these issues of absence and memory in a marriage.

76. Jack Kugelmass and Jonathan Boyarin, eds. and trans., *From a Ruined Garden: The Memorial Books of Polish Jewry* (Bloomington: Indiana University Press, 1998), 192.

77. Shmuel Yosef Agnon, "The Sign," trans. Arthur Green, in *A Book That Was Lost and Other Stories*, ed. Alan Mintz and Anne Golomb Hoffmann (New York: Schocken, 1995), 409.

78. Adam Michnik, "Poles and the Jews: How Deep the Guilt?" *New York Times*, March 17, 2001, B:7, 9.

79. Nicole Lapierre, *Le silence de la mémoire. À la recherche des Juifs de Płock* (Paris: Plon, 1989), 240; Germaine Tillion, *Ravensbrück*, 1st ed., (Neuchâtel: Éditions de la Baconnière, 1946), 19, 50; Patrick Modiano, *Dora Bruder* (Paris: Gallimard, 1999), 65. Klarsfeld located a photograph of Dora Bruder and wrote that "from now on, Patrick Modiano knows the face of Dora Bruder." Serge Klarsfeld, *Le mémorial des enfants juifs déportés de France* (Paris: Les fils et filles des déportés juifs de France, Beate Klarsfeld Foundation, 1995), 1535.

80. Wole Soyinka, "Thérapie collective de la mémoire en Afrique du Sud," in Barret-Ducrocq, *Pourquoi se souvenir?* 219; Soyinka, *The Burden of Memory, the Muse of Forgiveness* (Oxford: Oxford University Press, 1999), 37.

81. Czeslaw Milosz, "The Nobel Lecture," trans. Milosz, in *Beginning with My Streets* (New York: Farrar, Straus and Giroux, 1991), 281.

82. Carson, *Economy of the Unlost*, 40.

83. Alain Finkielkraut, *Le mécontemporain. Péguy, lecteur du monde moderne* (Paris: Gallimard, 1991), 14.

84. Henri Raczymow, *Contes d'exil et d'oubli* (Paris: Gallimard, 1979), 106.

85. Soyinka, *The Burden of Memory*, 13; Anthony Holiday, "Forgiving and Forgetting: The Truth and Reconciliation Commission," in *Negotiating the Past: The Making of Mem-*

ory in South Africa, ed. Sarah Nutall and Carli Coetzee (Oxford: Oxford University Press, 1998), 47. For a survey of some of the debates over truth and reconciliation processes, see Jonathan D. Tepperman, "Truth and Consequences," *Foreign Affairs* 81, no. 2 (March–April 2002): 128–45. John Kani's play "Nothing but the Truth" explores some of the dilemmas of the TRC process in South Africa. On the one hand, the niece, Mandisa, and the father, Sipho Makhaya, who lost a son to the apartheid-era police, both express grave reservations over the amnesty/truth-telling work of the TRC. And clearly the father would prefer revenge against his son's killers. On the other hand, the airing of long-hidden personal truths about his brother and wife seems deeply emancipatory for him, suggesting that disclosure about the past has a considerable value. John Kani, *Nothing But the Truth* (Johannesburg: Witwatersrand University Press, 2002), 27–29, 52–54, 58–60.

86. Soyinka, *The Burden of Memory*, 30–31, 36, 80.

87. Shklar, *The Faces of Injustice*, 93–94; Minow, *Between Vengeance and Forgiveness*, 5.

88. Huyssen suggests that allegations of the moral/political failure of Christa Wolf and other East German literary and intellectual figures to criticize the communist regime there were in part an echo of an earlier German failure to speak out against National Socialism. Andreas Huyssen, *Twilight Memories: Marking Time in a Culture of Amnesia* (New York: Routledge, 1995), 37ff.

89. Tony Judt, "The Past Is Another Country: Myth and Memory in Postwar Europe," in *The Politics of Retribution in Europe: World War II and Its Aftermath*, ed. István Deák, Jan T. Gross, and Tony Judt (Princeton: Princeton University Press, 2000), 308; Henry Rousso, *Le syndrome de Vichy de 1944 à nos jours* (Paris: Seuil, 1990), 18; Annette Wieviorka, *Auschwitz, 60 ans après* (Paris: Robert Laffont, 2005), 20.

90. Ricoeur, *La mémoire*, 420; Garapon, *Des crimes qu'on ne peut ni punir ni pardonner*, 255–56; Garapon, "La justice et l'inversion morale du temps," 122–23.

91. Quoted in Garapon, *Des crimes qu'on ne peut ni punir ni pardonner*, 177.

92. James E. Young, *The Texture of Memory: Holocaust Memorials and Meaning* (New Haven: Yale University Press, 1993), 28–37.

93. Henri Raczymow, *Un cri sans voix* (Paris: Gallimard, 1985), 213–14.

94. Certeau, *L'écriture de l'histoire*, 140–41. To name the absent, he continues, is to give the living a gift, to liberate them.

95. Walser, "Unser Auschwitz," 201; Garapon, *Des crimes qu'on ne peut ni punir ni pardonner*, 258, 260.

96. Osiel, *Mass Atrocity, Collective Memory, and the Law*, 6, 61; Smith, "Ein normatives Niemandsland?" 19.

97. Cohen, "State Crimes of Previous Regimes," 47; Gabriele Taylor, *Pride, Shame, and Guilt: Emotions of Self-Assessment* (Oxford: Clarendon Press, 1985), 89, 91.

98. See Bruce A. Ackerman, *The Future of Liberal Revolution* (New Haven: Yale University Press, 1992), 81; Osiel, *Mass Atrocity, Collective Memory, and the Law*, 61; Ginzburg, *The Judge and the Historian*, 14; Garapon, *Des crimes qu'on ne peut ni punir ni pardonner*, 199; Schlink, "Recht-Schuld-Zukunft," 58. I discussed earlier the issue of whether crimes committed under dictatorships belong on the community's historic ledger or only that of the responsible officials.

99. Walser, "Unser Auschwitz," 196–97, 199–200; Martin Walser, "Auschwitz und kein Ende" (1979), in *Deutsche Sorgen* (Frankfurt am Main: Suhrkamp, 1997), 228, 230, 232.

100. Williams, *Shame and Necessity*, 63–65, 94. See also Gordon's discussion of Primo Levi on the "grey zone" of accountability and the limits of legal justice. Robert S. C. Gordon, *Primo Levi's Ordinary Virtues: From Testimony to Ethics* (Oxford: Oxford University Press, 2001), 7–10.

101. Bernhard Schlink, *The Reader* (1995), trans. Carol Brown Janeway (New York: Pantheon Books, 1997), 170.

102. Habermas, "Warum ein 'Demokratiepreis' für Daniel J. Goldhagen?"; Williams, *Shame and Necessity*, 80; Schlink, "Recht-Schuld-Zukunft," 59; Herbert Morris, *On Guilt and Innocence* (Berkeley: University of California Press, 1976), 135.

103. Hannah Arendt, *Zur Zeit. Politische Essays* (Munich: Deutscher Taschenbuch Verlag, 1989), 45; Cohen, "State Crimes of Previous Regimes," 40.

104. Yerushalmi, "Réflexions sur l'oubli," 16.

105. Tillion, *Ravensbrück*, 2nd ed. (Paris: Seuil, 1973), 203–4; Tillion, *Ravensbrück*, 3rd ed. (Paris: Seuil, 1988), 12, 306.

106. François Bédarida, "La mémoire contra l'histoire," *Esprit* 193 (July 1993): 7; Garapon, *Des crimes qu'on ne peut ni punir ni pardonner*, 254.

107. Patrick Baudry, *La place des morts. Enjeux et rites* (Paris: Armand Colin, 1999), 159. And see Feinberg, *Harm to Others*, 94–95.

108. Milosz, "The Nobel Lecture," 281; Jankélévitch, *Le pardon*, 72, 75–76.

109. Avishai Margalit, *Ethik der Erinnerung (Max Horkheimer Vorlesungen)* (Frankfurt am Main: Fischer, 2002), 49; Wieviorka, *L'ère du témoin*, 81.

110. "The Attorney General's Opening Speech," in *The Trial of Adolf Eichmann: Record of Proceedings*, vol. 1 (Jerusalem: State of Israel, Ministry of Justice, 1992–1994), 62; Garapon, *Des crimes qu'on ne peut ni punir ni pardonner*, 162, 166; Douglas, *The Memory of Judgment*, 151; Gouri, *Face à la cage de verre*, 20. See Arendt's critique of Hausner's representing the voice of the victims as inimical to the workings of the law. Arendt, *Eichmann in Jerusalem*, 260–61.

111. Serge Klarsfeld, "Pouvoir juger (plaidoirie)," in *Archives d'un Procès. Klaus Barbie*, ed. Bernard-Henri Lévy (Paris: Globe, 1986), 132, 138; Claude Bochurberg, *Entretiens avec Serge Klarsfeld* (Paris: Stock, 1997), 287–90; Leïzer Aichenrand, "Paysage de destin," trans. Rachel Ertel, in *Dans la langue de personne. Poésie yiddish de l'anéantissement* (Paris: Seuil, 1993), 149; Claude Lanzmann, "*Shoah* et la shoah," in *Archives d'un Procès. Klaus Barbie*, ed. Bernard-Henri Lévy (Paris: Globe, 1986), 55.

112. Tillion, *Ravensbrück*, 3rd ed., 11.

113. Michèle Simondon, "Les modes du discours commémoratif en Grèce ancienne," in *Les Commémorations*, ed. Philippe Gignoux, Bibliothèque de l'Ecole des Hautes Études, Section des sciences religieuses, vol. 91 (Louvain: Peeters, 1988), 94. In ancient Egypt, burial stones asked passersby not to read silently the names of the dead but to speak them. "The warmth of breath is the blood that irrigates proper names." Pascal Quignard, *Petits traités II* (Paris: Gallimard, 1990), 213.

114. Margalit, *Ethik der Erinnerung*, 13–15; Emmanuel Kattan, *Penser le devoir de mémoire* (Paris: Presses Universitaires de France, 2002), 21, 29.

115. Brian Strawn and Karla Sierralta, *Dual Memory: World Trade Center Site, Memorial Competition*, Lower Manhattan Development Corporation, November 20, 2003, <http://www.wtcsitememorial.org/fin4.html>.

116. Klarsfeld, *Papon*, 114.

117. Quignard, *Sur le jadis*, 28; Tillion, *Ravensbrück*, 1st ed., 165; Lanzmann, "*Shoah* et la shoah," 51.

118. Ertel, *Dans la langue de personne*, 22; Human Rights Office, *Guatemala: Never Again!* 317.

119. Maurice Halbwachs, *Les cadres sociaux de la mémoire* (Paris: Librairie Félix Alcan, 1935), 227.

120. Alain Finkielkraut, *La mémoire vaine. Du crime contra l'humanité* (Paris: Gallimard, 1989), 12–13.

121. Garapon, "La justice et l'inversion morale du temps," 117.

122. Jean-Noël Jeanneny, *Le passé dans le prétoire* (Paris: Seuil, 1998), 7–8; Éric Conan, *Le procès Papon. Un journal d'audience* (Paris: Gallimard, 1998), 36–37; Denis Salas, "La justice entre histoire et mémoire," in *Barbie, Touvier, Papon . . . des procès pour la mémoire,* ed. Jean-Paul Jean and Denis Salas (Paris: Autrement, 2002), 21, 30; Thomas, "La vérité," 26; Garapon, *Des crimes qu'on ne peut ni punir ni pardonner,* 168.

123. Klarsfeld, *Papon,* 14; Garapon, *Des crimes qu'on ne peut ni punir ni pardonner,* 170, 172; Conan, *Le procès Papon,* 79, 96, 99–100, 102, 243, 302–3.

124. Conan, *Le procès Papon,* 113, 152–53, 243; Garapon, *Des crimes qu'on ne peut ni punir ni pardonner,* 173.

125. Klarsfeld, *Papon,* 159–60.

126. René Char, "Le bouge de l'historien," in *Commune présence* (Paris: Gallimard, 1978), 24. Veyne notes the significance of the wartime and Resistance context in which the poem was written. Paul Veyne, *René Char en ses poèmes* (Paris: Gallimard, 1990), 197–98.

127. Anne Applebaum, *Gulag: A History* (New York: Doubleday, 2003), 564–77; Denis Paillard, "URSS. Figures de la mémoire. *Mémorial* et *Pamiat,*" in Brossat, *À l'Est,* 365ff.; Stéphane Courtois, ed., *Du passé faisons table rase! Histoire et mémoire du communisme en Europe* (Paris: Robert Laffont, 2002); Courtois, ed., *Le livre noir du communisme: crimes, terreurs et répression* (Paris: Robert Laffont, 1997).

128. Jankélévitch, *Le pardon,* 75–76.

129. Detienne, *Les mâitres de la vérité dans la Grèce archaïque,* 76, 90; Ramnoux, *La nuit et les enfants de la nuit,* 115; Gesine Schwan, "Die Idee des Schlusstrichs—oder: Welches Erinnern und welches Vergessen tun der Demokratie gut?" in Smith and Margalit, *Amnestie oder die Politik der Erinnerung in der Demokratie,* 93; Jacques Le Goff, preface to Brossat, *À l'Est,* 10.

130. For an overview of both advocacy and critiques of forgetting, see Weinrich, *Lethe.*

131. Marcus Tullius Cicero, *De Oratore in Two Volumes,* vol. 1, trans. Edward William Sutton and Harris Rackham, Loeb Classical Library (Cambridge: Harvard University Press, 1988), 2.74.299–300. For a brief commentary, see Pascal Quignard, *Dernier royaume,* vol. 3, *Abîmes* (Paris: Grasset, 2002), 218–19.

132. Jorge Semprún, *L'écriture ou la vie* (Paris: Gallimard, 1994), 292, 332; Aharon Appelfeld, *Beyond Despair: Three Lectures and a Conversation with Philip Roth,* trans. Jeffrey M. Green (New York: Fromm International, 1994), ix; Appelfeld, *The Story of a Life,* 105, 120.

133. Améry, *Jenseits von Schuld und Sühne,* 111.

134. Hesiod, *Theogony,* in *Hesiod: Theogony, Works and Days, Shield,* ed. and trans. A. N. Athanassakis (Baltimore: Johns Hopkins University Press, 1983), ll. 54–55; Jean-Pierre Vernant, *Mythe et pensée chez les Grecs* (Paris: La Découverte, 1996), 117; Simondon, *La mémoire et l'oubli dans la pensée grecque,* 141.

135. Jean Giono, "Je ne peux pas oublier," in *Récits et essais* (Paris: Gallimard/Bibliothèque de la Pléiade, 1989), 261; Jean-Yves Le Naour, *Le soldat inconnu vivant* (Paris: Hachette Littératures, 2002), 101, 192.

136. Nietzsche, *On the Genealogy of Morals,* 38; Quignard, *Petits traités II,* 563.

137. Paul Valéry, *Cahiers,* vol. 1 (Paris: Gallimard/Bibliothèque de la Pléiade, 1973), 1234; Friedrich Nietzsche, *The Use and Abuse of History,* trans. Adrian Collins (Indianapolis: Library of Liberal Arts, 1957), 7–8; Nietzsche, *On the Genealogy of Morals,* 57–58.

138. Améry, *Jenseits von Schuld und Sühne,* 15; Ruth Klüger, *Weiter leben. Eine Jugend* (Munich: Deutscher Taschenbuch Verlag, 1997), 139; Alain Finkielkraut, *Le Juif imaginaire* (Paris: Seuil, 1980), 13, 19, 44; Finkielkraut, *Une voix vient de l'autre rive* (Paris: Gallimard, 2000), 107–8, 111.

139. Truth and Reconciliation Commission, "Reconciliation," in *Truth and Reconciliation Commission: Final Report* vol. 5 (1998), chap. 9, March 15, 2004, <http://www.chico.mweb.co.za/mg/projects/trc/5chap9.htm>.

140. Georges Perec, "Robert Antelme ou la vérité de la littérature," in *Robert Antelme. Textes inédits. Sur L'Espèce Humaine. Essais et témoignages*, ed. Daniel Dobbels (Paris: Gallimard, 1996), 175–77.

141. Siegfried Lenz, "Der Spielverderber," in *Siegfried Lenz: Die Erzählungen 1959–1964* (Munich: Deutscher Taschenbuch Verlag, 1986), 202–3; Lenz, *Über das Gedächtnis*, 11. The phenomenon of too much memory is also the central theme of two celebrated works: Jorge Luis Borges, "Funes, the Memorious," in *Ficciones*, ed. Anthony Kerrigan (New York: Grove Press, 1962), 107–15; and Aleksandr R. Luria, *The Mind of a Mnemonist: A Little Book about a Vast Memory*, trans. Lynn Solotaroff (New York: Basic Books, 1968). See also Weinrich, *Lethe*, 135–37.

142. Rousso, *Le syndrome de Vichy*, 40–42; Hans Magnus Enzensberger, *Civil Wars: From L.A. to Bosnia*, trans. Martin Chalmers (New York: New Press, 1990), 80; Robert Frank, "La mémoire empoisonnée," in *La France des années noires*, ed. Jean-Pierre Azéma and François Bédarida, vol. 2 (Paris: Seuil, 1993), 492, 507.

143. Raczymow, *Un cri sans voix*, 13–14, 213; Améry, *Jenseits von Schuld und Sühne*, 106, 111, 116; Vladimir Jankélévitch and Béatrice Berlowitz, *Quelque part dans l'inachevé* (Paris: Gallimard, 1978), 67; Minow, *Between Vengeance and Forgiveness*, 14, 63.

144. Friedrich Nietzsche, *The Will to Power*, trans. Walter Kaufmann and R. J. Hollingdale (New York: Vintage, 1968), 136; Nietzsche, *Thus Spoke Zarathustra*, 252–53; Vladimir Jankélévitch, *L'irréversible et la nostalgie* (Paris: Flammarion, 1974), 210, 328.

145. Raymond Aron, *Mémoires* (Paris: Julliard, 1983), 205.

146. Homer, *The Odyssey*, trans. Richmond Lattimore (New York: Harper and Row, 1977), bk. 4, ll. 220ff., bk. 24, ll. 480–85.

147. Achilles is never able to forget Patroklos, or to consign him to the past (despite the latter's accusation that Achilles has done just that). François Hartog, *Régimes d'historicité. Présentisme et expériences du temps* (Paris: Seuil, 2003), 56.

148. Loraux, "De l'amnistie et de son contraire," 31, 39; Nicole Loraux, "Eloge de l'anachronisme en histoire," *Le genre humain* 27 (1993): 34; Paul Ricoeur, "Gedächtnis-Vergessen-Geschichte," in *Historische Sinnbildung: Problemstellungen, Zeitkonzepte, Wahrnehmungshorizonte, Darstellungsstrategien*, ed. Klaus E. Müller and Jörn Rüsen (Hamburg: Rowolt, 1997), 452; Pierre Vidal-Naquet, *Réflexions sur le génocide*, vol. 3 of *Les Juifs, la mémoire et le présent* (Paris: La Découverte, 1995), 266–67.

149. Ernest Renan, *Qu'est-ce qu'une nation* (Paris: Agora, 1992), 41–42. Renan's insight about the importance of remembering and forgetting in the life of a political community applies not only to democracies, or to societies working toward a democratic regime. Ugrešić notes that in the emergence of nationalist politics and regimes from the rubble of the Yugoslav federation and its violent demise, forgetting of the former regime and a newly constructed nationalist memory (she calls this the terror of remembering and forgetting) played a key role. Dubravka Ugrešić, *The Culture of Lies*, trans. Celia Hawkesworth (University Park: Pennsylvania State University Press, 1998), 80–81, 108, 228.

150. See Alfonsín, "'Never Again,'" 18; Timothy Garton Ash, "Trials, Purges, and History Lessons: Treating a Difficult Past in Post-communist Europe," in *Memory and Power in Post-war Europe: Studies in the Presence of the Past*, ed. Jan-Werner Müller (Cambridge: Cambridge University Press, 2002), 267, 271; Michnik and Havel, "Justice or Revenge?"

151. Jankélévitch, *L'irréversible et la nostalgie*, 256.

152. Buruma writes about the passion for the *Heimatmuseum* as born of an attempt to fight off the identity-destroying ravages of change. Buruma, *The Wages of Guilt*, 209. In Lenz's *Heimatmuseum*, the museum is burnt down precisely because its close association with the history of one group readily spilled over into xenophobia. Siegfried Lenz, *Heimatmuseum* (Munich: DTV, 1992); in English, *The Heritage*, trans. Krishna Winston (New York: Hill and Wang, 1981).

153. Tzvetan Todorov, *Les abus de la mémoire* (Paris: Arléa, 1995), 18–19; Dimitri Nicolaïdis, "La Nation, les crimes, le mémoire," in *Oublier nos crimes. L'amnésie nationale, une spécificité française?* ed. Dimitri Nicolaïdis (Paris: Autrement, 1994), 21.

154. John Locke, *Second Treatise*, in *Two Treatises of Government*, ed. Peter Laslett (Cambridge: Cambridge University Press, 1963), §119–20.

155. Joshua F. Dienstag, *Dancing in Chains: Narrative and Memory in Political Theory* (Stanford: Stanford University Press, 1997), 52ff., interprets Locke as offering a counter-memory to the Filmerian account of the origins of legitimacy. See also Sheldon Wolin, *The Presence of the Past* (Baltimore: Johns Hopkins University Press, 1989), 40; Jean-Louis Déotte, *Oubliez! Les ruines, l'Europe, le Musée* (Paris: L'Harmattan, 1994), 21, 62; Michael Kammen, *Mystic Chords of Memory* (New York: Vintage, 1993), 42; Smith, "Ein normatives Niemandsland? 11.

156. In general, liberalism has difficulty with intergenerational obligations, whether of the future- or past-oriented kind, precisely because it has no notion of collective or corporate-like responsibility except as "legal fictions, shorthands for aggregations of natural persons." Peter A. French, *Responsibility Matters* (Lawrence: University of Kansas Press, 1992), 100; French, "The Corporation as a Moral Person," in *The Spectrum of Responsibility*, ed. French (New York: St. Martin's Press, 1991), 292–94; Thomas Nagel, *The View from Nowhere* (Oxford: Oxford University Press, 1986), 171; Kattan, *Penser le devoir de mémoire*, 37. On property, education, and intergenerational liberalism, see, for example, Bruce A. Ackerman, *Social Justice in the Liberal State* (New Haven: Yale University Press, 1980), 139ff., 201ff. I have previously discussed a different set of issues about intergenerational obligations, one centered on the proper subject of interests, harm, and obligations.

157. Stuart Hampshire, *Morality and Conflict* (Oxford: Basil Blackwell, 1983), 135; John Stuart Mill, *Considerations on Representative Government* (South Bend, Ind.: Gateway, 1962), 307; Edmund Burke, *Reflections on the Revolution in France* (1790; Indianapolis: Library of Liberal Arts, 1955), 38–39, 110.

158. On pardoning, mercy, and forgiveness, see Murphy, "Forgiveness and Resentment," 15, 17, 21, 24; Paul Ricoeur, *Le juste 1* (Paris: Esprit, 1995), 205–7; Avishai Margalit, "Gedenken, Vergessen, Vergeben," in Smith and Margalit, *Amnestie oder die Politik der Erinnerung in der Demokratie*, 204; Jacques Derrida, "Le Siècle et le Pardon. Entretien avec Michel Wieviorka," in *Foi et savoir suivi de la Le Siècle et le Pardon (Entretien avec Michel Wieviorka)* (Paris: Seuil, 2000), 101–33; Derrida, *On Cosmopolitanism and Forgiveness*, trans. Mark Dooley and Michael Hughes (New York: Routledge, 2001).

159. Murphy, "Forgiveness and Resentment," 20, 24.

160. Tutu, *No Future without Forgiveness*, 279; Gutmann and Thompson, "The Moral Foundations of Truth Commissions," 29. The epilogue to Sachs's autobiographical account of his part in the struggle for democracy in South Africa discusses retribution and forgiveness. Albie Sachs, epilogue to *The Soft Vengeance of a Freedom Fighter* (Berkeley: University of California Press, 2000), 205–45.

161. Tutu, *No Future without Forgiveness*, 50, 54; Jeffrie G. Murphy, "Mercy and Legal Justice," in Murphy and Hampton, *Forgiveness and Mercy*, 167; Peter E. Digeser, *Political Forgiveness* (Ithaca: Cornell University Press, 2001), 36ff.

162. Tutu writes that "in forgiving, people are not asked to forget. On the contrary,

it is important to remember." Tutu, *No Future without Forgiveness*, 271. See also Jankélévitch, *Le pardon*, 19, 31–32, 42, 205; Minow, *Between Vengeance and Forgiveness*, 15, 21–24.

163. Quoted in Anne Duruflé–Lozinski, "URSS/Pologne. Retour à Katyn," in Brossat, *À l'Est*, 50.

164. Joseph Brodsky argues differently. Discussing the work of Anna Akhmatova, he writes, "Forgiveness is . . . a property of time." Joseph Brodsky, "The Keening Muse," in *Less Than One: Selected Essays* (New York: Farrar, Straus and Giroux, 1986), 52. He also suggests that the source of forgiveness in her poetry is her Orthodox faith.

165. Homer, *The Odyssey*, bk. 24, ll. 480–90; Loraux, "De l'amnistie et de son contraire," 33. See Sophocles, *Works*, vol. 1, *Antigone*, trans. Hugh Lloyd–Jones, Loeb Classical Library (Cambridge: Harvard University Press, 1994), l. 150.

166. An equal number of votes are cast for and against acquittal. Even in the city of institutionalized justice, the Furies are not weak.

167. Aeschylus, *Eumenides*, ll. 825ff., 86off., 975; Vidal-Naquet, *Réflexions sur le génocide*, 266–67.

168. Aristotle, "The Athenian Constitution," trans. Harris Rackham, in *The Athenian Constitution, The Eudemian Ethics, On Virtues and Vices*, Loeb Classical Library (Cambridge: Harvard University Press, 1952), sec. xxxix; Thomas Clark Loening, "The Reconciliation Agreement of 403/402 B.C. in Athens," in *Hermes. Zeitschrift für klassische Philologie*, ed. Jürgen Blänsdorf, Jochen Bleicken, and Wolfgang Kullmann, vol. 53 (Stuttgart: Fritz Steiner, 1987); Jon Elster, "Coming to Terms with the Past: A Framework for the Study of Justice in the Transition to Democracy," *Archives européennes de sociologie* 39, no. 1 (1998): 9–13; Wilfred Nippel, "Bürgerkrieg und Amnestie: Athen 411–403," in Smith and Margalit, *Amnestie oder die Politik der Erinnerung in der Demokratie*, 103–19.

169. Loraux, *La cité divisée*, 38; Loraux, "De l'amnistie et de son contraire," 9, 22–23, 30.

170. Carl Schmitt, "Amnestie oder der Kraft des Vergessens," in *Staat, Großraum, Nomos. Arbeiten aus den Jahren 1916–1969*, ed. Gunter Maschke (Berlin: Duncker und Humblot, 1995), 219. The English word "amnesty" has its root in the Greek *amnēstia*, "the forgetfulness of wrong" or simply "oblivion." See Plato, *Menexenus* 239c: "but those exploits . . . which lie still buried in oblivion [*amnēstia*]." Loening remarks that the use of *amnēstia* for political-legal amnesties was a much later employment. Loening, "The Reconciliation Agreement of 403/402 B C. in Athens," 21. Bacon uses the term in that sense and ties it to reconciliation: "Reconcilement is better managed by an amnesty, and passing over that which is past." Francis Bacon, "The Advancement of Learning," in *The Advancement of Learning and New Atlantis*, ed. Geoffrey Cumberlege (London: Oxford University Press, 1951), 212.

171. Rousso, *Le syndrome de Vichy*, 67–68, 145–46; Norbert Frei, "Amnestiepolitik in den Anfangsjahren der Bundesrepublik," in Smith and Margalit, *Amnestie oder die Politik der Erinnerung in der Demokratie*, 120–37; Ash, "Trials, Purges, and History Lessons," 267; Stéphane Gacon, "L'oubli institutionnel," in *Oublier nos crimes. L'amnésie nationale, une spécificité française?* ed. Dimitri Nicolaïdis (Paris: Autrement, 1994), 98, 104.

172. Enzensberger, *Civil Wars*, 80.

173. Alfonsín, "'Never Again,'" 18; Waldron, "Superseding Historic Injustice," 4, 27.

174. Weschler, *A Miracle, a Universe*, 175, 184, 191.

175. Smith, "Ein normatives Niemandsland?" 11; Huntington, *The Third Wave*, 214; Minow, *Between Vengeance and Forgiveness*, 14; Cohen, "State Crimes of Previous Regimes," 29–30; Kendall Thomas, "Die Verfassung der Amnestie: der Fall

Südafrika," in Smith and Margalit, *Amnestie oder die Politik der Erinnerung in der Demokratie,* 180–81.

176. Ackerman, *The Future of Liberal Revolution,* 3, 69–71, 88. By contrast, Carlos Santiago Nino argues for the importance of retroactive justice in transitions to democracy. Nino, *Radical Evil on Trial,* x, 128ff., 131. Posner remarks on the oddity of instructing the "victims of communism to let bygones be bygones." Richard A. Posner, "Review of Bruce Ackerman's *The Future of Liberal Revolution,*" *East European Constitutional Review* 1, no. 3 (fall 1992): 36.

177. Ricoeur, "Gedächtnis-Vergessen-Geschichte," 452.

178. Jankélévitch, *Le pardon,* 25–26, 31, 33–34; Jankélévitch, *L'imprescriptible,* 48.

179. Emmanuel Lévinas, "A propos du Struthof," in *Difficile liberté. Essais sur le judaïsme* (Paris: Albin Michel, 1976), 211.

180. Ralph Ellison, "Going to the Territory," in *The Collected Essays of Ralph Ellison,* ed. John F. Callahan (New York: The Modern Library, 2003), 599–600; Ralph Ellison, "Blues People," in *The Collected Essays of Ralph Ellison,* ed. John F. Callahan, 280.

181. Elie Wiesel, preface to *Pourquoi se souvenir?* ed. Françoise Barret-Ducrocq (Paris: Grasset, 1998), 10; Jankélévitch, *L'imprescriptible,* 25, 59–60; Améry, *Jenseits von Schuld und Sühne,* 115.

182. Zbigniew Herbert, *Selected Poems,* trans. John Carpenter and Bogdana Carpenter (Oxford: Oxford University Press, 1977), 79; Michnik and Havel, "Justice or Revenge?" 25.

183. Samuel Pisar, "Nous-a-t-on seulement demandé pardon? Entretien avec Samuel Pisar," in *Archives d'un Procès. Klaus Barbie,* ed. Bernard-Henri Lévy (Paris: Globe, 1986), 72; Soyinka, *The Burden of Memory,* 26, 28; Derrida, *On Cosmopolitanism and Forgiveness,* 42; Ricoeur, *La mémoire,* 620. Closely related to this is the fact that we consider forgiveness something that could rightfully be given only by the person (or community) wronged. As Jeffrie Murphy observes, it would be odd to say that those born after World War II, and with no immediate connection to the victims of the Holocaust, could forgive Hitler for those crimes. Murphy, "Forgiveness and Resentment," 21.

184. Garapon, "La justice et l'inversion morale du temps," 115; Soyinka, "Thérapie collective de la mémoire en Afrique du Sud," 215, 218; Martens, "Temps, mémoire, oubli et droit," 732.

185. Jankélévitch, *L'irréversible et la nostalgie,* 294.

186. In Kani's play about post-apartheid South Africa, the father wants "everything that was mine given back to me now," including his murdered son. Kani, *Nothing But the Truth,* 54. The play suggests that neither the TRC nor the revenge that the father initially seeks will accomplish that end.

187. Aeschylus, *Eumenides,* 315–19. Translation slightly modified.

188. Ricoeur, *Le juste 1,* 208 quoting Hegel; Jankélévitch, *Le pardon,* 38–39, 137.

189. Semprún, *L'écriture ou la vie,* 297. See also Agnon, "The Sign."

190. Rousso, *Vichy,* 683, 694; Rousso, *Le syndrome de Vichy,* 71.

191. Benjamin Stora, *La gangrène et l'oubli. La mémoire de la guerre d'Algérie* (Paris: La Découverte, 1991), 8, 319. On the resurgence of the Algerian war in French collective memory, see Mohammed Harbi and Benjamin Stora, "La guerre d'Algérie: de la mémoire à l'histoire," in *La guerre d'Algérie. 1954–2004, la fin de l'amnésie,* ed. Harbi and Stora (Paris: Robert Laffont, 2004), 9–13; Benjamin Stora, "1999–2003, guerre d'Algérie, les accélérations de la mémoire," in Harbi and Stora, *La guerre d'Algérie,* 501–14.

192. Larry Rohter, "Now the Dirtiest of Wars Won't Be Forgotten," *New York Times,* June 18, 2003, A:4.

193. The trajectory of the passions surrounding the Holocaust, from neglect or indifference in the immediate postwar years to its powerful resurgence at the start of the

new millennium, suggests that the quiet of the Furies should not be mistaken for their disappearance. Consider Adam Michnik's comment on the furor in Poland over Jan Gross's book on the Polish massacre of Jews at Jedwabne: "It is a serious debate, full of sadness and sometimes terror—as if the whole society was suddenly forced to carry the weight of this terrible 60-year-old crime." Adam Michnik, "Poles and the Jews: How Deep the Guilt?" *New York Times*, March 17, 2001, B:79; Jan T. Gross, *Neighbors: The Destruction of the Jewish Community in Jedwabne* (New York: Penguin, 2001). The trial of General Wojciech Jaruzelski in Poland, the reopening of the issue of crimes committed during the "dirty war" in Argentina, and Truth Commissions in Peru and elsewhere all point to the persistence of the past.

194. Tutu, *No Future without Forgiveness*, 28.

195. Ralph Ellison, "Going to the Territory," 600.

196. Jankélévitch, *L'irréversible et la nostalgie*, 289; Jürgen Habermas, "Burdens of the Double Past," trans. Sidney Rosenfeld and Stella P. Rosenfeld, *Dissent* (fall 1994): 513.

197. Primo Levi, *The Drowned and the Saved*, trans. Raymond Rosenthal (New York: Vintage, 1989), 136; Jankélévitch, *Le pardon*, 24–25, 35–36; Thomas, "La vérité," 29; Garapon, *Des crimes qu'on ne peut ni punir ni pardonner*, 55.

198. Günter Grass, *Nobelvorlesung 1999*, Nobel e-Museum, April 13, 2004, <http://www.nobel.se/literature/laureates/1999/lecture-g.html>.

199. Quignard, *Abîmes*, 47, 210; Winfried Georg Sebald, *The Emigrants*, 1993, trans. Michael Hulse (London: Harvill, 1996), 23.

200. Eberhard Jäckel, "Nähe und Ferne der Hitlerzeit," in *Umgang mit Vergangenheit. Beiträge zur Geschichte* (Stuttgart: Deutsche Verlags-Anstalt, 1989), 93; Jankélévitch, *Le pardon*, 48.

201. Yerushalmi, "Réflexions sur l'oubli," 20.

202. Jankélévitch, *Le pardon*, 68–69.

203. Aeschylus, *Eumenides*, l. 154.

204. Jankélévitch, *L'imprescriptible*, 25, 54, 58–60, 62, 66, 79.

205. Améry, *Jenseits von Schuld und Sühne*, 110, 114–16, 129; Jankélévitch, *Le pardon*, 25, 68, 72–73, 75–76.

206. Emmanuel Lévinas, *Paul Celan de l'être à l'autre* (Paris: Fata Morgana, 2002), 26.

207. Manes Sperber, quoted in Lenz, *Über das Gedächtnis*, 59.

208. Lenz, *Über das Gedächtnis*, 9.

5. *Democratic Memory*

1. Hans-Georg Gadamer, *Truth and Method*, ed. Garrett Barden and John Cumming (New York: Crossroad, 1982), 16.

2. Jean-Yves Lacoste, *Note sur le temps. Essai sur les raisons de la mémoire et de l'espérance* (Paris: Presses Universitaires de France, 1990), 53.

3. Claude Lefort, "Société 'sans histoire' et historicité," in *Les formes de l'histoire. Essais d'anthropologie politique* (Paris: Gallimard, 1978), 64; François Hartog, *Régimes d'historicité. Présentisme et expériences du temps* (Paris: Seuil, 2003), 119.

4. "The philosophers of the Enlightenment . . . were slipping off the shackles of the past, destroying its pretensions and follies, but they also attempted to create out of the debris a more extended, a more rational, a more detached sense of human destiny. The old past is dying, its force weakening. . . . [I]t was compounded of bigotry, of national vanity, of class domination." John Harold Plumb, *The Death of the Past* (Boston: Houghton Mifflin, 1970), 144–45; Geraint Parry, "Tradition, Community, and Self-determination," *British Journal of Political Science* 12 (1982): 415–16.

5. Jürgen Habermas, *Theory of Communicative Action*, vol. 1, trans. Thomas McCarthy (Boston: Beacon Press, 1984), 340ff.; Habermas, "Können komplexe Gesellschaften eine vernünftige Identität ausbilden?" in *Zur Rekonstruktion des historischen Materialismus* (Frankfurt am Main: Suhrkamp, 1976), 116–17; Sheldon Wolin, *The Presence of the Past* (Baltimore: Johns Hopkins University Press, 1989), 43; Paul Connerton, *How Societies Remember* (Cambridge: Cambridge University Press, 1989), 96; Moses I. Finley, *The Ancestral Constitution* (Cambridge: Cambridge University Press, 1971), 54.

6. Pierre Nora, "Entre mémoire et histoire," in *Les lieux de mémoire*, ed. Nora, vol. 1, *La République* (Paris: Gallimard, 1984), xvii, xix, xxv–xxviii, xxxii.

7. Pascal Quignard, *Petits traités I* (Paris: Gallimard, 1990), 199–200.

8. Martin Heidegger, *Being and Time*, trans. John Macquarrie and Edward Robinson (Oxford: Basil Blackwell, 1973), 443; Jean Chesneaux, *Habiter le temps. Présent, passé, futur: esquisse d'un dialogue politique* (Paris: Bayard Éditions, 1996), 7, 128; Hartog, *Régimes d'historicité*, 112, 115, 158; Georges Balandier, *Le dédale. Pour en finir avec le XXe siècle* (Paris: Fayard, 1994), 39. The demand for remembering has been analyzed as a symptom of a crisis in the "presentism" of our way of living in time, a response and resistance to that loss of a sense of the long duration of the past and of the absence of the great projects of the future that characterized the past two centuries and more.

9. Winfried Georg Sebald, *Campo Santo*, trans. Anthea Bell (New York: Random House, 2005), 32–33.

10. Edmund Burke, *Reflections on the Revolution in France* (1790; Indianapolis: Library of Liberal Arts, 1955), 38.

11. Jürgen Habermas, "Konzeptionen der Moderne. Ein Rückblick auf zwei Traditionen," in *Die postnationale Konstellation* (Frankfurt am Main: Suhrkamp, 1998), 198; Paul Ricoeur, *La mémoire, l'histoire, l'oubli* (Paris: Seuil, 2000), 379, 397–98.

12. Friedrich Nietzsche, *Twilight of the Idols*, in *The Portable Nietzsche*, ed. and trans. Walter Kaufmann (New York: Penguin, 1954), 543; Nietzsche, *The Will to Power*, trans. Walter Kaufmann and R. J. Hollingdale (New York: Vintage, 1968), 43.

13. See Edward S. Casey, *Remembering: A Phenomenological Study*, 2nd ed. (Bloomington: Indiana University Press, 2000), 304–5; Jean-Yves Tadié and Marc Tadié, *Le sens de la mémoire* (Paris: Gallimard, 1999), 157; Roger Scruton, "In Defence of the Nation," in *The Philosopher on Dover Beach* (New York: St. Martin's Press, 1990), 303.

14. Burke, *Reflections*, 98ff., 171.

15. Rawls gestures toward something like this in discussing the "intimate and inexpressible knowledge" that ties us to our society and culture and that makes exit or exile so difficult. John Rawls, *Political Liberalism* (New York: Columbia University Press, 1993), 222.

16. Anne Gotman, *Hériter* (Paris: Presses Universitaires de France, 1988), 99, 145, 225; Charles Péguy, *Clio* (Paris: Gallimard, 1932), 35; Thomas Paine, "Rights of Man," in *The Complete Writings of Thomas Paine*, ed. Philip S. Foner, vol. 2 (New York: Citadel Press, 1945), 251.

17. Henri Raczymow, *Un cri sans voix* (Paris: Gallimard, 1985), 213.

18. Samuel Scheffler, *Boundaries and Allegiances: Problems of Justice and Responsibility in Liberal Thought* (Oxford: Oxford University Press, 2001), 98–99. Burke used the idea of "entailed inheritance" to express the notion of obligations between generations, and contrasted that to the model of political choice. It was this idea of intergenerational obligations that Paine criticized: "Every age and generation must be free to act for itself." Paine, "Rights of Man," 251; Burke, *Reflections*, 15–16, 37, 108.

19. "I inherited my religion and my nation without the least opportunity to opt for them." Mahmud Darwish, "Chronique de la tristesse ordinaire," trans. Olivier Carré, in *Chronique de la tristesse ordinaire. Poèmes palestiniens* (Paris: Cerf, 1989), 43.

20. Burke, *Reflections,* 110; Michael Walzer, "The Moral Standing of States," *Philosophy and Public Affairs* 9 (1980): 211; Scruton, "In Defence of the Nation," 302.

21. John Rawls, *A Theory of Justice* (Cambridge: Harvard University Press, 1971), 525; Rawls, *Political Liberalism,* 222.

22. Anthony D. Smith, "Gastronomy or Geology? The Role of Nationalism in the Reconstruction of Nations," *Nations and Nationalism* 1, no. 1 (1995): 4–5, 10ff.; David Miller, *On Nationality* (Oxford: Clarendon Press, 1995), 42; Benedict Anderson, *Imagined Communities* (London: Verso, 1991), 143.

23. On the rejection of the idea of identities beyond our control and a view of them as chosen and fluid, see the discussion in Scheffler, *Boundaries and Allegiances,* 105–6, 112–13.

24. Yael Tamir, *Liberal Nationalism* (Princeton: Princeton University Press, 1993), 29; Tzvetan Todorov, *Nous et les autres* (Paris: Seuil, 1989), 254. Nationalism, in its reflective appropriation of the past, is already post-traditional. Jürgen Habermas, "Historical Consciousness and Post-traditional Identity," trans. Shierry Weber Nicholsen, in *The New Conservatism* (Cambridge: MIT Press, 1989), 253, 261; Charles Taylor, "Nationalism and Modernity," in *The Morality of Nationalism,* ed. Robert McKim and Jeff McMahan (Oxford: Oxford University Press, 1997), 43.

25. Nicole Lapierre, *Changer de nom* (Paris: Stock, 1995), 52, 274.

26. Edmond Jabès, *Le livre des questions* (Paris: Gallimard, 1963), 42.

27. Françoise Zonabend, "Pourquoi nommer?" in *L'Identité,* ed. Claude Lévi-Strauss (Paris: Presses Universitaires de France, 1995), 262–63. In the archaic world, Bouvier writes, "the name served to unify the generations" but also "to call a person to his destiny." "The renown of the ancestors is an essential part of the identity of the descendants." David Bouvier, *Le sceptyre et la lyre: L'Iliade ou les héros de la mémoire* (Grenoble: Éditions Jérôme Millon, 2002), 363–64, 108.

28. In a similar vein is the passion to alter street and city names, and to remove memorials, after a regime change. Lapierre, *Changer de nom,* 26, 292, 367; Daniel Milo, "Le nom des rues," in *Les lieux de mémoire,* ed. Pierre Nora, vol. 2 (pt. 3), *La Nation (L'Idéel)* (Paris: Gallimard, 1986), 283, 292; Sophie Calle, *Souvenirs de Berlin-Est* (Paris: Actes Sud, 1999).

29. From that vantage point, the capacity to leave a place or to work in a language other than one's mother tongue is also a form of liberation from the weight of the past. Cioran argues that "to write in a foreign language is an emancipation, an emancipation from one's own past." Emile M. Cioran, *E. M. Cioran: Ein Gespräch. Geführt von Gerd Bergfleth* (Tübingen: Rive Gauche, 1985), 9. Jean Anouilh's play *Le voyageur sans bagage* critically portrays a family's attempt to force a past on a returning, memory-less soldier who would rather not be burdened with it: "I am refusing my past and the persons in it—me included. I can be as new as a baby . . . not a prisoner of any memory." Jean Anouilh, *Le voyageur sans bagage suivi de Le bal des voleurs* (Paris: La Table Rond, 1958), 99–100.

30. Mona Ozouf, "Allocution," in *Discours de réception de Pierre Nora à L'Académie Française et réponse de René Rémond* (Paris: Gallimard, 2002), 87; Pascal Quignard, *Dernier royaume,* vol. 3, *Abîmes* (Paris: Grasset, 2002), 259.

31. Dubravka Ugrešić, *The Culture of Lies,* trans. Celia Hawkesworth (University Park: Pennsylvania State University Press, 1998), 250n, 250. The first passage is quoted from a Croatian journal.

32. Czeslaw Milosz, "On Exile," *Parabola* 18, no. 2 (summer 1993): 26.

33. Maurice Halbwachs, *La mémoire collective* (Paris: Presses Universitaires de France, 1968), 77.

34. Alfred Grosser, *Le crime et la mémoire* (Paris: Flammarion, 1989), 27–28;

Françoise Zonabend, *La mémoire longue: temps et histoires au village* (Paris: Jean-Michel Place, 1999), 290–91; Zonabend, "Pourquoi nommer?" 261–62.

35. Bernard Williams, *Moral Luck* (Cambridge: Cambridge University Press, 1981), 15; Halbwachs, *La mémoire collective*, 119.

36. Habermas, "Können komplexe Gesellschaften eine vernünftige Identität ausbilden?" 96; Tzvetan Todorov, *Mémoire du mal, tentation du bien. Enquête sur le siècle* (Paris: Robert Laffont, 2000), 334; Tamir, *Liberal Nationalism*, 121. Needless to say, it is even more at odds with a cosmopolitanism of the sort urged, for example, by Martha Nussbaum. See also Anthony Smith's comment on the memory-lessness of the cosmopolitan standpoint. Martha C. Nussbaum, "Patriotism and Cosmopolitanism," in *For Love of Country: Debating the Limits of Patriotism*, ed. Joshua Cohen (Boston: Beacon Press, 1996), 3–17; Anthony D. Smith, *Myths and Memories of the Nation* (Oxford: Oxford University Press, 1999), 237.

37. John Schmid, "Etching the Notes of a New European Identity," *International Herald Tribune*, August 3, 2001, 1.

38. Sandra Pfister, "Kunst für die Geldbörse. Der Österreicher Robert Kalina hat die neuen Euro-Scheine kreiert," *Europa Info-online* (2001), May 5. 2004, <http://userpage.fu-berlin.de/~tmuehle/europa/euro/euron_01.htm>.

39. Jean Giraudoux, *Siegfried et le Limousin* (Paris: Grasset, 1959); Jean-Yves Le Naour, *Le soldat inconnu vivant* (Paris: Hachette Littératures, 2002), 94ff.

40. Annette Wieviorka, *Auschwitz, 60 ans après* (Paris: Robert Laffont, 2005), 16–17.

41. Smith, *Myths and Memories of the Nation*, 15, 58–61; Scruton, "In Defence of the Nation," 305.

42. Scruton, "In Defence of the Nation," 319; Charles R. Beitz, "Cosmopolitan Ideals and National Sentiment," *Journal of Philosophy* 80 (1983): 592–93.

43. Will Kymlicka, *Liberalism, Community, and Culture* (Oxford: Clarendon Press, 1991), 164ff.; Kymlicka, *Multicultural Citizenship: A Liberal Theory of Minority Rights* (Oxford: Oxford University Press, 1995), 82ff.; Tamir, *Liberal Nationalism*, 121.

44. See Dominique Schnapper, *La communauté des citoyens. Sur l'idée moderne de nation* (Paris: Gallimard, 1994), 36; Michael Walzer, "Nation and Universe," in *The Tanner Lectures on Human Values*, vol. 11 (Salt Lake City: University of Utah Press, 1990), 554; Smith, *Myths and Memories of the Nation*, 228; Scruton, "In Defence of the Nation," 301; David Lowenthal, "Identity, Heritage, and History," in *Commemorations: The Politics of National Identity*, ed. John R. Gillis (Princeton: Princeton University Press, 1994), 43.

45. Abraham Lincoln, "July 10, 1858 Speech," in *The Complete Lincoln-Douglas Debates of 1858*, ed. Paul M. Angle (Chicago: University of Chicago Press, 1958), 40–44; Miller, *On Nationality*, 44; Maurizio Viroli, *For Love of Country: An Essay on Patriotism and Nationalism* (Oxford: Oxford University Press, 1995), 9, 12–13.

46. Viroli, *For Love of Country*, 14; Smith, *Myths and Memories of the Nation*, 233–37, 241–42, 245, 261.

47. Miller, *On Nationality*, 141.

48. Emmanuel Lévinas, "Une religion d'adultes," in *Difficile liberté. Essais sur le judaïsme* (Paris: Albin Michel, 1976), 39, 40–41; Lévinas, "Textes messianiques," ibid., 136; Daniel Levy and Natan Sznaider, *Erinnerung im globalen Zeitalter: Der Holocaust* (Frankfurt am Main: Suhrkamp, 2001), 24, 54, 57.

49. Levy and Sznaider, *Erinnerung im globalen Zeitalter*, 9, 17, 27, 210.

50. Robert Antelme, *L'espèce humaine* (Paris: Gallimard, 1957), 11; Maurice Blanchot, "Dans la nuit surveillée," in *Robert Antelme. Textes inédits. Sur L'Espèce Humaine. Essais et témoignages*, ed. Daniel Dobbels (Paris: Gallimard, 1996), 72; Sarah Kofman, *Paroles suffoquées* (Paris: Galilée, 1987), 66.

51. Quoted in François Hartog and Jacques Revel, "Note de conjoncture histori-

ographique," in *Les usages politiques du passé*, ed. François Hartog and Jacques Revel (Paris: Éditions de l'École des Hautes Études en Sciences Sociales, 2001), 22.

52. Levy and Sznaider, *Erinnerung im globalen Zeitalter*, 15–17, 27, 224.

53. Cynthia Ozick, "Metaphor and Memory," in *Metaphor and Memory: Essays* (New York: Vintage, 1991), 278–79. Lévinas understands the remembering of slavery as a token of the humanity of the Jew, and of the Jew in every human. Emmanuel Lévinas, *L'au-delà du verset. Lectures et discours talmudiques* (Paris: Éditions de Minuit, 1982), 18, 172.

54. Cynthia Ozick, "Who Owns Anne Frank?" in *Quarrel and Quandary: Essays by Cynthia Ozick* (New York: Vintage, 2000), 74–102; Levy and Sznaider, *Erinnerung im globalen Zeitalter*, 27–28, 152, 155, 174ff., 218.

55. Halbwachs, *La mémoire collective*, 75.

56. Suzanne Citron, "Quelle mémoire pour quelle identité française," *Projet (Mémoires des Peuples)* (Paris) 248 (December 1996): 66–67; Michael Kammen, *Mystic Chords of Memory* (New York: Vintage, 1993), 10; Miller, *On Nationality*, 119ff.

57. Henry Sidgwick, *The Elements of Politics* (London: Macmillan, 1897), 308–9; Pierre Nora, "L'ère de la commémoration," in *Les lieux de mémoire*, ed. Pierre Nora, vol. 3 (pt. 3), *Les France (De L'archive à L'emblème)* (Paris: Gallimard, 1992), 984; Andreas Huyssen, *Twilight Memories: Marking Time in a Culture of Amnesia* (New York: Routledge, 1995), 5; Joël Candau, *Mémoire et identité* (Paris: Presses Universitaires de France, 1998), 191.

58. Czeslaw Milosz, "The Nobel Lecture," trans. Milosz, in *Beginning with My Streets* (New York: Farrar, Straus and Giroux, 1991), 280; Alain Brossat et al., introduction to *À l'Est, la mémoire retrouvée*, ed. Alain Brossat (Paris: La Découverte, 1990), 11, 24; Václav Havel, "Letter to Dr. Gustáv Husák," in *Václav Havel: Living in Truth*, ed. Jan Vladislav (London: Faber and Faber, 1986), 3–35. But see also Todorov's mixed evaluation of the impact of east European memory work in the West. Todorov, *Mémoire du mal, tentation du bien*, 132. The emancipatory dimensions of memory work are now widely understood, and it is no longer seen as the willing servant of the status quo. "The struggle of man against power is the struggle of memory against forgetting." Milan Kundera, *The Book of Laughter and Forgetting*, trans. Aaron Asher (New York: HarperCollins, 1996), 4; Alain Touraine, "Mémoire, histoire, à venir," in *Pourquoi se souvenir?* ed. Françoise Barret-Ducrocq (Paris: Grasset, 1998), 258; Geoffrey A. Hosking, "Memory in a Totalitarian Society: The Case of the Soviet Union," in *Memory: History, Culture, and the Mind*, ed. Thomas Butler (Oxford: Basil Blackwell, 1989), 119.

59. Jacques Ozouf and Mona Ozouf, "*Le Tour de la France par deux enfants*. Le petit livre rouge de la République," in Nora, *Les lieux de mémoire*, 1:296, 315; Ricoeur, *La mémoire*, 533.

60. See, for example, Paul Ricoeur, "Vulnérabilité de la mémoire," in *Patrimoines et passions identitaire*, ed. Jacques Le Goff (Paris: Librairie Arthème Fayard, 1998), 28; Jacqueline Costa-Lascoux, "Mémoires plurielles," in *Mémoire et intégration*, ed. Jacques Barou (Paris: Syros, 1993), 96, 100–101; Benjamin Stora, "La mémoire de la guerre d'Algérie chez les jeunes issus de l'immigration," in *Mémoire et intégration*, ed. Jacques Barou (Paris: Syros, 1993), 37; Kofi Yamgname, preface to Barou, *Mémoire et intégration*, 18; Candau, *Mémoire et identité*, 90; Levy and Sznaider, *Erinnerung im globalen Zeitalter*, 17, 27, 39, 46–47. Stora suggests an underlying relationship between French colonial memories and contemporary anti-Arab racism in France. Benjamin Stora, *Le transfert d'une mémoire. De l' "Algérie française" au racisme anti-arabe* (Paris: La Découverte, 1999), 101ff. On the United States and the politics of recognition, see Melissa S. Williams, *Voice, Trust, and Memory: Marginalized Groups and the Failings of Liberal Representation* (Princeton: Princeton University Press, 1998), 182ff.; Iris M. Young, *Justice and the Poli-*

tics of Difference (Princeton: Princeton University Press, 1990), 156ff.; Taylor, "Nationalism and Modernity," 45–47, 51; Charles Taylor, *Multiculturalism and the Politics of Recognition* (Princeton: Princeton University Press, 1992).

61. Levy and Sznaider, *Erinnerung im globalen Zeitalter*, 39.

62. Michel Foucault, "Nietzsche, la généalogie, l'histoire," in *Dits et écrits, 1954–1988*, vol. 1, *1954–1975* (Paris: Gallimard, 2001), 1008–9, 1020–22.

63. Hartog, *Régimes d'historicité*, 132. Joutard writes that it is the precariousness of modernity that motivates the attempt to find a sanctuary in tradition and memory. Philippe Joutard, *Ces voix qui nous viennent du passé* (Paris: Hachette, 1983), 157. See also Huyssen, *Twilight Memories*, 7; Schnapper, *La communauté des citoyens*, 194, 197; Balandier, *Le dédale*, 43; Tzvetan Todorov, *Les abus de la mémoire* (Paris: Arléa, 1995), 53.

64. Rushdie's essay on Lenz highlights points related to this reading. Salman Rushdie, "Siegfried Lenz," in *Imaginary Homelands: Essays and Criticism, 1981–1991* (London: Granta, 1991), 285–87.

65. Ugrešić, *The culture of lies*, 81.

66. Anderson, *Imagined Communities*, 205–6; Jeremy Waldron, "Superseding Historic Injustice," *Ethics* 103, no. 1 (October 1992): 6; Elie Wiesel, preface to Barret-Ducrocq, *Pourquoi se souvenir?* 10; Jonathan Glover, "Nations, Identity, and Conflict," in *The Morality of Nationalism*, ed. Robert McKim and Jeff McMahan (Oxford: Oxford University Press, 1997), 18.

67. Emmanuel Kattan, *Penser le devoir de mémoire* (Paris: Presses Universitaires de France, 2002), 128.

68. Milosz, "On Exile," 27.

69. Chesneaux, *Habiter le temps*, 6.

70. François Marcot, "Voix d'outre-tombe," in *La vie à en mourir. Lettres de fusillés (1941–1944)*, ed. Guy Krivopissko and François Marcot (Paris: Tallandier, 2003), 25.

71. Wallace Stevens, "A Clear Day and No Memories," in *The Palm at the End of the Mind*, ed. Holly Stevens (New York: Vintage, 1990), 397.

72. Lévinas writes of Judaism that through its moral sense it holds out the promise of a certain liberty in relation to history and a priority of justice over culture. From that same vantage point, Lévinas develops a critique of Heidegger's arguments concerning rootedness and space. See Lévinas, "Une religion d'adultes," 40–41; Emmanuel Lévinas, "Heidegger, Gagarine et nous," in *Difficile liberté*, 324–25.

73. Scheffler, *Boundaries and Allegiances*, 106; Jürgen Habermas, "Ethics, Politics, and History: An Interview with Jürgen Habermas, Conducted by Jean-Marc Ferry," *Philosophy and Social Criticism* 14 (1988): 439; Paul Ricoeur, *Le juste 1* (Paris: Esprit, 1995), 65.

74. Dimitri Nicolaïdis, "La Nation, les crimes, le mémoire," in *Oublier nos crimes. L'amnésie nationale, une spécificité française?* ed. Dimitri Nicolaïdis (Paris: Autrement, 1994), 29; Todorov, *Mémoire du mal, tentation du bien*, 331.

75. Alexis de Tocqueville, *Democracy in America*, trans. George Lawrence, ed. J.P. Mayer (New York: Anchor, 1969), 341. The literal visibleness of race, and so indirectly the reminder of injustice, both find their counterpart in Ellison's observation on the "blackness of my invisibility." "High visibility" is coupled, he says, with the "*un*-visible." Ralph Ellison, *Invisible Man* (New York: Vintage, 1995), xv, 13.

76. Chesneaux, *Habiter le temps*, 17, 260; Casey, *Remembering*, 290; Paul Ricoeur, *Le juste 2* (Paris: Esprit, 2001), 653.

77. There is a considerable literature on the reparations issue in the United States. For analysis of memory and reparations in the American context, see Lawrie Balfour, "Unreconstructed Democracy: W. E. B. Du Bois and the Case for Reparations," *American Political Science Review* 97, no. 1 (February 2003): 33–44; Thomas A. McCarthy, "Ver-

gangenheitsbewältigung in the USA: On the Politics of the Memory of Slavery," *Political Theory* 30, no. 5 (December 2002): 623–48; McCarthy, "Coming to Terms with Our Past, Part 2: On the Morality and Politics of Reparations for Slavery," *Political Theory* 32, no. 6 (December 2004): 750–72.

78. Jankélévitch, *L'irréversible et la nostalgie*, 294.

Index